George Berkeley, Alexander C. Fraser, Alexander Campbell Fraser

Selections

With an introd. and notes for the use of students in the universities

George Berkeley, Alexander C. Fraser, Alexander Campbell Fraser

Selections

With an introd. and notes for the use of students in the universities

ISBN/EAN: 9783337427740

Printed in Europe, USA, Canada, Australia, Japan

Cover: Foto ©Paul-Georg Meister /pixelio.de

More available books at **www.hansebooks.com**

SELECTIONS FROM BERKELEY

WITH

AN INTRODUCTION AND NOTES

FOR THE USE OF STUDENTS IN

THE UNIVERSITIES

BY

ALEXANDER CAMPBELL FRASER, D.C.L. Oxon.

Professor of Logic and Metaphysics in the University of Edinburgh

THIRD EDITION, REVISED

Oxford

AT THE CLARENDON PRESS

1884

[*All rights reserved*]

NOTE TO SECOND EDITION.

In this Edition the Introduction to the *Selections* has been rewritten, and the relevant parts of the Supplementary Note merged in it; the three Prefatory Notes have been revised; a number of foot-notes have been added, and the others amended or withdrawn. The volume has been kept nearly within its original dimensions by the subtraction of portions of the text, in the *Vindication* and in *Siris*, that seemed unnecessary. It is hoped that these changes may make the work less unworthy of the indulgent reception it has already met with in this country and in America.

October, 1878.

NOTE TO THIRD EDITION.

The demand for a third Edition of the *Selections* has afforded an opportunity for amending the expression of the thought contained in the General Introduction and in the Annotations. It is hoped that the book is now, thus and otherwise, better fitted for its intended office, as an aid to reflection on the fundamental questions raised in Berkeley's short and easy method with Materialists, or new metaphysical conception of the Universe.

November, 1883.

CONTENTS.

	PAGE
EDITOR'S GENERAL INTRODUCTION	vii

I.
Matter necessarily dependent on Mind.

PREFATORY NOTE BY THE EDITOR . . .	3
AUTHOR'S PREFACE TO THE PRINCIPLES OF HUMAN KNOWLEDGE	9
AUTHOR'S INTRODUCTION TO THE PRINCIPLES . .	11
PRINCIPLES OF HUMAN KNOWLEDGE: PART I. .	35

II.
Visual Phenomena significant of Mind.

PREFATORY NOTE BY THE EDITOR . .	147
ESSAY TOWARDS A NEW THEORY OF VISION . .	155
VISUAL LANGUAGE: A DIALOGUE	229
LETTER TO THE AUTHOR OF THE DIALOGUE . .	276
EXTRACTS FROM THE THEORY OF VISUAL LANGUAGE VINDICATED	283

III.
The Universe and the Universal Mind.

PREFATORY NOTE BY THE EDITOR . . .	309
EXTRACTS FROM SIRIS: A CHAIN OF PHILOSOPHICAL REFLEXIONS	313
INDEX	365

GENERAL INTRODUCTION TO THE SELECTIONS.

THE design of these *Selections* is to afford appropriate mental exercise to those who are engaged in Psychology and Metaphysics.

Berkeley may be used for this purpose for the following among other reasons :—

1. His philosophical writings, although only philosophical fragments, are English classics of true metaphysical genius, which present subtle thought in graceful and transparent language.

2. Their principal doctrine, about the metaphysical meaning of Matter, is itself an acknowledged 'touchstone of metaphysical sagacity,' while it is found on further reflection to raise the chief questions of physical and theological philosophy.

3. Berkeley is an important factor in the development of modern philosophy. Its sceptical crisis in Hume was precipitated by the new question about Matter that Berkeley raised, and the intellectual revolution followed in which Descartes, Hobbes, and Locke were exchanged for the transcendental criticism of Kant, the Association psychology or physiology, and Reid's appeal to the common rational sense.

The intrinsic freshness of Berkeley's thought, the literary charm of its expression, the romantic interest of his Immaterialism, its intellectual reach when it is pushed into its issues, with his historical importance, all unite in recommending him as a good companion for a student of philosophy at an early period in his course.

This estimate of the educational value of Berkeley does not of course oblige us to receive his most celebrated conclusion as final and sufficient; nor even as a profound answer to the ultimate question.

Berkeley's personal history is full of interest. His early years and ancestry are curiously shrouded in a mystery that is in keeping with the halo of romance in which his life is enveloped. The following facts are well known. He was born in the county of Kilkenny, in March, 1685. In March, 1700, he entered Trinity College, Dublin, where his next thirteen years were spent. Peter Browne, afterwards the philosophical bishop of Cork, was then provost of Trinity, and the seeds of modern thought were then finding their way into the College. Through the influence of Locke's friend and correspondent, William Molyneux, the *Essay of Human Understanding* had been introduced in Dublin, and Malebranche, the French philosophical contemporary of Locke, was not unknown there. The spirit of Descartes and of Bacon, the early operations of the Royal Society, and the discoveries of Newton and Leibnitz, were all rousing Irish intellect to action. Berkeley's published and unpublished writings show his early familiarity with Locke and Newton, Descartes and Malebranche.

When Berkeley was in Dublin, and before he reached his thirtieth year, he produced the three small volumes which state and defend his famous new conception of Matter. In 1709 his *Essay towards a New Theory of Vision* appeared, and opened the way for the other two. It was followed in 1710 by the *Principles of Human Knowledge*—the most systematically reasoned exposition of this new conception. In 1713 he popularly explained and illustrated it in *Three Dialogues between Hylas and Philonous*. Thus, like Descartes, Spinoza, and Hume, and in contrast to Locke, Kant, and Reid, the distinctive speculation of Berkeley was given to the world in early life, a fact in keeping with the fervid impetuosity of his temperament.

The stages of his intellectual growth in his first years at Trinity College may be traced in his metaphysical *Commonplace Book*. This is one of the most interesting records in existence of the juvenile struggles of philosophical genius. It was written in 1705 and the two or three following years, and was first published in 1871, in the Clarendon Press edition of his Works and Life.

In 1713 Berkeley visited London. The next twenty years of his life were spent for the most part in England, on the Continent, and in America. The accomplishment and charm of his conversation, as well as the surprise occasioned by his paradoxical expression of what is meant by the reality of the material world, attracted his most eminent contemporaries. During some of these years he indulged an artistic taste by a long stay in Italy. On his return, although in 1724 he became Dean of Derry, ardent philanthropy carried him to North America, at the age of forty-five, to devote the remainder of his life to spreading Christian civilisation and learning there, by a College at the Bermudas. After three years of delay in Rhode Island, withdrawal of the support on which the enterprise depended obliged him to return home.

His last twenty years were spent in comparative retirement, in the south of Ireland, as Bishop of Cloyne.

Neither in the twenty years of movement, nor in the closing twenty years of retirement, was philosophy forgotten by Berkeley. A Latin tract on the uncaused cause of Motion, the fruit of studies in Italy, appeared in 1721, on his return from the Continent. *Alciphron or the Minute Philosopher*, a book of dialogues, directed against sceptics in religion, containing important fragments of psychology and applications of his conception of Matter, was the fruit of studies in Rhode

Island. It was published in 1732, soon after his return from America. This was followed, the year after, by a subtle *Vindication* of his theory of vision. The latest development of his philosophical thought was the issue of his seclusion at Cloyne. It appeared in 1744, under the title of *Siris : a Chain of Philosophical Reflexions*. Here the Immaterialism of his youth, regarded now from the point of view of Plato and Plotinus rather than of Locke, becomes more comprehensive in its scope, and more ready to connect itself with speculations at the point of view of Kant or of Hegel.

Berkeley spent the evening of his days in works of philanthropy and in meditative quiet. For Cloyne he had a particular fondness. Its very obscurity and remoteness had a contemplative charm. But at last, when declining health needed change, his love for learned retirement carried him to Oxford, which for years had been before him in imagination as the ideal home of his old age. He enjoyed it only for a few months. There death suddenly closed this pious, ingenious, and beautiful life, in January 1753. His body rests in the Cathedral of Christ Church[1].

That all the things we see and touch, with their supposed inherent powers, are neither more nor less than appearances in the five senses, presented by Divine power, in what is called natural order ; and further, that the natural appearances so presented are dependent on living minds being percipient of them—this was the new conception of Matter announced and defended throughout Berkeley's philosophical works. It arose in his mind in the natural course of English metaphysical thought under the influence of Locke, and it was modified in his later life by sympathy with Plato. The

---

[1] For the details of Berkeley's history the reader is referred to my *Life of Berkeley*, in vol. iv of the Clarendon Press edition of his Works (published separately), which likewise contains his *Commonplace Book*. See also *Étude sur la Vie et les Œuvres Philosophiques de Georges Berkeley*, par A. Penjon (Paris, 1878).

historical consequences of its publication justify us in regarding it as one of the epoch-making doctrines that are springs of intellectual progress.

The history of modern philosophy as it was before and after Berkeley illustrates this. A survey of the history, with this in view, may prepare the reader for the *Selections*.

DESCARTES (1596-1650) was the father of modern philosophy. It originated in his famous endeavour to explode Dogmatism by means of tentative Doubt. As the first step in philosophy Descartes refused to accept without proof any belief which, after trial, he might find it intellectually possible to hold in suspense. He announced this as the best method for purifying conclusions from irrationality and prejudice in their premisses, and for finding the ultimate constitution of reason. He recommended it to others as a panacea for transforming the early life of blind trust in authority into the philosophic life of rational insight. This Cartesian spirit of free inquiry, stimulated by temporary doubt, is the distinctive mark of modern thought.

In trying what may be called the *mental experiment* of temporarily suspending all his ordinary beliefs, as well as all philosophical dogmas, Descartes found his tentative doubt arrested by one irresistible conviction—that of his own existence as a conscious person. This consciousness, and this only, it seemed to him that he could not even experimentally hold in suspense. He expressed the philosophical experience thus obtained in the celebrated formula—*cogito ergo sum*. This means that the ever-changing phenomena that each one is conscious of, so necessarily presuppose an unchanging *ego* or self, to sustain and connect them, that one cannot, even when one tries the experiment, conceive *them* appearing and the transcendent *ego* not existing. From this starting-point in consciousness, not thus recognised in the ancient world, the speculative philosophy of modern Europe has pursued its course.

One who had imbibed Cartesianism accordingly began with being surer of his own existence as a conscious person, than of any supposed reality external to himself and to the phenomena of which he was conscious. He was thus led to regard self-conscious existence as the ultimate assumption, and as a fact of more interest and importance than any unconscious thing. We know ourselves and our own conscious life with the most perfect assurance that is conceivable: we know our own bodies even, and all things external to them, only through this conscious or mental experience. For, if we were to cease to be conscious, the things of sense would cease to exist, as far as we were concerned. And if all the conscious life in the universe were to die, the dead universe which remained would be as good as non-existent. The things contained in space are unconscious of their own or any other existence; only conscious beings know themselves, and they give unconscious things their only *intelligible* reality, in feeling and knowing them. A conscious person, revealed to himself in the ideas of which he is conscious, is therefore the primary reality, at the Cartesian point of view. To be conscious is to have ideas—to have our own individual existence manifested to us. The existence of things external to himself and his ideas was a fallible inference, which Descartes vindicated on the ground of the innate idea that he supposed we have of our own existence as rooted in God or Perfect Being. This made him conclude we are not deceived, regarding what we have a clear and distinct conviction of, as we seemed to him to have of the substantial existence of extended things.

Descartes thus found *two* opposed substances and powers —the one conscious and unextended, and the other extended and unconscious—with the idea, and therefore (so he argues) the reality, of the Perfect Being or God, on whom both the opposed substances and powers depend. This ultimate Duality of two opposed and dependent beings in the universe was the great difficulty of early modern philosophy. How was the antithesis of a conscious substance and power and an extended substance and power—of living thought and dead matter—to be reconciled? This, in different phases of it, became the question of questions for modern philosophy. The world of extended substance was so opposed by the Cartesian to the self of which he was conscious, that the explanation of causal intercourse between them, and an intelligible theory of the universe, seemed impossible. Extension and conscious life are in their nature mutually exclusive. How can they be mixed in perception, and in our voluntary movements? How can extended things cause or be caused by conscious states, or how can our volitions either be changed by, or produce changes in, extended things? This Dualism was the perplexity of Cartesian philosophers.

Yet, as a matter of fact, it could not be denied that we perceive, and that external changes follow our volitions. The explanation of this offered by Cartesianism was, that the two mutually exclusive substances were perpetually dependent on Divine activity. All changes in the extended things were to be viewed as effects of which the will of God is the only efficient cause. The material world existed as a substance merely as an occasion for constant Divine efficiency. On occasion of an impression on the human body, God caused the corresponding perception in the human mind: when one exerted one's will, God made the body move. The one was the *occasional* cause of the other. This conception of causality in nature, as phenomenal and not efficient, was further developed by the Cartesians Geulinx and Malebranche. With Malebranche (1638–1715) matter, as extended, could not become an object of perception or consciousness, and as impotent and unintelligent, could not be itself the efficient cause of a perception of its existence. So he was led on to the hypothesis that, while our mere *sensations* of taste, smell, sound, and so on, are produced by Divine power, our *ideas*, or *cognitions* of things as extended and under space relations, are our actual participations in the Divine intelligence, and that thus we may be said to know the external or extended world 'in God.' This tendency of Cartesianism reached its extreme in SPINOZA (1632-77), who abolished as contradictory the supposed duality in substance, and treated thought and extension as necessary *modes* of One Substance—called by him God. LEIBNITZ (1646-1716) was dissatisfied with the merely modal existence of spirit and matter of Spinoza; and rejected the constant agency of God of the Cartesians, as involving the miraculousness of the common order of nature. He proposed the theory that the *monads* of existence were rationally prearranged by God, so that the thus necessitated changes in mind and matter correspond to one another in pre-established harmony. The original and eclectic genius of Leibnitz, the first great German philosopher, found points of agreement and of difference with the Cartesians, and also with Spinoza.

It was in this way that the material world was conceived in the development of Cartesian free thought represented by the speculative theory of Spinoza. Another development, chiefly in England, took the form of experiential and practical psychology; and thus Descartes was, indirectly at least, as Dugald Stewart describes him, 'the father of the experimental philosophy of the human mind.'

BACON (1561-1626) in his *Novum Organum* had urged the need for purifying the human mind from the prejudices generated by early and inevitable submission to authority. He too recommended preliminary doubt and inquiry, as essential to the philosophic spirit, and an indispensable first step in the analysis of experience. Bacon was the English prophet of the modern physical sciences, which men were learning to construct, by better calculated observation of the co-existences and sequences of phenomena in nature. He represented the spirit and the method which Locke—by his own account influenced much also by Descartes—afterwards applied to determine the origin and limits of our knowledge.

LOCKE (1632-1704) was the founder of modern experiential psychology. He addressed himself, in the Baconian spirit, not to the facts of external nature, but to the facts of consciousness, as manifested in the self-conscious being whose existence had arrested Cartesian doubt. These facts were for him facts beyond all others, for this reason, that only by their means were facts of whatever kind converted into knowledge, of which in consequence they formed the ultimate explanation. He sought for them above all in his own consciousness, but also in the expressed consciousness of other persons; not in order to construct an imposing speculative theory of Being, but modestly to mark the growth and take the measure of that power of knowing what exists, with which, as a matter of fact, human beings find themselves endowed. By thus investigating, 'in a plain historical way, the source of the ideas, notions, or whatever else you please to call them, which a man is conscious to himself he has in his own mind,' he hoped 'to show what knowledge the understanding hath by those ideas; the certainty, evidence, and extent of it; and the nature and grounds of faith or opinion, and the reasons and degrees of assent[1].'

The result of Locke's researches with this design in view, pursued systematically for nearly twenty years, appeared in his *Essay on Human Understanding* (1690)—one of the two most influential works of modern philosophy. He there argues, after a study of the facts, that all that each man can know is made up of simple or unanalysable ideas—

[1] See Introduction to Locke's *Essay*.

concerned either with what is presented to our five senses, or with what is presented when we reflect upon our mental operations; and that nothing can be even conceived by us that has not been present in one or other of these ways. He gives this as the verified issue of an examination of consciousness. He discards biological and ontological hypotheses,—avoiding 'the physical consideration of the mind,' and declining to examine 'wherein its essence consists, or by what motions of our spirits, or alterations of our bodies, we come to have any sensation by our organs, or any ideas in our understandings; and whether these ideas do in their formation, any or all of them, depend on matter or no[1].' In this way he separated from the materialistic psychology of Hobbes (1588–1679), who did not, like Descartes and Locke, make consciousness his starting-point and deepest fact, but treated 'minds' as visible organisms, fitted to last it might be for seventy or eighty years, which, through concourse of their atoms, had somehow mysteriously produced the Cartesian ultimate fact *cogito*—an ultimate fact fated to disappear in their dissolution.

Locke professed to explain our intuitive, our demonstrative, and our sense knowledge, as well as our judgments of probability, by what we get in experience. Our gradual acquisitions through the five senses and through reflection seemed to him to account for what we know, or can believe with reasonable probability. Nevertheless, with a semblance of inconsistency, he recognises and applies principles regulative of knowledge and belief, of the *universality* or *necessity* of which he has afforded no sufficient explanation. Take, for instance, his account of his 'knowledge' of his own existence, and of that of God and of Matter.

(*a*) The truth of his own existence he resolved, like Descartes, into irresistible 'intuition.' Experience shows us that we have an intuitive knowledge of our own existence—

[1] See *Essay*, b. I. ch. 1. § 2.

an internal, infallible perception that we are. 'If I doubt of all other things, that very doubt makes me perceive my own existence, and will not suffer me to doubt of that.'—(b) The existence of God or Eternal Mind he found to issue as a necessary consequence of a universal or necessary demand of reason for an eternal Cause of his own self-conscious existence.—(c) Our knowledge of Matter, or things that exist in space, independent of what we are conscious of, we have, he says, 'only by sensation.' Here too he virtually proceeds upon an unexplained principle of causality. For, no man can know the existence of any 'other being,' he argues, but only when, 'by its actual operating upon him,' that being 'makes itself felt by him.' The sense appearances, and 'ideas of sense,' which we thus passively receive, make us believe, through the principle of causality, that 'something' exists without us, at the time we have them, which is 'the cause' of our having them; and we believe in the existence of this external cause of our sensations with a certainty 'as great as human nature is capable of conceiving the existence of anything but a man's self alone and God[1].'—That God, and not this superfluous 'something,' is the constantly operative cause of the phenomena presented to us in our five senses, was, on the principle of parcimony, Berkeley's simplification of Locke's description of our knowledge of God and Matter.

Locke resolved into two classes the qualities of this 'something,' called Matter, which he supposed to exist in space, and to be the cause of what we are conscious of in sense. Those qualities in the external 'something' which were dogmatically assumed by him to be 'like' what we see and touch, he called *primary*, *real*, or *original;* the others, in themselves unlike our sensations, were called

---
[1] See *Essay*, b. IV. ch. 9, 10, 11, for Locke's explanation of our real 'knowledge' of ourselves, God, and 'other things.' Cf. ch. 2. § 14.

secondary or *imputed*. To the former class belong the sizes, figures, motions, impenetrability, and divisibility of things: these qualities (or rather relations of quantity) we cannot conceive any particle of matter to be destitute of: they belong to the things themselves, for they would be what we perceive them to be, even if there was no living person in the universe to perceive them. The others, such as the colours, sounds, tastes, and odours of things, are, so far as we have ideas of them, manifestations of our own sentient mind, which thus, by its varied sensations, all referable to extended things, gives variety and interest to the material world. The heat we feel cannot be felt by the atoms which form the visible fire, nor can our taste be in the visible orange. What heat and taste are in the 'something' without us, Locke cannot even imagine, if they are not unknown modifications of its primary qualities, or rather quantities. For, like the atomists, he conjectured that the secondary qualities might exist in the thing, in the form of subsensible modes of its primary atoms, connected by natural law with the colours, sounds, tastes, odours, heat and cold, to which they give rise. But even if we could discover these undiscoverable atoms, Locke insisted that we could never predict *à priori* the sensations to which they would give rise. It is therefore a fundamental doctrine in the *Essay* that a demonstrable science of the things of sense is impossible, consistently with the conditions of human knowledge: their laws, as discoverable by us, are arbitrary and only more or less probable.

Locke's doctrine of a 'something' or 'substance,' external to, and the cause of, what is present in the senses, was partly connected with what he taught about 'abstract' and 'general' ideas. 'Idea' was the vague name then commonly applied by philosophers to whatever we are conscious of, and was not confined to the internal representations of imagination and thought now popularly called ideas. The word in this wide meaning was naturally of frequent occurrence in Locke's *Essay*[1]. And he seemed to find, in the course of his researches in human 'understanding,' that men, especially philosophers, are conscious not only of ideas of individual things in sense, and of copies of these in imagination, but also of ideas that are not ideas of individual things, and which in consequence are difficult to apprehend. These are his 'abstract' ideas, reached only when we know the relations of individual things. The idea of a *triangle* was one of his examples. It is a figure 'neither oblique nor rectangle, neither equilateral, equicrural, nor scalenon, but all and none of these at once; something imperfect that cannot exist; an idea wherein some parts of different and inconsistent ideas are put together.' A more important example was the general idea of *substance*. This was an idea, made by abstraction, of a 'substratum which we accustom ourselves to suppose,' as that in which the qualities of things subsist, and from which they result; something related as a support and centre of unity to phenomena, but which is not itself got as a simple idea either in sensation or reflection. This abstract idea is one on which our knowledge of matter, or the 'something without us,' depends.

Locke describes it in terms which prepare for Berkeley's

[1] Students of the present day are apt to misconceive the psychology of the seventeenth century from want of due regard to the different meanings of the word *idea*. By Plato it was used objectively, to express the archetypal essence of things. Through the Aristotelian distinction of form and matter, it came gradually to lose its objective application for that of mental image or representation, until with Descartes, Locke, and others, it was applied indiscriminately to any phenomena of which we are conscious in sense or otherwise. Berkeley, in his earlier writings, uses 'idea' in this wide meaning. In *Siris* he reverts to its Platonic meaning, and uses *phenomenon* occasionally for the presentations of which we are conscious in sense.—Another term apt to mislead the reader is *perception*, now usually limited by the psychologist to sense. With Locke and Berkeley *immediate* perception is equivalent to consciousness of phenomena, mental or material; which with Berkeley developes, through what he calls *suggestion*, into our acquired perception of individual things in space—and at a more advanced stage, into inductive generalisation and scientific prevision.

reasonings about what is meant by Matter. 'The mind,' he says, 'being furnished with a great number of the simple ideas conveyed in by the senses, as they are found in exterior things, or by reflection on its own operations, takes notice also that a certain number of these ideas go constantly together; which—being presumed to belong to *one* thing— are called, so united in one subject, by one name; which, by inadvertency, we are apt afterward to talk of and consider as one simple idea, which indeed is a complication of many ideas together; because, not imagining how these simple ideas can subsist by themselves, we accustom ourselves to suppose some substratum wherein they do subsist, and from which they do result; which therefore we call Substance. So that if any one will examine himself concerning his notion of pure substance in general, he will find he has no other idea of it at all, but only a supposition of he knows not what support of such qualities, which are capable of producing simple ideas in us [1].'

Locke refers to other parts of his *Essay* for an answer to the question,—whether the fact 'that we *accustom* ourselves to suppose' a substance is all that can be said on behalf of material substance; as well as to the further question,—whether this 'custom' is (unconsciously) grounded upon reason or not. When treating of abstraction and general ideas, he shows that the 'general idea of substance' was formed 'by abstracting;'—that our idea of body or matter was of 'an extended solid substance,' and our idea of mind or soul that of 'a substance that thinks' or is conscious. But in none of these mental experiences does he profess to find a 'clear and distinct' idea of substance; he only finds that we are somehow obliged to suppose 'we know not what.' 'We have no other idea or notion of Matter but something wherein many sensible qualities which affect our senses do subsist.' In like manner, 'by sup-

[1] *Essay*, b. II. ch. 23. §§ 1, 2.

posing a substance wherein thinking, knowing, doubting, and a power of moving do subsist,' we have thus 'as clear a notion of Spirit as we have of Body, the one being supposed to be (without our knowing what it is) the substratum to those simple ideas we have from without; and the other supposed (with a like ignorance of what it is) to be the substratum to those operations we experiment in ourselves within.' It is plain 'that the idea of corporeal substance is as remote from our conceptions and apprehensions as that of spiritual substance or spirit; and therefore from our not having any notion of the substance of spirit, we can no more conclude its non-existence than we can for the same reason deny the existence of body.' It is 'as rational' to affirm there is no body, because we have no clear and distinct idea of the substance of matter, as to say there is no spirit, because we have no clear and distinct idea of the substance of a spirit.' But 'whatever be the secret abstract nature of substance in general, all the ideas we have of particular distinct sorts of substances are nothing but several combinations of simple ideas [1], coexisting in such, though unknown, cause of their union, so as to make the whole subsist of itself.' 'Powers make a great part of our complex ideas of substances.' — All this goes against a substance constitutive of conscious life, as well as against a substance constitutive of sensible qualities, if it is a ground of objection to either, though Berkeley applied it only to the latter.

The *Essay* of Locke was coming into vogue when Berkeley was beginning to think. At the time, it awakened his fresh and original mind more, probably, than any other philosophical book. But it failed to satisfy him in what it taught about the independent reality of the primary qualities of Matter; and also about abstract ideas, especially

[1] 'Simple ideas'—virtually the *qualities* coexisting, &c.

the 'obscure and relative' abstract idea of material Substance.

Certain contemporary tendencies increased Berkeley's dissatisfaction with these opinions of Locke. The age was prolific of atomic Materialism. The rise of the mixed mathematical sciences, and the intellectual habits formed by exclusive attention to external nature, were leading many to attribute their very consciousness itself—that consciousness which Descartes assumed as the ground of all knowledge, and among the facts of which Locke searched for the actual constitution of human knowledge and beliefs—to the powers of unconscious Matter—that external substance or 'something without us,' which Locke said was the cause of our sensations. This unintelligible Matter, it seemed, might be the source of all the phenomena of our conscious life, as well as of all that happens in extended nature. Locke himself had attributed our sensations to it: he had even suggested that God might give it, in some of its possible organisations, power to be conscious in all the other states of which we are conscious. 'It is not,' he says, 'much more remote from our comprehension to conceive this than to conceive that God should superadd to it *another* substance with a faculty of thinking; since we know not in what thinking consists, nor to what sort of substances the first eternal thinking Being has been pleased to give that power [1].' Locke here suggests, however, only a created, not an ultimate materialism, for he refers the ultimate dependence of matter and its powers to Supreme Mind and Will.

Such were some of the early issues of the endeavour of modern philosophy to explain conscious life and our knowledge of solid and extended things. It was unwilling to

[1] See *Essay*, b. IV. ch. 7. § 9; also b. I. ch. 4. § 18; II. ch. 23; III. 10. § 15.

accept external perception and free or moral agency as irreducible facts; and it saw that extended things could not be exactly what we now find them, if there were no percipient beings in existence to endow them with at least their *secondary* qualities. The tendency of Descartes, Malebranche, and Leibnitz was to explain perception by the agency of God —to find power *only* in Spirit—to assume the impotence of Matter. Hobbes, Gassendi, and other atomists or corpuscularians, at the opposite extreme, found power *only* in matter, and assumed that what is unconscious was the cause of conscious intelligence. Spinoza, in his higher speculative flight, emptied natural things and finite spirits of real substance and power, and even the *Unica Substantia* of any really free or moral agency. The moderate, cautious, and pious Locke found in physical impulse the phenomenal, but not the efficient or final, cause of our simple ideas of sense; for he somewhat incoherently referred this phenomenal causality of matter to the spiritual power of God. All this is disclosed in a retrospect of the seventy years' interval between Descartes and Berkeley.

It was at this juncture that it occurred to Berkeley to ask a question which had not been put, from the point of view at which he put it, by any ancient or modern. He found those presuppositions about *matter*—the supposed cause of our sensations—making men either materialists or sceptics. He pressed upon the world, with all the fervour of his Irish temperament, this New Question, to be answered before men could rest either in dogmatic materialism or in scepticism:—What in reason should we *mean* when we assume the *existence* of 'matter;' and to *what* power must we refer the phenomena that are daily presented to our senses?—if, in the spirit of Locke, we are to be faithful to the facts of our mental experience. In other words, what **is the true meaning of** 'external substance' and 'external cause'? A more faithful psychological examination of our experience might perhaps show that philosophers had been making an irrational assumption, in supposing that what we see and touch involves the existence of an *unconscious* substance of *unknown* power; or that we are obliged, as philosophers, to defend belief in this, when, with the mass of mankind, we affirm the real existence of the material world.

To convert our conception of Matter into an intelligible conception, and to determine the true function of the only intelligible material world, in the spiritual economy of the universe, was virtually what Berkeley attempted. His contemporaries and predecessors had been taking for granted that the things presented to sense exist substantially or unphenomenally; some had even thought that they were somehow the cause of self-consciousness or intelligence. He entreated them to doubt their dogma, and to cease to suppose that unreason could solve, in whole or in part, the mystery of the universe. Let them first ascertain that this Materialism could really explain anything, or, indeed, that it was an intelligible dogma. Instead of accepting meaningless propositions about the real existence, outwardness, and efficiency of material substance, he would first ask what *existence*, and being *real, external, substantial,* and *powerful,* can in reason mean, when these predicates are asserted of the things that we are daily seeing and touching.

What Berkeley tried to do was to get this, as a previous question, put in place of the old scientific and theological controversies about an unintelligible matter, and space, and power. He wanted to settle the *philosophical meaning* of 'material substance;' he did not want to prove the *practical reality* of the material world, which no sane person could doubt. He wanted, also, to settle the *philosophical meaning* of 'power' or 'cause,' when these terms are applied to sensible things; he did not doubt that there was a way in which even sensible things might be spoken of as powers or causes.

Berkeley's place in history cannot be understood by readers who do not see that what he tried to do was thus to change the (philosophical) question about the material world, with which his predecessors had been busy, into what he believed to be a deeper and more urgent one. With this question changed, he hoped that thinking men might be relieved from speculative perplexities about the external things we see and touch—which retarded the physical sciences; and that they might also discover the irrationality of referring self-conscious life, whether manifested in sense or in any other way, to blind unconscious matter as its cause. Find what matter means, when we are faithful to facts, and are not misled by empty words and metaphysical abstractions. This was his fervid entreaty. His promise was that when we have found this we shall at once see that we do not need to search for evidence of its 'reality;' and also that there is no room in reason for materialistic assumptions of 'power' in matter—because in truth the things we see and touch, as only caused causes, not uncaused or originating causes, can in reason have only a phenomenal and inefficient sort of power.

But what are the psychological facts to which we must be faithful? Here Berkeley started with Locke's ambiguous thesis, that human knowledge is the issue of experience —in our senses and in reflection[1].

When he reflected further upon our knowledge of the things presented to our senses, with which all physical and natural sciences are concerned, and which are commonly called *matter*, he said that he could not find in *this* matter Locke's abstract idea of substance. On the contrary, abstract or unphenomenal substance seemed to him either a

---

[1] See Berkeley's metaphysical *Commonplace Book* (*Works*, vol. iv). Compare *Principles of Human Knowledge*, §§ 1, 2.

meaningless term or to involve a contradiction; and what is either meaningless or contradictory cannot be real. He found sights and touches and sounds and tastes and smells. He found also—so he believed—*himself*, conscious of these sights and touches, and sounds, and tastes, and smells—conscious too of his own identity through all their changes, and of his own power to produce to some extent changes in what he saw and touched. When he reflected upon his experience of what is called *matter*, he found only sense-phenomena (sights, touches, &c.), presented according to natural laws, and necessarily dependent on some person being percipient of them. Space and its contents, he concluded, must be essentially what through our senses we perceive. Thus tested, they are essentially phenomena[1];—what we call 'external things' must therefore be the phenomena presented to us by the five senses. These we cannot without absurdity regard as either the representations or the effects of an abstract, unphenomenal, and therefore unintelligible, 'substance.'

It was thus that Berkeley melted 'matter' down into phenomena present to the senses. The existence of *this* matter was incapable even of Cartesian doubt. When we say that we see or touch a material object, all (according to his report) that we can truly mean is, that we are percipient, i.e. conscious in sense, of phenomena which have a very practical meaning. Of these, while we are percipient of them, we have the same sort of evidence that we have of our own existence. In being percipient, we find our mind and mental agency; we also find passive and mind-dependent sense-phenomena. We are *conscious* of the former: we are *percipient*—if this term is preferred to 'consciousness'—of the latter. There is as little room for doubt and problematical inference in the one case as in the other. Human knowledge begins with these two (for Berkeley)

[1] In Berkeley's nomenclature *ideas*.

irreducible facts—(a) self conscious of self, and (b) percipient of sense-phenomena that are in themselves unsubstantial and powerless.

But Berkeley found more than this, when he still further reflected upon our knowledge of solid and extended bodies, of different sizes, placed in space. For, we are obliged to believe that these continue to exist independently of the individual mind; but the sights or sounds present in actual perception are transitory. They cannot form a knowledge of solid and extended things that do not pass away. We are obliged to recognise in the things of sense more than a series of isolated sense-phenomena. We perceive *clusters* of phenomena, which we call individual things, and we regard the phenomena as their 'qualities.' Into what ultimate facts of our mental experience is this developed perception of *qualified things* to be resolved ? If things exist only while they actually appear to our senses, what is meant by their individual permanence and by their qualities ?

If the material world were reduced to nothing more than passing sensations, the existence of things would be intermittent and fragmentary, not permanent and individualised. The tree that I suppose I am looking at—from a distance, exists as *my* visual phenomena *only while I am looking at it*. And even then only in a very small number of the phenomena which, under the name of 'qualities,' I refer to it; for, being at a distance, the *invisible* qualities, which I find I can intelligibly attribute to it, are not, at the time, my actual sensations. Do *they* all the while exist? If not, the greater part of what is meant by the tree, which I suppose I am looking at, is (because external to my *present* sense-perceptions) not real, even at the very time that I say 'I see the tree.' If external matter means only *actual* sensations, all visible qualities of things must relapse into non-entity when they are left in the dark ; and their tangible ones too, in the light as well, unless a percipient is *always* in actual contact with every part of them. The external world could not have existed millions of ages before men, or other sentient beings, began to be conscious of sensations, if only *this* is what is meant by its real existence[1].

Here Berkeley acknowledges the validity of what he calls 'judgments' of 'suggestion,' but without offering any analysis of their rational ground. *Suggestion* is one of the terms he uses to express the mental tendency (by him unanalysed) that produces our expectation of a reappearance of phenomena, previously connected in our experience, when one or more of them has been again perceived. Perception through suggestion,—which presupposes memory and imagination, i.e. what has been called representative, in contrast to presentative, consciousness; and also the existence of rational order in the phenomenal world—developes thus into *acquired* or *expectant* perception, and ultimately into scientific *prevision*. The actual sight of the tree suggests the phenomenon of resistance, as naturally so connected with what is seen that we *expect* to encounter that phenomenon, after going through the locomotive experience required to bring us into collision with its trunk. The one sense-phenomenon is the *suggesting sign* of the other. This connexion between them is (so far as the sense of sight is concerned) what Berkeley means by 'visual language.' But significance is not confined (as he confines it) to visual phenomena. All phenomena in all the senses are significant. One sense virtually does duty for others. What is called the material world is thus found in experience to consist not of *mere* phenomena, but of *significant* phenomena. As such, it is interpretable in its nature. It is a cosmos and not a chaos of phenomena.

---

[1] This question is virtually raised by Locke (*Essay*, b. IV. ch. 11), when he assumes that the things of sense are 'known' by us only while they are actually present to our senses—their past and future existence being only 'presumed.' He fails to show how anything at all can be known in a so-called knowledge that is confined to present sensations.

It gradually emerges too as a cosmos of individual phenomenal things placed in space.

The most striking examples of this all-important general fact, that sense-phenomena constitute an interpretable language, are without doubt those presented by Sight. But one must never forget that this Symbolism constructs our whole sense-experience, and that we are continually translating the language of each sense above all into the original and fundamental data of Touch. The inductive inferences of previsive science are only more conscious and elaborate translations of this sort, founded ultimately on rational suggestion. External nature is sense symbolism. Every appearance of which we are conscious in our senses is significant of other appearances in sense, which at the time we are not conscious of, but only imagine. The significations are not indeed discoverable in the *mere* sensation, nor by any *à priori* reasoning. Our suggested or habitual interpretations are the result of custom; but it is a custom which is found on further analysis to be latent reason: what in its higher and calculated form is inductive reasoning commences in the form of mechanical habit.

The objective connexion between a present phenomenon in sense and expected phenomena which it signifies is said by Berkeley to be 'arbitrary.' He enlarges on this arbitrariness, and founds on it his favourite analogy of a visual language —the connexion between names and their meanings being also arbitrary. This may seem to imply that the natural laws which govern what is presented in sense are capricious, or not to be depended on. What he really intends appears to be, that there is no eternal reason in the nature of things why a tree seen from a distance should 'suggest' an expectation of the particular tactual and muscular phenomena which it does suggest; nor why any one of the constant connexions among phenomena which form the web of physical science should not have been other than it is in fact.

Physical causation is really physical signification,—a natural language. It is not more a *necessary* connexion than is the customary connexion between a word in any human language and the meaning which men have arbitrarily agreed to connect with the word. In both cases we have established custom. God, in the exercise of His free-will, is accustomed to maintain sensible things and their natural laws as we find them. He might have abstained from creation; or the physical laws might have been originally made different from what they are, including (Berkeley would add) even the spacial relations of things.

Belief in a divinely established connexion among sense-phenomena is Berkeley's expression for belief in natural law. This 'experienced' permanence in the relations between the *present* and the *expected*, among the different clusters of phenomena—assumed by him as common sense—is his (virtually common sense) explanation of our belief in the 'permanence' of sensible things, during the intervals in which they are not actually perceived. To illustrate expectations due to ordinary suggestion and habit is one use of his writings on Vision, making them an important contribution to psychology. There is neither contradiction nor meaninglessness, he would say, in a material world that is thus composed of the *significant sense-phenomena* which we all practically interpret: there must be either meaninglessness or contradiction in the material world of the philosophers, which consists of abstract, and therefore unintelligible, 'substances' and 'powers.'

But we find in our knowledge of the material world, Berkeley tells us, when we reflect still further, more even than this present perception, and this expectation or acquired perception. Causation, in its highest meaning, is more than the significance, that is to say the steady natural order, of the phenomena of sense. Indeed it is quite other than this. It is not phenomenal at all. It is unphenomenal, as I find it in my common sense conviction of my own responsible agency. It is involved in the use of the personal pronoun 'I,' and in the assertion 'I *can*.' The germ at least of this teaching may, I think, be attributed to Berkeley.

Besides the present and the suggested perceptions of sense, he finds that experience involves the 'notion' (not 'idea') of the perceiving active being that each one calls *myself*. I cannot indeed be percipient of myself in the phenomenal way I am percipient of sights or sounds. Still, I can use the personal pronoun with *meaning;* I can speak *intelligibly* of my own continued identity. I am obliged too, in my moral experience, to believe in my own free voluntary activity; so that I practically understand what *responsible power* means. It is only in this way indeed that the word power gathers meaning; for 'power' affirmed of *mere* phenomena, present or expected, is meaningless. My conviction of *my own* power is as certain as my conviction of my own existence, at least to the extent to which I acknowledge moral responsibility for my volitions.

But there must be Power in the universe other than each man's personal power; for we all find ourselves unable at will to produce the phenomena of which we are percipient in our senses, or to change the natural laws of their occurrence. We overcome external nature only by submission to the divinely established order in which its phenomena have to appear. In our experience of things we find ourselves able and yet unable; sometimes we *can* and sometimes we *cannot;* and our experienced ability is small indeed in its range compared to our experienced inability. But in this experience of his own limited power each one finds *himself;* we also have in this our one intelligible illustration of what the words power and impotence mean. That which is done, but which I am thus morally convinced is not done by *me*, must have been done (so **Berkeley argues**) by the *only kind* of power which experience gives me any example of. That is to say, it must be due to Mind in its moral agency. When we speak of any other sort of power than this, we are involving ourselves in meaningless abstractions[1]. Materialistic Causation is therefore impossible.

It thus becomes necessary in reason that the things of sense, in themselves unsubstantial and impotent, should be sustained and regulated by moral agency. This moral agency is what we mean by God. We cannot go deeper. The Divine or Perfect Agent presents to us the phenomena of which we are conscious in the five senses. God potentially holds, and ever and anon suggests, in and through custom based on reason, the phenomena which we expect. All the natural laws of the universe are simply manifestations of the Active Intelligence in which the universe centres, and in which its ultimate explanation is found. This is the efficient cause at work in those metamorphoses of sense-phenomena, and of the 'things' they constitute, with which the physical and natural sciences are concerned;—the formal cause of the relations which make natural law, and all real science;—their final cause too is this intending rational Will. In the knowledge of God or Supreme Reason, the material world becomes intelligible. Its permanence, amidst the constant changes of its constituent phenomena, is thus accounted for. Its primary qualities, as well as the propositions of science concerning things and their laws, which, on this theory, at first seemed dissolved in perishable sensations, are in the end restored in the Divine Rational Providence.

Such in its development would be Berkeley's explanation of what is implied in the *reality* we attribute to the material world. It virtually takes in the three connected objects of

---

[1] There is some analogy between what may thus be developed out of Berkeley, and the explanation of belief in the not-self long afterwards offered by Fichte.

metaphysical inquiry — Self, the World, and God — that is to say, the two opposed and dependent substances, and the one supreme Substance and Power of Cartesianism. But it is not worked out into a philosophy by Berkeley himself. What he attempted was done, he modestly says, 'with a view to giving hints to thinking men who have leisure and curiosity to go to the bottom of things, and pursue them in their own minds.' The final result of his new conception of Matter was the substitution of GOD for the unintelligible material substance and power of Locke. The report he made, after he had reflected upon 'the facts of consciousness'—freed from the bondage of abstract words, against which he vehemently protested—was in effect this:—We in this mortal life reach a practical knowledge of ourselves and of God, through our consciousness of the significant and interpretable phenomena of sense, commonly called the material world—the final moral end of whose significant and interpretable presence in the universe seems to be, to enable finite spirits who are percipient of them to become self-conscious, cognizant of one another, and cognizant of God, in whom we all live and move and have our being.

Berkeley, as we have seen, started from Locke's ambiguous formula which reduces human knowledge, in its last analysis, to human 'experience.' But both Locke and Berkeley, without critical analysis of what they thus assume, presuppose in experience more than *mere* phenomena. Locke's employment of the rational principle of causality, in his explanation of our knowledge of God, for instance, is a virtual acknowledgment of other than merely phenomenal elements in its constitution. Dr. Samuel Clarke (1675–1729), a philosophical theologian of Locke's School, worked out a 'demonstration' of the necessity for an eternal or uncaused Cause, in the form of an appeal to that in mind which intellectually obliges us—without a phenomenal experience of the fact—to believe that space and time must be ir finite, and that an eternal free cause is of the essence ci reason. The phenomena presented by God to the senses, along with the sense-interpretations of mere suggestion, do not exhaust the psychology of Berkeley. Custom induced suggestion was in the end contrasted by him with rational inference. 'To perceive,' he tells us in one of his later works, 'to perceive [1]' is one thing: to judge is another. So likewise to be suggested is one thing, and to be inferred another. Things are suggested and perceived by sense. We make judgments and inferences by the understanding. We infer causes from effects, effects from causes, and properties from one another, where the connexion is necessary [2].'

In *Siris* he puts present sense and the suggestions of custom still more in the background, and God and Reason becomes all in all. When he there attributes to Aristotle the doctrine 'that the mind of man is a *tabula rasa*, without innate ideas,' in contrast to Plato who found in the mind 'notions which never were nor can be in the sense,' he hints his own opinion. 'Some perhaps may think the truth to be this:—that there are properly no *ideas*, or passive objects [phenomena] in the mind but what were derived from sense, but that there are also besides these her own acts or operations. Such are *notions*.' (§ 308.) Again: 'The perceptions of sense are gross: but even in the senses there is a difference..... By experiments of sense we become acquainted with the lower faculties of the soul; and from them, whether by a gradual evolution or ascent, we arrive at the highest. Sense supplies images to memory. These become subjects for fancy to work upon. Reason considers and judges of the imaginations. And these acts of reason become new objects to the understanding. In this scale each lower faculty is a step that leads to one above it. And the uppermost naturally leads to the Deity; which is

---

[1] 'to perceive,' i.e. to have sensations.
[2] *Vindication of New Theory of Vision*, sect. 42.

rather the object of intellectual knowledge than even of the discursive faculty, not to mention the sensitive.' (§ 303.)

If Berkeley in his youth sometimes seems to resolve the material world and mind itself into Sensation, the pervading tendency of *Siris* is to find the essence of the universe in Reason, and to see in its phenomena an opportunity, through physical research and science, for the education of reason in the individual mind.

Such was Berkeley's philosophical conception of Matter, as it appears, first in the reasonings of his youth, and then in the more developed speculations of his later life. We may now look at some of its historical issues.

Six years before *Siris* appeared, Locke's vague formula regarding human knowledge, as in some way the issue of 'experience,' had been interpreted by DAVID HUME (1711-76) so as to include in experience only the transitory phenomena of sense and habit. Reason was melted down into impressions, and the suggested ideas of these impressions. 'Impressions,' or the original data of sense, and faint images of these called 'ideas'—through habit giving rise to new impressions—this was in the end his theory of knowledge[1]. The universe was pronounced 'a riddle, an ænigma, an inexplicable mystery.'—It was by this agnostic consequence, deduced from these premises, that Hume obliged metaphysicians to reconsider much that they had before taken for granted, and to search further for the roots of knowledge, if it was to remain rooted at all.

Hume's sceptical paralysis of intelligence and philosophical agnosticism was the crisis of the Modern or Cartesian movement of philosophy. His exposure of the impossibility of knowledge,—if knowledge at last means only experience, and if experience consists only of impressed and blindly suggested phenomena,—was the act in the history of philo-

[1] See Hume's *Inquiry concerning Human Understanding*, ch. 2-8.

sophy next following Berkeley's arguments for the absolute dependence of Matter and of the material world on percipient and active mind. Blind Materialism seemed, in Berkeley's theory of existence, to become impossible, and to be replaced by a mind-constituted universe, in which all solid and extended things, including our bodily organisms, can exist only as groups of dependent and powerless phenomena, perceived and changed in part by finite minds, and above all by ever-active Divine Mind. But Berkeley's mind-constituted universe, it was argued by Hume, involved assumptions which—on the hypothesis of pure empiricism, that all knowledge is merely phenomena connected by habit —might be proved (if proof of anything were possible on this hypothesis) to be as absurd as Berkeley had found abstract material substance to be.

Hume's attempt to show that, on Berkeley's original principles, mind or self is as merely phenomenal as matter—as unsubstantial and as impotent—is what gives him his epoch-making place in modern history. His sceptical account of knowledge was first proposed, without qualification, in his *Treatise on Human Nature*, in 1738; then, in a milder way, in 1748, in his *Inquiry concerning Human Understanding*. In both he refers to Berkeley's rejection of abstract ideas, and analysis of matter into the phenomena of sense, as new lessons in philosophy. Looking only at the negative part of what Berkeley taught about the meaning of the word 'real,' when applied to sensible things, he claims for him a place among the (unconscious) sceptics; adding, as evidence of this, that his 'arguments admit of no answer, and yet produce no conviction, their only effect being to produce that momentary amazement, irresolution, and confusion, which is the result of scepticism[1].'

The way in which Hume would bar Berkeley's ascent in *Siris* (a book to which he makes no reference), from the

[1] *Inquiry concerning Human Understanding*, sect. xii. pt. i., note.

'gross perceptions of sense' to 'the intellectual knowledge of Deity,' is argued and illustrated in detail throughout his *Treatise* and *Inquiry*.

A significant passage to begin with is that in which Hume deals with Berkeley's 'notion' of Self. This Berkeley takes for granted we are conscious of, finding as he thinks the evidence of it in a certain 'inward feeling or reflection.' Apart from this 'notion,' generated by the 'feeling,' a mind-constituted universe dissolves into mere phenomena, as readily as abstract matter did, at the point of view Berkeley occupied. 'There are,' argued Hume, 'some philosophers, who imagine we are every moment conscious of what we call our SELF; that we feel its existence and its continuance in existence; and are certain, beyond the evidence of a demonstration, both of its perfect identity and simplicity.... Unluckily all these positive assertions are contrary to that very experience, which is pleaded for them.... For my part, when I enter most intimately into what I call *myself*, I always stumble on some *particular* perception or other—of heat or cold, light or shade, love or hatred, pain or pleasure (i.e. something merely phenomenal). I never can catch *myself* at any time without a perception, and never can observe anything but the perception. When my perceptions are removed for any time, as by sound sleep, so long am I insensible of *myself*, and may truly be said not to exist. And were all my perceptions (i.e. phenomena) removed by death, and I could neither think, nor feel, nor see, nor love, nor hate; after the dissolution of my body I should be entirely annihilated; nor do I conceive what is farther requisite to make me a perfect nonentity[1].' Elsewhere he argues that 'the question concerning the *substance* of the *soul* is an absolutely unintelligible question,' as much so as Berkeley

---

[1] See Hume's *Treatise on Human Nature, being an attempt to introduce the Experimental Method of reasoning into Moral Subjects*, b. i. pt. iv. sect. 6.

had shown that about material substance, abstracted from its phenomena, to be.

We have Berkeley's reply to this, by anticipation, in the third of his *Three Dialogues between Hylas and Philonous.* 'It seems to me,' Hylas objects, 'that according to your own way of thinking, and in consequence of your own principles, it should follow that *you* are only a system of floating ideas, without any substance to support them. Words are not to be used without a meaning; and as there is no more meaning in *spiritual substance* than in *material substance*, the one ought to be exploded as well as the other.' 'How often,' replies Philonous (representing Berkeley), 'must I repeat that *I know or am conscious of* my own being; and that *I myself* am not my *ideas*, but somewhat else—a thinking active principle that perceives, knows, wills, and operates about ideas. I *know* that I—one and the same self—perceive both colours and sounds: that a colour cannot perceive a sound, nor a sound a colour: that I am therefore one individual principle, distinct from colour and sound; and, for the same reason, from all other sensible things and inert ideas. But I am not in like manner *conscious* either of the existence or essence of [abstract or unphenomenal] matter[1].'

Take, next, Hume's demand for evidence of that continual dependence of the coexistences and changes which constitute the World on supreme active Mind, which Berkeley had argued for.—'It seems to me,' he says, 'that this theory of the universal energy and operation of the Supreme Being is too bold ever to carry conviction with it, to a man sufficiently apprised of the weakness of human reason, and the narrow limits to which it is confined in its operations. . . . Our line is too short to fathom such immense abysses. And however we may flatter ourselves that we are guided

---

[1] See Berkeley's *Works*, vol. i. pp. 328-29. Berkeley has only partly met the objection that if unimaginable *matter* is absurd, all unimaginable *self* must be absurd too.

in every step we take by a kind of verisimilitude and experience; we may be assured that this fancied experience has no authority, when we thus apply it to subjects that lie entirely out of the reach of experience.... We are ignorant, it is true, of the manner in which *bodies* operate on each other: *their* " force" or " energy" is entirely incomprehensible. But are we not equally ignorant of the manner or force in which a *mind*—even the Supreme Mind—operates either on itself or on body? Whence, I beseech you, do we acquire any idea of it? We have no sentiment or consciousness of this power in ourselves. We have no idea of the Supreme Being but what we learn by reflection upon our own faculties. Were our ignorance therefore a good reason for rejecting anything, we should be led into that principle of denying all energy in the Supreme Being as much as in the grossest matter. We surely comprehend as little the operations of the one as of the other. Is it more difficult to conceive that motion may arise from *impulse* than that it may arise from *volition?* All we know is our profound ignorance in both cases.[1]'

Berkeley's favourite doctrine of a *Divine arbitrariness* in the original establishment of the significations of the phenomena presented to the senses is by Hume carried out into an *inexplicable arbitrariness*—in which anything may *a priori* be the ' cause' of anything that happens, either in matter or in mind. For this maxim is not confined, by Hume to causation between the things of sense only, but is applied also to the causation in a higher meaning, supposed by Berkeley necessarily to connect phenomena and their changes with mind and moral agency. All alike are inexplicably phenomena that are somehow practically significant; but there is no rational meaning involved in their developments. The conception of rationally willed connexion carries with it, when it disappears,—(*a*) Berkeley's implied contrast between natural signs and the rational will of God, which gives

[1] See Hume's *Inquiry concerning Human Understanding*, sect. vii.

them their significance, and (*b*) the dependence in reason of the orderly phenomenal world on Mind or Spirit, as the only formal, efficient, and final cause of the whole. There is no reason in the Universe recognised in Hume's philosophy, only blind uncertain fate. All so-called knowledge is only inexplicably produced belief, mechanically due to custom. Take the following :—'Whatever is *may* not be. No negation of a fact can involve a contradiction. The nonexistence of any being[1], without exception, is as clear and distinct an idea as its existence. The proposition which affirms it not to be, however false, is no less conceivable and intelligible than that which affirms it to be. The case is different with the sciences, properly so called. Every proposition which is not true is there unintelligible. That the cube of sixty-four is equal to the half of ten is a false proposition, and can never be distinctly conceived. But that Cæsar, or the angel Gabriel, or any being never existed, may be a false proposition, but still is perfectly conceivable, and implies no contradiction. The existence, therefore, of any *being* can only be proved by arguments from its cause or its effect[2]; and these arguments are founded entirely on experience. If we reason *a priori*, anything may appear able to produce anything. The falling of a pebble may, for aught we know, extinguish the sun; or the wish of a man controul the planets in their orbits. It is only experience which teaches us the nature and bounds of cause and effect, and enables us to infer the existence of one object [either 'material' or 'mental'] from that of another. . . . Not only the will of the Supreme Being may create matter; but for aught we know *a priori*, the will of any other being might create it, or any other cause that the most whimsical imagination can assign[3].'

[1] This includes of course the Divine Being.
[2] He means from its *phenomenal* or *caused* cause—its established sign, as Berkeley would say.
[3] *Inquiry*, sect. xii. pt. iii.—We find in Philosophy three divergent

Hume resolves Reason into Custom.

The principle that in the end determines all real inferences, Hume argues, can be nothing more than blind Custom in Nature, which occasions habits in us. 'For, wherever the repetition of any particular act or operation produces a propensity to renew the same act or operation, without being impelled by any reasoning or process of the understanding; we always say that this *propensity* is the *effect* of Custom. By employing that word, we pretend not to have given the *ultimate reason* of such propensity. We only point out a principle of human nature, which is universally acknowledged, and which is well known by its effects. *Perhaps we can push our enquiries no farther*[1].'

Berkeley's short and easy method with Materialism, in his explanation of the philosophical meaning of Matter, was thus followed—in the next great movement in European thought—not by a fuller development of Spiritual Philosophy, but by a Scepticism which professed inability to find more in experience than inexplicably associated phenomena, which, through 'custom,' inexplicably issue in beliefs that are ultimately blind. To this the modern philosophical movement, as represented in Locke, was conducted, when Locke and Berkeley were interpreted by Hume. This philosophical disintegration of rational belief surrendered all

views about Causality, corresponding severally to each of the two extreme positions—pure Empiricism and absolute Idealism, and to the 'broken system' which acknowledges an inexplicable duality, wisely resting satisfied with an acknowledgment of irreducible convictions, latent in our rational and moral nature, but ready to be developed by reflection.—According to one of these views, anything may, as far as we know, be the cause of anything, and it is presumptuous to speak of any alleged cause as 'sufficient' or 'insufficient.' This is Hume's account of the matter.—According to the opposite extreme view, each thing must be caused by everything that exists, in the infinite concatenation of existence, according to an immanent rational necessity. This is the outcome of the mathematical philosophy of Spinoza, and of the rational thought of Hegel. Berkeley tends towards it sometimes in *Siris*.—The third view finds the only true and 'sufficient' cause in the power of a moral agent—exemplified in our own moral experience of free personal agency.

[1] See *Inquiry*, sect. v. p. 1.

faith which depends on other elements in knowledge than phenomena connected by custom,—thus dissolving Berkeley's conception of a mind-constituted-universe.

In this way, in the middle of last century, the modern movement in quest of philosophy seemed to have exhausted itself.—The inductive psychology to which it had given rise, represented in Britain by the custom and association theory of Hume, had no further word to say—unless in due time, in Hartley and his school, to repeat the word 'association.' And in France an attenuated edition of Locke was maintaining a declining existence, in the school of Condillac.—On the other hand, the line of dogmatic demonstrative metaphysicians who succeeded Spinoza—after being represented in Germany, partly in reaction against him, by Leibnitz—seemed about to expire in the arid scholasticism of the German school of Wolff.

Thus one of the great intellectual tendencies which followed the original Cartesian impulse issued, in the middle of the eighteenth century, in the philosophical nescience of Hume, and the other in the dogmatic reasonings of the Wolffians.

But the disposition to seek for philosophy is permanent in human nature. In none of the preceding intellectual struggles had the complete philosophic form of knowledge been reached. Each of them contributed, however, to its disclosure. None was more effectual in this way than the empirical scepticism of Hume, which the Immaterialism of Berkeley occasioned if it did not justify. For this scepticism led to the reconsideration of ultimate principles, in the light either (a) of the actual constitution of our human nature, or (b) of the rational constitution of any possible experience.

One of the immediate and direct effects of Hume was the attempt of REID (1710–96), by patient reflection, to make patent principles latent in the human consciousness, some of which had been proceeded upon but not formally recognised in Locke's account of knowledge. Another was the attempt of KANT (1724-1804), by transcendental criticism, to explain by experience the constructive activity of universal reason. Reid says that he at first accepted Berkeley's system, till, finding 'other consequences' to follow from it (i.e. from his own interpretation of it), which gave him 'more uneasiness than the want of a material world,' it occurred to him to reconsider what he believed to be the pervading assumption of Cartesianism—that we can be immediately percipient only of *representative* ideas. Kant found his point of departure in Hume's empirical explanation of our belief in the causal connexion of the universe as the effect of custom.

It is beyond the design of this Introduction to trace philosophy in the second stage of its modern history—its revival after its sceptical dissolution by Hume. In this stage, which extends from the latter part of last century to the present day, Kant holds a place so far similar to that of Descartes in the preceding epoch. Each is related to the preceding condition of opinion somewhat as Socrates or Plato was to Heraclitus and Protagoras. Kant too tried to accomplish more thoroughly the work undertaken by Descartes; as Plato did that of Socrates, or Aristotle that of Plato. The reflective criticism of the first stage in modern philosophy was insufficient; its recognition of the contents of experience was inadequate. This gave rise to the scepticism, which professed its inability to find at last more than blindly-produced belief within our reach on any subject; and argued that, since 'knowledge' is the issue only of transitory phenomena of sense, associated by custom, there can be no true knowledge at all. Reid as well as Kant gave expression to the consequent need for reconsidering the postulates without which our physical and moral experience would be impossible. Some of these indeed had been proceeded upon, as the guarantees of scientific generalisation, and of theological belief, by philosophers who, like Locke, and Berkeley in his earlier works, vaguely professed to explain all knowledge from 'experience.' But a more faithful and thorough investigation of the constitution of reason in man, and in any possible experience, was induced by the reaction from Hume. In particular, it led to Kant's search for elements in pure reason that necessarily connect phenomena in physical experience, and for others, in moral or practical reason, which justify faith in God, and in the free agency and immortality of man.

The consequences of Kant's so-called 'transcendental criticism' of the rational constitution of experience, in the second epoch of modern philosophy, presents analogies to the historical issues, in the preceding century, of the more tentative speculation of Descartes—but with the advantage, on the whole, that is gained for each later development of philosophy over the more imperfect system which precedes it. In no single system of philosophy do we find the full realisation of the philosophical ideal—only an approach to this, and an approach that has probably been assisted by the collisions of previous thought. In the post-Kantian period, Hegelianism has been interpreted as developed Kantism, as Spinozism was interpreted as developed Cartesianism. Yet the influence of Kant, in another aspect of his philosophy, appears in Comte and Positivism, as that of Descartes did in Hume.

True philosophy must at least not be logically inconsistent with itself. It must also be in harmony with those universal judgments of reason which our physical and our moral experience can be proved to presuppose. And it ought not to reject practical beliefs, hitherto permanent in human nature (though often dormant in individuals), which are not shown to be inconsistent with the necessary judgments of pure reason. To these three conditions the student of philosophy should conform.

To awaken intelligently in individual minds such rational judgments and natural convictions is the chief aim of philosophical education. From Socrates onwards this has been the effort of the true teacher of philosophy. The genuine elements of reason and of human nature are not always recognised consciously. Some of them are dormant; or they are acted on without a distinct consciousness of what they mean. They are potentially rather than actually 'universal and necessary.' Thus the conviction that we are free rational beings, and therefore morally obliged and responsible, is often weak; or it is acted on without a philosophical recognition of what it implies. The same is true as to those convictions of God and the higher life that belong to our moral experience. (It is the office of philosophical education to assist in making patent in the individual consciousness what was latent in human nature, but implied in the Universal Reason in which we all more or less share.)

History is full of the records of reactions against principles thus latent, which have lost their influence for a time, through some transient turn in the course of philosophical thought, or in the habit of the popular imagination. Reason is eternal; our individual consciousness of the reason latent in nature and in spirit fluctuates and may be paralyzed. Thus the recluse, by habitual introspection, weakens his practical conviction of external reality, and of his own individual personality and responsibility. And a person who is exclusively devoted to physical science loses the power of apprehending the facts of spiritual experience—even the meaning wrapped up in the personal pronoun 'I.' All that transcends external experience becomes illusory, including the conviction of spiritual personality, and of the moral truths involved in *that*, which give meaning to faith in God or Moral Government.

In this latter part of the nineteenth century, the material world, and the means of making ourselves more comfortable, through skilful applications of its laws in our service, occupy people's imagination as perhaps they never did before—not even in the outbreak of physical research when Berkeley produced his Immaterialism. At a time like this, faith in metaphysical realities—God, free agency, and individual responsibility—dissolves in doubt, because it does not admit of verification by the senses, but only of verification by spirit. That certainty which is reached through verification by phenomena presented to the senses—*although* it involves faith, and postulates of reason—is held paramount; the certainty that is reached without any appeal to the facts of sense, *because* it involves faith, is rejected as illusory. That is to say, faith in physical government—the basis of our inferences in the sciences of nature—is strong. Faith in inferences which presume moral or spiritual government—not less lawfully rested on the postulates of our moral experience—is weak.

Materialism, as it has formerly done, must disappear, if it contradicts what, when men try through reflection, are found to be constituents of reason and of human nature—though often dormant—existing only potentially, not actually, in many individual minds. As philosophy has done before, it may even swing to the opposite extreme, in its current conceptions in the next age. For, its past history has been a succession of oscillations, between one-sided physics and one-sided metaphysics—between extreme Materialism, which explains consciousness and thought by motion, and extreme Idealism, which explains the phenomenal things of sense and their motions by pure thought. These two systems of Monism, in their successive reappearances, have been the subjects of the *reductio ad absurdum*, in the Scepticism to which each extreme has given rise. Sceptical Nescience too, in its turn, passes away, when the genuine convictions of human nature have been recovered, and philosophic insight of them probably deepened by the preceding collision of the two extremes, with its sceptical issue. Philosophy is then better prepared than before to pass through the ordeal of another and more enlightened development of extreme

The Three Divisions of the 'Selections.' xlvii

Materialism and extreme Idealism, which are in turn corrected by a new manifestation of sceptical despair. It is thus that it advances, in depth and comprehensiveness, through successive sceptical crises, consequent upon the collision of its own extreme developments. What is permanent in the spiritual nature of man may strengthen in the end, even through the series of philosophical eclipses.

These *Selections from Berkeley*, aided by the annotations, are meant to incite to further reflection about his conclusions and assumptions. They are so arranged as to carry the reader through Berkeley's reasoned conception of Matter as necessarily dependent on percipient and active Mind; his analysis of the growth of visual perception through habit and suggestion of visual meanings; and his speculative hints as to the ultimate constitution of the universe in Mind.

The Treatise on the *Principles of Human Knowledge* forms the First Division of the *Selections*. It is a defence and application, at Locke's point of view, of the hypothesis that Matter or the material world can consist only of ordered phenomena that are necessarily dependent on a percipient agent—that its *esse* is *percipi*[1].

Berkeley's analysis of the development of Visual Perception, in the form of interpretations of significant visual phenomena, follows in the Second Division of the *Selections*. The extracts illustrate his psychological explanation of our acquired perception in Sight of things in space, and (so far) of our inductive and theological judgments. They all conduct

[1] The reader is referred, under this head, to the *Dialogues between Hylas and Philonous*, in the 'Collected Works' of Berkeley. His explanation of what is meant by Matter is further explained and illustrated in that charming example of philosophical exposition.

to the conclusion that the phenomena presented to sight are significant of Mind[1].

Extracts from *Siris* form the Third Division of the *Selections*. These contain Berkeley's Platonic meditations, on the ultimate constitution of the universe in the Universal Mind, and on the organic unity of knowledge; with fragments of ancient and medieval metaphysics.

A more detailed account of the contents of these three Divisions is given in the Prefatory Notes prefixed to each. The foot-notes occasionally raise some of the ultimate questions which a philosophical student is supposed to be trying to settle for himself.

A. CAMPBELL FRASER.

---

[1] Some may prefer to begin with the psychological analyses of visual perception in the Second Division of the *Selections*, and then return to the metaphysical reasonings about Matter contained in the First Division.

I.

Matter necessarily dependent on Mind.

A TREATISE

CONCERNING THE

PRINCIPLES OF HUMAN KNOWLEDGE.

The same Principles which, at first view, lead to Scepticism, pursued to a certain point, bring men back to Common Sense.—BERKELEY's *Third Dialogue.*

EDITOR'S PREFATORY NOTE.

THIS Treatise is a reasoned statement and defence of the theory that the Material World depends for its actual existence on percipient and active Mind. The latter part of it is an application of this theory to the promotion of physical, psychological, and theological science.

The *Introduction* (pp. 14-34) contains an exposure of the abuse of terms and Language, by men in general, but particularly by philosophers. Language had been the shield of scholastic abstractions. The key to Berkeley's original point of view may be found in his attack on 'abstract ideas' in this Introduction—resumed in other places. The underlying principle is,—that real knowledge is concerned only with individual things; that there can be no intelligible reality in the things of sense apart from the perceptions of a living mind; and that to test the meaning of common terms, especially terms which have become so abstract as Matter and Mind, we must realise in actual perception, or in imagination, individual things which they denote. This means that all genuine knowledge of things may be individualised. It is what has been called his Nominalism.

Not to pretend in words to substantiate mere abstractions which cannot be individualised, and always to verify our terms by what is conceivable, is the lesson of the Introduction. (It warns those entering on philosophy that above all they must avoid empty verbal abstractions.)

The first two sections of the *Principles* (pp. 35, 36) offer a statement of the sorts of ideas we are capable of conceiving, which may be compared with Locke's account of the origin of our knowledge.

In the 154 sections which follow, the lesson of the Introduction is applied to the meaning of the abstract term Matter. Berkeley argues that the things of sense mean sensations, actual or imagined, of which some one must be conscious, and that no effort of abstraction can exclude sensation from what is meant by external things, and at the same time preserve intelligibility.

(*Things*, existing intelligibly, he calls *ideas*. (The term 'idea' is apt to mislead. We might substitute *significant sensation*, or *significant phenomenon presented in sense*.)

Now, is there, he asks, any reason for supposing, under the empty name of Matter, that to exist which cannot be individualised, either in sense or in imagination, and is therefore unintelligible? (We cannot have an *abstract* idea of Matter, or indeed any conception of it other than what is derived from its manifestations in the actual perceptions or consciousnesses of sense. (Must not the real material world then be the sense experience of living persons;) and in all our inferences about *matter*, should we not regard it as so constituted that its very *esse* is *percipi*?—This is the chief question of Berkeley's philosophy, raised in Sect. 3, and pursued through the *Principles*. It opens the whole theory of knowledge.

That and the sections which follow may be conveniently arranged thus:—

I. (Sect. 3–33). A reasoned statement of what is meant by the *real existence* of the material world. Here Matter is melted down into significant sensation, instead of being an irreducible and meaningless abstraction. The chief conclusions may be thus expressed:—

Prefatory Note.

1. Abstract Matter—unperceiving and unperceived 'something'—whether viewed as Substance or as Cause—is a meaningless abstraction. When we try to give it meaning we necessarily involve ourselves in a contradiction of terms.

2. The only intelligible Substance, i.e. independent and permanent existence, is conscious Mind or Spirit; and the only intelligible Cause of changes is Mind or Spirit in free voluntary action.

3. The only intelligible *material world* must thus consist of what is perceived in sense. (What is perceived in the senses, Berkeley calls *sensation*, or, because dependent on being perceived, *idea*.) These perceived sensations or ideas appear, disappear, and reappear (so common sense obliges us to believe) independently of our will, in an order commonly called the order of nature. The only possible *material substances* (if we are still to speak of material substance) are the clusters of them called 'things,' formed and kept together by a Will that is independent of the individual human will, and therefore called 'external;' and the only possible *material causes* and *effects* (if we are still to apply the terms cause and effect to matter) are sensations, and clusters of sensations, that are connected in an Order which common sense makes us regard as uniform, which true philosophy refers to the supreme rational Will[1].

These 31 sections contain reasons for adopting this conception of the necessary dependence of the material world on Mind. A logical analysis of the reasons, and refutation of objections, is a good intellectual exercise.

II. (Sect. 34-84). A criticism of this theory of the necessary dependence of Matter on Mind, and of the evidence

---

[1] In Berkeley's nomenclature, external things are *ideas*; we have *notions* of self-conscious mind as substance and as cause, and also of relations among our ideas; but we can have neither an *idea* nor a *notion* of Matter abstracted out of all relation to the conscious life of feeling and thought.

by which it is supported—in the form of a statement and refutation of fourteen Objections to it.

Other objections and difficulties, not conceived by Berkeley, and partly arising in later philosophical thought, might be added, and critically examined by the student. Some of them are referred to in foot-notes which I have introduced.

III. (Sect. 85-156). The conception of Matter as consisting of sensations, or phenomena of sense, necessarily dependent on a conscious mind for their intelligible existence, thus examined and guarded against objections, is next applied to expel Scepticism and restore Belief as well as to improve the Sciences. The relative sections may be thus subdivided :—

1. (Sect. 85-100). Application of the theory of the necessary dependence of the material world on percipient and active Mind—

(a) To restore, in an intelligible form, Beliefs which were dissolving in Scepticism (Sect. 85-96);

(b) To free language and thought from unmeaning abstractions (Sect. 97-100);

2. (Sect. 101-134). Its application to the Sciences of External Nature—

(a) In purifying and advancing Experimental Physics, impeded by empty abstractions of Matter, Causation, Space, Time, and Motion (Sect. 101-116);

(b) In making Mathematics more intelligible, by relieving perplexities and contradictions to which the abstraction of Quantitative Infinity had given rise, in reasonings about number and space. (117-134)

3. (Sect. 135-156). Its application to our knowledge of the world of Spirits—human and Divine—

(a) By explaining and sustaining faith in the natural Immortality of men (Sect. 137-144);

(b) By explaining the belief which each man has in the existence of other men (Sect. 145);

(c) By explaining and sustaining faith in the existence of God (Sect. 146-156).

This Treatise, intended as a short and easy method with Materialists, is the most systematic and comprehensive of Berkeley's philosophical works[1]. It is an attempt to analyse the meaning of the common term 'Matter,' in a severe adherence to our concrete experience, purified from the abstractions that empty words are so apt to conceal. The student may find some of his best philosophical education and discipline in trying to determine whether his conception of what Matter means is after all a sufficient philosophical representation of human experience.

A. C. F.

[1] It is, however, only Part *First* of the Treatise as originally designed. Three years later its leading Principle was placed in new lights in his *Three Dialogues* between Hylas and Philonous (*Works*, vol. I. pp. 241-360), as a further preparation for Part *Second*, which never appeared. Much of the Second Part was written, but the manuscript was lost when Berkeley was travelling in Italy. This is mentioned in a letter from Berkeley to Dr. Samuel Johnson of New York, lately recovered among Dr. Johnson's correspondence. See Beardsley's 'Life and Correspondence of Samuel Johnson, D.D.' (New York, 1874.)

THE AUTHOR'S PREFACE.

WHAT I here make public has, after a long and scrupulous inquiry, seemed to me evidently true, and not unuseful to be known—particularly to those who are tainted with Scepticism[1], or want a demonstration[2] of the Existence and Immateriality of God, or the Natural Immortality of the Soul. Whether it be so or no I am content the reader should impartially examine; since I do not think myself any farther concerned for the success of what I have written than as it is agreeable to truth. But, to the end this may not suffer, I make it my request that the reader suspend his judgment till he has once at least read the whole through with that degree of attention and thought which the subject-matter shall seem to deserve. For, as there are some passages that, taken by

---

[1] 'SCEPTICISM,' in the form of doubt or disbelief of dogmatic assumptions of Theology, was what gave rise to Berkeley's reconsideration of the meaning of what we call Matter. Hume afterwards, putting a purely empirical interpretation on the philosophy of Locke and Berkeley, transformed the spiritualised universe of the latter into universal sceptical nescience.

[2] Does he here use 'demonstration' in its looser meaning of analogical proof which leaves no room for reasonable doubt that a thing is true in fact, or in its strict sense of something shown to be necessary in itself, the opposite being contrary to the absolute nature of things ? It appears that Berkeley had intended to explain this in the *Principles*, but the intention was not carried out. 'I shall demonstrate all my doctrines. The *nature of demonstration* to be set forth and insisted on in the Introduction. In that I must differ from Locke, for he makes all demonstration to be about abstract ideas, which I say we have not and cannot have' (*Commonplace Book*, in *Works*, vol. IV. p. 439).—Locke held that we cannot *know* external things except while they are actually present to our senses: all beyond is *presumed* as more or less probable. Except the existence of God, only the relations of *abstract* ideas are demonstrable according to Locke.

themselves, are very liable (nor could it be remedied) to gross misinterpretation, and to be charged with most absurd consequences, which, nevertheless, upon an entire perusal will appear not to follow from them; so likewise, though the whole should be read over, yet, if this be done transiently, it is very probable my sense may be mistaken; but to a thinking reader I flatter myself it will be throughout clear and obvious.—As for the characters of novelty and singularity which some of the following notions may seem to bear, it is, I hope, needless to make any apology on that account. He must surely be either very weak, or very little acquainted with the sciences, who shall reject a truth that is capable of demonstration, for no other reason but because it is newly known, and contrary to the prejudices of mankind. Thus much I thought fit to premise, in order to prevent, if possible, the hasty censures of a sort of men who are too apt to condemn an opinion before they rightly comprehend it.

THE AUTHOR'S INTRODUCTION.

1. PHILOSOPHY being nothing else but the study of wisdom and truth[1], it may with reason be expected that those who have spent most time and pains in it should enjoy a greater calm and serenity of mind, a greater clearness and evidence of knowledge, and be less disturbed with doubts and difficulties than other men. Yet so it is, we see the illiterate bulk of mankind, that walk the high-road of plain common sense, and are governed by the dictates of nature, for the most part easy and undisturbed. To them nothing that is familiar appears unaccountable or difficult to comprehend. They com-

---

[1] The definitions of Philosophy which have been given are various. They imply in general that it is the deepest and truest insight into the ultimate meaning of our experience. Its aim, as distinguished from ordinary knowledge and science, is, if possible, to conceive the universe under the unity of a single rational principle.
But it does not follow that this aim is fully attainable, or that our experience *can* (by us) be reduced to a rational unity in which faith is entirely eliminated by being converted into reasoned knowledge. Philosophy as 'the study of wisdom' may issue in the discovery that this result is inconsistent with a due recognition of our physical and moral experience. Bacon thus puts it in speaking of theology :—'As for perfection or completeness in divinity it is not to be sought. For he that will reduce a knowledge into an art will make it round and uniform ; but in divinity many things must be left abrupt' (*Advancement of Learning*). The history of Philosophy has been the history of a struggle between, on the one side, Idealism or Materialism, as complete explanations, and, on the other side, those who find themselves obliged by the data of experience to leave many things 'abrupt.'—In this and the four sections which follow, the imaginative ardour of Berkeley too much encourages the expectation that philosophy *can* solve all difficulties; and in the end he professes to have done this—as far as the material world is concerned. All through, however, there is even with him an unexplained residuum—a *moral* duality in experience—and the recognition of an end higher than philosophical science.

plain not of any want of evidence in their senses, and are out
of all danger of becoming Sceptics. But no sooner do we
depart from Sense and Instinct to follow the light of a
superior principle—to reason, meditate, and reflect on the
nature of things, but a thousand scruples spring up in our
minds concerning those things which before we seemed fully
to comprehend. Prejudices and errors of sense do from all
parts discover themselves to our view; and, endeavouring to
correct these by Reason, we are insensibly drawn into uncouth
paradoxes, difficulties, and inconsistencies, which multiply
and grow upon us as we advance in speculation, till at length,
having wandered through many intricate mazes, we find
ourselves just where we were, or, which is worse, sit down in
a forlorn Scepticism [1].

2. The cause of this is thought to be the obscurity of
things, or the natural weakness and imperfection of our
understandings. It is said, 'the faculties we have are few,
and those designed by nature for the support and pleasure of
life, and not to penetrate into the inward essence and constitution of things. Besides, the mind of man being finite, when
it treats of things which partake of infinity, it is not to be
wondered at if it run into absurdities and contradictions, out
of which it is impossible it should ever extricate itself, it
being of the nature of infinite not to be comprehended by
that which is finite [2].'

---

[1] The aim of Berkeley was to reconcile Philosophy—the *ultimate*
meaning of the universe in which we find ourselves—with the unphilo-
sophised experience of common sense. He worked for this by trying to
substitute facts for empty verbal abstractions.

[2] Cf. Descartes' Third Meditation; also Locke's *Essay*, Introduction,
sect. 4-7. Locke attributes the perplexities and unprogressiveness of
Philosophy to our narrow faculties, which are meant only to regulate
our lives, and not to make the universe perfectly intelligible. The
uncertainty of metaphysics, and the inability of the mass of mankind to
understand its language, is a constant complaint, paralleled by the
constancy with which metaphysical speculation is nevertheless sustained
in each successive age—to satisfy a want that is deeply seated, if not
in many intelligently developed.

3. But, perhaps, we may be too partial to ourselves in placing the fault originally in our faculties, and not rather in the wrong use we make of them. It is a hard thing to suppose that right deductions from true principles should ever end in consequences which cannot be maintained or made consistent. We should believe that God has dealt more bountifully with the sons of men than to give them a strong desire for that knowledge which he had placed quite out of their reach. This were not agreeable to the wonted indulgent methods of Providence, which, whatever appetites it may have implanted in the creatures, doth usually furnish them with such means as, if rightly made use of, will not fail to satisfy them[1]. Upon the whole, I am inclined to think that the far greater part, if not all, of those difficulties which have hitherto amused philosophers, and blocked up the way to knowledge, are entirely owing to ourselves—that we have first raised a dust and then complain we cannot see.

4. My purpose therefore is, to try if I can discover what those Principles are which have introduced all that doubtfulness and uncertainty, those absurdities and contradictions, into the several Sects of Philosophy; insomuch that the wisest men have thought our ignorance incurable, conceiving it to arise from the natural dulness and limitation of our faculties. And surely it is a work well deserving our pains to make a strict inquiry concerning the First Principles of Human Knowledge, to sift and examine them on all sides; especially since there may be some grounds to suspect that those lets and difficulties, which stay and embarrass the mind in its

---

[1] Have we any reason *à priori* to suppose that our moral and physical experience is (by us) resolvable into an intelligible unity? Does it not at last issue in the moral trust that it is *somehow* capable of solution, though not by us, whose experience is intelligible only under relations of time? To take the universe as we find it, after we have exhausted reflection upon it, is 'wisdom,' even if we find that it consists at last of irreducible facts. We are not to assume that the chief end of man is to reach a knowledge which makes no demand upon faith, because purged of all that is mysterious or inexplicable.

search after truth, do not spring from any darkness and intricacy in the objects, or natural defect in the understanding, so much as from False Principles which have been insisted on, and might have been avoided[1].

5. How difficult and discouraging soever this attempt may seem, when I consider what a number of very great and extraordinary men have gone before me in the like designs, yet I am not without some hopes—upon the consideration that the largest views are not always the clearest, and that he who is short-sighted will be obliged to draw the object nearer, and may, perhaps, by a close and narrow survey, discern that which had escaped far better eyes.

6. In order to prepare the mind of the reader for the easier conceiving what follows, it is proper to premise somewhat, by way of Introduction, concerning the Nature and Abuse of Language. But the unravelling this matter leads me in some measure to anticipate my design, by taking notice of what seems to have had a chief part in rendering speculation intricate and perplexed, and to have occasioned innumerable errors and difficulties in almost all parts of knowledge. *And that is the opinion that the mind hath a power of framing abstract ideas or notions of things.* He who is not a perfect stranger to the writings and disputes of philosophers must needs acknowledge that no small part of them are spent about *abstract* ideas[2]. These are in a more especial manner thought to be the object of those sciences which go by the name of Logic and Metaphysics, and of all

---

[1] Berkeley, as we shall see, finds an explanation of the anarchy of Philosophy in assumptions—meaningless, and therefore impossible to believe—to which, under cover of empty names, it had helped to give currency.

[2] Berkeley's use of 'idea'—as equivalent to phenomenon present in sense, or represented in imagination—must be distinguished from the Platonic or the Kantian Idea, and from his own later use of the term 'notion.' By idea he here means phenomena either present in sense or imaginable. For him 'abstract ideas' would be abstract phenomena—phenomena that are not phenomena.

that which passes under the notion of the most abstracted and sublime learning, in all which one shall scarce find any question handled in such a manner as does not suppose their existence in the mind, and that it is well acquainted with them[1].

7. It is agreed on all hands that the qualities or modes of things do never *really exist* each of them apart by itself, and separated from all others, but are mixed, as it were, and blended together, several in the same object. But, we are told, the mind being able to *consider* each quality singly, or abstracted from those other qualities with which it is united, does by that means frame to itself abstract ideas. For example, there is perceived by sight an object extended, coloured, and moved: this mixed or compound idea the mind resolving into its simple, constituent parts, and viewing each by itself, exclusive of the rest, does frame the abstract ideas of extension, colour, and motion. Not that it is possible for colour or motion to exist without extension; but only that the mind can frame to itself by *abstraction* the *idea* of colour exclusive of extension, and of motion exclusive of both colour and extension.

8. Again, the mind having observed that in the particular extensions perceived by sense there is something common

[1] Compare with what follows against *abstract* ideas (as Berkeley understands idea), sect. 97-100, 118-132, 143; *New Theory of Vision*, sect. 122-125. See also *Alciphron*, Dial. vii. 5-7, and *Defence of Free Thinking in Mathematics*, sect. 45-48, in *Works*, vols. ii. iii. But in the end compare all this with *Siris*, sect. 335, and the sections in *Siris* which follow, on the 'Ideas' of Plato, to which Berkeley's 'notions' are nearer than his ideas.

In the following sections, on the abuse and legitimate use of words and of the faculty of abstraction, Berkeley has Locke much in view. What is said of 'abstract ideas' in Locke's *Essay* may be studied in this connexion. Hume refers to Berkeley (*Treatise of Human Nature*, b. I. part 1. chap. 7) as having, by bringing to light the absurdity of abstract ideas, produced 'one of the greatest and most valuable discoveries that has been made of late years in the republic of letters.' See also J. S. Mill, in *Fortnightly Review* for Nov. 1871, on Berkeley's 'discovery' of the true nature and office of abstraction in the formation of human knowledge.

and alike in all, and some other things peculiar, as this or that figure or magnitude, which distinguish them one from another; it considers apart or singles out by itself that which is common, making thereof a most abstract idea of extension, which is neither line, surface, nor solid, nor has any figure or magnitude, but is an idea entirely prescinded from all these[1]. So likewise the mind, by leaving out of the particular colours perceived by sense that which distinguishes them one from another, and retaining that only which is common to all, makes an idea of colour in abstract which is neither red, nor blue, nor white, nor any other determinate colour. And, in like manner, by considering motion abstractedly not only from the body moved, but likewise from the figure it describes, and all particular directions and velocities, the abstract idea of motion is framed; which equally corresponds to all particular motions whatsoever that may be perceived by sense.

9. And as the mind frames to itself abstract ideas of qualities or modes, so does it, by the same *precision* or mental separation, attain abstract ideas of the more compounded beings which include several co-existent qualities. For example, the mind having observed that Peter, James, and John resemble each other in certain common agreements of shape and other qualities, leaves out of the complex or compounded idea it has of Peter, James and any other particular man, that which is peculiar to each, retaining only what is common to all, and so makes an abstract idea wherein all the particulars equally partake—abstracting entirely from and cutting off all those circumstances and differences which might determine it to any particular existence. And after this manner it is said we come by the abstract idea of *man*, or, if you please, *humanity*, or *human nature;* wherein it is true

---

[1] 'Prescinded,' i. e. exclusively attended to. To *prescind* an idea or phenomenon is to attend to it to the exclusion of other ideas or phenomena.

there is included colour, because there is no man but has some colour, but then it can be neither white, nor black, nor any particular colour, because there is no one particular colour wherein all men partake. So likewise there is included stature, but then it is neither tall stature, nor low stature, nor yet middle stature, but something abstracted from all these. And so of the rest. Moreover, there being a great variety of other creatures that partake in some parts, but not all, of the complex idea of man, the mind, leaving out those parts which are peculiar to men, and retaining those only which are common to all the living creatures, frames the idea of *animal*, which abstracts not only from all particular men, but also all birds, beasts, fishes, and insects. The constituent parts of the abstract idea of animal are body, life, sense, and spontaneous motion. By *body* is meant body without any particular shape or figure, there being no one shape or figure common to all animals, without covering, either of hair, or feathers, or scales, &c., nor yet naked: hair, feathers, scales, and nakedness being the distinguishing properties of particular animals, and for that reason left out of the *abstract idea*. Upon the same account the spontaneous motion must be neither walking, nor flying, nor creeping; it is nevertheless a motion, but what that motion is it is not easy to conceive.

10. Whether others have this wonderful faculty of abstracting their ideas, they best can tell. For myself, I find indeed I have indeed a faculty of imagining, or representing to myself, the idea of those *particular* things I have perceived, and of variously compounding and dividing them. I can imagine a man with two heads, or the upper parts of a man joined to the body of a horse. I can consider the hand, the eye, the nose, each by itself abstracted or separated from the rest of the body.—But then whatever hand or eye I imagine, it must have some particular shape and colour.

Likewise the idea of man that I frame to myself must be either of a white, or a black, or a tawny, a straight, or a crooked, a tall, or a low, or a middle-sized man. I cannot by any effort of thought conceive[1] the *abstract* idea above described.—And it is equally impossible for me to form the abstract idea of motion distinct from the body moving, and which is neither swift nor slow, curvilinear nor rectilinear; and the like may be said of all other abstract general ideas whatsoever. To be plain, I own myself able to abstract *in one sense*, as when I consider some particular parts or qualities separated from others, with which, though they are united in some object, yet it is possible they may really exist without them. But I deny that <u>I can abstract from one another, or conceive separately, those qualities which it is impossible should exist so separated</u>; or that I can frame a <u>general notion[2] by abstracting from particulars in the manner aforesaid</u>—which last are the two proper acceptations of *abstraction*. And there is ground to think most men will acknowledge themselves to be in my case. The generality of men which are simple and illiterate never pretend to *abstract* notions[2]. It is said they are difficult and not to be attained without pains and study; we may therefore reasonably conclude that, if such there be, they are confined only to the learned.

11. I proceed to examine what can be alleged in defence of the doctrine of abstraction, and try if I can discover what it is that inclines the men of speculation to embrace an opinion so remote from Common Sense as that seems to be. There has been a late deservedly esteemed philosopher[3] who,

---

[1] 'Conceive' = realise in imagination.
[2] Here 'notion' = abstract idea = abstract image, which last is manifestly absurd. The so-called abstract *ideas* are really *relations* of ideas, and relations as such cannot be individualised either in sense or in imagination.
[3] Locke. Examine whether Locke means by 'abstract ideas' what

no doubt, has given it very much countenance, by seeming to think the having abstract general ideas is what puts the widest difference in point of understanding betwixt man and beast. 'The having of general ideas,' saith he, 'is that which puts a perfect distinction betwixt man and brutes, and is an excellency which the faculties of brutes do by no means attain unto. For, it is evident we observe no foot-steps in them of making use of general signs for universal ideas; from which we have reason to imagine that they have not the faculty of abstracting, or making general ideas, since they have no use of words or any other general signs.' And a little after : 'Therefore, I think, we may suppose that it is in this that the species of brutes are discriminated from men, and it is that proper difference wherein they are wholly separated, and which at last widens to so wide a distance. For, if they have any ideas at all, and are not bare machines (as some[1] would have them), we cannot deny them to have some reason. It seems as evident to me that they do, some of them, in certain instances reason as that they have sense; but it is only in particular ideas, just as they receive them from their senses. They are the best of them tied up within those narrow bounds, and have not (as I think) the faculty to enlarge them by any kind of abstraction.'—*Essay on Human Understanding*, b. II. ch. 11. §§ 10 and 11. I readily agree with this learned author, that the faculties of brutes can by no means attain to abstraction. But then if this be made the distinguishing property of that sort of animals, I fear a great many of those that pass for men must be reckoned into

---

Berkeley supposes he does. The objections in the text are due to Berkeley's arbitrary limitation of the term 'idea' to the perceived and the imagined, to the exclusion of the results of the mind's own elaborative activity, when we generalise from the data of sense and imagination, and form what are called *concepts*.

[1] The Cartesians, rejecting one of the alternatives open in their philosophy—that brutes are self-conscious spirits independent of and separable from their bodies, preferred the only other—that they are vital organisms without self-consciousness.

their number. The reason that is here assigned why we have no grounds to think brutes have abstract general ideas is, that we observe in them no use of words or any other general signs; which is built on this supposition—that the making use of words implies the having general ideas. From which it follows that men who use language are able to abstract or generalise their ideas. That this is the sense and arguing of the author will further appear by his answering the question he in another place puts: 'Since all things that exist are only particulars, how come we by general terms?' His answer is: 'Words become general by being made the signs of general ideas.'—*Essay on Human Understanding*, b. III. ch. 3. § 6.—But it seems that a word becomes general by being made the sign, not of an abstract general idea, but of several particular ideas, any one of which it indifferently suggests to the mind. For example, when it is said 'the change of motion is proportional to the impressed force,' or that 'whatever has extension is divisible,' these propositions are to be understood of motion and extension in general; and nevertheless it will not follow that they suggest to my thoughts an idea of motion without a body moved, or any determinate direction and velocity, or that I must conceive an abstract general idea of extension, which is neither line, surface, nor solid, neither great nor small, black, white, nor red, nor of any other determinate colour. It is only implied that whatever *particular* motion I consider, whether it be swift or slow, perpendicular, horizontal, or oblique, or in whatever object, the axiom concerning it holds equally true. As does the other of every *particular* extension, it matters not whether line, surface, or solid, whether of this or that magnitude or figure[1].

[1] 'A concept *as such* cannot be presented intuitively; but it must contain no attribute which is incompatible with the intuitive presentation of its object. It is not itself an individual, but it must comprehend such attributes as are capable of individualisation. ... The rule *individualise your concepts* does not mean *sensationalise them*, unless

12. By observing how ideas become general, we may the better judge how words are made so. And here it is to be noted that I do not deny absolutely there are general ideas, but only that there are any *abstract* general ideas; for, in the passages we have quoted wherein there is mention of general ideas, it is always supposed that they are formed by abstraction, after the manner set forth in sections 8 and 9. Now, if we will annex a meaning to our words, and speak only of what we can conceive, I believe we shall acknowledge that an idea which, considered in itself, is particular, becomes general by being made to represent or stand for all other particular ideas of the same sort.—To make this plain by an example, suppose a geometrician is demonstrating the method of cutting a line in two equal parts. He draws, for instance, a black line of an inch in length: this, which in itself is a particular line, is nevertheless with regard to its signification general, since, as it is there used, it represents all particular lines whatsoever; so that what is demonstrated of it is demonstrated of all lines, or, in other words, of a line in general. And, as *that particular line* becomes general by being made a sign, so the *name* 'line,' which taken absolutely is particular, by being a sign is made general. And as the former owes its generality not to its being the sign of an abstract or general line, but of all particular right lines that may possibly exist, so the latter must be thought to derive its generality from the same cause, namely, the various particular lines which it indifferently denotes[1].

the senses are the only sources of presentation.' (Mansel; see *Proleg. Logica*, pp. 23, 33.)

[1] Berkeley does not go so far as to say, with the extreme Nominalists, that a particular idea becomes general *only* by the fact of its being annexed to a general term, and that the 'generality' consists in the accident of this term being applied to many individuals in common. He here explains *how* a particular 'idea' may stand for an indefinite number of other particular 'ideas,' individualising the concept which thus logically connects them. Their common name, *itself a particular*

13. To give the reader a yet clearer view of the nature of abstract ideas, and the uses they are thought necessary to, I shall add one more passage out of the *Essay on Human Understanding*, which is as follows:—'Abstract ideas are not so obvious or easy to children or the yet unexercised mind as particular ones. If they seem so to grown men it is only because by constant and familiar use they are made so. For, when we nicely reflect upon them, we shall find that general ideas are fictions and contrivances of the mind, that carry difficulty with them, and do not so easily offer themselves as we are apt to imagine. For example, does it not require some pains and skill to form the general idea of a triangle (which is yet none of the most abstract, comprehensive, and difficult); for it must be neither oblique nor rectangle, neither equilateral, equicrural, nor scalenon, but all and none of these at once? In effect, it is something imperfect that cannot exist, an idea wherein some parts of several different and inconsistent ideas are put together. It is true the mind in this imperfect state has need of such ideas, and makes all the haste to them it can, for the conveniency of communication and enlargement of knowledge, to both which it is naturally very much inclined. But yet one has reason to suspect such ideas are marks of our imperfection. At least this is enough to shew that the most abstract and general ideas are not those that the mind is first and most easily acquainted with, nor such as its earliest knowledge is conversant about.'— B. IV. ch. 7. § 9. If any man has the faculty of framing in his mind such an idea of a triangle as is here described, it is in vain to pretend to dispute him out of it, nor would I go about it. All I desire is that the reader would fully and certainly inform himself whether he has such an idea or no.

---

thing, is connected with their concept by an arbitrary association—for the name—spoken or written—is not *itself* an individual example of the concept which it signifies. It is only arbitrarily associated with it by custom.

Inconsistency implied in Ideas of Things being Abstract. 23

And this, methinks, can be no hard task for any one to perform. What more easy than for any one to look a little into his own thoughts, and there try whether he has, or can attain to have, an idea that shall correspond with the description that is here given of the general idea of a triangle—which is neither oblique nor rectangle, equilateral, equicrural nor scalenon, but all and none of these at once[1]?

14. Much is here said of the difficulty that abstract ideas carry with them, and the pains and skill requisite to the forming them. And it is on all hands agreed that there is need of great toil and labour of the mind, to emancipate our thoughts from particular objects, and raise them to those sublime speculations that are conversant about abstract ideas. From all which the natural consequence should seem to be, that so difficult a thing as the forming abstract ideas was not necessary for *communication*, which is so easy and familiar to all sorts of men. But, we are told, if they seem obvious and easy to grown men, it is only because by constant and familiar use they are made so. Now, I would fain know at what time it is men are employed in surmounting that difficulty, and furnishing themselves with those necessary helps for discourse. It cannot be when they are grown up, for then it seems they are not conscious of any such painstaking; it remains therefore to be the business of their childhood. And surely the great and multiplied labour of framing abstract notions will be found a hard task for that tender age. Is it not a hard thing to imagine that a couple of children cannot prate together of their sugar-plums and rattles and the rest of their little trinkets, till they have first tacked together

---

[1] The language of Locke is awkward; but does it mean more than that the concept of a triangle *may* be individualised in any one of its many possible applications—oblique, equilateral, &c.—all of which it is potentially, but no one of them actually, till it is exemplified in that particular application? No concept, formed by *generalisation*, can be represented in *imagination* except in an individual example. In itself it belongs to the formal constitution, not to the phenomenal material, of human knowledge.

numberless inconsistencies, and so framed in their minds abstract general ideas, and annexed them to every common name they make use of?

15. Nor do I think them a whit more needful for the *enlargement of knowledge* than for communication. It is, I know, a point much insisted on, that all knowledge and demonstration are about universal notions, to which I fully agree: but then it does not appear to me that those notions are formed by abstraction in the manner premised—*universality*, so far as I can comprehend, not consisting in the absolute, positive nature or conception of anything; but in the relation it bears to the particulars signified or represented by it; by virtue whereof it is that things, names, or notions[1], being in their own nature *particular*, are rendered *universal*. Thus, when I demonstrate any proposition concerning triangles, it is to be supposed that I have in view the universal idea of a triangle; which ought not to be understood as if I could frame an idea of a triangle which was neither equilateral, nor scalenon, nor equicrural; but only that the particular triangle I consider, whether of this or that sort it matters not, doth equally stand for and represent all rectilinear triangles whatsoever, and is *in that sense universal*. All which seems very plain and not to include any difficulty in it[2].

16. But here it will be demanded, how we can know any proposition to be true of all particular triangles, except we have first seen it demonstrated of the abstract idea of a triangle which equally agrees to all? For, because a property may be demonstrated to agree to some one particular triangle,

---

[1] 'Notions' here = Berkeley's ideas, i. e. individual perceptions and imaginations.

[2] This and the next are important sections. They touch the great question—*what* that is in the objective constitution of things which enables us to find the universal in the particular, and to extend our real knowledge beyond the data of sense and memory, by deductive or inductive inferences. This question lies at the root of mediæval Realism, and also of modern inductive logic.

it will not thence follow that it equally belongs to any other triangle, which in all respects is not the same with it. For example, having demonstrated that the three angles of an isosceles rectangular triangle are equal to two right ones, I cannot therefore conclude this affection agrees to all other triangles which have neither a right angle nor two equal sides. It seems therefore that, to be certain this proposition is universally true, we must either make a particular demonstration for every particular triangle, which is impossible, or once for all demonstrate it of the abstract idea of a triangle, in which all the particulars do indifferently partake and by which they are all equally represented.—To which I answer, that, though the idea I have in view whilst I make the demonstration be, for instance, that of an isosceles rectangular triangle whose sides are of a determinate length, I may nevertheless be certain it extends to all other rectilinear triangles, of what sort or bigness soever. And that because neither the right angle, nor the equality, nor determinate length of the sides are at all concerned in the demonstration. It is true the diagram I have in view includes all these particulars, but then there is not the least mention made of them in the proof of the proposition. It is not said the three angles are equal to two right ones, because one of them is a right angle, or because the sides comprehending it are of the same length. Which sufficiently shews that the right angle might have been oblique, and the sides unequal, and for all that the demonstration have held good. And for this reason it is that I conclude that to be true of any obliquangular or scalenon which I had demonstrated of a particular right-angled equicrural triangle, and not because I demonstrated the proposition of the abstract idea of a triangle. [[1] And here it must be acknowledged that a man may consider a figure merely as triangular, without attending to the particular qualities of

---

[1] What follows to the end of this section was added in Berkeley's third edition.

the angles, or relations of the sides. So far he may abstract[1]; but this will never prove that he can frame an abstract, general, inconsistent idea of a triangle. In like manner we may consider Peter so far forth as man, or so far forth as animal, without framing the forementioned abstract idea, either of man or of animal, inasmuch as all that is perceived is not considered.]

17. It were an endless as well as an useless thing to trace the Schoolmen, those great masters of abstraction, through all the manifold inextricable labyrinths of error and dispute which their doctrine of abstract natures and notions seems to have led them into. What bickerings and controversies, and what a learned dust have been raised about those matters, and what mighty advantage has been from thence derived to mankind, are things at this day too clearly known to need being insisted on. And it had been well if the ill effects of that doctrine were confined to those only who make the most avowed profession of it. When men consider the great pains, industry, and parts that have for so many ages been laid out on the cultivation and advancement of the sciences, and that notwithstanding all this the far greater part of them remain full of darkness and uncertainty and disputes that are like never to have an end, and even those that are thought to be supported by the most clear and cogent demonstrations contain in them paradoxes which are perfectly irreconcilable to the understandings of men, and that, taking all together, a very small portion of them does supply any real benefit to mankind, otherwise than by being an innocent diversion and amusement—I say, the consideration of all this is apt to throw them into a despondency and perfect contempt

---

[1] Here Berkeley grants that without abstraction there can be no scientific knowledge of things, provided that by abstraction is meant no more than exclusive attention to the *common* attributes or relations of *individual* things—a spontaneous process at first, afterwards matured in scientific researches, by help of common terms and their definitions, through logically calculated experiments and induction.

of all study. But this may perhaps cease upon a view of the False Principles that have obtained in the world, amongst all which there is none, methinks, hath a more wide and extended sway over the thoughts of speculative men than this of *abstract* general ideas[1].

18. I come now to consider the *source* of this prevailing notion, and that seems to me to be Language. And surely nothing of less extent than reason itself could have been the source of an opinion so universally received. The truth of this appears as from other reasons so also from the plain confession of the ablest patrons of abstract ideas, who acknowledge that they are made in order to naming; from which it is a clear consequence that if there had been no such thing as speech or *universal* signs there never had been any thought of abstraction. See b. III. ch. 6. § 39, and elsewhere of the *Essay on Human Understanding*. Let us examine the manner wherein Words have contributed to the origin of that mistake[2].—First then, it is thought that every name has, or ought to have, one only precise and settled signification; which inclines men to think there are certain abstract, determinate ideas that constitute the true and only immediate signification of each general name, and that it is by the mediation of these abstract ideas that a general name comes to signify any particular thing. Whereas, in truth, there is no such thing as one precise and definite signification annexed to any general name, they all signifying

---

[1] To say that the abstract *ideas* against which Berkeley argues are impossible is to say that abstract *phenomena*, or *substances* abstracted from phenomena, are impossible. But this does not prove that isolated phenomena constitute real knowledge; or that they can become knowledge without connecting or constituting judgments of relations being involved; or that progress in real knowledge is other than an ever widening and deepening apprehension of such relations.

[2] What follows on thought and language is a commentary on the abuse of abstraction, especially in verbal controversies of metaphysics and theology, and on the need for 'individualising our concepts,' if we are to keep within the boundary of good sense and positive knowledge.

indifferently a great number of particular ideas[1]. All which does evidently follow from what has been already said, and will clearly appear to any one by a little reflexion. To this it will be objected that every name that has a definition is thereby restrained to one certain signification. For example, a triangle is defined to be 'a plain surface comprehended by three right lines,' by which that name is limited to denote one certain idea and no other. To which I answer, that in the definition it is not said whether the surface be great or small, black or white, nor whether the sides are long or short, equal or unequal, nor with what angles they are inclined to each other; in all which there may be great variety, and consequently there is no one settled idea which limits the signification of the word triangle. It is one thing for to keep a name constantly to the same definition, and another to make it stand everywhere for the same idea; the one is necessary, the other useless and impracticable[2].

19. But, to give a farther account how words came to produce the doctrine of abstract ideas, it must be observed that it is a received opinion that language has no other end but the communicating our ideas, and that every significant name stands for an idea. This being so, and it being withal certain that names which yet are not thought altogether insignificant do not always mark out particular conceivable ideas, it is straightway concluded that they stand for abstract notions. That there are many names in use amongst speculative men which do not always suggest to others determinate particular ideas, or in truth anything at all, is what nobody will deny. And a little attention will discover that it is not

---

[1] This must be understood of the denotation rather than the connotation and definition of a name. The same connotation may be found exemplified in any one of many particular objects, irrespectively of their individual differences.

[2] Yet a definition *virtually* determines the individual objects ('ideas,' as Berkeley would say) to which the name is applicable, although the *relations* which constitute the concept expressed by the name defined cannot be individualised in imagination.

necessary (even in the strictest reasonings) significant names which stand for ideas should, every time they are used, excite in the understanding the ideas they are made to stand for—in reading and discoursing, names being for the most part used as letters are in Algebra, in which, though a particular quantity be marked by each letter, yet to proceed right it is not requisite that in every step each letter suggest to your thoughts that particular quantity it was appointed to stand for[1].

20. Besides, the communicating of ideas marked by words is not the chief and only end of language, as is commonly supposed. There are other ends, as the raising of some passion, the exciting to or deterring from an action, the putting the mind in some particular disposition—to which the former is in many cases barely subservient, and sometimes entirely omitted, when these can be obtained without it, and I think does not unfrequently happen in the familiar use of language. I entreat the reader to reflect with himself, and see if it does not often happen, either in hearing or reading a discourse, that the passions of fear, love, hatred, admiration, and disdain, and the like, arise immediately in his mind upon the perception of certain words, without any ideas coming between[2]. At first, indeed, the words might have occasioned ideas that were fitting to produce those emotions; but, if I mistake not, it will be found that, when language is once grown familiar, the hearing of the sounds, or

[1] The 'symbolical knowledge' of Leibnitz (*Opera Philosophica*, pp. 79-80, Erdmann), and Stewart on 'Abstraction' (*Elements*, vol. I. chap. 4. §§ 1 and 2)—where he treats of signs, resembling and verbal or non-resembling, and of the analogies of algebra and verbal signs—may be compared with this.

[2] That is to say, without any 'ideas' (particular examples) of the sort of objects denoted by the words being suggested in his imagination in the act of hearing or of reading—the *word* doing service instead. Thought in this way proceeds more rapidly and easily; but we are apt, in consequence, to accept words that are meaningless or nonsensical. To escape this we should test our supposed concepts by individualising them, meantime dismissing the names till their intelligibility has been verified.

sight of the characters, is oft immediately attended with those passions which at first were wont to be produced by the intervention of ideas that are now quite omitted. May we not, for example, be affected with the promise of a *good thing*, though we have not an idea of what it is? Or is not the being threatened with *danger* sufficient to excite a dread, though we think not of any particular evil likely to befall us, nor yet frame to ourselves an idea of danger in abstract? If any one shall join ever so little reflexion of his own to what has been said, I believe that it will evidently appear to him that general names are often used in the propriety of language without the speaker's designing them for marks of ideas in his own, which he would have them raise in the mind of the hearer. Even proper names themselves do not seem always spoken with a design to bring into our view the ideas of those individuals that are supposed to be marked by them. For example, when a schoolman tells me 'Aristotle hath said it,' all I conceive he means by it is to dispose me to embrace his opinion with the deference and submission which custom has annexed to that name. And this effect is often so instantly produced in the minds of those who are accustomed to resign their judgment to authority of that philosopher, as it is impossible any idea either of his person, writings, or reputation should go before. So close and immediate a connexion may custom establish betwixt the very *word* Aristotle and the motions of assent and reverence in the minds of some men. Innumerable examples of this kind may be given, but why should I insist on those things which every one's experience will, I doubt not, plentifully suggest unto him[1]?

---

[1] Compare *Alciphron*, Dial. VII. sect. 8-10. Berkeley here shows how names—especially in politics, theology, and metaphysics—may impose upon the uneducated and half-educated, determining their feelings and conduct independently of their intelligence. History records theological controversies, and also social changes which were largely due to the influence on ill-educated minds of verbal shibboleths used without meaning.

21. We have, I think, shewn the impossibility of Abstract Ideas. We have considered what has been said for them by their ablest patrons; and endeavoured to shew they are of no use for those ends to which they are thought necessary. And lastly, we have traced them to the source from whence they flow, which appears evidently to be language.—It cannot be denied that words are of excellent use, in that by their means all that stock of knowledge which has been purchased by the joint labours of inquisitive men in all ages and nations may be drawn into the view and made the possession of one single person. But most parts of knowledge have been strangely perplexed and darkened by the *abuse* of words and general ways of speech wherein they are delivered. Since therefore words are so apt to impose on the understanding, whatever *ideas* I consider, I shall endeavour to take *them* bare and naked into my view, keeping out of my thoughts, so far as I am able, those *names* which long and constant use hath so strictly united with them; from which I may expect to derive the following advantages :—

22. *First*, I shall be sure to get clear of all controversies purely verbal—the springing up of which weeds in almost all the sciences has been a main hindrance to the growth of true and sound knowledge. *Secondly*, this seems to be a sure way to extricate myself out of that fine and subtle net of *abstract ideas* which has so miserably perplexed and entangled the minds of men; and that with this peculiar circumstance, that by how much the finer and more curious was the wit of any man, by so much the deeper was he likely to be ensnared and faster held therein. *Thirdly*, so long as I confine my thoughts to my own ideas divested of words, I do not see how I can easily be mistaken. The objects I consider, I clearly and adequately know. I cannot be deceived in thinking I have an idea which I have not. It is not possible for me to imagine that any of

my own ideas are alike or unlike that are not truly so. To discern the agreements or disagreements there are between my ideas, to see what ideas are included in any compound idea and what not, there is nothing more requisite than an attentive perception of what passes in my own understanding[1].

23. But the attainment of all these advantages does presuppose an entire deliverance from the deception of words which I dare hardly promise myself; so difficult a thing it is to dissolve an union so early begun, and confirmed by so long a habit as that betwixt words and ideas. Which difficulty seems to have been very much increased by the doctrine of *abstraction*. For, so long as men thought abstract ideas were annexed to their words, it does not seem strange that they should use words for ideas—it being found an impracticable thing to lay aside the word, and retain the *abstract* idea in the mind, which in itself was perfectly inconceivable.

This seems to me the principal cause why those who have so emphatically recommended to others the laying aside all use of words in their meditations, and contemplating their bare ideas, have yet failed to perform it themselves. Of late many have been very sensible of the absurd opinions and insignificant disputes which grow out of the abuse of words. And, in order to remedy these evils, they advise well, that we attend to the ideas signified, and draw off our attention from the words which signify them[2]. But, how good soever this advice may be they have given others, it is plain they could not have a due regard to it themselves, so long as they

---

[1] Berkeley appeals throughout to this test. He everywhere entreats the student to examine his own consciousness and find whether he can conceive clearly and distinctly the meanings of his philosophical terms.

[2] See Locke, *Essay*, b. II. ch. 13. §§ 18, 28; also b. III. ch. 10. The drift of Berkeley's exhortation is good so far as it is fitted to guard us against the dangerous tendency to accept empty words instead of concepts that can be individualised.

thought the only immediate use of words was to signify ideas, and that the immediate signification of every general name was a determinate abstract idea.

24. But, these being known to be mistakes, a man may with greater ease prevent his being imposed on by words. He that knows he has no other than *particular* ideas, will not puzzle himself in vain to find out and conceive the *abstract* idea annexed to any name. And he that knows names do not always stand for ideas will spare himself the labour of looking for ideas where there are none to be had. It were, therefore, to be wished that every one would use his utmost endeavours to obtain a clear view of the ideas he would consider, separating from them all that dress and imcumbrance of words which so much contribute to blind the judgment and divide the attention[1]. In vain do we extend our view into the heavens and pry into the entrails of the earth, in vain do we consult the writings of learned men and trace the dark footsteps of antiquity—we need only draw the curtain of words, to behold the fairest tree of knowledge, whose fruit is excellent, and within the reach of our hand.

25. Unless we take care to clear the First Principles of Knowledge from the embarras and delusion of words, we may make infinite reasonings upon them to no purpose; we may draw consequences from consequences, and be never the wiser. The farther we go, we shall only lose ourselves the more irrecoverably, and be the deeper entangled in difficulties and mistakes. Whoever therefore designs to read the following sheets, I entreat him that he would make my words the occasion of his own thinking, and endeavour to attain the same train of thoughts in reading that I had in writing them.

---

[1] The student may perhaps ask here what he is to do when his words signify what Berkeley afterwards called *notions*, and not *ideas*, if it is true that all words must at bottom signify what is representable in imagination, under conditions of time.

By this means it will be easy for him to discover the truth or falsity of what I say. He will be out of all danger of being deceived by my words, and I do not see how he can be led into an error by considering his own naked, undisguised ideas.

OF THE

PRINCIPLES

OF

HUMAN KNOWLEDGE.

PART I.

1. IT is evident to any one who takes a survey of the *objects* of human knowledge, that they are either *ideas*[1] actually imprinted[2] on the senses; or else such as are perceived[3] by attending to the passions and operations of the mind; or lastly, *ideas* formed by help of memory and imagination—either compounding, dividing, or barely representing those originally perceived in the aforesaid ways[4].—By

---

[1] Berkeley assumes at the outset with Locke that all we can know must consist of *ideas*, meaning by ideas what Locke means. He afterwards (§§ 3-24) goes on to argue that there *can* be nothing hyperphenomenal in the things of sense, consistently with that acceptance of experience and rejection of abstractions void of ideas on which he had insisted in his Introduction. He does not raise the question, whether unrelated phenomena *can* be knowledge.

[2] What precisely is here meant by 'imprinted'? So Hume's prominent use afterwards of 'impression,' as distinguished from 'idea'—in Hume's meaning of idea.

[3] The term 'perception' is here applied to consciousness of internal as well as of external phenomena.

[4] This sentence expresses Locke's thesis about our 'ideas' in the second book of the *Essay*. According to him they are all either *simple ideas*, got either by the senses, or by reflexion on the 'passions and operations of the mind;' or they are *complex ideas*, 'formed by help of

sight I have the ideas of light and colours, with their several degrees and variations. By touch I perceive hard and soft, heat and cold, motion and resistance, and of all these more and less either as to quantity or degree. Smelling furnishes me with odours; the palate with tastes; and hearing conveys sounds to the mind in all their variety of tone and composition.—And as several of these are observed to accompany each other, they come to be marked by one name, and so to be reputed as one THING [1]. Thus, for example, a certain colour, taste, smell, figure and consistence having been observed to go together, are accounted one distinct thing, signified by the name *apple;* other collections of ideas constitute a stone, a tree, a book, and the like sensible things—which as they are pleasing or disagreeable excite the passions of love, hatred, joy, grief, and so forth.

2. But, besides all that endless variety of ideas or objects of knowledge, there is likewise something which knows or perceives them; and exercises divers operations, as willing, imagining, remembering, about them. This perceiving, active being is what I call MIND, SPIRIT, SOUL, or MYSELF. By which words I do not denote any one of my ideas, but a thing entirely distinct from them, wherein they exist, or, which is the same thing, whereby they are perceived—for the existence of an idea consists in being perceived [2].

memory and imagination,' and some (Locke adds) by abstraction. This thesis is ambiguous as expressed both by Locke and by Berkeley; and Berkeley even more than Locke fails, in his earlier writings, to recognise *theoretically* elements in knowledge on which he proceeds in his reasoning.

[1] Is *mere* 'observation' enough to account for this synthesis, in which *ideas* or *phenomena* are aggregated, and thus converted into *things?* Nothing is here said of *suggestion*—which has a function so important in his explanation of visual perception—nor of *notions* and their office. See *Commonplace Book* (p. 444) on 'thing' and 'idea' as equivalents.

[2] We have here rudiments of Berkeley's early Psychology—a rough outline of sorts of ideas of which we can be conscious. He recognises three sorts :—(a) those 'actually imprinted on the senses,' afterwards (sect. 3) called 'sensations'—as when what we are conscious of is

3. That neither our thoughts, nor passions, nor ideas formed by the imagination, exist without the mind, is what everybody will allow. And to me it is no less evident that the various SENSATIONS, or *ideas imprinted on the sense,* however blended or combined together (that is, whatever *objects* they compose), cannot exist otherwise than in a mind perceiving them—I think an intuitive knowledge may be obtained of this by any one that shall attend to what is meant

something coloured, hard, odorous, &c.; (*b*) 'passions and operations of the mind'—as when we are conscious of pleasurable or painful feelings, or of exerting ourselves corporeally or intellectually; (*c*) mental representations and elaborations—as when we remember a scene we have witnessed, or imagine one of our own creation, or generalise with the help of words. These ideas are, as in Locke's *Essay,* the simple and complex material of our knowledge. Their rational elaboration is made to presuppose consciousness of self as its intellectual centre and the principle of causality, which Berkeley afterwards used as universal, like Locke, but without critical examination of the origin of its universality.

All this may be compared with Locke's 'plain historical' account of our *ideas* in the second and third books of his *Essays,* and with his account of our *knowledge* in the fourth book; also with Hume's 'impressions and ideas,' and their blind 'associations' directed by custom; and with Kant's manifold of sense, understanding and its categories, and reason.

The necessary correlate of all 'ideas' or 'phenomena'—that in and through which they are intelligible, and in which their changes originate—is, according to Berkeley, self-conscious MIND—of which each sense-conscious self is an example.—Phenomena are phenomena, and are phenomenal things, only on condition of the existence of mind; for the known necessarily implies a knower.—He does not ask whether knowing may not equally require a something known (not necessarily an idea of *sense,* however), in order to its realisation.—Note that Berkeley's 'Mind' is an individual spirit—living and conscious—not abstract thought relations of an impersonal Ego. Compare with Kant's synthetical unity of apperception.

Berkeley's analysis of the constitution of human knowledge thus in a manner recognises (a) phenomena given in sense, (b) reproduced in memory and imagination, (c) logically elaborated in generalisations, (d) through reason and rational insight. The last is, in the *Principles,* obscurely, if at all, recognised, in an undeveloped doctrine of 'notions.' It is different in *Siris.*

The triplicity of Cognition, Feeling or Desire, and Will or moral agency, including the contrast of passive and active consciousness, also dimly appears in these sections. The actual relations of these three among themselves, in the individual, give rise to the facts with which Psychology deals.

by the term *exist* when applied to *sensible things*. The table I write on I say exists, that is, I see and feel it; and if I were out of my study I should say it existed—meaning thereby that if I was in my study I might perceive it, or that some other spirit actually does perceive it. There was an odour, that is, it was smelt; there was a sound, that is, it was heard; a colour or figure, and it was perceived by sight or touch. This is all that I can understand by these and the like expressions.—For as to what is said of the absolute existence of unthinking things without any relation to their being perceived, that is to me perfectly unintelligible. Their *esse is percipi*, nor is it possible they should have any existence out of the minds or thinking things which perceive them [1].

---

[1] It is in this third section that Berkeley first raises the characteristic question of his philosophy, which might be thus expressed:—Do the phenomena present in the five senses, and the individual things of sense, which seem to be composed of what is presented to our senses, *really* exist as *substances*, i.e. as entities that are independent of a percipient mind; or, if not, do they at least *represent* what so exists? Are what we call 'solid and extended things'—which we actually touch and see—independent of mind, in a way that imaginations and feelings of the mind itself are not? His answer is, that they cannot exist otherwise than as phenomena of which a (not necessarily *my*) mind must be percipient: their *esse* is *percipi* (he does not define what is ultimately and necessarily involved in *percipi*, or in *percipere*, as Kant has tried to do); for the supposition of a cluster of phenomena, or even a single phenomenon, existing—as an abstraction—when no one is percipient of it, is a meaningless supposition. To say 'the table *exists*' means, if it has any meaning, 'that it is seen or felt.' Out of all conscious relation to its qualities—i.e. the phenomena of which it is made up—the word 'table' is an empty abstraction. (But what, one may ask, is implied in the 'it;' and is Berkeley entitled, on his principles, to mean by 'it' more than *I see or feel in a particular way?* He has to explain the transformation of mere sensations into perceptions of things existing in space—the transformation of *feelings* which are subjective into *knowledge* which is objective.)

Ueberweg charges Berkeley with begging his whole question because he sets out by calling the things of sense *sensations* or *ideas*, thus implying in the very connotation of their name that they have only a subjective and phenomenal reality. But Berkeley need not, at setting out, be supposed to mean more than that all that we are conscious of must at any rate be present in consciousness, and must therefore be, *so far*, idea—leaving it still open to inquire, whether what is perceived

4. [1]It is indeed an opinion strangely prevailing amongst men, that houses, mountains, rivers, and in a word all sensible objects, have an existence, natural or real, distinct from their being perceived by the understanding. But, with how great an assurance and acquiescence soever this principle may be entertained in the world, yet whoever shall find in his heart to call it in question may, if I mistake not, perceive it to involve a manifest contradiction. For, what are the forementioned objects but the things we perceive by sense? and what do we perceive besides our own ideas or sensations? and is it not plainly repugnant that any one of *these*, or any combination of them, should exist unperceived[2]?

5. If we thoroughly examine this tenet it will, perhaps, be found at bottom to depend on the doctrine of *abstract ideas*. For can there be a nicer strain of abstraction than to distinguish the *existence* of sensible objects from their *being perceived*, so as to conceive[3] them existing unperceived? Light and colours, heat and cold, extension and figures—in a word the things we see and feel—what are they but so many sensations, notions, ideas, or impressions on the sense[4]? and is

in the five senses is *more* than this—whether it is, or at least represents, an independent entity.

[1] Sections 4-24 contain Berkeley's *reasoned exposition* of his answer to the question about Matter raised in sect. 3. The truth of his own answer to the question must, he thinks, be *self-evident* to any one who should attend to what must be meant by the word 'exist' when applied to sensible things. That people are notwithstanding disposed to give a different answer, he attributes (sect. 5) to our tendency to substantiate verbal abstractions, on which he had enlarged in the Introduction.

[2] How does Berkeley in thus limiting our 'perceptions' to the 'ideas' or phenomena of which we are individually conscious in sense —'*our own* ideas'—explain the objectivity of the material world? His theory of vision would make it a 'suggestion' of 'experience.'

[3] Must 'conceive' here mean have an *idea* or *mental image* of, or may it mean have a (Berkeleian) *notion* of?

[4] Here the 'things' of sense are vaguely called 'notions,' as well as 'sensations,' 'ideas,' 'impressions on sense.' In *Siris* he calls them 'phenomena.' Berkeley has not defined what he means, here and elsewhere, by the metaphor 'impressions on sense,' which taken literally makes perception *motion in the organism* instead of *consciousness*.

it possible to separate, even in thought, any of these from perception? For my part, I might as easily divide a thing from itself. I may, indeed, divide in my thoughts, or conceive apart from each other, those things which, perhaps, I never perceived by sense so divided. Thus, I imagine the trunk of a human body without the limbs, or conceive the smell of a rose without thinking on the rose itself. So far, I will not deny, I can abstract—if that may properly be called *abstraction* which extends only to the conceiving separately such objects as it is possible may really exist or be actually perceived asunder. But my conceiving or imagining power does not extend beyond the possibility of real existence or perception [1]. Hence, as it is impossible for me to see or feel anything without an actual sensation of that thing, so is it impossible for me to conceive in my thoughts any sensible thing or object distinct from the sensation or perception of it. [[2] In truth, the object and the sensation are the same thing and cannot therefore be abstracted from each other.]

6. Some truths there are so near and obvious to the mind that a man need only open his eyes to see them. Such I take this important one to be, viz. that all the choir of heaven and furniture of the earth, in a word all those bodies which compose the mighty frame of the world, have not any subsistence without a mind—that their *being* is *to be perceived or known;* that consequently so long as they are not actually perceived by me, or do not exist in my mind or that of any other created spirit, they must either have no existence at all, or else subsist in the mind of some Eternal Spirit—it being perfectly unintelligible, and involving all the absurdity of abstraction, to attribute to any single part of them an existence independent of a spirit. To be convinced of which, the reader need only reflect, and try to separate in his own

---

[1] But does our power of forming 'notions' not extend beyond what is phenomenal; and may we not 'consider separately' in thought what in the perceptions of sense is always found united with something else?

[2] This sentence is omitted in Berkeley's Second Edition.

of Human Knowledge.   41

thoughts the *being* of a sensible thing from its *being perceived* [1].

7. From what has been said it is evident there is not any other Substance [2] than SPIRIT, or *that which perceives* [3]. But, for the fuller demonstration of this point, let it be considered the sensible qualities are colour, figure, motion, smell, taste, &c., *i. e.* the ideas perceived by sense. Now, for an idea to exist in an unperceiving thing is a manifest contradiction, for to have an idea is all one as to perceive; that therefore wherein colour, figure, &c. exist must perceive them; hence it is clear there can be no unthinking substance or *substratum* of those ideas.

8. But, say you, though the ideas themselves do not exist without the mind [4], yet there may be things like them,

[1] Ueberweg grants Berkeley's argument as regards the necessary dependence of phenomena of sense, severally or in aggregates, on percipient mind: he denies that he has proved that there may not *also* be external things, existing independently of their being perceived, which may so operate on our senses that—in consequence of the organic agitation produced—the spirit which animates every part of the organism generates the perceptions of phenomena.

Berkeley has not here given articulate reason for adopting the alternative, that sensible things subsist 'in the mind of some Eternal Spirit,' during intervals in which they are not perceived by finite spirits —instead of the counter supposition of their having 'no existence at all,' during such intervals. He does not even ask *why* we are obliged to suppose their continuity. Still less does he explain the *manner* in which things exist in the Eternal Mind, which might be objected to as equally unintelligible with their abstract or unperceived existence. Do they exist as perceptions of sense, or as abstractions of reason, in the mind of God? Of this afterwards.

[2] He does not say distinctly what he means by existing *substantially*. He seems (like Descartes) to suppose a relative as well as an absolute substance or independence—the absolute Substance being God, or Substance in its highest meaning.

[3] It is implied that a mind or spirit must be *always* conscious of phenomena—that mind must think always. Otherwise, in *unconscious spirit* we should still, on Berkeley's premises, have an empty abstraction open to his objections against *unperceived things*. Indeed he argues elsewhere that the essence of mind is conscious activity;—an 'unthinking substance or substratum of ideas' being a 'manifest contradiction.' See *Commonplace Book*, pp. 439, 444, &c.

[4] As Sir W. Hamilton, for instance, says the object present in perception does. That 'object' is with him the animated and extended organism of the percipient, which is at once within and without the

whereof they are copies or resemblances, which things exist
without the mind in an unthinking substance [1]. I answer,
an idea can be like nothing but an idea; a colour or figure
can be like nothing but another colour or figure [2]. If we look
but never so little into our own thoughts, we shall find it
impossible for us to conceive a likeness except only between
our ideas. Again, I ask whether those supposed originals or
external things, of which our ideas are the pictures or representations, be themselves perceivable or no? If they are,
then they are ideas and we have gained our point; but if you
say they are not, I appeal to any one whether it be sense to
assert a colour is like something which is invisible; hard or
soft, like something which is intangible; and so of the rest.

9. Some there are who make a distinction betwixt *primary*
and *secondary* qualities [3]. By the former they mean exten-

animating mind (see Hamilton's Reid, pp. 860, &c.). There are curious
analogies between Berkeley and Hamilton in their view of external
perception.

[1] As those say who hold that our perception of the sensible world is
essentially mediate, implying either that external things are *like* our
feelings and cognitions, and thus literally *representations* of them; or
else that the medium is something mysterious—neither a conscious
state or act, nor the extended external entity. Berkeley goes on to
argue that perception of sensible things can be *like nothing but itself*.
'An idea can be like nothing but an idea.'

[2] The reader may reflect on this assumption, illustrating it to himself
and examining its reason, as a useful exercise in psychology. Compare
with Locke's doctrine that our ideas of the *primary* qualities of matter
are resemblances of what really exists in bodies that are external. Is
Berkeley justified in putting 'figure' on the same footing as 'colour,'
as a mere 'idea or sensation'?

[3] Locke is more immediately in his view. See *Essay*, b. II. ch. 8.
We have here Berkeley's own treatment of the Qualities of Matter—
classed by Locke and other philosophers, according to their supposed independence of, or dependence on, a sentient mind. By the *primary*
(called also *objective* and *mathematical*) qualities of external things, of
which a list is here given, they meant properties of matter as such,
inhering in the thing—which exist unperceiving, and do not need to be
perceived. The *secondary* qualities comprehend indefinitely numerous
properties of matter, as it is this, that, or the other kind of body, which
are manifested in our individual sensations. We *know* the primary
and we *feel* the secondary qualities; objective perception, it is said,
is only of the former. Now, Berkeley tries, in what follows, to melt
down the primary into sense-dependent phenomena like the secondary,

sion, figure, motion, rest, solidity or impenetrability, and number; by the latter they denote all other sensible qualities, as colours, sounds, tastes, and so forth. The ideas we have of these last they acknowledge not to be the resemblances of anything existing without the mind, or unperceived, but they will have our ideas of the primary qualities to be patterns or images of things which exist without the mind, in an unthinking substance which they call Matter.—By Matter, therefore, we are to understand *an inert*[1], *senseless substance, in which extension, figure, and motion do actually subsist*. But it is evident, from what we have already shewn, that extension, figure, and motion are only[2] ideas existing in the mind, and that an idea can be like nothing but another idea, and that consequently neither they nor their archetypes can exist in an unperceiving substance. Hence, it is plain that the very notion of what is called *Matter* or *corporeal substance* involves a contradiction in it[3].

10. They who assert that figure, motion, and the rest of the primary or original qualities do exist without the mind in unthinking substances, do at the same time acknowledge that colours, sounds, heat, cold, and suchlike secondary qualities, do not—which they tell us are sensations existing in the affirming at the same time the practical reality of both. The argument which follows is more fully unfolded in the First of his *Three Dialogues*, in which the sensuous or phenomenal nature of the primary is maintained on the same grounds as that of the secondary qualities of things. (See *Works*, vol. I. pp. 278-85.)

[1] The *necessary powerlessness* of the solid and extended things of sense, with the consequent absurdity of all materialistic explanations of the universe, is the essence of Berkeley's own philosophy.

[2] 'Only.' Has he shewn that the phenomenal things of sense may not presuppose necessary mathematical relations, without which they could not enter an intelligible experience?

[3] In this section Berkeley has defined the *sort* of 'Matter' against which his reasoning is directed. It is inert, and senseless or unperceiving; yet extension, figure, and motion are supposed to exist in it, as its objective qualities, so that *it* is *per se* extended, figured, and moved. He tries to show that the very notion of *this* Matter is self-contradictory. The reasoning implies that even our mathematical knowledge of sensible things may be melted down into phenomena in sense, which can exist only when and as perceived.

mind alone, that depend on and are occasioned by the different size, texture, and motion of the minute particles of matter[1]. This they take for an undoubted truth, which they can demonstrate beyond all exception. Now, if it be certain that those original qualities are inseparably united with the other sensible qualities, and not, even in thought, capable of being abstracted from them, it plainly follows that they exist only in the mind. But I desire any one to reflect and try whether he can, by any abstraction of thought, conceive the extension and motion of a body without all other sensible qualities[2]. For my own part, I see evidently that it is not in my power to frame an idea of a body extended and moving, but I must withal give it some colour or other sensible quality which is acknowledged to exist only in the mind. In short, extension, figure, and motion, abstracted from all other qualities, are inconceivable. Where therefore the other sensible qualities are, there must these be also, to wit, in the mind and nowhere else.

11. Again, *great* and *small*, *swift* and *slow*, are allowed to exist nowhere without the mind, being entirely relative, and changing as the frame or position of the organs of sense varies. The extension therefore which exists without the mind is neither great nor small, the motion neither swift nor slow, that is, they are nothing at all. But, say you, they are extension in general, and motion in general: thus we see

---

[1] See Locke's *Essay*, b. II. ch. 8. sect. 16-18; ch. 23. sect. 11; b. IV. ch. 3. sect. 24-26, for his opinion, here alluded to, about the *relation* of the secondary to the primary qualities of matter—the former being the supposed causal issue of (by us) unperceivable modifications of the latter. Locke consequently denies the possibility *for man* of any strictly demonstrative science of nature, holding that inferences in physical science can ultimately only be inductive presumptions. Berkeley puts all qualities—secondary and primary—on the same footing. Their essence is *percipi*.

[2] That we cannot be percipient of extension and motion unless they are blended with sensations of secondary qualities may be granted. There is another question as to the possibility of *objective relations* of extension and motion, and of our having *notions* of these.

how much the tenet of extended moveable substances existing without the mind depends on that strange doctrine of *abstract* ideas [1]. And here I cannot but remark how nearly the vague and indeterminate description of Matter or corporeal substance, which the modern philosophers are run into by their own principles, resembles that antiquated and so much ridiculed notion of *materia prima*, to be met with in Aristotle and his followers [2]. Without extension solidity cannot be conceived; since therefore it has been shewn that extension exists not in an unthinking substance, the same must also be true of solidity.

12. That number is entirely the creature of the mind [3], even though the other qualities be allowed to exist without, will be evident to whoever considers that the same thing bears a different denomination of number as the mind views it with different respects. Thus, the same extension is one, or three, or thirty-six, according as the mind considers it with reference to a yard, a foot, or an inch. Number is so visibly relative, and dependent on men's understanding, that it is strange to think how any one should give it an absolute existence without the mind. We say one book, one page, one line, &c.; all these are equally units, though some contain several of the others. And in each instance, it is plain, the unit relates to some particular combination of ideas arbitrarily put together by the mind.

[1] Does it follow that the Extension, which, viewed relatively to the sense-perceptions of individual sentients is neither great nor small, or the Motion which, also viewed relatively is neither swift nor slow—must absolutely, or in the light of pure intelligence, be 'nothing at all'?

[2] For a definition of Aristotle's πρώτη ὕλη, see his *Phys.* I. 9; also *Metaph.* VII. 3. See also *De Anima*, III. 4, for what he says of the relation of the actual (not potential) reality of things to a knowledge of them by individuals.

[3] If Number is entirely a 'creature of the mind,' how does Berkeley reconcile this with what he says elsewhere about a plurality of *finite* spirits? Does not this relativity of number, if meant as relating to individual mind, make God immanent in spirits as well as in sensible things

13. Unity I know some[1] will have to be a simple or uncompounded idea, accompanying all other ideas into the mind. That I have any such idea answering the word *unity* I do not find; and if I had, methinks I could not miss finding it: on the contrary, it should be the most familiar to my understanding, since it is said to accompany all other ideas, and to be perceived by all the ways of sensation and reflexion. To say no more, it is an *abstract* idea[2].

14. I shall further add, that, after the same manner as modern philosophers prove (certain sensible qualities to have no existence in Matter, or without the mind, the same thing may be likewise proved of all other sensible qualities whatsoever. Thus, for instance, it is said that heat and cold are affections only of the mind, and not at all patterns of real beings, existing in the corporeal substances which excite them, for that the same body which appears cold to one hand seems warm to another[3]. Now, why may we not as well argue that figure and extension are not patterns or resemblances of qualities existing in Matter, because to the same eye at different stations, or eyes of a different texture at the same station, they appear various, and cannot therefore be the images of anything settled and determinate without the mind? Again, it is proved that sweetness is not really in the

---

[1] Locke for instance. See *Essay*, b. II. ch. 7. § 7.
[2] The dependence of Number—another of the primary qualities—on the elaborative activity of the *understanding*, i. e. on the way in which mind 'considers' the 'objects' numbered, is affirmed, in this and the preceding section; just as the dependence on *sense* of other primary qualities is inferred, in what precedes and follows, from their being necessarily blended with the 'sensations' of the percipient. It may be urged, as an objection to this, that mind does not proceed by a *capricious* elaboration, but according to essential relations in nature, when it considers three trees, for instance, as three things, and not as ten or twenty things, determined by some accidents of the phenomena; and also that 'number,' as such, is a necessary constructive form of understanding. In sec. 13 Berkeley opposes Locke. Cf. Locke's *Essay*, b. II. ch. 7. § 7; ch. 13. § 26; ch. 16. § 1.
[3] Yet we find a standard in the thermometer, in which *motion* (a primary quality) is substituted for *individual sensations* of heat and cold (secondary qualities).

sapid thing, because the thing remaining unaltered the sweetness is changed into bitter, as in case of a fever or otherwise vitiated palate. Is it not as reasonable to say that motion is not without the mind, since if the succession of ideas in the mind become swifter, the motion, it is acknowledged, shall appear slower without any alteration in any external object.

15. In short, let any one consider those arguments which are thought manifestly to prove that colours and tastes exist *only* in the mind, and he shall find they may with equal force be brought to prove the same thing of extension, figure, and motion.—Though it must be confessed this method of arguing does not so much prove that there is no extension or colour in an outward object, as that we do not know by *sense* which is the *true* extension or colour of the object. But the arguments foregoing plainly shew it to be impossible that any colour or extension at all, or other sensible quality whatsoever, should exist in an unthinking subject without the mind, or in truth, that there should be any such thing as an outward object[1].

16. But let us examine a little the received opinion.—It is said extension is a mode or accident of Matter, and that Matter is the *substratum* that supports it. Now I desire that you would explain to me what is meant by Matter's *supporting* extension. Say you, I have no idea of Matter and therefore cannot explain it. I answer, though you have no positive, yet, if you have any meaning at all, you must at least have a relative idea of Matter; though you know not what it is, yet you must be supposed to know what relation it bears to accidents, and what is meant by its supporting them. It is evident 'support' cannot here be taken in its usual or

---

[1] His conclusion, in this part of the argument, which turns on the Qualities of Matter, is that *all* its so-called qualities—the primary or mathematical as much as the secondary—must be resolved into phenomena of sense, which presuppose a perceiving subject. Otherwise they become meaningless; and the supposed residual 'Matter' becomes an unintelligible abstraction.

literal sense—as when we say that pillars support a building; in what sense therefore must it be taken[1]?

17. If we inquire into what the most accurate philosophers declare themselves to mean by *material substance*, we shall find them acknowledge they have no other meaning annexed to those sounds but the idea of *being in general*, together with the relative notion of its *supporting accidents*. The general idea of Being appeareth to me the most abstract and incomprehensible of all other; and as for its supporting accidents, this, as we have just now observed, cannot be understood in the common sense of those words; it must therefore be taken in some other sense, but what that is they do not explain. So that when I consider the two parts or branches which make the signification of the words *material substance*, I am convinced there is no distinct meaning annexed to them. But why should we trouble ourselves any farther, in discussing this material *substratum* or 'support' of figure, and motion, and other sensible qualities? Does it not suppose they have an existence without the mind? And is not this a direct repugnancy, and altogether inconceivable[2]?

18. But, though it were possible that solid, figured, moveable substances may exist without the mind, corresponding

---

[1] He argues in this and next section as if the difficulty in question applies exclusively to *material substance*, and is not of force against *spiritual substance*. He accepts spiritual substance, on grounds defended in his *Third Dialogue*.

[2] This 'repugnancy' or 'contradiction' consists in the supposition of what is perceived existing without being perceived—the phenomenal being unphenomenal. He seems to have Locke in view. Cf. Locke's *Essay*, b. I. ch. 4. § 18; b. II. ch. 12. §§ 3-6; ch. 13. § 19; ch. 23, where our idea of substance, as distinct from qualities, is said to be dark, confused, and of little use. Yet Locke hesitates to dismiss entirely this obscure idea—as Hume afterwards did; or even to exclude it from our knowledge of the material world—as Berkeley is here doing. Locke's 'substance' is 'one knows not what support' of 'those qualities we find existing—a "support" which we are somehow intellectually obliged to suppose.' Berkeley does not here refer, as he might, to the difference between propositions which are self-contradictory and those which express a meaning that, because of the finitude of human intelligence, is necessarily incomplete and mysterious.

to the ideas we have of bodies, yet how is it possible for us to know this? Either we must know it by Sense or by Reason.—As for our senses, by them we have the knowledge only of our sensations, ideas, or those things that are immediately perceived by sense, call them what you will: but they do not inform us that things exist without the mind, or unperceived, like to those which are perceived. This the Materialists themselves acknowledge[1].—It remains therefore that if we have any knowledge at all of external things, it must be by Reason inferring their existence from what is immediately perceived by sense. But what reason can induce us to believe the existence of bodies without the mind, from what we perceive, since the very patrons of Matter themselves do not pretend there is any *necessary* connexion betwixt them and our ideas? . I say it is granted on all hands—and what happens in dreams, frenzies, and the like, puts it beyond dispute—that it is possible we might be affected with all the ideas we have now, though there were no bodies existing without resembling them. Hence, it is evident the supposition of external bodies is not necessary for the producing our ideas; since it is granted they are produced sometimes, and might possibly be produced always in the same order we see them in at present, without their concurrence.

19. But, though we might possibly have all our sensations without them, yet perhaps it may be thought easier to conceive and explain the manner of their production, by supposing external bodies in their likeness[2] rather than otherwise, and so it might be at least probable there are such things

---

[1] 'Materialist' includes all who maintain the existence of what is impercipient and unperceived; for the designation is not here limited, as it commonly is, to those who recognise *no other* than impercipient and unperceived substance.—Materialism is a term vaguely and ambiguously used. The hypothesis that God, by divinely established law in nature, has made human organisms self-conscious, however incoherent, must be distinguished from the absolute Materialism which substitutes unconscious atoms for God.

[2] 'In their likeness,' i. e. in the likeness of the phenomena of which we are percipient in the five senses.

as bodies that excite their ideas in our minds. But neither can this be said; for, though we give the materialists their external bodies, they by their own confession are never the nearer knowing *how* our ideas are produced; since they own themselves unable to comprehend in what manner body can act upon spirit, or how it is possible it should imprint any idea in the mind. Hence it is evident the production of ideas or sensations in our minds can be no reason why we should suppose Matter or corporeal substances, since *that* is acknowledged to remain equally inexplicable with or without this supposition. If therefore it were possible for bodies to exist without the mind, yet to hold they do so must needs be a very precarious opinion; since it is to suppose, without any reason at all, that God has created innumerable beings that are entirely useless, and serve to no manner of purpose[1].

20. In short, if there were external bodies, it is impossible we should ever come to know it; and if there were not, we might have the very same reasons to think there were that we have now. Suppose—what no one can deny possible— an intelligence *without the help of external bodies*, to be affected with the same train of sensations or ideas that you are, imprinted in the same order and with like vividness in his mind. I ask whether that intelligence hath not all the reason to believe the existence of corporeal substances, represented by his ideas, and exciting them in his mind, that you can possibly have for believing the same thing? Of this there can be no question—which one consideration were enough to make any reasonable person suspect the strength of whatever arguments he may think himself to have, for the existence of bodies without the mind[2].

---

[1] Not 'useless' if it can be shown that the existence of things as independent entities is presupposed in the acknowledged fact of social intercourse between intelligent beings; in the existence of law or continuity in nature; and even in the realization of our individual existence as conscious persons. Of all which afterwards.

[2] Although 'sensations' may not reveal to us either 'solid, extended,

21. Were it necessary to add any farther proof against the Existence of Matter, after what has been said, I could instance several of those errors and difficulties (not to mention impieties) which have sprung from that tenet. It has occasioned numberless controversies and disputes in philosophy, and not a few of far greater moment in religion. But I shall not enter into the detail of them in this place, as well because I think arguments *a posteriori* are unnecessary for confirming what has been, if I mistake not, sufficiently demonstrated *a priori*, as because I shall hereafter find occasion to speak somewhat of them[1].

22. I am afraid I have given cause to think I am needlessly prolix in handling this subject. For, to what purpose is it to dilate on that which may be demonstrated with the utmost evidence in a line or two, to any one that is capable of the least reflection? It is but looking into your own thoughts, and so trying whether you can conceive it possible for a sound, or figure, or motion, or colour to exist without the mind or unperceived. This easy trial may perhaps make you see

and moveable' substance, or 'abstract' material substance without qualities—are there any *permanent relations* so involved in the phenomena of sense as to constitute *notions* of 'things,' converting mere sensation into perception, and thus explaining sense-knowledge? Berkeley does not rise to this question. Dreams, for example, as interpreted during the dream by the dreamer, are not in harmony with the natural laws which determine the ordered dream of real life, by which natural reality is distinguished from illusions of fancy. Whether Berkeley's conception of what the material world means can be reconciled with *law* in nature, without presupposing (unconsciously) what it professedly rejects, is a consideration which here begins to suggest itself. If the reality of law in nature presupposes the *unperceived* or *independent* existence of what is manifested to us as extended, solid, and moveable, Berkeley must not say that phenomenal things as independent entities are 'entirely useless,' and 'serve no manner of purpose.' Consider whether, under Berkeley's conception of the material world, objective law does not dissolve into subjective association of ideas.

[1] In the old meaning of the terms, 'reasoning *a priori*' is from the essential nature or real definition of a cause, prior to any experience of its effects; 'reasoning *a posteriori*' is based upon a comparative observation of effects. The premisses of the former are principles; those of the latter facts. The method of the former is deductive; that of the latter inductive.

that what you cor*nd for is a downright contradiction. Insomuch that I am content to put the whole upon this issue:—If you can but conceive it possible for one extended moveable substance, or, in general, for any one idea, or anything like an idea, to exist otherwise than in a mind perceiving it; I shall readily give up the cause. And, as for all that compages of external bodies you contend for, I shall grant you its existence, though you cannot either give me any reason why you believe it exists, or assign any use to it when it is supposed to exist. I say, the bare possibility of your opinions being true shall pass for an argument that it is so[1].

23. But, say you, surely there is nothing easier than for me to imagine trees, for instance, in a park, or books existing in a closet, and nobody by to perceive them. I answer, you may so, there is no difficulty in it; but what is all this, I beseech you, more than framing in y ur mind certain ideas which you call books and trees, and at the same time omitting to frame the idea of any one that may perceive them? But do not you yourself perceive or think of them all the while? This therefore is nothing to the purpose: it only shews you have the power of imagining or forming ideas in your mind; but it does not shew that you can conceive it possible the objects of your thought may exist without the mind. To make out this, it is necessary that *you* conceive them existing unconceived or unthought of, which is a manifest repugnancy. When we do our utmost to conceive the existence of external bodies, we are all the while only contemplating our own ideas. But the mind, *taking no notice of itself*, is deluded to think it can and does conceive bodies existing

---

[1] In all this Berkeley takes for granted that he has already sufficiently shown that neither an object phenomenal in sense, nor anything like one, can exist as an independent entity. This assumed, it is of course a contradiction to say that it can so exist—or that we can imagine its continued existence, after the withdrawal of the perception in and through which phenomena of sense are possible.

unthought of or without the mind, though at the same time they are apprehended by or exist in itself[1]. A little attention will discover to any one the truth and evidence of what is here said, and make it unnecessary to insist on any other proofs against the existence of *material substance*[2].

24. It is very obvious, upon the least inquiry into our own thoughts, to know whether it be possible for us to understand what is meant by the *absolute* existence of sensible objects *in themselves* or *without the mind*. To me it is evident those words mark out either a direct contradiction, or else nothing at all. And to convince others of this, I know no readier or fairer way than to entreat they would calmly attend to their own thoughts; and if by this attention the emptiness or repugnancy of those expressions does appear, surely nothing more is requisite for their conviction. It is on this therefore that I insist, to wit, that the absolute existence of unthinking things are words without a meaning, or which include a contradiction[3]. This is what I repeat

[1] It may be asked whether this argument does not equally apply to the existence, independently of me, of *other conscious persons*, whose existence it is nevertheless one aim of Berkeley's philosophy to vindicate. A self-conscious life external to my own, is not *meaningless*, however, in the way in which his supposed unphenomenal matter is. It is, he would maintain, an intelligible externality, of which we can have a 'notion,' derived from our notion of our own self-conscious existence.

[2] Is there not in this section a confusion of existence in *sense* with existence in *imagination?* What we imagine exists, but it exists only subjectively—not as part of the universal system of ordered or objective things. Now, it is the *interrupted phenomenal* existence, in human experience, of the *things* which exhibit this order that Berkeley has to reconcile with their permanence and identity.

[3] A 'contradiction' if it means that sensible objects are at once perceived and yet not perceived—that they are phenomenal and yet not phenomenal; 'words without a meaning' if what is intended is, that 'Matter in itself' is something not phenomenal or qualified. The argument rests on the assumption that what cannot be sensibly phenomenal is not merely unimaginable by us, but must in itself be an empty verbal abstraction. But for Berkeley's recognition elsewhere of our 'notion' of Mind it would involve the empirical phenomenalism of Hume.

Berkeley rejects, as meaningless, a material world that may exist without being phenomenal in any sentient intelligence. He takes no account of the distinction between existence that is only *potential* and

and inculcate, and earnestly recommend to the attentive thoughts of the reader.

25. All our ideas, sensations, notions, or the things which we perceive, by whatsoever names they may be distinguished, are visibly inactive—there is nothing of Power or Agency included in them. So that one idea or object of thought cannot produce or make any alteration in another.—To be satisfied of the truth of this, there is nothing else requisite but a bare observation of our ideas. For, since they and every part of them exist only in the mind, it follows that there is nothing in them but what is perceived: but whoever shall attend to his ideas, whether of sense or reflection, will not perceive in them any power or activity; there is, therefore, no such thing contained in them. A little attention will discover to us that the very being of an idea implies passiveness and inertness in it, insomuch that it is impossible for an idea to do anything, or, strictly speaking, to be the cause of anything: neither can it be the resemblance or pattern of any active being, as is evident from sect. 8. Whence it plainly follows that extension, figure, and motion cannot be the cause of our sensations. To say, therefore, that these are the effects of powers resulting from the configuration, number, motion, and size of corpuscles, must certainly be false[1].

existence that is *actual*. The function of x in finite knowledge is a subject to be here pondered, and also the question whether any progress of philosophical speculation can ever eliminate x from a knowledge that is finite.

[1] We have here the rudiments of that theory of Causality and Power from which Berkeley deduces the *impotence* as well as the unsubstantiality of Matter. In section 25 he turns from Mind, giving actual reality to the material world in and through the perceptions of sense, to Mind as the only *independent originating cause* and *actual agent*. Here his first position is, that there can be no power or efficient causality in phenomena of sense: 'bare observation' of these is to him proof of their inactivity. Customary connexion, established by God among phenomenal things, independently of human will, is the only sort of

26. We perceive a continual *succession* of ideas; some are anew excited, others are changed or totally disappear. There is therefore some Cause of these ideas, whereon they depend, and which produces and changes them. That this cause cannot be any quality, or idea, or combination of ideas is clear from the preceding section. It must therefore be a substance; but it has been shewn that there is no corporeal or material substance: it remains therefore that the cause of ideas is an incorporeal active substance or Spirit[1].

'causality' which Berkeley recognises in the material world, which is with him a divinely established system of sensible signs, in which a *priori* anything might by God have been made the sign of anything. 'Established connexion' is the conception of causality afterwards professed by Hume, Brown, Comte, the Mills, and others, and is in harmony with Bacon's favourite conception of external nature as interpretable. With them, however, it was not, as with Berkeley, limited to the material world, and so with them independent originating causality or free agency is left out of account.

[1] Berkeley, like Locke, here assumes, without analysis of the *metaphysical principle* of Causality—that every change necessarily presupposes the existence of something in which it originates, and out of which it issues. Causality with him is not, however, merely a relation of established signs under which phenomena happen to be connected. He sees in tangible and visible phenomena ordered signs, Spirit *alone* being the ultimate cause. The material world is thus emptied of power, its supposed 'powers' being refunded into Spirit. Every appearance in sense is caused: only Spirit causes. Except metaphorically, he does not attribute any sort of efficacy to any sensible thing: the material world contains substances and causes only in a figurative way. He grants, indeed, that metaphorically each phenomenal thing may be called a 'substance,' and each instance of uniform phenomenal succession a case of 'causality.' Spirits themselves are not phenomena, he seems to say; for each *ego* remains the same, while the phenomena of which it is conscious, in sense and otherwise, are changing.

In these sections Berkeley seems to found our notion of Power and Causation on our conviction of our own free voluntary activity—akin to the solution adopted afterwards by Reid, Stewart, Maine de Biran, and others. Elsewhere (e.g. *Siris*, 257) he seems to trace it more to our moral experience of responsibility. His views (more developed in the *Vindication* and in *Siris*) may be compared with those of Locke, *Essay*, b. 11. ch. 21 and ch. 26; also with the reduction of the causal relation afterwards proposed by Hume; with the analysis of causation by Kant, as a 'category' constitutive of experience; or (turning to ancient speculation) with the Aristotelian Four Causes. Hume tries to shew that any supposed *necessity* of connexion among phenomena is an illusion, generated by custom, as a necessary relation cannot be phenomenalised, or resolved into an impression: Kant finds the notion of cause,

27. A Spirit is one simple, undivided, active being—as it *perceives* ideas it is called the *Understanding*, and as it *produces* or otherwise *operates* about them it is called the *Will*. Hence there can be no *idea* formed of a soul or spirit; for, all ideas whatever, being passive and inert, (vid. sect. 25,) cannot represent unto us, by way of image or likeness, that which acts. A little attention will make it plain to any one that to have an idea which shall be *like* that active principle of motion and change of ideas is absolutely impossible. Such is the nature of Spirit, or that which acts, that it cannot be of itself perceived, but only by the effects which it produceth. —If any man shall doubt of the truth of what is here delivered, let him but reflect and try if he can frame the idea of any Power or Active Being; and whether he has ideas of two principal powers, marked by the names *Will* and *Understanding*, distinct from each other, as well as from a third idea of Substance or Being in general, with a relative notion of its supporting or being the subject of the aforesaid powers —which is signified by the name Soul or Spirit[1]. This is what some hold; but, so far as I can see, the words *will, soul, spirit,* do not stand for different ideas, or, in truth, for any idea at all, but for something which is very different from ideas, and which, being an Agent, cannot be like unto, or represented by, any idea whatsoever. [Though it must be owned at the same time that we have some *notion*[2] of soul,

like that of substance, in a necessity of the understanding, presupposed in the very possibility of intelligible experience. According to Aristotle, everything presupposes *matter* of which it is made; *form* or *essence* by which it may be defined; *force* or *efficiency* by which the matter and form have been united in its constitution; and *end* or *purpose* which it is its function to fulfil;—so that a full knowledge of a thing would be a knowledge of it in these four relations of its causality.

[1] According to Locke we have no *positive idea* either of corporeal or of spiritual substance, yet he recognises a sort of *negative idea* of both. Berkeley accepts, in the form of *consciousness of self*, the 'notion' of spiritual substance. Hume afterwards rejected, or at least proclaimed ignorance of both. Kant recalled the notion of substance, as a relation involved in an intelligible experience.

[2] According to Berkeley, the notions of substance and cause are given

spirit, and the operations of the mind; such as willing, loving, hating—inasmuch as we know or understand the meaning of these words[1].]

28. I find I can excite ideas in my mind at pleasure, and vary and shift the scene as oft as I think fit. It is no more than willing, and straightway this or that idea arises in my fancy; and by the same power it is obliterated and makes way for another. This making and unmaking of ideas doth very properly denominate the mind active. Thus much is certain and grounded on experience: but when we talk of unthinking agents, or of exciting ideas exclusive of Volition, we only amuse ourselves with words.

29. But, whatever power I may have over my own thoughts, I find the ideas actually perceived by Sense have not a like dependence on my will[2]. When in broad daylight I open my eyes, it is not in my power to choose whether I shall see or no, or to determine what particular objects shall present themselves to my view; and so likewise as to the hearing and other senses, the ideas imprinted on them are not creatures of my will. There is therefore some *other* Will or Spirit that produces them[3].

30. The ideas of Sense are more strong, lively, and distinct

---

to us in the fact of our being conscious of ourselves as freely acting spirits, not as categories necessarily involved in an experience of phenomena. He says that we have 'notions,' not 'ideas,' of them; for Spirit cannot be phenomenalised. Ueberweg suggests that Berkeley's reasoning implies that I can know only *my individual* notions of what I call *other* spirits—thus leading, as a *reductio ad absurdum*, to Egoism or Solipsism.

[1] This sentence was added in the Second Edition of the *Principles*. It introduces the term *notion* in its strict Berkeleian meaning of an intelligent apprehension of Mind, and of relations among phenomena.

[2] Here 'thoughts,' as individual mental images, are contrasted with phenomena actually perceived in the senses. Cf. Locke, *Essay*, b. IV. ch. 11.

[3] In this and the following sections we have Berkeley's account of the difference between Perception and Imagination. He tries to explain the objectivity of the former in contrast with the subjectivity of the latter.

than those of the Imagination; they have likewise a steadiness, order, and coherence, and are not excited at random, as those which are the effects of human wills often are, but in a regular train or series—the admirable connexion whereof sufficiently testifies the wisdom and benevolence of its Author. Now the set rules or established methods wherein the Mind we depend on excites in us the ideas of sense, are called the *laws of nature;* and these we learn by experience [1], which teaches us that such and such ideas are attended with such and such other ideas, in the ordinary course of things.

31. This gives us a sort of foresight which enables us to regulate our actions for the benefit of life. And without this we should be eternally at a loss; we could not know how to act anything that might procure us the least pleasure, or remove the least pain of sense. That food nourishes, sleep refreshes, and fire warms us; that to sow in the seed-time is the way to reap in the harvest; and in general that to obtain such or such ends, such or such means are conducive —all this we know, not by discovering any *necessary connexion* between our ideas, but only by the *observation* of the settled laws of nature, without which we should be all in uncertainty and confusion, and a grown man no more know how to manage himself in the affairs of life than an infant just born [2].

32. And yet this consistent uniform working, which so evidently displays the goodness and wisdom of that Governing Spirit whose Will constitutes the laws of nature, is so far from leading our thoughts to Him, that it rather sends them wandering after second causes. For, when we perceive

---

[1] Something more than the merely phenomenal is here tacitly included in 'experience.' For, how does experience explain our conviction of the *universality* of order, if it means only particular phenomena that are present as transient sensations?

[2] This reduction of Perception into observationally reached expectation or prevision may be compared with J. S. Mill's 'psychological' theory of belief in the external world (*Examination of Hamilton*, ch. XII).

certain ideas of Sense constantly followed by other ideas, and we know this is not of our own doing, we forthwith attribute power and agency to the ideas themselves, and make one the cause of another, than which nothing can be more absurd and unintelligible. Thus, for example, having observed that when we perceive by sight a certain round luminous figure we at the same time perceive by touch the idea or sensation called heat, we do from thence conclude the sun to be the *cause* of heat. And in like manner perceiving the motion and collision of bodies to be attended with sound, we are inclined to think the latter the *effect* of the former.

33. The ideas imprinted on the Senses by the Author of nature are called *real things:* and those excited in the Imagination being less regular, vivid, and constant, are more properly termed *ideas,* or *images of things,* which they copy and represent. But then our sensations, be they never so vivid and distinct, are nevertheless ideas, that is, they exist in the mind[1], or are perceived by it, as truly as the ideas of its own framing. The ideas of Sense are allowed to have more reality in them, that is, to be more strong, orderly, and coherent than the creatures of the mind; but this is no argument that they exist without the mind. They are also less dependent on the spirit, or thinking substance which perceives them, in that they are excited by the will of another and more powerful Spirit; yet still they are *ideas,* and certainly no idea, whether faint or strong, can exist otherwise than in a mind perceiving it[2].

---

[1] 'In the mind' is here and elsewhere used figuratively for being actually perceived; not of course in the sense of being locally within the mind, to which the terms 'within' and 'without,' in this meaning, are foreign.

[2] Such is Berkeley's account of the difference between real and merely imaginary things—between the actually perceived and the merely imagined, in our mental experience. 'Sensations'—the real phenomena of which we are actually percipient—are, he says, (*a*) involuntary, as far as each individual percipient is concerned, while the creatures of imagination are not; (*b*) they are more strong, lively, and distinct than the latter, thus differing from them in degree; (*c*) they are units in the

34 [1]. Before we proceed any farther it is necessary we spend some time in answering Objections which may probably be made against the principles we have hitherto laid down. In doing of which, if I seem too prolix to those of quick apprehensions, I desire I may be excused, since all men do not equally apprehend things of this nature, and I am willing to be understood by every one.

First, then, it will be objected that by the foregoing principles all that is real and substantial in nature is banished out of the world, and instead thereof a chimerical scheme of *ideas* takes place. All things that exist exist only in the mind, that is, they are purely notional. What therefore becomes of the sun, moon, and stars? What must we think of houses, rivers, mountains, trees, stones; nay, even of our own bodies? Are all these but so many chimeras and illusions on the fancy?—To all which, and whatever else of the same sort may be objected, I answer, that by the principles premised we are not deprived of any one thing in nature. Whatever we see, feel, hear, or any wise conceive or under-

---

universal system of coherent relations which constitutes objective Nature. The second of these distinguishing marks was afterwards emphasised by Hume, in his contrast between *impressions* and (their representative) *ideas* in imagination (*Treatise of Human Nature*, b. I. pt. I. sect. 1, 3. pt. 4. sect. 7; *Inquiry concerning Human Understanding*, sect. 2). Hume explains all *belief* as the issue of an inexplicable tendency of custom 'to enliven some ideas beyond others.' 'The memory, senses, and understanding are,' he says, 'all of them *founded* on the imagination, or the vivacity of our ideas.'—See also Leibnitz, *De modo distinguendi Phenomena Realia ab Imaginariis*, and Locke, *Essay*, b. IV. ch. 2. § 14; ch. 4; ch. 11, for opinions antecedent to Berkeley.

The result of the preceding argumentation (Sect. 3-33) might be thus expressed:—Phenomenal things can be substantiated and caused only by self-conscious spirit, for no other substantiation or causation is intelligible; to affirm that the phenomenal things of which alone we are immediately percipient can be, or can represent, non-phenomenal or abstract substances, and originating causes, would be to affirm a contradiction in terms.

[1] Sect. 34-84 contain Berkeley's answers to a series of supposed *objections* to the conception of Matter that has been reasoned out in the preceding sections.

stand, remains as secure as ever, and is as real as ever. There is a *rerum natura*, and the distinction between realities and chimeras retains its full force. This is evident from sect. 29, 30, and 33, where we have shewn what is meant by *real things*, in opposition to *chimeras* or ideas of our own framing; but then they both equally exist in the mind, and in that sense are alike *ideas*.

35. I do not argue against the existence of any one thing that we can apprehend either by sense or reflection. That the things I see with my eyes and touch with my hands do exist, really exist, I make not the least question. The only thing whose existence we deny is that which *philosophers* call Matter or corporeal substance. And in doing of this there is no damage done to the rest of mankind, who, I dare say, will never miss it. The Atheist indeed will want the colour of an empty name to support his impiety; and the Philosophers may possibly find they have lost a great handle for trifling and disputation.

36. If any man thinks this detracts from the existence or reality of things, he is very far from understanding what hath been premised in the plainest terms I could think of. Take here an abstract of what has been said:—There are spiritual substances, minds, or human souls, which will or excite ideas[1] in themselves at pleasure; but these are faint, weak, and unsteady in respect of others they perceive by Sense—which, being impressed upon them according to certain Rules or Laws of Nature, speak themselves the effects of a Mind more powerful and wise than human spirits. These latter are said to have *more reality* in them than the former;—by which is meant that they are more affecting, orderly, and distinct, and that they are not fictions[2] of the mind perceiving them. And in this sense the sun that I see by day is the real sun, and that

---

[1] 'Ideas,' i. e. phenomena of imagination.
[2] 'Not fictions,' because they are the ultimate data, immediately presented in sense; and *these* cannot misrepresent, because they are not representative of what is beyond themselves. They *are* the sensible reality.

which I imagine by night is the idea of the former[1]. In the sense here given of *reality*, it is evident that every vegetable, star, mineral, and in general each part of the mundane system, is as much a *real being* by our principles as by any other. Whether others mean anything by the term *reality* different from what I do, I entreat them to look into their own thoughts and see.

37. It will be urged that thus much at least is true, to wit, that we take away all corporeal substances. To this my answer is, that if the word *substance* be taken in the vulgar sense—for a combination of sensible qualities, such as extension, solidity, weight, and the like—this we cannot be accused of taking away; but if it be taken in a philosophic sense—for the support of accidents or qualities without the mind—then indeed I acknowledge that we take it away, if one may be said to take away that which never had any existence, not even in the imagination[2].

38. But after all, say you, it sounds very harsh to say we eat and drink ideas, and are clothed with ideas. I acknowledge it does so—the word *idea* not being used in common discourse to signify the several combinations of sensible qualities which are called *things;* and it is certain that any expression which varies from the familiar use of language will seem harsh and ridiculous. But this doth not concern the truth of the proposition, which in other words is no more than to say, we are fed and clothed with those things which we perceive immediately by our senses. The hardness or

---

[1] Here again we have the difference between Imagination and Perception insisted on, and sought to be reconciled with the already argued *necessary* unsubstantiality and impotence of sensible things apart from percipient and active mind.

[2] The 'observed' existence of established aggregates of phenomena of sense, actual and potential, commonly called 'things,' is acknowledged; but a 'substance' abstracted out of all relation to a percipient is rejected as meaningless, if not self-contradictory. We cannot, he argues, find any substance or power in *ideas* or *phenomena;* but we have *notions* of both substance and power notwithstanding, implied in our consciousness of self and belief in our own personal agency.

softness, the colour, taste, warmth, figure, or suchlike qualities, which, combined together, constitute the several sorts of victuals and apparel, have been shewn to exist only in the mind that perceives them; and this is all that is meant by calling them *ideas;* which word if it was as ordinarily used as *thing*, would sound no harsher nor more ridiculous than it. I am not for disputing about the propriety, but the truth of the expression. If therefore you agree with me that we eat and drink and are clad with the immediate objects of sense, which cannot exist unperceived or without the mind, I shall readily grant it is more proper or conformable to custom that they should be called *things* rather than *ideas*[1].

39. If it be demanded why I make use of the word *idea*, and do not rather in compliance with custom call them *things;* I answer, I do it for two reasons:—first, because the term *thing*, in contradistinction to *idea*, is generally supposed to denote somewhat existing without the mind; secondly, because *thing* hath a more comprehensive signification than *idea*, including spirit or thinking things as well as ideas[2]. Since therefore the objects of sense exist only in the mind, and are withal thoughtless and inactive[3], I chose to mark them by the word *idea*, which implies those properties[4].

40. But, say what we can, some one perhaps may be apt to reply, he will still believe his senses, and never suffer any arguments, how plausible soever, to prevail over the certainty

[1] The point for consideration here is, whether this deviation from the ordinary custom of language does not necessarily imply a deviation from rational suppositions on which all experience of things depends. What is meant by eating phenomena presented in sense? and is not the eater as ideal or phenomenal as the thing eaten? Berkeley might say that 'I am eating' involves the 'notion' of will and personality, and is not a mere phenomenon.
[2] Spirits are more properly called *persons* than *things*.
[3] He takes for granted that he has already proved their unsubstantiality and impotence.
[4] The terms 'sensation,' 'sense idea,' 'real idea,' 'impression,' 'percept,' 'phenomenon,' might be substituted, though objections are open to them all. As in some respects the least objectionable, I prefer *phenomenon present in sense*.

of them. Be it so; assert the evidence of sense as high as you please, we are willing to do the same. That what I see, hear, and feel doth exist, that is to say, is perceived by me, I no more doubt than I do of my own being. But I do not see how the testimony of sense can be alleged as a proof for the existence of anything which is *not* perceived by sense. We are not for having any man turn sceptic and disbelieve his senses; on the contrary, we give them all the stress and assurance imaginable; nor are there any principles more opposite to Scepticism than those we have laid down, as shall be hereafter clearly shewn [1].

41. *Secondly*, it will be objected that there is a great difference betwixt real fire for instance, and the idea of fire, betwixt dreaming or imagining oneself burnt, and actually being so: if you suspect it to be only the idea of fire which you see, do but put your hand into it and you will be convinced with a witness [2]. This and the like may be urged in opposition to our tenets.—To all which the answer is evident from what hath been already said, and I shall only add in this place, that if real fire be very different from the idea of fire, so also is the real pain that it occasions very different from the idea of the same pain, and yet nobody will pretend that real pain either is, or can possibly be, in an unperceiving thing, or without the mind, any more than its idea [3].

[1] Berkeley argues that to suppose phenomenal things still existing phenomenally, which nevertheless are not perceived by *any* mind, is as absurd as to suppose an actual perception of them without their perceived existence. But if he resolves matter into present phenomena of sense only, his real world is without any principle for their synthesis, and so unintelligible. How does this eject Scepticism? Is it with his vague theory of 'suggestion' of which he makes so much in his writings on visual perception; or with his undeveloped doctrine of 'notions' and reason, as in *Siris;* or with both, that he would meet this question?
[2] So Locke, *Essay*, b. IV. ch. 11. §§ 7, 8.
[3] But is there no more *objectivity* in the extended things of sense than there is in our private and purely personal pains and pleasures —though both, it is granted, are different from the bare imagination of either?

42. *Thirdly*, it will be objected that we *see* things actually without or at a distance from us, and which consequently do not exist in the mind; it being absurd that those things which are seen at the distance of several miles should be as near to us as our own thoughts. In answer to this, I desire it may be considered that in a dream we do oft perceive things as existing at a great distance off, and yet for all that, those things are acknowledged to have their existence only in the mind.

43. But, for the fuller clearing of this point, it may be worth while to consider *how* it is that we perceive distance and things placed at a distance by sight. For, that we should in truth see external space, and bodies actually existing in it—some nearer, and others farther off—seems to carry with it some opposition to what hath been said of their existing nowhere without the mind. The consideration of this difficulty it was that gave birth to my *Essay towards a New Theory of Vision*, which was published not long since—wherein it is shewn that *distance* or *outness* is neither immediately of itself perceived by sight, nor yet apprehended or judged of by lines and angles, or anything that hath a necessary connexion with it; but that it is only suggested[1] to our thoughts by certain visible ideas and sensations attending vision, which in their own nature have no manner of similitude or relation either with distance or things placed at a distance; but, by a connexion taught us by experience[2], they come to signify and suggest them to us, after the same manner that words of any language suggest the ideas they are made to stand for; insomuch that a man born blind and afterwards made to see, would not, at first sight, think the things he saw to be with-

---

[1] Note that the term *suggestion*, so significant in the psychology of Berkeley, here first makes its appearance in the *Principles*. See *New Theory of Vision*, sect. 16, *note*, and *Vindication*, sect. 42.—The term 'suggestion'—simple and relative—was much employed long afterwards, in the subtle psychology of Dr. Thomas Brown.

[2] 'Suggestion' is here rested upon 'experience' or custom, and is then made the constructive principle in the explanation of visual perception, if not ultimately of all human knowledge.

out his mind, or at any distance from him. See sect. 41 of the forementioned treatise.

44. The ideas of sight and touch make two species entirely distinct and heterogeneous. The former are marks and prognostics of the latter. That the proper objects of sight neither exist without the mind, nor are the images of external things, was shewn even in that treatise. Though throughout the same the contrary be supposed true of tangible objects—not that to suppose that vulgar error was necessary for establishing the notion therein laid down, but because it was beside my purpose to examine and refute it in a discourse concerning *Vision*[1]. So that in strict truth the ideas of sight, when we apprehend by them distance and things placed at a distance, do not suggest or mark out to us things actually existing at a distance, but only admonish us what ideas of touch[2] will be imprinted in our minds at such and such distances of time, and in consequence of such and such actions. It is, I say, evident from what has been said in the foregoing parts of this *Treatise*, and in sect. 147 and elsewhere of the *Essay* concerning Vision, that visible ideas are the Language whereby the Governing Spirit on whom we depend informs us what tangible ideas he is about to imprint upon us, in case we excite this or that motion in our own bodies. But for a fuller information in this point I refer to the *Essay* itself[3].

45. *Fourthly*, it will be objected that from the foregoing

---

[1] In the *Essay on Vision* he was inserting the thin end of the wedge of his new conception of *reality* and *externality*.

[2] Under 'touch' and 'tangible ideas' he includes our (active) sense-consciousness of locomotion. He virtually treats Space as consisting in a succession of phenomena presented in touch and signified in what we see. Thus mathematics becomes the science of number, which is itself, as he had argued, dependent on percipient mind.

[3] Berkeley's theory of visual *perception* (virtually visual *expectation*) may be developed into one of *universal* sense symbolism, based on an assumption of physical causality as consisting of ordered phenomenal signs, and of the consequent interpretability of nature by an inductive comparison of the orderly or significant phenomena.

principles it follows things are every moment annihilated and created anew. The objects of sense exist only when they are perceived; the trees therefore are in the garden, or the chairs in the parlour, no longer than while there is somebody by to perceive them. Upon shutting my eyes all the furniture in the room is reduced to nothing, and barely upon opening them it is again created.—In answer to all which, I refer the reader to what has been said in sect. 3, 4, &c., and desire he will consider whether he *means* anything by the actual existence of an idea distinct from its being perceived. For my part, after the nicest inquiry I could make, I am not able to discover that anything else is meant by those words; and I once more entreat the reader to sound his own thoughts, and not suffer himself to be imposed on by words. If he can conceive it possible either for his ideas or their archetypes to exist without being perceived, then I give up the cause; but if he cannot, he will acknowledge it is unreasonable for him to stand up in defence of he knows not what, and pretend to charge on me as an absurdity the not assenting to those propositions which at bottom have no meaning in them[1].

46. It will not be amiss to observe how far the received principles of philosophy are themselves chargeable with those pretended absurdities. It is thought strangely absurd that upon closing my eyelids all the visible objects around me should be reduced to nothing; and yet is not this what philosophers commonly acknowledge, when they agree on all hands that light and colours, which alone are the proper and immediate objects of sight, are mere sensations[2] that exist no longer

---

[1] This repeats the warning with which he introduced us to philosophy —against empty abstractions; for such, according to his argument, material substances and powers that are supposed to exist unperceived by any mind must be.

[2] But the 'extended thing' said to excite these sensations was supposed to exist as an independent entity, and its secondary qualities (by Locke and others regarded as unknown modifications of the primary) were assumed to be the cause of the sensations. Berkeley's recognition of power or independent causality as existing only in Spirit dissolves the

than they are perceived? Again, it may to some perhaps seem very incredible that things should be every moment creating, yet this very notion is commonly taught in the schools. For the Schoolmen, though they acknowledge the existence of matter, and that the whole mundane fabric is framed out of it, are nevertheless of opinion that it cannot subsist without the divine conservation, which by them is expounded to be a continual creation[1].

47. Farther, a little thought will discover to us that though we allow the existence of Matter or corporeal substance, yet it will unavoidably follow, from the principles which are now generally admitted, that the particular bodies, of what kind soever, do none of them exist whilst they are not perceived. For, it is evident, from sect. 11 and the following sections, that the Matter philosophers contend for is an incomprehensible somewhat, which hath none of those particular qualities whereby the bodies falling under our senses are distinguished one from another. But, to make this more plain, it must be remarked that the infinite divisibility of Matter is now universally allowed, at least by the most approved and considerable philosophers, who, on the received principles, demonstrate it beyond all exception. Hence, it follows there is an infinite number of parts in each particle of Matter which are not perceived by sense[2]. The reason therefore that any particular body seems to be of a finite magnitude, or exhibits only a finite number of parts to sense, is, not because it contains no more, since in itself it contains an infinite number of parts,

supposed power of the 'extended thing,' and substitutes the constant activity of God as the cause of the phenomena which are presented to us in our senses (sect. 6, 48, &c.)

[1] It is the implied want of *phenomenal* continuity in sensible existence that is objected to Berkeley's view; but this does not fully apply to that constant preservation of *things supposed continuously to exist indépendently of perception*, which is meant by many who speak of 'constant creation.'

[2] The divisibility of matter was supposed to be potentially, not actually, infinite; for it is of the essence of infinite division that it can never be completed, and that every actual division may be carried further. The *divisibility*, not any actual division ever observable by us, is infinite.

but because the sense is not acute enough to discern them. In proportion therefore as the sense is rendered more acute, it perceives a greater number of parts in the object, that is, the object appears greater, and its figure varies, those parts in its extremities which were before unperceivable appearing now to bound it in very different lines and angles from those perceived by an obtuser sense. And at length, after various changes of size and shape, when the sense becomes infinitely acute the body shall seem infinite. During all which there is no alteration in the body, but only in the sense. Each body therefore, considered in itself, is infinitely extended, and consequently void of all shape and figure[1].—From which it follows that, though we should grant the existence of Matter to be never so certain, yet it is withal as certain, the Materialists themselves are by their own principles forced to acknowledge, that neither the particular bodies perceived by sense, nor anything like them, exists without the mind. Matter, I say, and each particle thereof, is according to them infinite and shapeless, and it is the mind that frames all that variety of bodies which compose the visible world, any one whereof does not exist longer than it is perceived.

48. But, after all, if we consider it, the objection proposed in sect. 45 will not be found reasonably charged on the principles we have premised, so as in truth to make any objection at all against our notions. For, though we hold indeed the objects of sense to be nothing else but ideas which cannot exist unperceived, yet we may not hence conclude they have no existence except only while they are perceived by us; since there may be some other spirit that perceives them though we do not. Wherever bodies are said to have no existence without the mind, I would not be understood to mean this or that particular mind, but *all minds whatsoever*. It does not therefore follow from the foregoing principles that bodies

---

[1] Does this follow, if the parts diminish in size in an infinite ratio? This reasoning about an infinity of parts becomes obscure.

are annihilated and created every moment, or exist not at all during the intervals between *our* perception of them[1].

49. *Fifthly*, it may perhaps be objected that if extension and figure exist only in the mind, it follows that the mind is extended and figured; since extension is a mode or attribute which (to speak with the schools) is predicated of the *subject* in which it exists.—I answer, those qualities are in the mind only as they are perceived by it—that is, not by way of *mode* or *attribute*, but only by way of *idea*; and it no

[1] To explain our common sense belief in the *permanence* and *identity* of the things we see and touch, notwithstanding the constant flux of their constituent phenomena in our senses, and to shew *how* they exist during intervals in which there may be no perception of them by any finite mind, is *the* difficulty, under Berkeley's conception of what the material world means. What amount of phenomenal change in the 'things of sense' is consistent with the individual identity of each thing?

With reference to Berkeley's reply to the fourth objection, it might be urged that if sensible things exist continuously, either potentially, or supernaturally in God's will and thought; and if, as actual, they are dependent on our (often interrupted) sense-perceptions,—then, what we call the *same* thing is for each of us *many* things, each of them annihilated and created anew with every opening and closing of our eyes. Did the Herculanean manuscripts, Ueberweg asks, not exist actually during the centuries in which they were buried, and shall we say that when they were discovered God created them anew? Can this restoration be consistently explained by Berkeley merely by the fact that all phenomena in sense are governed by natural law? Is law in nature possible except on the supposition that things exist independently of all *finite* percipients *during the intervals* of their being perceived? and would not their supposed Divine Ideal (potential, as concerns us) existence imply their eternal and necessary existence, because the Ideas of God are eternal and necessary?—Kant, in a passage in his *Critique of Pure Reason* ('Transcendental Dialectic,' b. II. ch. 2. sect. 6), accepts a position not unlike Berkeley's. 'The objects of experience are not,' he concludes, 'things in themselves (*dinge an sich*), but are given in experience, independently of which they have no existence. That there may be inhabitants in the moon, though no one has ever observed them, must be admitted; but this means only that in the progress of knowledge we may discover them at some future time. That which stands in connexion with a present perception according to the progress of the laws of experience is real.' ('Inhabitants of the moon' are hardly in point, for, if they are conscious, their own conscious life maintains their existence.)

On the 'sameness' of sensible things, see *Third Dialogue* (*Works*, vol. I. pp. 343-345); also on the opinions of the Schoolmen on 'constant creation,' see *Life of Berkeley*, p. 108.

more follows the soul or mind is extended, because extension exists in it alone, than it does that it is red or blue, because those colours are on all hands acknowledged to exist in it, and nowhere else. As to what philosophers say of 'subject' and 'mode,' that seems very groundless and unintelligible. For instance, in this proposition—'a die is hard, extended, and square,' they will have it that the word *die* denotes a subject or substance, distinct from the hardness, extension, and figure which are predicated of it, and in which they exist. This I cannot comprehend: to me a die seems to be nothing distinct from those things which are termed its modes or accidents. And, to say 'a die is hard, extended, and square' is not to attribute those qualities to a subject distinct from and supporting them, but only an explication of the meaning of the word *die*[1].

50. *Sixthly*, you will say there have been a great many things explained by matter and motion; take away these and you destroy the whole corpuscular philosophy, and undermine those mechanical principles which have been applied

[1] If Space and extended things are phenomenal only in and through percipient mind, it may seem that mind is itself extended, so that after all we are landed in Materialism.—Berkeley's reply here throws light on his conception of the relation between percipients and perceived phenomena—between the conscious self and the flux of 'sensations' of which self is cognisant. A *percipient* is not, he assumes, related to what is *perceived* either (*a*) under the unmeaning relation of *subject* (ὑποκείμενον) and *attributes*, which scholastics, who substantiate abstractions, talk about; or (*b*) as one phenomenon is related to another, in those steady aggregates of presented phenomena which compose 'things.' On the contrary, percipient mind is related to the phenomena of extension, figure, and what else is given in sense, simply *as* percipient and perceived—knower and known-object—with whatever 'otherness' that altogether *sui generis* relation may involve. But it is not so related as that the extended phenomenon is an *attribute* of the *ego*.

(Berkeley here means by *subject* 'substratum,' or impercipient and unperceived subject; not the conscious or percipient subject,—the ὑποκείμενον of the Peripatetics; not their οὐσία or τί ἐστιν, which includes also the essence which makes a thing what it is, and which is expressed in its definition. The term is also used, as he shews, to designate a grammatical term in a proposition. The deep question of the ontological import of judgments rises here.)

with so much success to account for the phenomena. In short, whatever advances have been made, either by ancient or modern philosophers, in the study of Nature do all proceed on the supposition that corporeal substance or Matter doth really exist.—To this I answer that there is not any one phenomenon explained on that supposition which may not as well be explained without it, as might easily be made appear by an induction of particulars[1]. To explain the phenomena, is all one as to shew why, upon such and such occasions, we are affected with such and such ideas. But how Matter should operate on a Spirit, or produce any idea in it, is what no philosopher will pretend to explain; it is therefore evident there can be no use of Matter in Natural Philosophy[2]. Besides, they who attempt to account for things do it not by corporeal substance, but by figure, motion, and other qualities, which are in truth no more than mere ideas, and therefore cannot be the *cause* of anything, as hath been already shewn. See sect. 25.

51. *Seventhly*, it will upon this be demanded whether it

[1] It has been objected to this—that all physico-mathematical explanations of events in nature rest on the hypothesis that changes in the material world are independent of every percipient mind—that they are in an objective causal relation to one another and to our organism—and in particular that Berkeley's conception of what 'reality' of the material world means is inconsistent with the conservation of 'force' through its successive metamorphoses.

[2] The question for Materialism is—whether conscious life, in all its rational and voluntary manifestations, more probably issues (*a*) from a power like itself, or is (*b*) the blind outcome of phenomenal organization —by actual but inexplicable law. And the most plausible and consistent materialism professes only its own probability, rather than to be a demonstrable explanation of the universe : we have probable evidence, it argues, that molecular motions, on the one side, and states or acts of conscious life, on the other, are related as constant antecedent and consequent, and we probably cannot go deeper than this probable fact. —With Berkeley the organism, in itself unsubstantial and impotent, is ultimately dependent on Mind ; though each individual mind may be conditioned by its own organism, as healthy or diseased. The Materialist assumes with regard to power in the universe that, *a priori*, anything may be caused by anything, instead of its being necessarily the issue of elements in its productive cause which are *rationally adequate* for its production.

does not seem absurd to take away Natural Causes, and ascribe everything to the immediate operation of Spirits? We must no longer say upon these principles that fire heats, or water cools, but that a Spirit heats, and so forth. Would not a man be deservedly laughed at, who should talk after this manner?—I answer, he would so; in such things we ought to 'think with the learned, and speak with the vulgar.' They who to demonstration are convinced of the truth of the Copernican system do nevertheless say 'the sun rises,' 'the sun sets,' or 'comes to the meridian;' and if they affected a contrary style in common talk it would without doubt appear very ridiculous. A little reflection on what is here said will make it manifest that the common use of language would receive no manner of alteration or disturbance from the admission of our tenets.

52. In the ordinary affairs of life, any phrases may be retained, so long as they excite in us proper sentiments, or dispositions to act in such a manner as is necessary for our well-being, how false soever they may be if taken in a strict and speculative sense. Nay, this is unavoidable, since, propriety being regulated by custom, language is suited to the received opinions, which are not always the truest. Hence it is impossible—even in the most rigid, philosophic reasonings—so far to alter the bent and genius of the tongue we speak as never to give a handle for cavillers to pretend difficulties and inconsistencies. But a fair and ingenuous reader will collect the sense from the scope and tenor and connexion of a discourse, making allowances for those inaccurate modes of speech which use has made inevitable.

53. As to the opinion that there are no Corporeal Causes, this has been heretofore maintained by some of the Schoolmen, as it is of late by others among the modern philosophers, who, though they allow Matter to exist, yet will have God *alone* to be the immediate efficient cause of all things. These men saw that amongst all the objects of sense there

was none which had any power or activity included in it; and that by consequence this was likewise true of whatever bodies *they* supposed to exist without the mind, like unto the immediate objects of sense. But then, that they should suppose an innumerable multitude of created beings, which they acknowledge are not capable of producing any one effect in nature, and which therefore are made to no manner of purpose, since God might have done everything as well without them—this I say, though we should allow it possible, must yet be a very unaccountable and extravagant supposition [1].

54. In the *eighth* place, the universal concurrent Assent of Mankind may be thought by some an invincible argument in behalf of Matter, or the existence of external things [2]. Must we suppose the whole world to be mistaken? And if so, what cause can be assigned of so widespread and predominant an error?—I answer, first, that, upon a narrow inquiry, it will not perhaps be found so many as is imagined do really believe the existence of Matter or things without the mind. Strictly speaking, to believe that which involves

[1] The reference in this section is to Malebranche, Geulinx, and other so-called Occasionalists in the seventeenth century, who, while they argued for the sub*stantial existence* of sensible things, denied, like Berkeley, but on other grounds, their *proper efficiency*. They inferred from the Cartesian assumption of the perfect heterogeneity of what is extended and what is conscious, the impossibility of action or reaction between the two. They concluded that, on occasion of the affection of the organism, the corresponding perception in us is produced by God— that He moves our limbs for us, on occasion of our desire to move them.
[2] This is the argument from 'common sense' for the reality of the material world, afterwards put by Reid and other Scottish psychologists. The point in question is not, however, whether the material world really exists, but what we must mean, if we mean anything, and do not indulge in empty verbal abstraction, when we affirm its real existence. That the unreflecting part of mankind should have a confused view of what matter and external reality mean is not to be wondered at. It is the very office of philosophical meditation to improve their conception, making it deeper and truer. But it does not follow from this that Berkeley has not emptied perception of elements which are essential to it, in his desire for unity and simplicity, and to avoid verbal abstrac-

a contradiction, or has no meaning in it, is impossible; and whether the foregoing expressions are not of that sort, I refer it to the impartial examination of the reader. In one sense, indeed, men may be said to believe that Matter exists; that is, they act as if the immediate cause of their sensations, which affects them every moment, and is so nearly present to them, were some senseless unthinking being. But, that they should clearly apprehend any *meaning* marked by those words, and form thereof a settled speculative opinion, is what I am not able to conceive. This is not the only instance wherein men impose upon themselves, by imagining they believe those propositions which they have often heard, though at bottom they have no meaning in them [1].

55. But secondly, though we should grant a notion to be never so universally and stedfastly adhered to, yet this is but a weak argument of its truth to whoever considers what a vast number of prejudices and false opinions are everywhere embraced with the utmost tenaciousness, by the unreflecting (which are the far greater) part of mankind. There was a time when the antipodes and motion of the earth were looked upon as monstrous absurdities even by men of learning: and if it be considered what a small proportion they bear to the rest of mankind, we shall find that at this day those notions have gained but a very inconsiderable footing in the world.

56. But it is demanded that we assign a Cause of this Prejudice, and account for its obtaining in the world.—To this I answer, that men knowing they perceived several ideas, whereof *they themselves* were not the authors—as not being excited from within nor depending on the operation of *their* wills—*this* made them maintain those ideas or objects of perception had an existence independent of and without the mind, without ever dreaming that a contradiction was involved

---

[1] That our perceptions of the material world are perceptions of ordered phenomena dependent on percipient and active mind is hardly what Reid set himself to refute.

in those words. But, philosophers having plainly seen that the *immediate objects* of perception do not exist without the mind, they in some degree corrected the mistake of the vulgar, but at the same time run into another which seems no less absurd, to wit, that there are certain objects really existing without the mind, or having a subsistence distinct from being perceived, of which our ideas are only images or resemblances, imprinted by those objects on the mind. And this notion of the philosophers owes its origin to the same cause with the former, namely, their being conscious that *they* were not the authors of their own sensations, which they evidently knew were imprinted from without, and which therefore must have some cause distinct from the minds on which they are imprinted [1].

57. But why they should suppose the ideas of sense to be excited in us by *things in their likeness*, and not rather have recourse to *Spirit* which alone can act, may be accounted for, first, because they were not aware of the repugnancy there is, as well in supposing things like unto our ideas existing without, as in attributing to them power or activity. Secondly, because the Supreme Spirit which excites those ideas in our minds, is not marked out and limited to our view by any particular finite collection of sensible ideas, as human agents are by their size, complexion, limbs, and motions. And thirdly, because His operations are regular and uniform. Whenever the course of nature is interrupted by a miracle, men are ready to own the presence of a superior agent. But, when we see things go on in the ordinary course they do not excite in us any reflection; their order and concatenation, though it be an argument of the greatest wisdom, power, and goodness in their creator, is yet so constant and familiar to us that we do not think them the immediate effects of a

[1] A representative perception in sense presupposes 'things in themselves'—unperceived things—existing *behind* the perceived phenomena which they are supposed to cause. Compare with this section the close of the *Third Dialogue* (*Works*, vol. I. pp. 339-360).

FREE SPIRIT; especially since inconsistency and mutability in acting, though it be an imperfection, is looked on as a mark of *freedom*[1].

58. [2] *Tenthly*, it will be objected that the notions we advance are inconsistent with several sound truths in Philosophy and Mathematics. For example, the motion of the earth is now universally admitted by astronomers as a truth grounded on the clearest and most convincing reasons. But, on the foregoing principles, there can be no such thing. For, motion being only an idea, it follows that if it be not perceived it *exists* not : but the motion of the earth is not perceived by sense.—I answer, that tenet, if rightly understood, will be found to agree with the principles we have premised ; for, the question whether the earth moves or no amounts in reality to no more than this, to wit, whether we have reason to conclude, from what has been observed by astronomers, that if we were placed in such and such circumstances, and such or such a position and distance both from the earth and sun, we should perceive the former to move among the choir of the planets, and appearing in all respects like one of them ; and this, by the established rules of nature which we have no reason to mistrust, is reasonably collected from the phenomena.

59. We may, from the experience we have had of the train and succession of ideas[3] in our minds, often make, I

---

[1] Some confound Divine 'arbitrariness' with caprice. Hence their difficulty in allowing that Divine Will originates and maintains the laws of nature. Philosophy struggles to resolve the seeming contingencies of nature into a rational unity that is at first only dimly revealed in what we are conscious of in sense. Sense in us is confused thought, which the rational constitution latent in nature enables our intelligence more or less to convert into physical science. Whether the intellectual power of man can ever entirely eliminate contingency from our knowledge of nature is another question. Locke denied that it could.

[2] The *ninth* objection seems to be in sect. 56.

[3] 'Succession of ideas,' i. e. of phenomena presented in sense. Our actual experience is here supposed to consist in the divinely established

will not say uncertain conjectures, but sure and well-grounded predictions concerning the ideas we shall be affected with pursuant to a great train of actions, and be enabled to pass a right judgment of what would have appeared to us, in case we were placed in circumstances very different from those we are in at present. Herein consists the knowledge of nature, which may preserve its use and certainty very consistently with what hath been said. It will be easy to apply this to whatever objections of the like sort may be drawn from the magnitude of the stars, or any other discoveries in astronomy or nature.

60. In the *eleventh* place, it will be demanded to what purpose serves that curious organization of plants, and the animal mechanism in the parts of animals; might not vegetables grow, and shoot forth leaves and blossoms, and animals perform all their motions as well without as with all that variety of internal parts so elegantly contrived and put together; which, being ideas, have nothing powerful or operative in them, nor have any *necessary* connexion with the effects ascribed to them? If it be a Spirit that immediately produces every effect by a *fiat* or act of his will, we must think all that is fine and artificial in the works, whether of man or nature, to be made in vain. By this doctrine, though an artist has made the spring and wheels, and every movement of a watch, and adjusted them in such a manner as he knew would produce the motions he designed, yet he must think all this done to no purpose, and that it is an Intelligence which directs the index, and points to the hour of the day. If so, why may not the Intelligence do it without his being at the pains of making the movements and

---

associations of *those* phenomena—not in what is commonly meant by 'association of ideas.' This might be Berkeley's answer to the objection that the possibility of forming reasonable expectations cannot be explained merely by association of *ideas*, but presupposes *objects* that exist independently, *i.e.* universally or for all, and not privately or only for me.

putting them together? Why does not an empty case serve as well as another? And how comes it to pass that whenever there is any fault in the going of a watch, there is some corresponding disorder to be found in the movements, which being mended by a skilful hand all is right again? The like may be said of all the Clockwork of Nature, great part whereof is so wonderfully fine and subtle as scarce to be discerned by the best microscope. In short, it will be asked, how, upon our principles, any tolerable account can be given, or any final cause assigned, of an innumerable multitude of bodies and machines, framed with the most exquisite art, which in the common philosophy have very apposite uses assigned them, and serve to explain abundance of phenomena?

61. To all which I answer, first, that though there were some difficulties relating to the administration of Providence, and the uses by it assigned to the several parts of nature, which I could not solve by the foregoing principles, yet this objection could be of small weight against the truth and certainty of those things which may be proved *a priori*, with the utmost evidence and rigour of demonstration[1]. Secondly, but neither are the received principles free from the like difficulties; for, it may still be demanded to what end God should take those roundabout methods of effecting things by instruments and machines, which no one can deny might have been effected by the mere command of His will without all that apparatus: nay, if we narrowly consider it, we shall find the objection may be retorted with greater force on those who hold the existence of those machines without the mind; for it has been made evident that solidity, bulk, figure, motion, and the like have no *activity* or *efficacy* in them, so as to be capable of producing any one effect in nature. See sect 25[2]. Whoever therefore supposes them to exist (allowing

[1] He here assumes that his proof of the unsubstantiality and impotence of the material world, grounded on its essence being only phenomenal, offered in sect. 3-33, is strictly demonstrative.

[2] This proof, in sect. 25, rests on reflex 'observation' of consciousness.

the supposition possible) when they are not perceived does it manifestly to no purpose; since the only use that is assigned to them, as they exist unperceived, is that they produce those perceivable effects which in truth cannot be ascribed to anything but Spirit.

62. But, to come nigher the difficulty, it must be observed that though the fabrication of all those parts and organs be not absolutely necessary to the producing *any* effect, yet it is necessary to the producing of things *in a constant regular way according to the laws of nature*. There are certain general laws that run through the whole chain of natural effects: these are learned by the observation and study of nature, and are by men applied as well to the framing artificial things for the use and ornament of life as to the explaining the various phenomena—which explanation consists only in shewing the conformity any particular phenomenon hath to the general laws of nature, or, which is the same thing, in discovering the *uniformity* there is in the production of natural effects; as will be evident to whoever shall attend to the several instances wherein philosophers pretend to account for appearances. That there is a great and conspicuous *use* in these regular constant methods of working observed by the Supreme Agent hath been shewn in sect. 31. And it is no less visible that a particular size, figure, motion, and disposition of parts are necessary, though not absolutely to the producing any effect, yet to the producing it according to the standing mechanical laws of nature. Thus, for instance, it cannot be denied that God, or the Intelligence that sustains and rules the ordinary course of things, might, if He were minded to produce a miracle, cause all the motions on the dial-plate of a watch, though nobody had ever made the movements and put them in it: but yet, if He will act agreeably to the rules

---

It assumes, as proved, that solidity, bulk, figure, motion—the primary qualities in short—*can* exist *only* as phenomena of which there is a sense-consciousness or perception.

of mechanism—by Him for wise ends established and maintained in the creation—it is necessary that those actions of the watchmaker, whereby he makes the movements and rightly adjusts them, precede the production of the aforesaid motions; as also that any disorder in them be attended with the perception of some corresponding disorder in the movements, which being once corrected all is right again[1].

63. It may indeed on some occasions be necessary that the Author of nature display His overruling power in producing appearances out of the ordinary series of things. Such exceptions from the general rules of nature are proper to surprise and awe men into an acknowledgment of the Divine Being; but then they are to be used but seldom, otherwise there is a plain reason why they fail of that effect. Besides, God seems to choose the convincing our reason of His attributes by the works of nature, which discover so much harmony and contrivance in their make, and are such plain indications of wisdom and beneficence in their Author, rather than to astonish us into a belief of His Being by anomalous and surprising events[2].

[1] This reply, good in itself according to Ueberweg, contains, he argues, a principle the application of which breaks up the whole Berkeleian conception of what an external world really means. When Berkeley recognizes rational order in nature, his position, it is urged, is untenable, because he can only *assume*, not prove, the conformity of the phenomena presented in sense to that order;—and further, this assumption implies that things exist independently of being perceived: knowledge of phenomenal things that express law presupposes their independent existence. Between our perceptions in eating and our perceptions of the consequent growth of our bodies, for instance, many processes are interposed, which exist unperceived by any finite mind, but which, as each had a beginning and an end, cannot, it is argued, *when thus existing unperceived*, be identified with the Eternal Ideas of God.—On the other hand, Berkeley might ask in reply, whether the material world could maintain an *intelligible* existence after the extinction of all conscious intelligence, finite and Divine; also whether there is more difficulty in explaining (consistently with his philosophical conception of the material world) the unperceived growth of our bodies, or the early geological periods, than there is in explaining the existence of the *invisible* qualities of a house or a mountain when one is only *seeing* it.

[2] The nature and educational office of miracles is here touched. If

64. To set this matter in a yet clearer light, I shall observe that what has been objected in sect. 60 amounts in reality to no more than this:—ideas are not anyhow and at random produced, there being a certain order and connexion between them, like to that of cause and effect : there are also several combinations of them made in a very regular and artificial manner, which seem like so many *instruments* in the hand of nature that, being hid as it were behind the scenes, have a secret operation in producing those appearances which are seen on the theatre of the world, being themselves discernible only to the curious eye of the philosopher. But, since one idea cannot be the *cause* of another, to what purpose is that connexion? And, since those instruments—being barely *inefficacious perceptions* in the mind—are not subservient to the production of natural effects, it is demanded why they are made; or, in other words, what reason can be assigned why God should make us, upon a close inspection into His works, behold so great variety of ideas so artfully laid together, and so much according to rule; it not being credible that He would be at the expense (if one may so speak) of all that art and regularity to no purpose?

65. To all which my answer is, first, that the connexion of ideas does not imply the relation of *cause* and *effect*, but only of a *mark* or *sign* with the *thing signified*[1]. The fire which I see is not the cause of the pain I suffer upon my approaching it, but the mark that forewarns me of it. In like manner the noise that I hear is not the effect of this or that

---

the whole evolution of events in nature is *perpetually* caused by God, where, it may be asked, is the room for supernatural events? Berkeley's answer to this may be gathered from sect. 62, where room is left for extraordinary physical events. These, in the system of spiritual government, may be fitted to develope our spiritual insight. Faith, in itself independent of sensible signs, may thus be evoked and trained by them.

[1] When it is objected that what is *unperceived by me* must have existed independently of *my* perception, it should be remembered that the sense-symbolism here supposed to constitute externality in nature is shared in by all human minds.

motion or collision of the ambient bodies, but the sign thereof. Secondly, the reason why ideas are formed into machines, that is, artificial and regular combinations, is the same with that for combining letters into words. That a few original ideas may be made to signify a great number of effects and actions, it is necessary they be variously combined together. And, to the end their use be permanent and universal, these combinations must be made by *rule*, and with *wise contrivance*. By this means abundance of information is conveyed unto us, concerning what we are to expect from such and such actions, and what methods are proper to be taken for the exciting such and such ideas—which in effect is all that I conceive to be distinctly meant when it is said[1] that, by discerning the figure, texture, and mechanism of the inward parts of bodies, whether natural or artificial, we may attain to know the several uses and properties depending thereon, or the nature of the thing[2].

66. Hence, it is evident that those things which, under the motion of a cause co-operating or concurring to the production of effects, are altogether inexplicable, and run us into great absurdities, may be very naturally explained, and have a proper and obvious use assigned to them, when they are considered only as marks or signs for our information. And it is the searching after and endeavouring to understand this Language (if I may so call it) of the Author of Nature, that ought to be the employment of the natural philosopher[3]; and not the pretending to explain things by corporeal causes[4], which doctrine seems to have too much estranged the minds

---

[1] By Locke, for instance, in his view of the established dependence of the secondary on the primary qualities of matter.

[2] This section expresses well the office of an orderly system of phenomena in educating finite spirits, morally as well as intellectually—which perhaps is the final cause of the existence of the material world.

[3] Compare this with the 'homo naturae minister et interpres' of Bacon, and with Berkeley himself on Visual Language.

[4] 'Corporeal causes'—which Berkeley has already disposed of in his 'proof' that productive *power* cannot be found within the world of sense, and that mind—moral agency—is the only real power in nature.

of men from that Active Principle, that supreme and wise Spirit 'in whom we live, move, and have our being[1].'

67. In the *twelfth* place, it may perhaps be objected that—though it be clear from what has been said that there can be no such thing as an inert, senseless, extended, solid, figured, moveable substance existing without the mind, such as philosophers describe Matter,—yet, if any man shall leave out of his idea of matter the positive ideas of extension, figure, solidity and motion, and say that he means only by that word an inert, senseless substance, that exists without the mind or unperceived, which is the *occasion* of our ideas, or at the presence whereof God is pleased to excite ideas in us—it doth not appear but that Matter taken in this sense may possibly exist.—In answer to which I say, first, that it seems no less absurd to suppose a substance without accidents, than it is to suppose accidents without a substance. But secondly, though we should grant this unknown substance may possibly exist, yet *where* can it be supposed to be? That it exists not in the *mind* is agreed; and that it exists not in *place* is no less certain—since all place or extension exists only in the mind[2], as hath been already proved. It remains therefore that it exists nowhere at all.

68. Let us examine a little the description that is here given us of *Matter*. It neither acts, nor perceives, nor is perceived; for this is all that is meant by saying it is an inert, senseless, unknown substance; which is a definition entirely made up of negatives[3], excepting only the relative

---

[1] The search for physical 'causes' thus becomes a search for the meaning of the 'language' of the Author of Nature—a figure which is carried by Berkeley through all the speculations about physical causation implied in his Theory of Visual Language. Does the causality that belongs to the material world mean no more than is signified by this metaphor?

[2] i. e. exists intelligibly only so far forth as it is actually perceived.

[3] This approaches Kant's 'thing in itself' (*ding an sich*), made up of negatives, though he seems to assume its power to produce sensations.

notion of its standing under or supporting. But then it must be observed that it supports nothing at all, and how nearly this comes to the description of a *nonentity* I desire may be considered. But, say you, it is the *unknown occasion*, at the presence of which ideas are excited in us by the will of God. Now, I would fain know how anything can be present to us, which is neither perceivable by sense nor reflection, nor capable of producing any idea in our minds, nor is at all extended, nor hath any form, nor exists in any place. The words 'to be present,' when thus applied, must needs be taken in some abstract and strange meaning, and which I am not able to comprehend.

69. Again, let us examine what is meant by *occasion*. So far as I can gather from the common use of language, that word signifies either the agent which produces any effect, or else something that is observed[1] to accompany or go before it in the ordinary course of things. But when it is applied to Matter as above described, it can be taken in neither of those senses; for Matter is said to be passive and inert, and so cannot be an agent or efficient cause. It is also unperceivable, as being devoid of all sensible qualities, and so cannot be the occasion of our perceptions in the latter sense—as when the burning my finger is said to be the occasion of the pain that attends it. What therefore can be meant by calling Matter an *occasion*? This term is either used in no sense at all, or else in some very distant from its received signification.

70. You will perhaps say that Matter, though it be not perceived by us, is nevertheless perceived by God, to whom it is the *occasion* of exciting ideas in our minds. For, say you, since we observe our sensations to be imprinted in an orderly and constant manner, it is but reasonable to suppose

[1] That which is the *occasion* of Divine activity need not lie within the sphere of our observation, though it may be reached by our inferences.

that there are certain constant and regular occasions of their being produced. That is to say, that there are certain permanent and distinct parcels of Matter, corresponding to our ideas, which, though they do not excite them in our minds, or anywise immediately affect us, as being altogether passive and unperceivable to *us*, they are nevertheless to God, *by whom they are perceived*, as it were so many occasions to remind Him when and what ideas to imprint on our minds—that so things may go on in a constant uniform manner.

71. In answer to this, I observe that, as the notion of Matter is here stated, the question is no longer concerning the existence of a thing distinct from *Spirit* and *idea*, from perceiving and being perceived; but whether there are not certain Ideas, of I know not what sort, in the mind of God, which are so many marks or notes that direct Him how to produce sensations in our minds in a constant and regular method—much after the same manner as a musician is directed by the notes of music to produce that harmonious strain and composition of sound which is called a tune, though they who hear the music do not perceive the notes, and may be entirely ignorant of them. But, this notion of Matter (which after all is the only intelligible one that I can pick from what is said of unknown occasions) seems too extravagant to deserve a confutation[1]. Besides, it is in effect no objection against what we have advanced, viz. that there is no *senseless unperceived* substance.

72. If we follow the light of reason, we shall, from the constant uniform method of our sensations, collect the goodness and wisdom of the Spirit who excites them in our minds; but this is all that I can see reasonably concluded from thence. To me, I say, it is evident that the being of a Spirit infinitely wise, good, and powerful is abundantly

---

[1] Here Berkeley rejects the suggestion that the supposed 'things in themselves' can be Ideas of God—an objection to this by others being, that the Ideas of God are eternal, while the material world is transitory. Afterwards he seems more favourable to it (see sect. 76, *note*).

sufficient to explain all the appearances of nature. But, as for *inert, senseless Matter*, nothing that I perceive has any the least connexion with it, or leads to the thoughts of it. And I would fain see any one explain any the meanest phenomenon in nature by *it*, or shew any manner of reason, though in the lowest rank of probability, that he can have for its existence, or even make any tolerable sense or meaning of that supposition. For, as to its being an occasion, we have, I think, evidently shewn that with regard to us it is no occasion. It remains therefore that it must be, if at all, the occasion to God of exciting ideas in us; and what this amounts to we have just now seen[1].

73. It is worth while to reflect a little on the motives which induced men to suppose the existence of *material substance;* that so having observed the gradual ceasing and expiration of those motives or reasons, we may proportionably withdraw the assent that was grounded on them. First, therefore, it was thought that colour, figure, motion, and the rest of the sensible qualities or accidents, did really exist without the mind[2]; and for this reason it seemed needful to suppose some unthinking *substratum* or substance wherein they did exist—since they could not be conceived to exist by themselves[3]. Afterwards, in process of time, men being convinced that colours, sounds, and the rest of the sensible, *secondary* qualities had no existence without the mind, they stripped this *substratum* or material substance of those qualities—leaving only the *primary* ones, figure, motion, and suchlike, which they still conceived to exist without the mind, and consequently to stand in need of a material support. But, it having been shewn that none even of these

---
[1] Compare with this and the preceding sections Berkeley's *Second Dialogue* (*Works*, vol. I. pp. 308-314).
[2] This is the uneducated supposition, which assumes that the material world would be exactly what we experience in sense, if no one was experiencing it—ignoring even what is added by our sensations in the case of the secondary qualities.
[3] He nowhere explains the ground of this assumption.

can possibly exist otherwise than in a Spirit or Mind which perceives them, it follows that we have no longer any reason to suppose the being of Matter, nay, that it is utterly impossible that there should be any such thing—so long as that word is taken to denote an *unthinking substratum* of qualities or accidents wherein they exist without the mind[1].

74. But—though it be allowed by the Materialists themselves that Matter was thought of only for the sake of supporting accidents, and, the reason entirely ceasing, one might expect the mind should naturally, and without any reluctance at all, quit the belief of what was solely grounded thereon—yet the prejudice is riveted so deeply in our thoughts, that we can scarce tell how to part with it, and are therefore inclined, since the *thing* itself is indefensible, at least to retain the *name*, which we apply to I know not what abstracted and indefinite notions of Being, or Occasion, though without any show of reason, at least so far as I can see. For, what is there on our part, or what do we perceive, amongst all the ideas, sensations, notions which are imprinted on our minds, either by sense or reflection[2], from whence may be inferred the existence of an inert, thoughtless, unperceived occasion? and, on the other hand, on the part of an All-sufficient Spirit, what can there be that should make us believe or even suspect He is directed by an inert occasion to excite ideas in our minds?

75. It is a very extraordinary instance of the force of prejudice, and much to be lamented, that the mind of man retains so great a fondness, against all the evidence of reason,

---

[1] It has been argued, in opposition to this, that although none of the sensible qualities can exist *per se* as they do in our experience in sense, yet the steady order of the phenomena that are presented when we perceive, implies existence of *a* 'thing in itself,' endowed with unperceivable attributes.—Instead of this 'thing in itself,' with unknown attributes, Berkeley finds God. See also sect. 78.

[2] Here he uses 'idea, sensation, and notion' as synonymous, and speaks metaphorically of ideas of *reflection* even, as 'imprinted' on our minds.

for a *stupid thoughtless Somewhat*, by the interposition whereof it would as it were screen itself from the Providence of God, and remove Him farther off from the affairs of the world. But, though we do the utmost we can to secure the belief of Matter; though, when reason forsakes us, we endeavour to support our opinion on the bare possibility of the thing, and though we indulge ourselves in the full scope of an imagination not regulated by reason to make out that poor possibility, yet the upshot of all is—that there are certain *unknown*[1] *Ideas* in the mind of God; for this, if anything, is all that I conceive to be meant by *occasion* with regard to God. And this at the bottom is no longer contending for the thing, but for the name.

76. Whether therefore there are such Ideas in the mind of God, and whether *they* may be called by the name *Matter*, I shall not dispute. But, if you stick to the notion of an unthinking substance or support of extension, motion, and other sensible qualities, then to me it is most evidently impossible there should be any such thing; since it is a plain repugnancy that those qualities should exist in or be supported by an unperceiving substance[2].

77. But, say you, though it be granted that there is no thoughtless support of extension and the other qualities or accidents which we perceive, yet there may perhaps be some inert, unperceiving substance or *substratum* of some other qualities, as incomprehensible to us as colours are to a man

[1] But which become more or less known to us in natural science.
[2] Berkeley says years afterwards that he has 'no objection to calling the Ideas in the mind of God archetypes of ours,' and that he objects only to those [unthinking] archetypes supposed by philosophers to exist without any consciousness at all of them. (*Life of Berkeley*, pp. 176 177.) And in truth his conception of what the reality of the material world means presupposes Divine conceptions, towards which human science in its successful search for the laws of nature is approximating. The assertion that 'the material world exists' would when so understood, be simply the assertion, that what we perceive is part of an interpretable universe. It is actually interpreted to the extent that our scientific conceptions are in harmony with the divinely established laws obeyed by phenomenal things. Cf. *Siris*, sect. 335.

born blind, because we have not a sense adapted to them. But, if we had a new sense, we should possibly no more doubt of their existence than a blind man made to see does of the existence of light and colours.—I answer, first, if what you mean by the word *Matter* be only the unknown support of *unknown* qualities, it is no matter whether there is such a thing or no, since it no way concerns us; and I do not see the advantage there is in disputing about what we know not *what*, and we know not *why*.

78. But, secondly, if we had a new sense it could only furnish us with new ideas or sensations; and then we should have the same reason against *their* existing in an unperceiving substance that has been already offered with relation to figure, motion, colour, and the like. 'Qualities,' as hath been shewn, are nothing else but *sensations* or *ideas*, which exist only in a *mind* perceiving them; and this is true not only of the ideas we are acquainted with at present, but likewise of all possible ideas whatsoever.

79. But, you will insist, what if I have no reason to believe the existence of Matter? what if I cannot assign any use to it or explain anything by it, or even conceive what is meant by that word? yet still it is no contradiction to say that Matter exists, and that this Matter is in general a *substance*, or *occasion* of ideas; though indeed to go about to unfold the meaning or adhere to any particular explication of those words may be attended with great difficulties. I answer, when words are used without a meaning, you may put them together as you please without danger of running into a contradiction. You may say, for example, that twice two is equal to seven, so long as you declare you do not take the words of that proposition in their usual acceptation but for marks of you know not what. And, by the same reason, you may say there is *an inert thoughtless substance without accidents* which is the occasion of our ideas. And we shall understand just as much by one proposition as the other.

80. In the *last* place, you will say, what if we give up the cause of material *Substance*, and stand to it that Matter is an unknown *Somewhat*—neither substance nor accident, spirit nor idea, inert, thoughtless, indivisible, immoveable, unextended, existing in no place? For, say you, whatever may be urged against *substance* or *occasion*, or any other positive or relative notion of Matter, hath no place at all, so long as this *negative* definition of Matter is adhered to.—I answer, you may, if so it shall seem good, use the word 'Matter' in the same sense as other men use 'nothing,' and so make those terms convertible in your style. For, after all, this is what appears to me to be the result of that definition—the parts whereof when I consider with attention, either collectively or separate from each other, I do not find that there is any kind of effect or impression made on my mind different from what is excited by the term *nothing*.

81. You will reply, perhaps, that in the aforesaid definition is included what doth sufficiently distinguish it from nothing —the positive abstract idea of *quiddity, entity,* or *existence*. I own, indeed, that those who pretend to the faculty of framing abstract general ideas do talk as if they had such an idea, which is, say they, the most abstract and general notion of all; that is, to me, the most incomprehensible of all others[1]. That there are a great variety of spirits of different orders and capacities, whose faculties both in number and extent are far exceeding those the Author of my being has bestowed on me, I see no reason to deny. And for me to pretend to determine, by my own few, stinted, narrow inlets of perception, what ideas the inexhaustible power of the Supreme Spirit may imprint upon them were certainly the utmost folly and presumption—since there may be, for aught that I know, innumerable sorts of ideas or sensations, as different from one another, and from all that I have perceived, as colours are from sounds. But, how ready soever I may be to acknow-

[1] Being = Nothing.

ledge the scantiness of my comprehension with regard to the endless variety of spirits and ideas that may possibly exist, yet for any one to pretend to a notion of Entity or Existence, *abstracted* from *spirit* and *idea*, from perceived and being perceived, is, I suspect, a downright repugnancy and trifling with words[1].

It remains that we consider the objections which may possibly be made on the part of Religion.

82. Some there are who think that, though the arguments for the real existence of bodies which are drawn from Reason be allowed not to amount to demonstration, yet the Holy Scriptures are so clear in the point as will sufficiently convince every good Christian that bodies do really exist, and are something more than mere ideas; there being in Holy Writ innumerable facts related which evidently suppose the reality of timber and stone, mountains and rivers, and cities, and human bodies. To which I answer that no sort of writings whatever, sacred or profane, which use those and the like words in the vulgar acceptation, or so as to have a meaning in them, are in danger of having their truth called in question by our doctrine. That all those things do really exist, that there are bodies, even corporeal substances, when taken in the vulgar sense, has been shewn to be agreeable to our Principles: and the difference betwixt *things* and *ideas*, *realities* and *chimeras*, has been distinctly explained. See sect. 29, 30, 33, 36, &c. And I do not think that either what philosophers call *Matter*, or the existence of objects without the mind, is anywhere mentioned in Scripture.

83. Again, whether there be or be not external things, it is agreed on all hands that the proper use of words is the marking our conceptions, or things only as they are known

---

[1] Compare this and the preceding section with the *Second Dialogue* (*Works*, vol. I. pp. 315-320).

and perceived by us; whence it plainly follows that in the tenets we have laid down there is nothing inconsistent with the right use and significancy of language, and that discourse, of what kind soever, so far as it is intelligible, remains undisturbed. But all this seems so very manifest, from what has been largely set forth in the premises, that it is needless to insist any farther on it.

84. But, it will be urged that Miracles do, at least, lose much of their stress and import by our principles. What must we think of Moses' rod? was it not *really* turned into a serpent, or was there only a change of *ideas* in the minds of the spectators? And, can it be supposed that our Saviour did no more at the marriage-feast in Cana than impose on the sight, and smell, and taste of the guests, so as to create in them the appearance of idea only of wine? The same may be said of all other miracles; which, in consequence of the foregoing principles, must be looked upon only as so many cheats, or illusions of fancy.—To this I reply, that the rod was changed into a real serpent, and the water into real wine. That this does not in the least contradict what I have elsewhere said will be evident from sect. 34 and 35. But this business of *real* and *imaginary* has been already so plainly and fully explained, and so often referred to, and the difficulties about it are so easily answered from what has gone before, that it were an affront to the reader's understanding to resume the explication of it in its place. I shall only observe that if at table all who were present should see, and smell, and taste, and drink wine, and find the effects of it, with me there could be no doubt of its reality;—so that at bottom the scruple concerning real miracles has no place at all on ours, but only on the received principles, and consequently makes rather for than against what has been said [1].

---

[1] Participation in similar sense experiences by all human beings, according to an established order of nature, is here offered as a test of the 'reality' of these sense experiences. Ueberweg allows that

85. Having done with the Objections[1], which I endeavoured to propose in the clearest light, and gave them all the force and weight I could, we proceed in the next place to take a view of our tenets in their Consequences[2].

Some of these appear at first sight—as that several difficult and obscure questions, on which abundance of speculation has been thrown away, are entirely banished from philosophy. 'Whether corporeal substance can think,' 'whether Matter be infinitely divisible,' and 'how it operates on spirit'—these and

---

Berkeley's principles can be reconciled with miracles, but reiterates that they (and miracles too) are irreconcilable with a thorough-going recognition of law in nature. He proposes an ingenious theory for harmonizing Berkeley's philosophical conception of the reality of the material world with the Catholic miracle of transubstantiation—with which that conception is usually assumed to be inconsistent. Its consistency with a resurrection of the human body is also a question. See sect. 95.

[1] In the eighty-two foregoing sections, we have many arguments for and against Berkeley's philosophical explanation of the terms 'reality' and 'externality,' as applicable to the material world. Instead of the unreflecting assumption, that things around us would be what we now perceive, although no conscious being was perceiving—he argues that they must be composed of the significant phenomena present to our senses, whose significance was established and is constantly sustained by God, without any independent substance or power in themselves. The meaninglessness of 'external reality,' on any other view than this of what matter and force mean, and the contradiction involved in any attempt to introduce meaning into the meaningless, might be called his metaphysical argument. The need for resolving the primary or mathematical, as much as the secondary qualities of matter, into the passive and transitory, although significant, phenomena present in sense is his psychological argument. There is besides the practical argument, that the existence of sensible things as independent entities would after all make no difference in our actions.

The chief objections to all this (only some of which are seen by Berkeley in the preceding sections) are—(a) the difficulty of reconciling it with the continuous identity of things, and with the universality of their mathematical, or even their physical laws ; (b) its elimination of presuppositions implied in our belief of the existence of other finite persons ; (c) the unsubstantiality and impotence of *persons* as well as of *things* if the new conception of matter is to be consistently carried out. Berkeley's *Commonplace Book* shows that this last difficulty at first influenced him enough to make his starting-point like Hume's.

[2] Sect. 85-156 contain Berkeley's *application* of the new conception of the meaning and function of the material world.—And first he shows its efficacy as against theological scepticism (sect. 86-96), and in purifying thought of empty abstractions (sect. 97-100).

the like inquiries have given infinite amusement to philosophers in all ages; but, depending on the existence of Matter, they have no longer any place on our principles. Many other advantages there are, as well with regard to religion as the sciences, which it is easy for any one to deduce from what has been premised; but this will appear more plainly in the sequel.

86. From the Principles we have laid down it follows Human Knowledge may naturally be reduced to two heads— that of IDEAS[1] and that of SPIRITS. Of each of these I shall treat in order.

And *first* as to IDEAS or *unthinking things*. Our knowledge of these has been very much obscured and confounded, and we have been led into very dangerous errors, by supposing a two-fold existence of the objects of sense—the one *intelligible* or in the mind; the other *real* and without the mind, whereby unthinking things are thought to have a natural subsistence of their own, distinct from being perceived by spirits[2]. This, which, if I mistake not, hath been shewn to be a most groundless and absurd notion, is the very root of Scepticism; for, so long as men thought that real things subsisted without the mind, and that their knowledge was only so far forth *real* as it was *conformable to real things*, it follows they could not be certain that they had any real knowledge at all. For, how can it be *known* that the things which are perceived are conformable to those which are not perceived, or exist without the mind[3]?

---

[1] Berkeley's use of *idea* to signify what is present to sense, and his conclusion that the material world consists of what is thus present, has led to his being called an Idealist. But, on the same ground, he might be called a Phenomenalist, or a Sensationist—negatively an Immaterialist—so far as this half of his philosophy is concerned.—It is with reference to the other (constructive and terminal) side of his philosophy that he becomes Idealist in the higher meaning.

[2] Kant reversely views the things which are independent of perceptions as the *intelligible* world, while he regards phenomenal things as the *objectively* real for us.

[3] This question expresses what has been regarded as an insuperable objection to a *representative* perception.—How can we be assured of the

87. Colour, figure, motion, extension, and the like, considered only as so many *sensations* in the mind, are perfectly known, there being nothing in them which is not perceived. But, if they are looked on as notes or images, referred to *things* or *archetypes existing without the mind*, then are we involved all in scepticism. We see only the appearances, and not the real qualities of things. What may be the extension, figure, or motion of anything really and absolutely, or in itself, it is impossible for us to know, but only the proportion or relation they bear to our senses. Things remaining the same, our ideas vary, and which of them, or even whether any of them at all, represent the true quality really existing in the thing, it is out of our reach to determine. So that, for aught we know, all we see, hear, and feel, may be only phantom and vain chimera, and not at all agree with the real things existing *in rerum natura*. All this sceptical cant follows from our supposing a difference between *things* and *ideas*, and that the former had a subsistence without the mind or unperceived. It were easy to dilate on this subject, and shew how the arguments urged by sceptics in all ages depend on the supposition of external objects.

88. So long as we attribute a real existence to unthinking things, distinct from their being perceived, it is not only impossible for us to know with evidence the nature of any real unthinking being, but even that it exists. Hence it is that we see philosophers distrust their senses, and doubt of the existence of heaven and earth, of everything they see or feel, even of their own bodies. And, after all their labouring and struggle of thought, they are forced to own we cannot attain to any self-evident or demonstrative knowledge of the existence of sensible things. But all this doubtfulness, which so bewilders and confounds the mind and makes philosophy ridiculous in the eyes of the world, vanishes if we annex a

harmony of the representation with the real thing—*if the real thing exists unperceived?* We cannot in that case compare the two.

meaning to our words, and not amuse ourselves with the terms 'absolute,' 'external,' 'exist,' &c.—signifying we know not what. For my part, I can as well doubt of my own being as of the being of those *things which I actually perceive by sense*[1]; it being a manifest contradiction that any sensible object should be immediately perceived by sight or touch, and at the same time have no existence in nature, since the very *existence* of an unthinking being consists in *being perceived*[2].

89. Nothing seems of more importance towards erecting a firm system of sound and real knowledge, which may be proof against the assaults of Scepticism, than to lay the beginning in a distinct explication of *what is meant by* THING, REALITY, EXISTENCE; for in vain shall we dispute concerning the 'real existence' of things, or pretend to any knowledge

---

[1] i.e. as long, at least, as I am in the act of perceiving them. See Locke's *Essay*, b. IV. ch. 11. § 9.

[2] The difficulty of supposing that we can have a knowledge of things, if our knowledge of them may be melted down into phenomena, has been acknowledged by philosophers. The difficulty raises the chief question in philosophy, which has to *shew* the rationality of what we assume to be knowledge. Berkeley argues that the favourite hypothesis of philosophers—that matter is not directly perceived, but has to be inferred from *representative* phenomena of which we are conscious—needlessly increases the difficulty. Let us, he says, recognise the reality as *already given phenomenally* in perception,—not as something dependent on a 'conformity'—impossible to ascertain—between an unperceivable 'matter' and the representation of which alone, on this hypothesis, we are supposed to be percipient,—and then the difficulty is relieved. But does Berkeley's conception of the phenomena, which he assumes to be thus given, include all that is essential to objective reality?

On the connexion between scepticism and this 'representative perception' which Berkeley rejects, see Hume's *Inquiry concerning Human Understanding*, sect. xii. pt. 1 (which might be a text for discussing the 'immediate perception' of Reid and Hamilton, and for comparing it with the 'perception' and 'suggestion' of Berkeley); also Hamilton's *Discussions*, 'Philosophy of Perception.'—For an account of various modifications of this representative Perception, see Reid's Second Essay on the Intellectual Powers, and Hamilton's Dissertations B and C. These Scotch psychologists taught that an immediate revelation of the material world in sense-perception is an ultimate fact of consciousness, the rejection of which is of the essence of a universal scepticism, as involving distrust in the ultimate criterion of belief; but they did not, like Berkeley, try to explain what they meant philosophically by Matter.

H

thereof, so long as we have not fixed the meaning of those words[1]. THING or BEING is the most general name of all: it comprehends under it two kinds entirely distinct and heterogeneous, and which have nothing common but the name, viz. SPIRITS and IDEAS. The former are active, indivisible [[2] incorruptible] substances: the latter are inert, fleeting, or dependent beings, which subsist not by themselves, but are supported by, or exist in minds or spiritual substances. [[3] We comprehend our own existence by inward feeling or Reflection, and that of other spirits by Reason[4].—We may be said to have some knowledge or *notion* of our own minds, of spirits and active beings—whereof in a strict sense we have not ideas. In like manner, we know and have a *notion* of relations between things or ideas—which relations are distinct from the ideas or things related, inasmuch as the latter may be perceived by us without our perceiving the former[5]. To me it seems that *ideas, spirits,* and *relations* are all, in their respective kinds, the object of human knowledge and subject of discourse, and that the term *idea* would be improperly extended to signify *everything* we know or have any notion of.]

90. Ideas imprinted on the senses are 'real' things, or do really exist: this we do not deny; but we deny they can subsist without the minds which perceive them, or that they are resemblances of any archetypes[6] existing without the

---

[1] This throws light on Berkeley's purpose, which was not to *prove* the reality of the material world, but—by showing what intelligible 'reality' involves, and what we are entitled to *mean* when we say that an external thing 'exists'—to make proof superfluous.
[2] Withdrawn in Second Edition of *Principles*.
[3] The remainder of this section was added in the Second Edition of the *Principles*, when he began to recognise a distinction between *ideas* and *notions* which, in one form of expression or another, goes deep into his and every philosophy. For his reasons for recognising independent substance in Spirit, while he rejects it in the material world, see his *Third Dialogue* (*Works*, vol. I. pp. 327-329).
[4] i. e. reasoning or inference.
[5] This seems to say that we may have knowledge of mere phenomena.
[6] i. e. unperceived and unperceiving archetypes.

mind; since the very being of a sensation or idea consists in being perceived, and an idea can be like nothing but an idea. —Again, the things perceived by sense may be termed 'external,' with regard to their origin, in that they are not generated from within by the mind itself[1], but imprinted by a Spirit distinct from that which perceives them.—Sensible objects may likewise be said to be 'without the mind' in another sense, namely when they exist in some other mind; thus, when I shut my eyes, the things I saw may still exist, but it must be in another mind[2].

91. It were a mistake to think that what is here said derogates in the least from the reality of things. It is acknowledged, on the received principles, that extension, motion, and in a word all sensible qualities, have need of a support, as not being able to subsist by themselves. But the objects perceived by sense are allowed to be nothing but combinations of those qualities, and consequently cannot subsist by themselves. Thus far it is agreed on all hands. So that in denying the things perceived by sense an existence independent of a substance or support wherein they may exist[3], we detract nothing from the received opinion of their reality, and are guilty of no innovation in that respect. All the difference is that, according to us, the unthinking beings perceived by sense have no existence distinct from being perceived, and cannot therefore exist in any other substance than those unextended indivisible substances or *Spirits* which act and think and perceive them; whereas philosophers vulgarly hold the sensible qualities do exist in an inert, extended, unperceiving substance which they call *Matter*—to which they

---

[1] Here Berkeley's view differs from Fichte's, so far as the latter considers the individual (?) mind—the subjective (?) Ego—as the origin of what we call the *external* world, and thus lands in Egoism.

[2] This takes for granted our individuality. Berkeley in this section offers various intelligible meanings of 'real'—'external'—'without the mind.'

[3] Which, in the next sentence, he concedes to conscious life, inherent in an *Ego* or spiritual substance. Cf. sect. 16, 17.

attribute a natural subsistence, exterior to all thinking beings, or distinct from being perceived by any mind whatsoever, even the eternal mind of the Creator, wherein they suppose only Ideas of the corporeal substances created by Him: if indeed they allow them to be at all created.

92. For, as we have shewn the doctrine of Matter or Corporeal Substance to have been the main pillar and support of Scepticism, so likewise upon the same foundation have been raised all the impious schemes of Atheism and Irreligion. Nay, so great a difficulty has it been thought to conceive Matter[1] produced out of nothing, that the most celebrated among the ancient philosophers, even of those who maintained the being of a God, have thought Matter to be uncreated and coeternal with Him. How great a friend *material substance* has been to Atheists in all ages were needless to relate. All their monstrous systems have so visible and necessary a dependence on it that, when this corner-stone is once removed, the whole fabric cannot choose but fall to the ground, insomuch that it is no longer worth while to bestow a particular consideration on the absurdities of every wretched sect of Atheists[2].

93. That impious and profane persons should readily fall in with those systems which favour their inclinations, by deriding immaterial substance, and supposing the soul to be divisible and subject to corruption as the body; which exclude all freedom, intelligence, and design from the formation of things, and instead thereof make a self-existent, stupid, unthinking substance the root and origin of all beings; that

---

[1] That is to say, Matter abstracted from phenomena.
[2] Yet with Hume, and in later Positive Philosophy, the analysis of the material world into significant phenomena dependent on a percipient—on the ground of the inconceivability of the hyper-phenomenal, has, on this same ground, been used for analysing the percipient spirit too into transitory conscious states, with a confession of ultimate philosophical nescience. Berkeley of course alleges reason for retaining moral substance and agency, while he rejects the supposed substance and power of matter.

they should hearken to those who deny a Providence, or inspection of a Superior Mind over the affairs of the world, attributing the whole series of events either to blind chance or fatal necessity arising from the impulse of one body on another—all this is very natural. And, on the other hand, when men of better principles observe the enemies of religion lay so great a stress on *unthinking Matter*, and all of them use so much industry and artifice to reduce everything to it[1], methinks they should rejoice to see them deprived of their grand support, and driven from that only fortress, without which your Epicureans, Hobbists[2], and the like, have not even the shadow of a pretence, and become the most cheap and easy triumph in the world[3].

94. The existence of Matter, or bodies unperceived, has not only been the main support of Atheists and Fatalists, but on the same principle doth Idolatry likewise in all its various forms depend. Did men but consider that the sun, moon, and stars, and every other object of the senses, are *only* so many sensations in their minds, which have no other existence but barely being perceived, doubtless they would never fall down and worship their own *ideas*—but rather address their homage to that Eternal Invisible Mind which produces and sustains all things.

95. The same absurd principle, by mingling itself with the articles of our faith, has occasioned no small difficulties to Christians. For example, about the Resurrection, how many scruples and objections have been raised by Socinians and others? But do not the most plausible of them depend on the supposition that a body is denominated the *same*, with regard

---

[1] Rather, now-a-days, it is the fashion to get rid of all ultimate difficulties by assuming our necessary ignorance of other than negative answers to the ultimate questions.

[2] Epicurus, following Democritus, resolved thought, as well as sensible things, ultimately into inexplicable concourse of atoms, and the teaching of Hobbes was akin to this.

[3] Does Berkeley's account of what the material world means really accomplish so much?

not to the *form*, or that which is perceived by sense, but the *material substance*, which remains the same under several forms? Take away this *material substance*—about the identity whereof all the dispute is—and mean by *body* what every plain ordinary person means by that word, to wit, *that which is immediately seen and felt*, which is only a combination of sensible qualities or ideas, and then their most unanswerable objections come to nothing[1].

96. Matter[2] being once expelled out of nature drags with it so many sceptical and impious notions, such an incredible number of disputes and puzzling questions, which have been thorns in the sides of divines as well as philosophers, and made so much fruitless work for mankind, that if the arguments we have produced against it are not found equal to demonstration (as to me they evidently seem), yet I am sure all friends to knowledge, peace, and religion have reason to wish they were.

97. Beside the external existence of the objects of perception, another great source of errors and difficulties with regard to *ideal* knowledge[3] is the doctrine of 'abstract ideas,' such as it hath been set forth in the Introduction. The plainest things in the world, those we are most intimately acquainted with and perfectly know, when they are considered in an abstract way, appear strangely difficult and incomprehensible. Time, Place, and Motion, taken in particular or concrete, are what everybody knows; but, having passed through the hands of a metaphysician, they become too abstract and fine to be apprehended by men of ordinary sense. Bid your servant meet you at such a *time* in such a *place*,

---

[1] On the meaning of the word 'same,' in its application to sensible things, see *Third Dialogue* (*Works*, vol. I. pp. 343-345). He does not inquire however what, on his new conception of things, the *sameness* of the self or *ego* means.

[2] Not the phenomena presented to our senses and their established order, of course, but only a supposed abstract Matter, is here meant.

[3] 'Ideal knowledge'—knowledge of significant and interpretable

of Human Knowledge. 103

and he shall never stay to deliberate on the meaning of those words; in conceiving that particular time and place, or the motion by which he is to get thither, he finds not the least difficulty. But if Time be taken exclusive of all those *particular* actions and ideas that diversify the day, merely for the continuation of existence, or duration in abstract, then it will perhaps gravel even a philosopher to comprehend it.

98. For my own part, whenever I attempt to frame a simple idea of Time, abstracted from the succession of ideas in my mind, which flows uniformly and is participated by all beings, I am lost and embrangled in inextricable difficulties[1]. I have no notion of it at all: only I hear others say it is infinitely divisible, and speak of it in such a manner as leads me to harbour odd thoughts of my existence;—since that doctrine lays one under an absolute necessity of thinking, either that he passes away innumerable ages without a thought, or else that he is annihilated every moment of his life, both which seem equally absurd. Time therefore being *nothing*, abstracted from the succession of ideas in our minds, it follows that the duration of any finite spirit must be estimated by the number of ideas or actions succeeding each other in that same spirit or mind. Hence, it is a plain consequence that *the soul always thinks;* and in truth whoever shall go about to divide in his thoughts, or abstract the *existence* of a spirit from its *cogitation*, will, I believe, find it no easy task[2].

[1] Locke's account of Time (*Essay*, b. II. ch. 14. §§ 3, 5, 17) may be compared with this. See also Berkeley's Commonplace Book, in *Life of Berkeley*, pp. 439, 468. Though observed changes in phenomena of which we are conscious or percipient may, as a matter of fact, *develope* in us the notion of time, it does not follow that they philosophically *explain* it.
[2] Berkeley says elsewhere:—'A succession of ideas I take to *constitute* time, and not be only the sensible measure thereof, as Mr. Locke and others think. One of my earliest enquiries was about time, which led me into several paradoxes that I did not think fit or necessary to publish.' (*Life of Berkeley*, p. 177.) 'Si non rogas intelligo' may be

99. So likewise when we attempt to abstract Extension and Motion from all other qualities, and consider them by themselves, we presently lose sight of them, and run into great extravagances. All which depend on a twofold abstraction;—first, it is supposed that extension, for example, may be abstracted from all other sensible qualities; and secondly, that the entity of extension may be abstracted from its being perceived. But, whoever shall reflect, and take care to understand what he says, will, if I mistake not, acknowledge that all sensible qualities are alike *sensations* and alike *real*—that where the extension is, there is the colour too, *i.e.* in his mind; that their archetypes can exist only in some *other mind;* and that the objects of sense are nothing but those sensations combined, blended, or (if one may so speak) concreted together[1]—none of all which can be supposed to exist unperceived.

100. What is it for a man to be happy, or an object good, every one may think he knows. But to frame an *abstract* idea of happiness, prescinded from all particular pleasure, or of goodness from everything that is good, this is what few can pretend to. So likewise a man may be just and virtuous without having precise ideas of justice and virtue. The opinion that those and the like words stand for general notions, abstracted from all particular persons and actions, seems to have rendered Morality very difficult, and the study thereof of small use to mankind. And in effect one may make a great progress in school-ethics without ever being the wiser or better man for it, or knowing how to behave himself in the affairs of life more to the advantage of himself

said of Time, in itself inconceivable when we try to abstract it, and yet necessarily mixed up with our experience.

With Berkeley 'the soul always thinks;' for 'time' abstracted from change of conscious state would not be time at all. (Here he differs from Locke. See *Essay*, b. II. ch. 1, §§ 9-19.) Hence too, since the essence of things is *percipi*—or (as in *Siris*) *intelligi*, so the esse of spirits would be *percipere*—or *intelligere*.

[1] By Supreme Mind and Will.

or his neighbours than he did before. This hint may suffice to let any one see the doctrine of *abstraction* has not a little contributed towards spoiling the most useful parts of knowledge[1].

101. The two great provinces of speculative science conversant about *ideas received from Sense*, are Natural Philosophy and Mathematics; with regard to each of these I shall make some observations[2].

And first I shall say somewhat of Natural Philosophy. On this subject it is that the sceptics triumph. All that stock of arguments they produce to depreciate our faculties and make mankind appear ignorant and low, are drawn principally from this head, namely, that we are under an invincible blindness as to the *true* and *real* nature of things. This they exaggerate, and love to enlarge on. We are miserably bantered, say they, by our senses, and amused only with the outside and show of things. The real essence—the internal qualities and constitution—of every the meanest object, is hid from our view; something there is in every drop of water, every grain of sand, which it is beyond the power of human understanding to fathom or comprehend. But, it is evident from what has been shewn that all this complaint is groundless, and that we are influenced by false principles to that degree as to mistrust our senses, and think we know nothing of those things which we perfectly comprehend.

102. One great inducement to our pronouncing ourselves ignorant of the nature of things is the current opinion that

[1] The substitution of facts for empty abstractions is, with Berkeley, the beginning and end of philosophy. This is the lesson of the 'Introduction' to the *Principles*, here made one of their applications. There is great value in his condemnation of our disposition to substantiate meaningless abstractions, even if, here and elsewhere, he too much attempts to eliminate all mystery from our ultimate convictions.

[2] In Kant's 'Aesthetic' and 'Analytic' we have *his* explanation and defence of mathematical and physical science, as against the sceptical dissolution of it into phenomena habitually connected—all which may be compared with sect. 101-134, which is at the point of view of Locke.

everything includes within itself the cause of its properties; or that there is in each object an inward *essence* which is the source whence its discernible qualities flow, and whereon they depend[1]. Some have pretended to account for appearances by occult qualities: but of late they are mostly resolved into mechanical causes, to wit, the figure, motion, weight, and suchlike qualities[2], of insensible particles ;—whereas, in truth, there is no other agent or efficient cause than *spirit*, it being evident that motion, as well as all other *ideas*, is perfectly inert. See sect. 25. Hence, to endeavour to explain the production of colours or sounds, by figure, motion, magnitude and the like, must needs be labour in vain. And accordingly we see the attempts of that kind are not at all satisfactory. Which may be said in general of those instances wherein one idea or quality is assigned for the cause of another. I need not say how many hypotheses and speculations are left out, and how much the study of nature is abridged by this doctrine[3].

103. The great *mechanical* principle now in vogue is Attraction. That a stone falls to the earth, or the sea swells towards the moon, may to some appear sufficiently explained thereby. But how are we enlightened by being told this is done by attraction? Is it that that word signifies the manner of the tendency, and that it is by the mutual drawing of bodies instead of their being impelled or protruded towards

---

[1] This is the Aristotelian and Scholastic teaching, according to which the essential nature or formal cause of anything (οὐσία, τὸ τί ἦν εἶναι) explains its *secondary* qualities (ποία), and is unfolded in its definition. The *form* or *essence* of a thing thus consists of what is essential to its existence as *that* thing, and is *always* present in all its developments.

[2] i. e. the primary qualities, regarded as the explanation of the differences in the secondary qualities of things, as even Locke suggests.

[3] Berkeley's conception of the material world is a sort of Spiritual Positivism, which eliminates all real substance and power from the things we see and touch, and finds it in Mind. He sees in the order or significance of the phenomena presented to the senses laws according to which the Supreme Power regulates their coexistences and successions, in the experience of finite percipients.

each other? But nothing is determined of the manner or action, and it may as truly (for aught we know) be termed 'impulse,' or 'protrusion,' as 'attraction.' Again, the parts of steel we see cohere firmly together, and this also is accounted for by attraction; but, in this as in the other instances, I do not perceive that anything is signified besides the effect itself; for as to the manner of the action whereby it is produced, or the cause which produces it, these are not so much as aimed at[1].

104. Indeed, if we take a view of the several phenomena, and compare them together, we may observe some likeness and conformity between them. For example, in the falling of a stone to the ground, in the rising of the sea towards the moon, in cohesion, crystallization, &c., there is something alike, namely, an union or mutual approach of bodies. So that any one of these or the like phenomena may not seem strange or surprising to a man who has nicely observed and compared the effects of nature. For that only is thought so which is uncommon, or a thing by itself, and out of the ordinary course of our observation. That bodies should tend towards the centre of the earth is not thought strange, because it is what we perceive every moment of our lives. But, that they should have a like gravitation towards the centre of the moon may seem odd and unaccountable to most men, because it is discerned only in the tides. But a philosopher, whose thoughts take in a larger compass of nature, having observed a certain similitude of appearances, as well in the heavens as the earth, that argue innumerable bodies to have a mutual tendency towards each other, which he denotes by the general name 'attraction,' whatever can be reduced to *that* he thinks justly accounted for. Thus he explains the tides by the attraction of the terraqueous globe towards the moon, which to him

[1] Whether Gravitation is included in the 'essence' or 'form' of the material world has been a disputed question, which, like others about physical causation, Berkeley summarily disposes of by referring all law in nature to an Agent that is rational and free.

does not appear odd or anomalous, but only a particular example of a general rule or law of nature.

105. If therefore we consider the difference there is betwixt natural philosophers and other men, with regard to their knowledge of the phenomena, we shall find it consists not in an exacter knowledge of the *efficient cause* that produces them—for that can be no other than the *will of a spirit*—but only in a greater largeness of comprehension, whereby analogies, harmonies, and agreements are discovered in the works of nature, and the particular effects explained, that is, *reduced to general rules*, see sect. 62; which rules, grounded on the analogy and uniformness observed in the production of natural effects, are most agreeable and sought after by the mind; for that they extend our prospect beyond what is present and near to us, and enable us to make very probable conjectures touching things that may have happened at very great distances of time and place, as well as to predict things to come; which sort of endeavour towards Omniscience is much affected by the mind [1].

106. But we should proceed warily in such things, for we are apt to lay too great a stress on analogies [2], and, to the prejudice of truth, humour that eagerness of the mind whereby it is carried to extend its knowledge into general theorems. For example, in the business of gravitation or mutual attraction, because it appears in many instances, some are straight-

---

[1] The Modern Physical Sciences, with their hypothetical and inductive inferences of past, distant, and future phenomena, are here referred to, and the method of their formation is suggested. The ideal of inductive research would be reached, in the discovery of the relation of each event to the Divine conception of the whole. But our scientific generalisations are only partial, and this ideal belongs to philosophy.

[2] 'Analogy.' He implies that our knowledge of nature and its laws is based on analogy. See *Siris*, sect. 252. It is thus presumption and not demonstrable science. This is Locke's doctrine, founded on his view of the causal dependence of the secondary qualities on the primary qualities. Our so-called science of nature is therefore only probable, not rationally necessary. 'That which chiefly constitutes probability,' says Butler, 'is expressed in the word *likely*, i. e. like (analogous to) some truth' or real event. (*Analogy*, p. 2.)

way for pronouncing it *universal;* and that to attract and be attracted by every other body is an essential quality inherent in all bodies whatsoever. Whereas it is evident the fixed stars have no such tendency towards each other; and, so far is that gravitation from being *essential* to bodies that in some instances a quite contrary principle seems to shew itself; as in the perpendicular growth of plants, and the elasticity of the air. There is nothing necessary or essential in the case[1], but it depends entirely on the Will of the Governing Spirit, who causes certain bodies to cleave together or tend towards each other according to various laws, whilst He keeps others at a fixed distance; and to some He gives a quite contrary tendency to fly asunder just as He sees convenient[2].

107. After what has been premised, I think we may lay down the following conclusions.—First, it is plain philosophers amuse themselves in vain, when they enquire for *any* natural efficient cause, distinct from a *Mind* or *Spirit.* Secondly, considering the whole creation is the workmanship of a *wise and good Agent,* it should seem to become philosophers to employ their thoughts (contrary to what some hold) about the final causes of things; and I must confess I see no reason why pointing out the various ends to which natural things are adapted, and for which they were originally with unspeakable wisdom contrived, should not be thought one good way of accounting for them, and altogether worthy a philosopher. Thirdly, from what has been premised no reason can be drawn why the history of nature should not still be studied, and observations and experiments made—which, that they

---

[1] It may well be that we are *intellectually obliged to think* that each new event must have previously existed in the form of a preceding phenomenon, but not necessarily in this, that, or the other particular phenomenon; for a knowledge of this last we are dependent on observation.

[2] Physical research has outgrown Berkeley's examples in this section. The movement of the solar system and of the fixed stars is now recognised by astronomers: neither the growth of plants nor the elasticity of the air contradicts gravity.

are of use to mankind, and enable us to draw any general conclusions, is not the result of any immutable habitudes or relations between things themselves, but only of God's goodness and kindness to men in the administration of the world. See sect. 30 and 31. Fourthly, by a diligent observation of the phenomena within our view, we may discover the general laws of nature, and from them deduce the other phenomena; I do not say *demonstrate*, for all deductions of that kind depend on a supposition that the Author of Nature always operates uniformly, and in a constant observance of those rules we take for principles—which we cannot evidently know [1].

108. Those men who frame general rules for the phenomena, and afterwards derive the phenomena from those rules, seem to consider Signs rather than Causes. A man may well understand natural signs without knowing their analogy, or being able to say by what rule a thing is so or so. And, as it is very possible to write improperly, through too strict an observance of general grammar-rules; so, in arguing from general laws of nature, it is not impossible we may extend the analogy too far, and by that means run into mistakes.

109. As in reading other books a wise man will choose to fix his thoughts on the sense and apply it to use, rather than lay them out in grammatical remarks on the language; so, in perusing the Volume of Nature, methinks it is beneath the dignity of the mind to affect an exactness in reducing each particular phenomenon to general rules, or shewing how it follows from them. We should propose to ourselves nobler

---

[1] What right has one to take for granted (in opposition to teaching like Berkeley's) that the material world is something that is ultimately independent of Reason and Will, or that physical laws are in themselves necessary and eternal? Can we assert that the things we see and touch must gravitate, or else that experience would be impossible; or that, by a like necessity of all possible experience, matter is indestructible, and force identical through all its metamorphoses?

views, namely, to recreate and exalt the mind with a prospect of the beauty, order, extent, and variety of natural things: hence, by proper inferences, to enlarge our notions of the grandeur, wisdom, and beneficence of the Creator; and lastly, to make the several parts of the creation, so far as in us lies, subservient to the ends they were designed for—God's glory, and the sustentation and comfort of ourselves and fellow-creatures[1].

110. The best key for the aforesaid Analogy or Natural Science will be easily acknowledged to be a certain celebrated Treatise of *Mechanics*[2]. In the entrance of which justly admired treatise, Time, Space, and Motion are distinguished into *absolute* and *relative*, *true* and *apparent*, *mathematical* and *vulgar*;—which distinction, as it is at large explained by the author, does suppose those Quantities to have an existence without the mind, and that they are ordinarily conceived with relation to sensible things, to which nevertheless in their own nature they bear no relation at all.

111. As for *Time*, as it is there taken in an absolute or abstracted sense, for the duration or perseverance of the existence of things, I have nothing more to add concerning it after what has been already said on that subject. Sect. 97 and 98. For the rest, this celebrated author holds there is an *Absolute Space*, which, being unperceivable to sense, remains in itself similar and immoveable; and *relative space* to be the measure thereof, which being moveable, and defined by its situation in respect of sensible bodies, is vulgarly taken for immoveable space. *Place* he defines to be that part of space which is occupied by any body; and according as the space is absolute or relative so also is the place. *Absolute*

---

[1] So Bacon, in passages which, like this one, illustrate the broad humanity which animates the best English philosophy, and its wise contentment with 'broken knowledge,' when the facts of experience refuse to submit to 'our little systems.'

[2] Newton's *Principia*, published in 1687, on which Berkeley comments in the following sections.

Motion is said to be the translation of a body from absolute place to absolute place, as *relative motion* is from one relative place to another. And, because the parts of Absolute Space do not fall under our senses, instead of them we are obliged to use their sensible measures, and so define both place and motion with respect to bodies which we regard as immoveable. But, it is said in philosophical matters we must abstract from our senses, since it may be that none of those bodies which seem to be quiescent are truly so, and the same thing which is moved relatively may be really at rest ; as likewise one and the same body may be in relative rest and motion, or even moved with contrary relative motions at the same time, according as its place is variously defined. All which ambiguity is to be found in the apparent motions, but not at all in the true or absolute, which should therefore be alone regarded in philosophy. And the true we are told are distinguished from apparent or relative motions by the following properties.—First, in true or absolute motion all parts which preserve the same position with respect of the whole, partake of the motions of the whole. Secondly, the place being moved, that which is placed therein is also moved; so that a body moving in a place which is in motion doth participate the motion of its place. Thirdly, true motion is never generated or changed otherwise than by force impressed on the body itself. Fourthly, true motion is always changed by force impressed on the body moved. Fifthly, in circular motion barely relative there is no centrifugal force, which nevertheless, in that which is true or absolute, is proportional to the quantity of motion.

112. But, notwithstanding what has been said, I must confess it does not appear to me that there can be any motion other than *relative ;* so that to conceive motion there must be at least conceived two bodies, whereof the distance or position in regard to each other is varied. Hence, if there was one only body in being it could not possibly be moved.

This to me seems very evident, in that the idea I have of motion does necessarily include relation [1].

113. But, though in every motion it be necessary to conceive more bodies than one, yet it may be that one only is moved, namely, that on which the force causing the change in the distance or situation of the bodies is impressed. For, however some may define relative motion, so as to term that body *moved* which changes its distance from some other body, whether the force or action causing that change were impressed on *it* or no, yet as relative motion is that which is perceived by sense, and regarded in the ordinary affairs of life, it follows that every man of common sense knows what it is as well as the best philosopher. Now, I ask any one whether, in his sense of motion as he walks along the streets, the stones he passes over may be said to *move*, because they change distance with his feet? To me it appears that though motion includes a relation of one thing to another, yet it is not necessary that each term of the relation be denominated from it. As a man may think of somewhat which does not think, so a body may be moved to or from another body which is not therefore *itself* in motion.—I mean relative motion, for other I am not able to conceive.

114. As the place happens to be variously defined, the motion which is related to it varies. A man in a ship may be said to be quiescent with relation to the sides of the vessel, and yet move with relation to the land. Or he may move eastward in respect of the one, and westward in respect of the other. In the common affairs of life men never go beyond the Earth to define the place of any body; and what is quiescent *in respect of that* is accounted *absolutely* to be so. But philosophers, who have a greater extent of thought, and juster notions of the system of things, discover even the

---

[1]. What has been alleged as to all this is, that 'experience' presupposes objective relations which constitute and are in a manner embedded in all real knowledge. On Motion, cf. Berkeley, *De Motu* (*Works*, vol. III. pp. 75-100).

Earth itself to be moved. In order therefore to fix their notions, they seem to conceive the Corporeal World as finite, and the utmost unmoved walls or shell thereof to be the place whereby they estimate true motions. If we sound our own conceptions, I believe we may find all the absolute motion we can frame an idea of to be at bottom no other than relative motion thus defined. For, as has been already observed, absolute motion, exclusive of all external relation, is incomprehensible; and to this kind of relative motion all the above-mentioned properties, causes, and effects ascribed to absolute motion will, if I mistake not, be found to agree. As to what is said of the centrifugal force, that it does not at all belong to circular relative motion, I do not see how this follows from the experiment which is brought to prove it. See *Philosophiæ Naturalis Principia Mathematica, in Schol. Def. VIII*. For the water in the vessel at that time wherein it is said to have the greatest relative circular motion, has, I think, no motion at all; as is plain from the foregoing section.

115. For, to denominate a body *moved* it is requisite, first, that it change its distance or situation with regard to some other body; secondly, that the force occasioning that change be impressed on *it*. If either of these be wanting, I do not think that, agreeably to the sense of mankind, or the propriety of language, a body can be said to be in motion. I grant indeed that it is possible for us to think a body which we see change its distance from some other to be moved, though it have no force applied to it (in which sense there may be apparent motion); but then it is because the force causing the change of distance is imagined by us to be applied or impressed on that body thought to move; which indeed shews we are capable of mistaking a thing to be in motion which is not, and that is all.

116. From what has been said it follows that the philosophic consideration of motion does not imply the being of

an Absolute Space, distinct from that which is perceived by sense and related to bodies; which that *it* cannot exist without the mind is clear upon the same principles that demonstrate the like of all other objects of sense.—And perhaps, if we inquire narrowly, we shall find we cannot even frame an idea of Pure Space exclusive of all body. This I must confess, seems impossible, as being a most abstract idea. When I excite a motion in some part of my body, if it be free or without resistance, I say there is *Space;* but if I find a resistance, then I say there is *Body :* and in proportion as the resistance to motion is lesser or greater, I say the space is more or less *pure.* So that when I speak of pure or empty space, it is not to be supposed that the word 'space' stands for an idea distinct from or conceivable without body and motion—though indeed we are apt to think every noun substantive stands for a distinct idea that may be separated from all others; which has occasioned infinite mistakes. When, therefore, supposing all the world to be annihilated besides my own body, I say there still remains *Pure Space*, thereby nothing else is meant but only that I conceive it possible for the limbs of my body to be moved on all sides without the least resistance; but if that too were annihilated then there could be no motion, and consequently no Space[1]. Some, perhaps, may think the sense of seeing does furnish them with the idea of Pure Space; but it is plain from what we have elsewhere shewn, that the ideas of Space and Distance are not obtained by that sense. See the *Essay concerning Vision.*

117. What is here laid down seems to put an end to all those disputes and difficulties that have sprung up amongst the learned concerning the nature of Pure Space. But the chief advantage arising from it is that we are freed from that dangerous dilemma, to which several who have em-

[1] Though pure space is unimaginable, it does not follow that the mathematical relations embedded in our experience are unintelligible: for experience of external things cannot be intelligibly formed independently of their geometrical relations.

ployed their thoughts on that subject imagine themselves reduced, viz. of thinking either that Real Space is God, or else that there is something beside God which is eternal, uncreated, infinite, indivisible, immutable. Both which may justly be thought pernicious and absurd notions. It is certain that not a few divines, as well as philosophers of great note, have, from the difficulty they found in conceiving either limits or annihilation of space, concluded it must be Divine. And some of late have set themselves particularly to shew the incommunicable attributes of God agree to it[1]. Which doctrine, how unworthy soever it may seem of the Divine Nature, yet I must confess I do not see how we can get clear of it, so long as we adhere to the received opinions[2].

118. Hitherto of Natural Philosophy: we come now to make some inquiry concerning that other great branch of speculative knowledge, to wit, Mathematics. These, how celebrated soever they may be for their clearness and certainty of demonstration, which is hardly anywhere else to be found, cannot nevertheless be supposed altogether free from mistakes, if so be that in their principles there lurks some secret error which is common to the professors of those sciences with the rest of mankind. Mathematicians, though they deduce their theorems from a great height of evidence, yet their first principles are limited by the consideration of

[1] See Dr. Samuel Clarke's *Demonstration of the Being and Attributes of God*, which appeared in 1706.

[2] 'Abstract Space' is with Berkeley space out of relation to the empirical data of sense—neither seen nor touched. His own view is that space is at last only a certain succession of phenomena, its relations being thus resolvable into those of time and change.

The mathematical type of atheism then prevalent accounts for Berkeley's recurrence to space, and his endeavours to melt it down into phenomena. He thus got rid of an abstraction which seemed to him the essence of Materialism. (See *Commonplace Book*, p. 490.)—Yet space suggests the Infinite, or at least the inability of man to rest satisfied with what is finite, and our intellectual obligation to think of something beyond any limited space. Some have even found the origin of religion in our mental experience of inability to arrest imagination by an absolute limit when we contemplate space.

Quantity: and they do not ascend into any inquiry concerning those transcendental maxims which influence all the particular sciences, each part whereof, Mathematics not excepted, does consequently participate of the errors involved in them. That the principles laid down by mathematicians are true, and their way of deduction from those principles clear and incontestible, we do not deny; but, we hold there may be certain erroneous maxims of greater extent than the object of Mathematics, and for that reason not expressly mentioned, though tacitly supposed throughout the whole progress of that science; and that the ill effects of those secret unexamined errors are diffused through all the branches thereof[1]. To be plain, we suspect the mathematicians are no less deeply concerned than other men in the errors arising from the doctrine of abstract general ideas, and the existence of objects without the mind.

119. Arithmetic has been thought to have for its object *abstract* ideas of *Number*; of which to understand the properties and mutual habitudes, is supposed no mean part of speculative knowledge. The opinion of the pure and intellectual nature of numbers in abstract has made them in esteem with those philosophers who seem to have affected an uncommon fineness and elevation of thought. It hath set a price on the most trifling numerical speculations, which in practice are of no use, but serve only for amusement; and hath heretofore so far infected the minds of some, that they have dreamed of mighty mysteries involved in numbers, and attempted the explication of natural things by them[2]. But, if we narrowly inquire into our own thoughts, and consider

---

[1] The preceding sentences imply the difference between philosophy and science. As concerned only with science, mere mathematicians do not, as metaphysical philosophers are obliged to do, ascend into an inquiry concerning those transcendental maxims which influence all the particular sciences. It is this 'transcendental' inquiry that Berkeley is here engaged in.

[2] The Pythagoreans for instance, in the beginnings of philosophy.

what has been premised, we may perhaps entertain a low opinion of those high flights and abstractions, and look on all inquiries about numbers only as so many *difficiles nugæ*, so far as they are not subservient to practice, and promote the benefit of life.

120. Unity in abstract we have before considered, in sect. 13, from which, and what has been said in the Introduction, it plainly follows there is not any such idea. But, number being defined a 'collection of units,' we may conclude that, if there be no such thing as unity or unit in abstract, there are no ideas of number in abstract denoted by the numeral names and figures. The theories therefore in Arithmetic, if they are abstracted from the names and figures, as likewise from all use and practice, as well as from the particular things numbered, can be supposed to have nothing at all for their object; hence we may see how entirely the science of numbers is subordinate to practice, and how jejune and trifling it becomes when considered as a matter of mere speculation[1].

121. However, since there may be some who, deluded by the specious show of discovering abstracted verities, waste their time in arithmetical theorems and problems which have not any use, it will not be amiss if we more fully consider and expose the vanity of that pretence; and this will plainly

---

[1] As in treating of Space, which he resolves into an aggregate of sensible minima, thus making geometry an application of arithmetic, so now, in treating of Number itself, he fails to recognise in it elements not given as phenomena, or to distinguish between ideas or sensations which call forth the 'notion' of number and the notion itself—between an experience *involving* numerical relations and mere phenomena themselves *being* those relations. Even Locke had assigned a humbler function to sense in arithmetical knowledge, and spoke of the idea of number as 'suggested' by the data of experience. 'Amongst all the ideas we have, as there is none suggested to the mind by more ways, so there is none more simple than unity or one. Every object our senses are employed about, every idea in our understandings, brings this idea along with it. It is the most universal idea we have. For number applies itself to everything that either doth exist or can be imagined' (*Essay*, b. II. ch. 16. § 1).

appear by taking a view of Arithmetic in its infancy, and observing what it was that originally put men on the study of that science, and to what scope they directed it. It is natural to think that at first, men, for ease of memory and help of computation, made use of counters, or in writing of single strokes, points, or the like, each whereof was made to signify an unit, *i. e.* some one thing of whatever kind they had occasion to reckon. Afterwards they found out the more compendious ways of making one character stand in place of several strokes or points. And, lastly, the notation of the Arabians or Indians came into use, wherein, by the repetition of a few characters or figures, and varying the signification of each figure according to the place it obtains, all numbers may be most aptly expressed; which seems to have been done in imitation of language, so that an exact analogy is observed betwixt the notation by figures and names, the nine simple figures answering the nine first numeral names and places in the former, corresponding to denominations in the latter. And agreeably to those conditions of the simple and local value of figures, were contrived methods of finding, from the given figures or marks of the parts, what figures and how placed are proper to denote the whole, or *vice versa*. And having found the sought figures, the same rule or analogy being observed throughout, it is easy to read them into words; and so the number becomes perfectly known. For then the number of any particular things is said to be known, when we know the name or figures (with their due arrangement) that according to the standing analogy belong to them. For, these signs being known, we can, by the operations of arithmetic, know the signs of any part of the particular sums signified by them; and, thus computing in signs, (because of the connexion established betwixt them and the distinct multitudes of things whereof one is taken for an unit), we may be able rightly to sum up, divide, and proportion the things themselves that we intend to number.

122. In Arithmetic, therefore, we regard not the *things* but the *signs*, which nevertheless are not regarded for their own sake, but because they direct us how to act with relation to things, and dispose rightly of them. Now, agreeably to what we have before observed of words in general (sect. 19, Introd.) it happens here likewise that *abstract ideas* are thought to be signified by numeral names or characters, while they do not suggest *ideas of particular things* to our minds. I shall not at present enter into a more particular dissertation on this subject, but only observe that it is evident, from what has been said, those things which pass for abstract truths and theorems concerning numbers, are in reality conversant about no object distinct from particular numerable things, except only names and characters, which originally came to be considered on no other account but their being signs, or capable to represent aptly whatever particular things men had need to compute. Whence it follows that to study them for their own sake would be just as wise, and to as good purpose, as if a man, neglecting the true use or original intention and subserviency of language, should spend his time in impertinent criticisms upon words, or reasonings and controversies purely verbal[1].

123. From numbers we proceed to speak of *Extension*, which is the object of Geometry. The *infinite* divisibility of *finite* extension, though it is not expressly laid down either as an axiom or theorem in the elements of that science, yet is throughout the same everywhere supposed and thought to have so inseparable and essential a connexion with the principles and demonstrations in Geometry, that mathematicians never admit it into doubt, or make the least question of it. And, as this notion is the source from whence do spring all those amusing geometrical paradoxes which have such a direct

---

[1] This is his old argument against abstractions, applied to pure as distinguished from mixed arithmetic, from which he concludes that the former is a sham science of empty verbal signs.

repugnancy to the plain common sense of mankind, and are admitted with so much reluctance into a mind not yet debauched by learning; so is it the principal occasion of all that nice and extreme subtilty which renders the study of Mathematics so very difficult and tedious. Hence, if we can make it appear that *no finite extension contains innumerable parts, or is infinitely divisible*, it follows that we shall at once clear the science of Geometry from a great number of difficulties and contradictions which have ever been esteemed a reproach to human reason, and withal make the attainment thereof a business of much less time and pains than it hitherto has been.

124. Every particular finite extension which may possibly be the object of our thought is an *idea* existing only in the mind, and consequently each part thereof must be perceived. If, therefore, I cannot perceive innumerable parts in any finite extension that I consider, it is certain they are not contained in it; but, it is evident that I cannot distinguish innumerable parts in any particular line, surface, or solid, which I either perceive by sense, or figure to myself in my mind: wherefore I conclude they are not contained in it. Nothing can be plainer to me than that the extensions I have in view are no other than my own ideas; and it is no less plain that I cannot resolve any one of my ideas into an infinite number of other ideas, that is, that they are not infinitely divisible. If by finite extension be meant something distinct from a finite idea, I declare I do not know what that is, and so cannot affirm or deny anything of it. But if the terms 'extension,' 'parts,' &c., are taken in any sense conceivable, that is, for ideas, then to say a finite quantity or extension consists of parts infinite in number is so manifest and glaring a contradiction, that every one at first sight acknowledges it to be so[1]; and it is impossible it should ever gain

---

[1] The contradiction is not so manifest. Locke more cautiously remarks, that 'the divisibility *in infinitum* of any finite extension involves

the assent of any reasonable creature who is not brought to it by gentle and slow degrees, as a converted Gentile to the belief of transubstantiation. Ancient and rooted prejudices do often pass into principles; and those propositions which once obtain the force and credit of a *principle*, are not only themselves, but likewise whatever is deducible from them, thought privileged from all examination. And there is no absurdity so gross, which, by this means, the mind of man may not be prepared to swallow.

125. He whose understanding is prepossessed with the doctrine of *abstract* general ideas may be persuaded that (whatever be thought of the *ideas of sense*) extension in *abstract* is infinitely divisible. And any one who thinks the objects of sense exist without the mind will perhaps in virtue thereof be brought to admit that a line but an inch long may contain innumerable parts—really existing, though too small to be discerned. These errors are grafted as well in the minds of geometricians as of other men, and have a like influence on their reasonings; and it were no difficult thing to shew how the arguments from Geometry made use of to support the infinite divisibility of extension are bottomed on them. At present we shall only observe in general whence it is the mathematicians are all so fond and tenacious of that doctrine.

us, whether we grant or deny it, in consequences impossible to be explicated, or made in *our* apprehensions consistent.' *Essay*, b. II. ch. 23. § 31. What Berkeley teaches is that infinitely divided extension, being in its infinite division unperceived, must be non-existent—as existence necessarily depends on a percipient. The only possible extension must be a perceived extension, which can of course be divided only down to the point at which its parts cease to be perceived.

He thus makes sense and imagination the criterion of possibility, and seeks to eliminate the puzzles and paradoxes of the infinitely little in space (so too of the infinitely great) by applying his phenomenalist test to space as well as to matter. Locke had illustrated the consciousness of infinity through number and numerical quantity. 'The *endless* addition or addibility of numbers, so apparent to the mind, is that,' he says, 'which gives us the clearest and most distinct idea of infinity' (*Essay*, b. II. ch. 16. § 8). And endlessness of course cannot be mentally imaged, as every mental image is bounded.

126. It has been observed in another place that the theorems and demonstrations in Geometry are conversant about *universal ideas* (sect. 15. Introd.); where it is explained in what sense this ought to be understood, to wit, the *particular* lines and figures included in the diagram are supposed to stand for innumerable others of different sizes; or, in other words, the geometer considers *them* abstracting from their magnitude—which does not imply that he forms an abstract idea, but only that he cares not what the particular magnitude is, whether great or small, but looks on that as a thing indifferent to the demonstration. Hence it follows that a line in the scheme but an inch long must be spoken of as though *it* contained ten thousand parts, since it is regarded not in itself, but as it is universal; and it is universal only in its signification, whereby it represents innumerable lines greater than itself, in which may be distinguished ten thousand parts or more, though there may not be above an inch in it. After this manner, the properties of the lines signified are (by a very usual figure) transferred to the sign, and thence, through mistake, thought to appertain to it considered in its own nature [1].

127. Because there is no number of parts so great but it is possible there may be *a* line containing more, the *inch*-line is said to contain parts more than any assignable number; which is true, not of the inch taken absolutely, but only for the things signified by it. But men, not retaining that distinction in their thoughts, slide into a belief that the small particular line described on paper contains in itself parts innumerable. There is no such thing as the ten thousandth part of an inch; but there is of a mile or diameter of the earth, which may be signified by that inch. When therefore I delineate a triangle on paper, and take one side not above an inch, for example, in length to be the radius, this

---

[1] This is using an imaginable individual as a *relative image* or specimen of a class. It is thinking by help of a *resembling* sign.

I consider as divided into 10,000 or 100,000 parts or more; for, though the ten thousandth part of *that* line considered in itself is nothing at all, and consequently may be neglected without any error or inconveniency, yet these described lines, being only marks standing for greater quantities, whereof it may be the ten thousandth part is very considerable, it follows that, to prevent notable errors in practice, the radius must be taken of 10,000 parts or more.

128. From what has been said the reason is plain why, to the end any theorem become universal in its use, it is necessary we speak of the lines described on paper as though they contained parts which really they do not. In doing of which, if we examine the matter thoroughly, we shall perhaps discover that we cannot conceive an inch itself as consisting of, or being divisible into, a thousand parts, but only some other line which is far greater than an inch, and represented by it; and that when we say a line is infinitely divisible, we must mean a line which is infinitely great[1]. What we have here observed seems to be the chief cause why, to suppose the infinite divisibility of finite extension has been thought necessary in geometry.

129. The several absurdities and contradictions which flowed from this false principle might, one would think, have been esteemed so many demonstrations against it. But, by I know not what logic, it is held that proofs *a posteriori* are not to be admitted against propositions relating to infinity— as though it were not impossible even for an infinite mind to reconcile contradictions; or as if anything absurd and repugnant could have a necessary connexion with truth or flow from it. But, whoever considers the weakness of this pre-

---

[1] But what, on his own principles, and using his criterion, is meant by 'a line infinitely great'? Is the boundlessness of space more comprehensible in imagination than the infinite divisibility of any finite portion of it? The antinomies of Kant, in his 'Dialectic,' and the contradictions found by Hamilton and Mansel, are the issue of the attempt to construe quantitative infinity in terms of finite quantity and of the imagination.

tence will think it was contrived on purpose to humour the laziness of the mind which had rather acquiesce in an indolent scepticism than be at the pains to go through with a severe examination of those principles it has ever embraced for true.

130. Of late the speculations about Infinites have run so high, and grown to such strange notions, as have occasioned no small scruples and disputes among the geometers of the present age. Some there are of great note who, not content with holding that finite lines may be divided into an infinite number of parts, do yet farther maintain that each of those infinitesimals is itself subdivisible into an infinity of other parts or infinitesimals of a second order, and so on *ad infinitum*. These, I say, assert there are infinitesimals of infinitesimals of infinitesimals, &c., without ever coming to an end: so that according to them an inch does not barely contain an infinite number of parts, but an infinity of an infinity of an infinity *ad infinitum* of parts. Others there be who hold all orders of infinitesimals below the first to be nothing at all; thinking it with good reason absurd to imagine there is any positive quantity or part of extension which, though multiplied infinitely, can never equal the smallest given extension. And yet on the other hand it seems no less absurd to think the square, cube, or other power of a positive real root, should itself be nothing at all; which they who hold infinitesimals of the first order, denying all of the subsequent orders, are obliged to maintain.

131. Have we not therefore reason to conclude they are *both* in the wrong, and that there is in effect no such thing as parts infinitely small, or an infinite number of parts contained in any finite quantity? But you will say that if this doctrine obtains it will follow the very foundations of Geometry are destroyed, and those great men who have raised that science to so astonishing a height, have been all the while building a castle in the air. To this it may be replied

that whatever is useful in geometry, and promotes the benefit of human life, does still remain firm and unshaken on our principles—that science considered as practical will rather receive advantage than any prejudice from what has been said. But to set this in a due light, and shew how lines and figures may be measured, and their properties investigated, without supposing finite extension to be infinitely divisible, may be the proper business of another place [1]. For the rest, though it should follow that some of the more intricate and subtle parts of Speculative Mathematics may be pared off without any prejudice to truth, yet I do not see what damage will be thence derived to mankind. On the contrary, I think it were highly to be wished that men of great abilities and obstinate application would draw off their thoughts from those amusements, and employ them in the study of such things as lie nearer the concerns of life, or have a more direct influence on the manners.

132. If it be said that several theorems undoubtedly true are discovered by methods in which Infinitesimals are made use of, which could never have been if their existence included a contradiction in it—I answer that upon a thorough examination it will not be found that in any instance it is necessary to make use of or conceive infinitesimal parts of finite lines, or even quantities less than the *minimum sensibile;* nay, it will be evident this is never done, it being impossible.

133. By what we have hitherto said, it is plain that very numerous and important errors have taken their rise from those false Principles which were impugned in the foregoing parts of this treatise; and the opposites of those erroneous

[1] In Berkeley's *Analyst*, published more than twenty years after the *Principles,* the consequences which follow where Infinitesimals are accepted as fixed quantities are deduced. But are they quantities, as Berkeley's objections would imply, and do his contradictions disappear when they cease to be so regarded? Cf. Hume's *Treatise of Human Nature*, pt. II. sect. 1, 2, for his reasoning about the infinite divisibility of finite spaces and times.

tenets at the same time appear to be most fruitful Principles, from whence do flow innumerable consequences highly advantageous to true philosophy, as well as to religion. Particularly *Matter*, or the *absolute* existence of corporeal objects, hath been shewn to be that wherein the most avowed and pernicious enemies of all knowledge, whether human or divine, have ever placed their chief strength and confidence [1]. And surely if by distinguishing the *real* existence of unthinking things from their *being perceived*, and allowing them a subsistence of their own out of the minds of spirits, no one thing is explained in nature, but on the contrary a great many inexplicable difficulties arise; if the supposition of Matter is barely precarious, as not being grounded on so much as one single reason; if its consequences cannot endure the light of examination and free inquiry, but screen themselves under the dark and general pretence of Infinites being incomprehensible; if withal the removal of this Matter be not attended with the least evil consequence; if it be not even missed in the world, but everything as well, nay much easier, conceived without it; if, lastly, both Sceptics and Atheists are for ever silenced upon supposing only SPIRITS and IDEAS [2], and this scheme of things is perfectly agreeable both to Reason and Religion—methinks we may expect it should be admitted and firmly embraced, though it were

[1] A question by which modern thought is troubled is partly raised in these sections, in connexion with the infinite divisibility of finite extension, to wit, the possibility of a knowledge by man of the Infinite in Quantity. Is the term 'infinite' the sign of a meaningless abstraction, or does it correspond to something in our mental experience; and if so, what is that to which it corresponds? Is it rational intuition or mysterious belief? Is space or time infinite in the same way as we suppose God infinite? or does the infinite mean the rational relations which constitute experience? Do space and time, as infinite, transcend the category of quantity altogether?

[2] They are 'for ever silenced' if it has been *proved* that Moral Reason and Moral Government is supreme in the universe. But is that necessarily involved in the supposition that only *spirits* and *phenomena dependent on a percipient* can exist; and is this supposition the only one that effectually silences atheistic rejection of the supremacy of moral government?

proposed only as an *hypothesis*, and the existence of Matter had been allowed possible—which yet I think we have evidently demonstrated that it is not.

134. True it is that, in consequence of the foregoing Principles, several disputes and speculations which are esteemed no mean parts of learning, are rejected as useless. But, how great a prejudice soever against our notions this may give to those who have already been deeply engaged and made large advances in studies of that nature, yet by others we hope it will not be thought any just ground of dislike to the principles and tenets herein laid down—that they abridge the labour of study, and make human Sciences far more clear, compendious, and attainable than they were before.

135. Having despatched what we intended to say concerning the knowledge of IDEAS, the method we proposed leads us in the next place to treat of SPIRITS—with regard to which, perhaps, human knowledge is not so deficient as is vulgarly imagined[1]. The great reason that is assigned for our being thought ignorant of the nature of Spirits is—our not having an *idea* of it. But, surely it ought not to be looked on as a defect in a human understanding that it does not perceive the idea of spirit, if it is manifestly impossible there should be any such idea. And this if I mistake not has been demonstrated in section 27; to which I shall here add—that a spirit has been shewn to be the only substance or support wherein unthinking beings or ideas can exist; but that this *substance* which supports or perceives ideas should itself be an idea or like an idea is evidently absurd.

[1] In sections 101-34 Berkeley has mentioned improvements in the sciences of nature which might follow a general acceptance of his philosophical conception of matter. He proceeds, in sections 135-56, to trace the consequences of the conception in its application in studies which are concerned with the origin and destiny of men, and with the being and attributes of God. Sections 101-56 may be compared with Locke's *Essay*, b. IV. ch. 2-11, and with Kant's 'Dialectic,' b. II. ch. 1, 3.

136. It will perhaps be said that we want a *sense* (as some have imagined) proper to know substances withal, which, if we had, we might know our own soul as we do a triangle. To this I answer, that, in case we had a new sense bestowed upon us, we could only receive thereby some new sensations or ideas of sense. But I believe nobody will say that what he means by the terms *soul* and *substance* is only some particular sort of idea or sensation. We may therefore infer that, all things duly considered, it is not more reasonable to think our faculties defective, in that they do not furnish us with an *idea* of spirit or active thinking substance, than it would be if we should blame them for not being able to comprehend a *round square*.

137. From the opinion that spirits are to be known after the manner of an idea or sensation have risen many absurd and heterodox tenets, and much scepticism about the nature of the soul. It is even probable that this opinion may have produced a doubt in some whether they had any soul at all distinct from their body, since upon inquiry they could not find they had an idea of it. That an *idea*, which is inactive and the existence whereof consists in being perceived, should be the image or likeness of an agent subsisting by itself, seems to need no other refutation than barely attending to what is meant by those words. But perhaps you will say that though an idea cannot resemble a spirit in its thinking, acting, or subsisting by itself, yet it may in some other respects; and it is not necessary that an idea or image be in all respects like the original.

138. I answer, if it does not in those mentioned, it is impossible it should represent it in any other thing. Do but leave out the power of willing, thinking, and perceiving ideas, and there remains nothing else wherein the idea can be like a spirit. For, by the word *spirit* we mean only that which thinks, wills, and perceives; this, and this alone, constitutes the signification of that term. If therefore it is impossible

that any degree of those powers should be represented in an idea, it is evident there can be no idea of a spirit.

139. But it will be objected that, if there is no *idea* signified by the terms 'soul,' 'spirit,' and 'substance,' they are wholly insignificant, or have no meaning in them[1]. I answer, those words do mean or signify a real thing—which is neither an idea nor like an idea, but that which perceives ideas, and wills, and reasons about them. What I am myself—that which I denote by the term *I*—is the same with what is meant by *soul* or *spiritual substance*. But if I should say that *I* was nothing, or that *I* was an idea, nothing could be more evidently absurd than either of these propositions. If it be said that this is only quarrelling at a word, and that, since the *immediate* significations of other names are by common consent called *ideas*, no reason can be assigned why that which is signified by the name *spirit* or *soul* may not partake in the same appellation, I answer—All the unthinking objects of the mind agree in that they are entirely passive, and their existence consists only in being perceived; whereas a soul or spirit is an active being, whose existence consists, not in being perceived, but in perceiving ideas and thinking[2]. It is therefore necessary—in order to prevent equivocation and confounding natures perfectly disagreeing and unlike—that we distinguish between SPIRIT and IDEA. See sect. 27.

140. In a large sense indeed, we may be said to have an idea [or rather a notion[3]] of *spirit;* that is, we understand the meaning of the word, otherwise we could not affirm or deny

---

[1] 'Rational psychology,' says Kant, 'has its origin in a mere misunderstanding. The unity of self-consciousness is confused with intuition of the subject as an object, and the object thus supposed to be intuited is, moreover, substantiated. But this 'subject' is really nothing more than a unity in thought, in which no object is given, and to which therefore the category of substance, which presupposes an object, cannot be applied. Therefore the subject cannot be known as a substance.'

[2] If it consists in *actual* perception, or being conscious, one cannot be unconscious without ceasing to exist.

[3] Added in Second Edition of the *Principles*.

anything of it[1]. Moreover, as we conceive the ideas that are in the minds of other spirits by means of our own, which we suppose to be resemblances of them; so we know *other* spirits by means of *our own soul*—which in that sense is *the image or idea of them;* it having a like respect to other spirits that blueness or heat by me perceived has to those ideas perceived by another[2].

141. The Natural Immortality of the Soul is a necessary consequence of the foregoing doctrine. But before we attempt to prove this, it is fit that we explain the meaning of that tenet. It must not be supposed that they who assert the natural immortality of the soul are of opinion that it is absolutely incapable of annihilation even by the infinite power

---

[1] By spiritual substance Berkeley means 'what I denote by the personal pronoun I.' This cannot, he urges, be an *idea* or *phenomenon.* The knower cannot be also an object phenomenally known; yet, as I am presupposed in all my knowledge, I cannot be ignorant of *myself.* Hume afterwards applied Berkeley's own reasoning against abstract matter to this 'notion' of self, and argued that the knower as well as the known may be resolved into passing phenomena, whose union in imagination gives rise to the illusion of individuality. (*Treatise of Human Nature,* b. IV. sect. 6.)—Berkeley's answer to this is given by anticipation in his *Third Dialogue* (*Works,* vol. I. pp. 327-29), where he meets the objection that 'as there is no more *meaning* in spiritual substance than in material substance, the one is to be exploded as well as the other.' Kant (Dialec. II. 1) argues that our having the notion of self is indispensable to our having experience, but that it is impossible to settle whether we exist as substance or as accident.

[2] That is to say, we become aware of the existence of other human spirits, not as phenomena perceived, but by inference based partly on our consciousness of self, and partly on the *signs* of a similar self-conscious life in them presented in our perceptions of their corporeal actions. We can conceive *another conscious life,* while *unperceiving* and *unperceived matter* is at the most a meaningless negation.

Berkeley's account of the relations of free human spirits to the Supreme Spirit, and to the system of nature, is obscure. The question whether each human spirit is part of the Cosmos, its birth being an event in time, he does not touch;—nor yet our relation to the Universal Consciousness or God, of which, Pantheists say, we are the individuals —God being the universal form of which each of us is the phenomenal manifestation, and human individuality an illusion.—Is not the root of individuality to be found in the freedom of action through which man is able to destroy his true spiritual life by sin?

of the Creator who first gave it being, but only that it is not liable to be broken or dissolved by the ordinary laws of nature or motion. They indeed who hold the soul of man to be only a thin vital flame, or system of animal spirits, make it perishing and corruptible as the body; since there is nothing more easily dissipated than such a being, which it is naturally impossible should survive the ruin of the tabernacle wherein it is enclosed. And this notion has been greedily embraced and cherished by the worst part of mankind, as the most effectual antidote against all impressions of virtue and religion. But it has been made evident that *bodies*, of what frame or texture soever, are barely passive ideas in the *mind*—which is more distant and heterogeneous from them than light is from darkness. We have shewn that the soul is indivisible, incorporeal, unextended, and it is consequently incorruptible. Nothing can be plainer than that the motions, changes, decays, and dissolutions which we hourly see befall natural bodies (and which is what we mean by the *course of nature*) cannot possibly affect an active, simple, uncompounded substance: such a being therefore is indissoluble by the force of nature; that is to say—the soul of man is *naturally immortal*[1].

[1] This is Berkeley's application of his philosophy of perception to the awful ænigma of the grave—the continued existence or not of self-conscious life after the dissolution of our bodily organism in Death. From the necessary dependence of body on conscious spirit, and the independence of self-conscious spirit of the phenomena presented to our *five senses* (all which he assumes that he has already proved), he argues the conclusion of the *natural* immortality of man. There is therefore no absurdity in supposing our continued self-consciousness as *unbodied spirit*, without connexion between the dissolution of the body and extinction of consciousness; though, as far as power to do so goes, God may, at death, or afterwards, cause self-conscious life to cease. 'I see no difficulty,' he says elsewhere, 'in conceiving a change of state, such as is vulgarly called Death, as well without as with material substance. It is sufficient for that purpose that we allow sensible bodies; the existence of which I am so far from questioning (as philosophers are used to do) that I establish it, I think, upon evident principles. Now, it seems very easy to conceive the *soul* to exist in a separate state (i.e. diverted from those limits and laws of motion and perception with which she is embarrassed here), to exercise herself

142. After what has been said, it is, I suppose, plain that our souls are not to be known in the same manner as senseon new ideas, without the intervention of those tangible things we call bodies. It is even very possible to conceive how the soul may have ideas of colour without an eye, or of sounds without an ear.' (*Life of Berkeley*, p. 181.)

It was common among philosophers and theologians of the Cartesian period to defend faith in life after death by the indivisibility of mind, its independence of extended things, or its connexion with them merely in the way of occasional causation. Hence the then prevailing view of the connexion between our bodies and our selfconscious life as only temporary and instrumental. Thus Bishop Butler takes for granted that 'all presumption of death's being the destruction of living beings must go upon the supposition that they are compounded and so discerptible;' adding as he does that, since consciousness 'is a single and indivisible power, it should seem that the subject in which it resides must be so too.' And even if it should not be 'absolutely indiscerptible,' we have no way, he argues, of determining by experience 'what its bulk in space is; and till it can be shown that what I call *myself* is larger in bulk than the solid elementary particles of matter (atoms), which there is no ground to think any *natural* power can dissolve, there is no sort of reason to think death to be *our* dissolution.' Referring to our connexion with our bodies, he says that 'upon the supposition that the living being each man calls *himself* is a single being . . . *our organised bodies are no more ourselves, or part of ourselves, than any other matter around us.*' 'It is as easy to conceive,' he continues, 'that we may exist out of bodies as in them; that we might have animated bodies of any other organs, and senses wholly different from those now given us; and that we may hereafter animate these same or new bodies variously modified and organised, as to conceived how we can animate such bodies as our present; and the dissolution of all these several organised bodies, supposing ourselves to have successively animated them, would have no more conceivable tendency to destroy the living beings, ourselves, or deprive us of living faculties, than the dissolution of any foreign matter' (*Analogy*, pt. I. ch. 1).

This train of thought is more foreign to the present generation, when physical research insists that the organic unity of self-conscious life in dependence on the corporeal frame is proved by a sufficient induction of facts, whatever may be the abstract possibility of conceiving the conscious being to exist independently of the body. The only conscious life we have any experience of, it would be argued, is one that is known in organic union with the corporeal structure in correlation with which it developes. Speculations like those of Berkeley and Butler would be condemned as unverified hypotheses regarding abstractions.

One may still reply that in the *moral* experience of the organised unity I call *myself*, there is evidence that the organic change called Death is not the end of me. In one view the rising of the sun tomorrow, and the conscious life after death of any person who has not yet died, are both 'beyond experience.' In another definition of experience, neither is 'beyond' it, if the one is involved in the rational constitution of natural and the other in that of moral experience.

less, inactive objects, or by way of *idea*. *Spirits* and *ideas* are things so wholly different, that when we say 'they exist,' 'they are known,' or the like, these words must not be thought to signify anything common to both natures. There is nothing alike or common in them; and to expect that by any multiplication or enlargement of our faculties we may be enabled to know a spirit as we do a triangle, seems as absurd as if we should hope to see a sound. This is inculcated because I imagine it may be of moment towards clearing several important questions, and preventing some very dangerous errors concerning the Nature of the Soul. [[1] We may not, I think, strictly be said to have an *idea* of an active being, or of an action, although we may be said to have a *notion* of them. I have some knowledge or notion of my mind, and its acts about ideas—inasmuch as I know or understand what is meant by these words. What I know, that I have some notion of. I will not say that the terms *idea* and *notion* may not be used convertibly, if the world will have it so; but yet it conduceth to clearness and propriety that we distinguish things very different by different names. It is also to be remarked that, all *relations* including an act of the mind, we cannot so properly be said to have an idea, but rather a notion of the relations and habitudes between things [2]. But if, in the modern way, the word *idea* is extended to *spirits*, and *relations* and *acts*, this is, after all, an affair of verbal concern [3].]

---

[1] What follows to the end of this section was introduced in the second edition of the *Principles*, like the other passages in which *notion* is distinguished from *idea*.

[2] There is perhaps a faint anticipation of Kantism in this. But a transcendental analysis of rational relations presupposed in real knowledge is foreign to the method and spirit of Berkeley.

[3] Berkeley does not after all so explain in what way spiritual substance is 'known' as to prove that we cannot in the same way have a 'notion' of substance in sensible phenomena. What he says goes rather to establish that we find in the fact called *self* that to which there is nothing analogous in the phenomena of which we are conscious in any of our five senses. He seems to mean that our continuous individual

143. It will not be amiss to add, that the doctrine of *abstract* ideas has had no small share in rendering those sciences intricate and obscure which are particularly conversant about spiritual things. Men have imagined they could frame abstract notions of the *powers* and *acts* of the mind, and consider them prescinded as well from the mind or spirit itself, as from their respective objects and effects. Hence a great number of dark and ambiguous terms, presumed to stand for abstract notions, have been introduced into metaphysics and morality, and from these have grown infinite distractions and disputes among the learned [1].

144. But, nothing seems more to have contributed towards engaging men in controversies and mistakes with regard to the nature and operations of the mind, than the being used to speak of those things in terms borrowed from sensible ideas. For example, the will is termed the *motion* of the soul: this infuses a belief that the mind of man is as a ball in motion, impelled and determined by the objects of sense, as necessarily as that is by the stroke of a racket. Hence arise endless scruples and errors of dangerous consequence in morality. All which, I doubt not, may be cleared, and truth appear plain, uniform, and consistent, could but philosophers be prevailed on to depart from some received prejudices and modes of speech, and retire into themselves, and attentively consider their own meaning.

personality is an irreducible fact, *sui generis*, and untranslatable into the language of mere phenomena.

[1] In this section Berkeley refers to the so-called 'powers' or 'faculties' in mind, by which some psychologists account for experience. These 'powers' *per se* he regards as substantiated abstractions, which no more *explain* our cognitions than the supposition of 'forces' inherent in matter ultimately explains the phenomena of external nature. Shall we then—abandoning mental 'powers' or 'faculties'—account for our experience not by them but by *laws of association* among sensations and ideas, determined perhaps ultimately by physical evolution, as with Herbert Spencer; or shall we explain it by *categories of thought*, involved as necessary elements in experience, as with Kantists? Berkeley does not touch this question.—Compare sect. 1, 2; also *Siris*, sect. 303.

145. From what has been said, it is plain that we cannot know the existence of *other spirits* otherwise than by their operations, or the ideas by them excited in us. I perceive several motions, changes, and combinations of ideas, that inform me there are certain particular agents, like myself, which accompany them and concur in their production. Hence, the knowledge I have of other spirits is not immediate, as is the knowledge of my ideas; but depending on the intervention of ideas, by me referred to agents or spirits distinct from myself, as effects or concomitant signs [1].

146. But, though there be some things which convince us *human* agents are concerned in producing them, yet it is evident to every one that those things which are called the Works of Nature—that is, the far greater part of the ideas or sensations perceived by us—are not produced by, or dependent on, the wills of men. There is therefore some other Spirit that causes them; since it is repugnant that they should subsist by themselves. See sect. 29. But, if we attentively consider the constant regularity, order, and concatenation of natural things, the surprising magnificence, beauty and perfection of the larger, and the exquisite contrivance of the smaller parts of the creation, together with the exact harmony and correspondence of the whole; but above all the

[1] This is one of the most interesting sections in the *Principles*. How can one individual mind communicate with another individual mind? It has been alleged that, on Berkeley's conception of what the material world is, I have no reason to believe in the existence of other men; —that, at most, I can discover only my own existence and that of God. I find that *I* intend or will—all in nature that my will fails to determine being God's doing, *my* volitions and *His* determine all changes.— Berkeley, however, might argue that, under his view of nature, the concurrence of divine or perfectly reasonable Will is a security that we are not deceived when significant changes in our sensations *suggest* the intentions and meanings of other conscious agents like ourselves as their cause. (Is this, we may ask, mere 'suggestion' or is it 'inference'? See *Vindication of Theory of Vision*, §§ 11, 12, 42.) The difficulty still is to understand *how* the phenomena of which I am conscious when I use my senses—if they are numerically different from those of which any other mind is conscious—can be media of communication with another mind. In sect. 147 he says vaguely that God 'maintains that intercourse between spirits whereby they are able to perceive the existence of each other.'

never-enough-admired laws of pain and pleasure, and the instincts or natural inclinations, appetites, and passions of animals—I say.if we consider all these things, and at the same time attend to the meaning and import of the attributes One, Eternal, Infinitely Wise, Good, and Perfect, we shall clearly perceive that they belong to the aforesaid Spirit, 'who works all in all,' and 'by whom all things consist.'

147. Hence, it is evident that God is known as certainly and immediately as any other mind or spirit whatsoever distinct from ourselves. We may even assert that the existence of God is far more evidently perceived than the existence of men; because the effects of Nature are infinitely more numerous and considerable than those ascribed to human agents. There is not any one mark that denotes a man, or effect produced by him, which does not more strongly evince the being of that Spirit who is the Author of Nature[1]. For, it is evident that in affecting other persons the will of man has no other object than barely the motion of the limbs of his body; but that such a motion should be attended by, or excite any idea in the mind of another, depends wholly on the will of the Creator. He alone it is who, 'upholding all things by the word of His power,' maintains that intercourse between spirits whereby they are able to perceive the existence of each other. And yet this pure and clear light which enlightens every one is itself invisible.

148. It seems to be a general pretence of the unthinking herd that they cannot *see* God. Could we but see Him, say they, as we see a man, we should believe that He is, and believing obey His commands. But alas, we need only open our eyes to see the Sovereign Lord of all things, with a more full and clear view than we do any one of our fellow-creatures. Not that I imagine we see God (as some will have it) by a direct and immediate view; or see corporeal things, not by

---

[1] The reasoning in this and the two next sections is expanded in the Dialogue on *Divine Visual Language*.

themselves, but by seeing that which represents them in the essence of God, which doctrine is, I must confess, to me incomprehensible[1]. But I shall explain my meaning:—A human spirit or person is not perceived by sense, as not being an idea; when therefore we see the colour, size, figure, and motions of a man, we perceive only certain sensations or ideas excited in our own minds; and these being exhibited to our view in sundry distinct collections, serve to mark out unto us the existence of finite and created spirits like ourselves. Hence it is plain we do not *see* a man—if by *man* is meant that which lives, moves, perceives, and thinks as we do—but only such a certain collection of ideas as directs us to think there is a distinct principle of thought and motion, like to ourselves, accompanying and represented by it. And after the same manner we *see* God; all the difference is that, whereas some one finite and narrow assemblage of ideas denotes a particular human mind, whithersoever we direct our view, we do at all times and in all places perceive manifest tokens of the Divinity—everything we see, hear, feel, or anywise perceive by Sense, being a *sign* or *effect* of the power of God; as is our perception of those very motions which are produced by men[2].

[1] He refers to Malebranche, whose doctrine—that we perceive the material world in and through God—was an attempt to reconcile the Cartesian duality of finite substances—self-conscious and unextended, extended and unconscious—with the unity of our perception. Berkeley does not, like Malebranche, say that we perceive things by perceiving God, but only that phenomena are presented to us in our perceptions, according to what we call 'natural order,' but which is really the immediate issue and expression of the Will and Ideas of God. The phenomena present in our senses, which are wholly passive, cannot, he argues, be like the divine substance, which is wholly active. See Berkeley's *Works*, vol. I. p. 308.

[2] The *eternal* existence of God and the *present* existence of *other* human spirits are thus both reached through phenomena of sense, according to Berkeley, and at first only in the way of 'suggestion.' The *Dialogue on Visual Language* is an expansion of this section. Neither here nor there does he refer to the evidence of God in conscience, as Butler does in his supremacy of conscience, which is practically the supremacy of God, or as Kant does in his Practical Reason. Berkeley's ethical theory is inadequate.

149. It is therefore plain that nothing can be more evident to any one that is capable of the least reflection than the existence of God, or a Spirit who is intimately present to our minds—producing in them all that variety of ideas or sensations which continually affect us, on whom we have an absolute and entire dependence, in short 'in whom we live, and move, and have our being.' That the discovery of this great truth, which lies so near and obvious to the mind, should be attained to by the reason of so very few, is a sad instance of the stupidity and inattention of men, who, though they are surrounded with such clear manifestations of the Deity, are yet so little affected by them that they seem, as it were, blinded with excess of light.

150. But you will say, Hath Nature no share in the production of natural things, and must they be all ascribed to the immediate and sole operation of God? I answer, if by *Nature* is meant only the *visible series* of effects or sensations imprinted on our minds, according to certain fixed and general laws, then it is plain that Nature, taken in this sense, cannot produce anything at all. But, if by *Nature* is meant some being distinct from God, as well as from the laws of nature, and things perceived by sense, I must confess that word is to me an empty sound without any intelligible meaning annexed to it. Nature, in this acceptation, is a vain chimera, introduced by those heathens who had not just notions of the omnipresence and infinite perfection of God[1]. But, it is more unaccountable that it should be received among Christians, professing belief in the Holy Scriptures, which constantly ascribe those effects to the immediate hand of God that heathen philosophers are wont to impute to Nature.

[1] Thus in Aristotle's conception of Nature (φύσις) as something intermediate between Necessity and Chance—as the efficient cause of the Cosmos, of which God is the final cause. So too in the impersonal 'force' of modern scientific assumption. Are conservation and transformation of force more than names for a supposed *law* of changes in the universe, under which every perishing phenomenon has its equivalent in a new one?

'The Lord He causeth the vapours to ascend; He maketh lightnings with rain; He bringeth forth the wind out of His treasures.' Jerem. x. 13. 'He turneth the shadow of death into the morning, and maketh the day dark with night.' Amos v. 8. 'He visiteth the earth, and maketh it soft with showers : He blesseth the springing thereof, and crowneth the year with His goodness ; so that the pastures are clothed with flocks, and the valleys are covered over with corn.' See Psal. lxv. But, notwithstanding that this is the constant language of Scripture, yet we have I know not what aversion from believing that God concerns Himself so nearly in our affairs. Fain would we suppose Him at a great distance off, and substitute some *blind unthinking* deputy in His stead, though (if we may believe Saint Paul) 'He be not far from every one of us.'

151. It will, I doubt not, be objected that the slow, gradual, and roundabout methods observed in the production of natural things do not seem to have for their cause the *immediate* hand of an Almighty Agent. Besides, monsters, untimely births, fruits blasted in the blossom, rains falling in desert places, miseries incident to human life, and the like, are so many arguments that the whole frame of nature is not immediately actuated and superintended by a Spirit of infinite wisdom and goodness[1]. But the answer to this objection is in a good measure plain from sect. 62 ; it being visible that the aforesaid Methods of Nature are absolutely necessary, in order to working by the most simple and general rules, and after a steady and consistent manner ; which argues both the wisdom and goodness of God. Such is the artificial contrivance of this mighty Machine of Nature that, whilst its motions and various phenomena strike on our senses, the hand which actuates the whole is itself unperceivable to men

[1] So J. S. Mill, in his *Autobiography* and posthumous *Essays*, in which he conjectures a Manichæist solution of the difficulties of our moral experience, instead of referring them to the immoral agency of finite spirits. See note on p. 143, on Manichæism.

of flesh and blood. 'Verily' (saith the prophet) 'thou art a God that hidest thyself[1].' Isaiah xlv. 15. But, though the Lord conceal Himself from the eyes of the sensual and lazy, who will not be at the least expense of thought, yet to an unbiassed and attentive mind nothing can be more plainly legible than the intimate presence of an All-wise Spirit, who fashions, regulates, and sustains the whole system of beings. It is clear, from what we have elsewhere observed, that the operating according to general and stated laws is so necessary for our guidance in the affairs of Life, and letting us into the secret of Nature, that without it all reach and compass of thought, all human sagacity and design, could serve to no manner of purpose; it were even impossible there should be any such faculties or powers in the mind. See sect. 31. Which one consideration abundantly outbalances whatever particular inconveniences may thence arise[2].

152. But we should further consider that the very blemishes and defects of Nature are not without their use, in that they make an agreeable sort of variety, and augment the beauty of the rest of the creation, as shades in a picture serve to set off the brighter and more enlightened parts. We would likewise do well to examine whether our taxing the waste of seeds and embryos, and accidental destruction of plants and animals, before they come to full maturity, as an imprudence in the Author of Nature, be not the effect of prejudice contracted by our familiarity with impotent and saving mortals. In man indeed a thrifty management of those things which he cannot procure without much pains and industry may be esteemed wisdom. But, we must not imagine that the inexplicably fine machine of an animal or vegetable costs the great Creator any more pains or trouble in its production

[1] So Pascal in the *Pensées*, on God as a God 'that hideth himself.'
[2] We should be virtually irrational if we lived in a physical Chaos instead of the Cosmos; for sense-phenomena would then have no meaning on which our cognitive power might be exercised. The objective Cosmos is the correlate of our personal reason.

than a pebble does; nothing being more evident than that an Omnipotent Spirit can indifferently produce everything by a mere *fiat* or act of his will [1]. Hence, it is plain that the splendid profusion of natural things should not be interpreted weakness or prodigality in the agent who produces them, but rather be looked on as an argument of the riches of his power.

153. As for the mixture of pain or uneasiness which is in the world, pursuant to the general Laws of Nature, and the actions of finite, imperfect spirits, this, in the state we are in at present, is indispensably necessary to our well-being. But our prospects are too narrow. We take, for instance, the idea of some one particular pain into our thoughts, and account *it* evil; whereas, if we enlarge our view, so as to comprehend the various ends, connexions, and dependencies of things, on what occasions and in what proportions we are affected with pain and pleasure, the nature of human freedom, and the design with which we are put into the world; we shall be forced to acknowledge that those particular things which, considered in themselves, appear to be evil, have the nature of good, when considered as linked with the whole system of beings [2].

154. From what has been said, it will be manifest to any considering person, that it is merely for want of attention and comprehensiveness of mind that there are any favourers

---

[1] By a power that, as Berkeley views it, is not *immanent* but independent of nature. He supposes nature to be freely sustained, not necessarily evolved.

[2] So afterwards Butler. '*Our whole nature* leads us to ascribe moral perfection to God, and to deny all imperfection of Him. And *this* must for ever be a practical proof of His moral character. From thence we conclude that virtue must be the happiness and vice the misery of every creature; and that regularity, order, and right cannot but prevail finally, in a universe under His government. *But we are in no sort judges what are the necessary means of accomplishing this end.*' (*Analogy*, Introduction.) See also his Sermon on the 'Ignorance of Man.'—In the *Theodicée* of Leibnitz, published in the same year as the *Principles* of Berkeley, the difficulties of this and next section are discussed.

of Atheism or the Manichæan Heresy to be found [1]. Little and unreflecting souls may indeed burlesque the works of Providence—the beauty and order whereof they have not capacity, or will not be at the pains, to comprehend; but those who are masters of any justness and extent of thought, and are withal used to reflect, can never sufficiently admire the divine traces of Wisdom and Goodness that shine throughout the Economy of Nature. But what truth is there which glares so strongly on the mind that, by an aversion of thought—a wilful shutting of the eyes—we may not escape seeing it, at least with a full and direct view? Is it therefore to be wondered at, if the generality of men, who are ever intent on business or pleasure, and little used to fix or open the eye of their mind, should not have all that conviction and evidence of the Being of God which might be expected in reasonable creatures?

155. We should rather wonder that men can be found so stupid as to neglect, than that neglecting they should be unconvinced of such an evident and momentous truth. And yet it is to be feared that too many of parts and leisure, who live in Christian countries, are, merely through a supine and dreadful negligence, sunk into Atheism [2]. They cannot say

[1] Manichæism, the doctrine of Manes, a Persian philosopher of the third century, who appears to have held the eternal Duality of the Supreme Power to be the explanation of the mingled good and evil that is in the universe. The existence of free agents, who, as free, must be able to act immorally as well as virtuously, might seem to be a modified Manichæism;—especially if accompanied by the supposition that the universe into which finite agents can thus introduce evil is incapable of ultimate restoration, and that unrestored it is absolutely a failure, which last it is doubtful whether the Manichæans themselves meant to say. Is the existence of creators of actions which may be evil as well as good the existence of potential evil? A sense of the importance of responsible human agents in the government (physical and moral) of the universe has, through Christianity, grown in medieval and modern times, as compared with the indifferent feeling towards *persons* of Greek and other ancient philosophers.

[2] Our ultimate ignorance of the origin, constitution, and destiny of the universe is the assumption at the root of objections at the present day to the recognition of Perfect Mind as its ultimate explanation. Hume proceeds partly on this, when he treats the universe as a 'singular

there is not a God, but neither are they convinced that there is. Since it is downright impossible that a soul pierced and enlightened with a thorough sense of the omnipresence, holiness, and justice of that Almighty Spirit should persist in a remorseless violation of His laws. We ought, therefore, earnestly to meditate and dwell on those important points; that so we may attain conviction without all scruple 'that the eyes of the Lord are in every place beholding the evil and the good; that He is with us and keepeth us in all places whither we go, and giveth us bread to eat and raiment to put on;' that He is present and conscious to our innermost thoughts; in fine, that we have a most absolute and immediate dependence on Him. A clear view of which great truths cannot choose but fill our hearts with an awful circumspection and holy fear, which is the strongest incentive to VIRTUE and the best guard against VICE.

156. For, after all, what deserves the first place in our studies is the consideration of GOD and our DUTY; which to promote, as it was the main drift and design of my labours, so shall I esteem them altogether useless and ineffectual if, by what I have said, I cannot inspire my readers with a pious Sense of the Presence of God; and, having shewn the falseness or vanity of those barren speculations which make the chief employment of learned men, the better dispose them to reverence and embrace the salutary truths of the Gospel, which to know and to practise is the highest perfection of human nature.

effect,' which can be interpreted only so far as this present life of sense is concerned (and even that in a merely probable interpretation), but which at last dissolves in 'a riddle, an ænigma, an inexplicable mystery.' Does not the true philosophical analysis show that our knowledge of the universe cannot be even so much as this without being more than this?

II.

Visual Phenomena significant of Mind.

SELECTIONS

FROM

BERKELEY'S WRITINGS

ON

VISUAL SUGGESTION;

ALSO ON THE

THEISTIC INTERPRETATION

OF THE

VISUAL SIGNS.

It was the great object of Berkeley's *Theory of Vision* to shew the effect of constant and early *habits*, and it is this which gives to that work its chief value when considered in connexion with the philosophy of the human mind.—Stewart's *Dissertation*.

In Him we live, and move, and have our being.—*Acts* xvii. 28.

PREFATORY NOTE.

THE *Essay towards a New Theory of Vision* was published in 1709, a year before the *Principles*. It is the first in chronological order of those writings of Berkeley which, ostensibly concerned with Visual Perception, treat by implication of the nature of inductive science and our belief in the Order of Nature, in relation to our theistic belief. Twenty-three years after the publication of the juvenile *Essay on Vision*—in which the student is introduced to the psychology of the Five Senses, especially of seeing and touching—certain theological inferences involved in the *Essay* were followed out in the Fourth Dialogue of *Alciphron*, on 'Visual Language.' And in the following year he gave his last word on these subjects in his *Theory of Visual Language Vindicated and Explained*. The selections which follow are taken from these three works.

According to Berkeley's *Principles of Knowledge*, the supposition that body exists unperceived is unintelligible: the existence of a material world divorced from perception involves the absurdity of conscious experience existing without any one to be conscious of it.

Yet all bodies exist 'without mind,' if what is meant by 'without' is, that they exist 'in space.' And that they exist in space, or consist of *partes extra partes*, cannot be doubted. Do we not *see* them so existing—in seeing that they are extended; and also in seeing that each extra-organic body is *placed* relatively to other extra-organic bodies, and to the living body of the percipient? Now what, Berkeley asks, is the deepest and truest meaning of that 'outness' or 'externality' which consists in occupying space; and is the space which bodies occupy originally seen? This question leads us into the heart of the philosophy of Perception.

The *Essay on Vision* is part of Berkeley's answer. In this *Essay* he holds in reserve the more sweeping doctrine of the *Principles*—that the material world cannot in *any* of its qualities exist actually or intelligibly without being perceived: he is satisfied with the more limited thesis, that its *visible* extension is dependent on a percipient. The claims of what is perceived by touch to independent externality are meanwhile reserved. He argues that, because the relations of space are unintelligible apart from the experience we have when we touch things, and when we move our bodies, therefore space cannot be perceived originally by sight. The *Essay* is concerned with the origin—whether in sight, or touch, or otherwise—of our perception of Extension, as well as with the suggestions and judgments which this perception involves when it is developed. It may be used for mental exercises in the part of psychology that relates to the Five Senses and the growth of Perception.

The reader has to observe that what Berkeley has written —nominally about Vision—in the *Essay*, the *Dialogue*, and the *Vindication*, advances from the qualities of the things of sense, through the theory of their natural laws as inductively interpreted in the physical sciences, to our faith in the Supreme Mind, here alleged as the ultimate or philosophical explanation of all the changes of the sensible world. Our power of seeing things in 'ambient space' is thus explained to be virtually a power of seeing sensible signs of the constant regulative activity of God, and one is thus led from the lower to the higher faculties of Intellect.

The *Essay on Vision* was the first elaborate attempt by any philosopher to shew that our ordinary visual 'perceptions' of extended things, existing outside of our bodies, are not our *original* visual perceptions; that, on the contrary, they are expectations of perceptions of touch, which have, by habit and 'suggestion,' become connected with what we originally see. Berkeley traces the early growth of our knowledge of space, in its three dimensions of length, breadth, and thickness, out of our habit of associating the phenomena of colour and organic sensations in the eye, with phenomena of muscular resistance and locomotion which have previously accompanied them. The former in process of time do duty for the latter, so that by habit we can be 'admonished by what we see of what sensations of touch will affect us, at such and such distances of time, in consequence of such and such actions.' Our educated or acquired power of Visual Perception is thus explained as the issue of Habit and Suggestion.

Locke had said that 'men perceive by sight distance between bodies, and between parts of the same body,' and that it was 'as unnecessary to prove this as to prove that we see colours themselves.' He had added that our idea of Space was derived from sight and touch.

Berkeley started with the permitted assumption that Colour and Colour only is the proper and immediate object of sight. Without denying that the colour we see is in a sort extended, he analysed this coloured extension, in order to show that it is different in kind from the phenomenon of resistant extension, on which our knowledge of real 'outness' is based by him. He tries to shew that when one says that a thing is 'at a distance,' what is meant is that he *foresees* that, in order to touch the thing, he must pass through sensations of movement, more or less numerous according to the length of the distance from him at which the thing is placed. Seeing is thus foreseeing. If people had never experienced locomotive sensations, they could not, he argues, understand what the word Space means; for it means *room to move in*, a notion we could not have had without some experience of movement. The so-called 'sight' of distance is therefore the acquired power of interpreting visual phenomena that are found by experience to signify that we have to pass through so much locomotive experience before we can touch the distant object. Our knowledge of what the visual appearances signify, he further argues, is not instinctive; nor is it connected with what we see by an abstract necessity of reason, so that it can be demonstrated *a priori*: it is the gradual issue of the habit of connecting in thought what has previously coexisted regularly in sense; in the same way as words by habit suggest their established meanings.

This is the answer given by Berkeley to the question, How it comes to pass that we apprehend, by what we see, what is not originally seen; and what neither resembles, nor causes, nor is caused by, nor has any necessary connexion with what is originally seen? This answer implies, however, that what we see is connected with its tactual meaning, *objectively*, or by natural law; not merely *subjectively*, or by the tendency to associate in imagination ideas that have by accident often been together in our minds. The objective ground and meaning of Law in Nature, and not merely the 'laws of association' in the individual mind, is (almost unconsciously on the part of Berkeley) thus proposed for reflection. Natural law is resolved into divinely established association among sense-phenomena; and *this* association is said to be 'arbitrary' because God might have connected *any* meaning with the significant phenomena, thus making the laws of nature different from what they actually are. This *arbitrariness* is what Berkeley intends in his metaphor of 'Visual Language.' But one difference between the spoken or written words of men and the visible words daily addressed to us by God in the language of the senses is, that the connexion between words and their meanings is due to human convention, whereas the connexion between what we see and the muscular and locomotive experience which we expect is grounded on the rational will of God. As he puts it, 'visible ideas are the language whereby the Governing Spirit, on whom we depend, informs us what tangible ideas He is about to imprint upon us, in case we excite this or that motion in our own bodies.' When applied to all the phenomena presented in the five senses, and not merely to those of sight, this means that Order in Nature is contingent on Rational Will—that the physical government of external things is subordinate to the moral government of persons—and that our knowledge of the natural laws of the material world is incapable of ever becoming demonstrable *a priori*.

The early *Essay on Vision*, which only opens this vista of speculation, consists of a series of psychical analyses, meant to bring out the antithesis between coloured or visible extension and resistant or tangible extension. These analyses all lead up to Divine Will as being the objective basis of the 'suggestions' through which our original sense of sight becomes our visual perception of things existing under space relations. This implies that Space in the abstract is a meaningless word, and that all actual spaces can be resolved into significance in the phenomena presented to sight.

The conclusions argued for in the *Essay* may be conveniently presented as follows:—

I. (Sect. 2-51). *Distance*, meaning by that depth or thickness of space and things in space, as distinguished from plane superficial extension, is originally invisible: it is 'suggested' by association between tactual phenomena and visual phenomena, which are the established signs of what is thus suggested.

II. (Sect. 52-87). *Magnitude*, or size of sensible things, is necessarily invisible: what we see is only a larger or smaller number of coloured points (*minima visibilia*): our supposed power of seeing magnitude is a gradually acquired power of 'suggesting' the tactual meaning of colours and of organic sensations which we experience in seeing.

III. (Sect. 88–120). The *Situations* of sensible things are necessarily invisible: all that we can see is variety in colours: our supposed power of seeing places is really a power acquired by 'suggestion' of interpreting visible and organic signs of locality.

IV. (Sect. 121–146). There is no phenomenon in sense common to sight and touch: space or extension, which has the strongest claim to be both visible and tangible, and which is nominally both seen and touched, is not merely numerically different but different in kind in these two senses: and the supposition of an extension that is neither seen nor touched involves the absurdity of an 'abstract' idea.

V. (Sect. 147–148). The ultimate explanation of the established connexion between visible and tangible phenomena is found in the fact that the visual are, through laws in nature which are really laws of God, the signs to us of tactual phenomena, and may therefore be said to form a Divine Language, significant of the relations of things as extended.

VI. (Sect. 149–160). What is studied in Geometry is the resistant extension of touch, not the coloured extension of sight.

Berkeley's account of how we learn to see the places of things implies that if a person born blind was enabled to see, he could at first have no knowledge of outness, sizes, or situations by his eyes; that the sun and stars, with all else, near or remote, must seem to be 'in his mind.' This is a conclusion which might be tested by experiments on individuals as well as by psychological analysis. Appropriate tests would be—(*a*) cases of persons relieved from born-blindness; (*b*) investigation of the conception of space possessed by those not so relieved; (*c*) experiments on persons able to see, but who had no sense of contact or of movement in their bodily organs (if such could be found); (*d*) the facts of sight in human infants; (*e*) in the lower animals. Berkeley contributes no original observations gathered on any of these fields.

The *Essay* and the other writings on Visual Language which follow may be used by the student as aids to a psychological analysis ascending from the lower to the higher faculties of knowledge:—the Five Senses and their original Perceptions; the development of perceptions through Suggestion; the meaning of Law in Nature, with the ground of our expectation of its constancy; the relation between the natural order of the phenomena of Sense and free or supernatural agency; and the ground of our belief in God in whom 'we live and move and have our being.'

A. C. F.

AN ESSAY

TOWARDS

A NEW THEORY OF VISION.

1. My *design* is to shew the manner wherein we perceive by Sight the Distance, Magnitude, and Situation of objects; also to consider the difference there is betwixt the ideas of Sight and Touch, and whether there be any idea common to both senses [1].

2. It is, I think, agreed by all that Distance of itself, and immediately, cannot be seen. For, distance being a line directed endwise to the eye, it projects only one point in the fund of the eye—which point remains invariably the same, whether the distance be longer or shorter [2].

---

[1] The design of this *Essay* is, to compare the phenomena presented in Sight and in Touch, and to shew how we learn to see the primary or mathematical qualities of things. But we are led to consider the office of all the Five Senses in the formation of knowledge, in the course of this analysis of Sight, 'the most perfect and delightful' of them all.

[2] Sect. 2-51 explain how we learn to 'see' Distance, or an interval between two visible points. (Cf. *Vindication*, sect. 62-69.) Sect. 2 takes for granted, but without distinct proof, that distance is necessarily invisible. It must be noted that the 'distance' of which this can be assumed is space in its third|dimension—depth or thickness; not space merely as plane superficial extension. In relation to the distance which Berkeley says cannot be seen,—that which is in the line of sight, the percipient is at the end of a straight line, the interval between the two points of which must, it is argued, be invisible, because only one of them can be seen. When we see superficial distance, on the other hand, we are at the side, and not at the end of the line—at a point where it forms a larger or smaller angle with the eye; so that this sort of distance is called *lateral, transverse,* or *angular.* Any

3. I find it also acknowledged that the estimate we make of the distance of objects *considerably remote* is rather an act of judgment[1] grounded on experience than of sense. For example, when I perceive a great number of intermediate objects, such as houses, fields, rivers, and the like, which I have experienced to take up a considerable space, I thence form a judgment or conclusion, that the object I see beyond them is at a great distance. Again, when an object appears faint and small which at a near distance I have experienced to make a vigorous and large appearance, I instantly conclude it to be far off.—And this, it is evident, is the result of experience; without which, from the faintness and littleness, I should not have inferred anything concerning the distance of objects[2].

4. But, when an object is placed at so near a distance as that the interval between the eyes bears any sensible proportion to it, the opinion of speculative men is, that the two optic axes (the fancy that we see only with one eye at once

distance that is strictly in the line of sight must, in order to become visible, be as it were transformed into lateral distance—from a relation in the third dimension of space into plane superficial extension. But it has then ceased to be the distance or outness here alleged to be invisible.

Some of Berkeley's critics have referred to sect. 2 as if it expressed his famous 'theory of vision,' and his 'sole argument in support of it.' It is merely a statement of one of several assumptions on which the theory rests. He does not here say whether the 'point in the fund of the eye' is itself visible: in the *Vindication* (sect. 50) he denies that, properly speaking, it can be seen, 'being tangible, and apprehended only by imagination.'

[1] See the account of what Locke calls *judgment* (i. e. presumption of probability) in his *Essay*, b. IV. ch. 14, 15, 16. Like Berkeley here, he opposes it to *knowledge* strictly so called.

[2] What does Berkeley here and in what follows intend by a '*necessary* connexion'? Is it too a factitious, a *posteriori* necessity, generated, as Hume, Mill, or Herbert Spencer might say, by the habits of the individual, or of the race? Or is it a transcendental necessity, due to the rational constitution of mind as mind? That it is meant to be more than the former seems implied in the subsequent analysis of our beliefs in laws of nature into mere suggestions of our habit. Necessary inference he here grants seemingly to mathematics, although the outcome of his *Essay* tends to reduce mathematical necessity itself to the creative will of God.

being exploded), concurring at the object, do there make an angle, by means of which, according as it is greater or lesser, the object is perceived to be nearer or farther off.

5. Betwixt which and the foregoing manner of estimating distance there is this remarkable difference;—that, whereas there was no apparent *necessary connexion*[1] between small distance and a large and strong appearance, or between great distance and a little and faint appearance, there appears a very necessary connexion between an obtuse angle and near distance, and an acute angle and farther distance. It does not in the least depend upon experience, but may be evidently known by any one before he had experienced it, that the nearer the concurrence of the optic axes the greater the angle, and the remoter their concurrence is the lesser will be the angle comprehended by them[2].

6. There is another way, mentioned by optic writers, whereby they will have us judge of those distances in respect of which the breadth of the pupil hath any sensible bigness. And that is the greater or lesser divergency of the rays, which, issuing from the visible point, do fall on the pupil—that point being judged nearest which is seen by most diverging rays, and that remoter which is seen by less diverging rays; and so on, the apparent distance still

---

[1] What artists call aerial and linear perspectives are here taken as acknowledged signs of 'considerably remote' distances. But the main question is, the manner in which we learn to see *near* distances outwards. In Berkeley's day even, it was 'agreed by all' that 'the remoter distances' outwards are 'suggested' by 'arbitrary signs;' near distances were supposed to be inferred from (not suggested by) 'necessary connexions' with lines and angles. This last supposition Berkeley proceeds to refute in the following sections.

[2] Here again, what *sort* of 'necessity' does he intend in the 'connexion' (sect. 5, 7) between angles and distances, and between divergency of rays and degrees of distance? The varieties in the possible meaning of the ambiguous term 'necessity' should be here distinguished by the student. Is there ground for *ultimately* distinguishing the necessity in virtue of which *this* is the cause of *that* from the necessity for *a* cause of *every* change; also for distinguishing mathematical from metaphysical necessity, and both from the intellectual obligation to avoid a contradiction in terms.

increasing, as the divergency of the rays decreases, till at length it becomes infinite when the rays that fall on the pupil are to sense parallel. And after this manner it is said we perceive distance when we look only with one eye.

7. In this case also it is plain we are not beholden to experience: it being a certain, necessary truth that, the nearer the direct rays falling on the eye approach to a parallelism, the farther off is the point of their intersection, or the visible point from whence they flow.

8. Now, though the accounts here given of perceiving near distance by sight are received for true, and accordingly made use of in determining the apparent places of objects, they do nevertheless seem to me very unsatisfactory, and that for these following reasons :—

9. *First*, It is evident that, when the mind perceives any idea, not immediately and of itself, it must be by the means of some other idea. Thus, for instance, the passions which are in the mind of another are of themselves to me invisible. I may nevertheless perceive them by sight, though not immediately, yet by means of the colours they produce in the countenance. We often see shame or fear in the looks of a man, by perceiving the changes of his countenance to red or pale.

10. Moreover, it is evident that no idea which is not itself perceived can be to me the means of perceiving any other idea [1]. If I do not perceive the redness or paleness of a man's face themselves, it is impossible I should perceive by them the passions which are in his mind.

11. Now, from sect. 2, it is plain that distance is in its

---

[1] Here 'perceived' means being actually conscious of phenomena present in sense; 'perceiving' means being aware (through what he afterwards calls suggestion) of what is signified by them. So in the following sections what is 'imperceptible' is yet 'perceived,' or judged through suggestion. The former is immediate and the latter developed or acquired perception.

own nature imperceptible; and yet it is perceived by sight. It remains, therefore, that it be brought into view by means of some other idea, that is itself immediately perceived in the act of vision.

12. But those lines and angles by means whereof some men pretend to explain the perception of distance, are themselves not at all perceived, nor are they in truth ever thought of by those unskilful in optics. I appeal to any one's experience, whether, upon sight of an object, he computes its distance by the bigness of the angle made by the meeting of the two optic axes? or whether he ever thinks of the greater or lesser divergency of the rays which arrive from any point to his pupil? nay, whether it be not perfectly impossible for him to perceive by sense the various angles wherewith the rays, according to their greater or lesser divergence, do fall on the eye? Every one is himself the best judge of what he perceives, and what not. In vain shall any man tell me, that I perceive certain lines and angles which introduce into my mind the various ideas of distance, so long as I myself am conscious of no such thing.

13. Since therefore those angles and lines are not themselves perceived by sight, it follows, from sect. 10, that the mind does not by them judge of the distance of objects.

14. *Secondly*, The truth of this assertion will be yet farther evident to any one that considers those lines and angles have no real existence in nature, being only an hypothesis framed by the mathematicians, and by them introduced into optics that they might treat of that science in a geometrical way.

15. The *third* and last reason I shall give for rejecting that doctrine is, that though we should grant the real existence of those optic angles, &c., and that it was possible for the mind to perceive them, yet these principles would not be found sufficient to explain the phenomena of distance, as shall be shewn hereafter.

16. Now, it being already shewn that distance is *suggested*[1] to the mind, by the mediation of some other idea which is

[1] Note in sect. 16 the first use in the *Essay* of the term *suggestion*—already referred to as expressive of the way in which our acquired power of interpreting what we see, and thus going beyond *pure visual sense*, has been explained by Berkeley. He explains our acquired visual perception of things by resolving it into what he calls suggestion.—The next question is, What does he mean by Suggestion? Is it more than the blind issue of unconscious habit? Does it mean a special faculty? Is it an exercise of thought? (See *Vindication*, sect. 42.) The answer to this question goes so far to settle Berkeley's place as (unconsciously) a mere phenomenalist, like Hume, or as (unconsciously) anticipating Reid, if not Kant, in the foundation of his philosophy.—Reid, in his *Inquiry*, often uses the word 'suggestion' when treating of the five senses and the relations of their phenomenal data to one another, making it mean the common rational convictions of which no further explanation can be given. 'I know no word,' he says, ' more proper to express a power of the mind which seems entirely to have escaped the notice of philosophers, and to which we owe many of our simple ideas which are neither impressions nor ideas, as well as many original principles of belief. . . . There is suggestion which is not natural or original : it is the result of experience and habit. . . . But I think it appears that there are [also] *natural suggestions:*—that sensation suggests the notion of present existence, and the belief that what we perceive or feel does now exist; that memory suggests the notion of past existence, and the belief that what we remember did exist in time past ; and that our sensations and thoughts suggest the notion of a mind, and the belief of its existence, and of its relation to our thoughts. By a like natural principle it is that a beginning of existence, or any change in nature, suggests to us the notion of a cause, and compels our belief of its existence. And in like manner, certain sensations of touch, *by the constitution of our nature*, suggest to us extension, solidity, and motion, which are nowise like sensations, although they have been hitherto confounded with them' (*Inquiry*, ch. II. sect 7). 'This class of intimations,' says Stewart, with reference to this passage, ' result from *the original frame of the human mind*, and ' were quite overlooked by Berkeley.'—The question which Berkeley would solve by ' suggestion ' is really the great one afterwards proposed by Hume, in his *Inquiry concerning Human Understanding*, section IV, and which the remainder of that work is an attempt to answer:—' What is the nature of that evidence which assures us of any matter of fact that lies beyond the present testimony of our senses or the records of our memory?' This is just to ask what the ultimate constitutive principle of our knowledge of nature is, in virtue of which phenomena of sense become acquired perceptions and physical science. That Hume says is custom and mental association. With Berkeley perception is developed by 'suggestion,' to which the origin of our judgments of Extension is thus referred. What the term Suggestion is used by Berkeley to connote, and whether, with this connotation, these judgments are adequately explained by him, is what the critical reader of Berkeley has to consider.—The analysis may be compared with Kant's, by whom phenomena of sense were supposed

itself perceived in the act of seeing, it remains that we inquire *what* ideas or sensations there be that attend vision unto which we may suppose the ideas of distance are connected, and by which they are introduced into the mind[1].

And, *first*, it is certain by experience, that when we look at a near object with both eyes, according as it approaches or recedes from us, we alter the disposition of our eyes, by lessening or widening the interval between the pupils. This disposition or turn of the eyes is attended with a sensation[2], which seems to me to be that which in this case brings the idea of greater or lesser distance into the mind.

17. Not that there is any natural or necessary connexion between the sensation we perceive by the turn of the eyes and greater or lesser distance. But—because the mind has, by constant experience, found the different sensations corresponding to the different dispositions of the eyes to be attended each with a different degree of distance in the object—there has grown an habitual or customary connexion[3] between those two sorts of ideas; so that the mind no sooner perceives the sensation arising from the different turn it gives the eyes, in order to bring the pupils nearer or farther asunder, but it withal perceives the different idea of distance which was wont

to be translated into perceptions, under 'forms' that belong to mind and not to phenomena, but which are objectively valid because they are forms under which phenomena, as matter of experience, *must* be presented; also with the transformed sensations of Condillac; and with the antithesis of extension and sensation of Reid.

[1] Sect. 16-27 give three sorts of arbitrary signs of 'near distances' —recognition of their *arbitrariness* being what Berkeley considers the important outcome of his whole investigation into vision, as it empties natural law and physical science of *a priori* necessity.

[2] This 'sensation' of organic movement in the eye is of course not itself seen. It belongs to our tactual experience—in Berkeley's wide meaning of 'touch.' It may be called *visual*, but it is not *visible*. Thus the visual signs through which we learn to see things in their places are some of them invisible while others are visible.

[3] This 'customary connexion,' elsewhere called arbitrary, need not therefore be capricious. The 'suggestions' to which it gives rise may involve reason; and 'arbitrary' may be understood to mean the expression of will, as opposed to *blind necessity*—so that in rational will would thus be the essence of the visible universe.

to be connected with that sensation. Just as, upon hearing a certain sound, the idea is immediately suggested to the understanding which custom had united with it.

18. Nor do I see how I can easily be mistaken in this matter. I know evidently that distance is not perceived of itself—that, by consequence, it must be perceived by means of some other idea, which is immediately perceived, and varies with the different degrees of distance. I know also that the sensation arising from the turn of the eyes is of itself immediately perceived, and various degrees thereof are connected with different distances, which never fail to accompany them into my mind, when I view an object distinctly with both eyes whose distance is so small that in respect of it the interval between the eyes has any considerable magnitude.

19. I know it is a received opinion that, by altering the disposition of the eyes, the mind perceives whether the angle of the optic axes, or the lateral angles comprehended between the interval of the eyes or the optic axes, are made greater or lesser; and that, accordingly, by a kind of natural geometry, it judges the point of their intersection to be nearer or farther off. But that this is not true I am convinced by my own experience, since I am not conscious that I make any such use of the perception I have by the turn of my eyes. And for me to make those judgments, and draw those conclusions from it, without knowing that I do so, seems altogether incomprehensible.

20. From all which it follows, that the judgment we make of the distance of an object viewed with both eyes is entirely the result of experience[1]. If we had not constantly found certain sensations, arising from the various dispositions of the eyes, attended with certain degrees of distance, we should never make those sudden judgments from them concerning

---

[1] 'Experience,' i. e. phenomena of sense organised into experience by 'suggestion,' which he held sufficient to explain this 'judgment' or presumption.

the distance of objects; no more than we would pretend to judge of a man's thoughts by his pronouncing words we had never heard before.

21. *Secondly*, an object placed at a certain distance from the eye, to which the breadth of the pupil bears a considerable proportion, being made to approach, is seen more confusedly. And the nearer it is brought the more confused appearance it makes. And, this being found constantly to be so, there arises in the mind an habitual connexion between the several degrees of confusion and distance; the greater confusion still implying the lesser distance, and the lesser confusion the greater distance of the object[1].

22. This confused appearance of the object doth therefore seem to be the medium whereby the mind judges of distance, in those cases wherein the most approved writers of optics will have it judge by the different divergency with which the rays flowing from the radiating point fall on the pupil. No man, I believe, will pretend to see or feel those imaginary angles that the rays are supposed to form according to their various inclinations on his eye. But he cannot choose seeing whether the object appear more or less confused. It is therefore a manifest consequence from what has been demonstrated that, instead of the greater or lesser divergency of the rays, the mind makes use of the greater or lesser confusedness of the appearance, thereby to determine the apparent place of an object.

23. Nor doth it avail to say there is not any necessary connexion between confused vision and distance great or small. For I ask any man what necessary connexion he sees between the redness of a blush and shame? And yet no sooner shall he behold that colour to arise in the face of

---

[1] The explanation here, so far as it goes, turns upon what has since been called Inseparable Association. See Mill's *Examination of Hamilton*, ch. XIV. But can belief be resolved into habit and association? This may explain, in a physical way, connexions between thoughts in an individual mind but not the conviction of objective reality.

another but it brings into his mind the idea of that passion which hath been observed to accompany it.

24. What seems to have misled the writers of optics in this matter is, that they imagine men judge of distance as they do of a conclusion in mathematics; betwixt which and the premises it is indeed absolutely requisite there be an apparent, necessary connexion[1]. But it is far otherwise in the sudden judgments men make of distance. We are not to think that brutes and children, or even grown reasonable men, whenever they perceive an object to approach or depart from them, do it by virtue of geometry and demonstration.

25. That one idea may suggest another to the mind, it will suffice that they have been observed to go together, without any demonstration of the necessity of their coexistence, or without so much as knowing what it is that makes them so to coexist. Of this there are innumerable instances, of which no one can be ignorant[2].

26. Thus, greater confusion having been constantly attended with nearer distance, no sooner is the former idea perceived but it suggests the latter to our thoughts. And, if it had been the ordinary course of nature that the farther off an object were placed the more confused it should appear, it is certain the very same perception that now makes us think an object approaches would then have made us to imagine it

---

[1] Is this consistent with Berkeley's ultimate explanation of mathematical science, and the intellectual necessity of its demonstrations?

[2] Here and throughout Berkeley presupposes a natural tendency to connect together ever after phenomena of sense which have often been present simultaneously, or in immediate succession—a tendency the strength of which may be so confirmed through repetition, that we at last become *unable* to separate them mentally. This is the *associative* tendency, since made so much of by some psychologists, which thus with Berkeley as with Aristotle is mixed up with the psychology of the senses. Because it is dependent on the variable experience of each person, it has been called a *subjective* law or tendency, in contrast to relations which issue from irreversible necessities that are of the essence of reason. The difference between the subjective tendency to associate and the objective relations of reason is obscured by association psychology.

went farther off—that perception, abstracting from custom and experience, being equally fitted to produce the idea of great distance, or small distance, or no distance at all.

27. *Thirdly*, an object being placed at the distance above specified, and brought nearer to the eye, we may nevertheless prevent, at least for some time, the appearance's growing more confused, by straining the eye. In which case that sensation supplies the place of confused vision, in aiding the mind to judge of the distance of the object; it being esteemed so much the nearer by how much the effort or straining of the eye in order to distinct vision is greater.

28. I have here set down those sensations or ideas that seem to be the constant and general occasions of introducing into the mind the different ideas of near distance. It is true, in most cases, that divers other circumstances contribute to frame our idea of distance, viz. the particular number, size, kind, &c. of the things seen [1]. Concerning which, as well as all other the forementioned occasions which suggest distance, I shall only observe, they have none of them, in their own nature, any relation or connexion with it: nor is it possible they should ever signify the various degrees thereof, otherwise than as by experience they have been found to be connected with them [2].

*   *   *   *   *

[1] *Visible* signs mix with those that are merely *visual*. The latter are *felt* in the organ of sight, but are not themselves *seen*.

[2] The visual 'signs' given in the preceding sections are all either (*a*) visible or (*b*) invisible. Under neither head is Berkeley's list exhaustive, nor even accurate as far as it goes. Recent German and British physiologists have discovered others: Müller, Helmholtz, and Lotze have mentioned visual signs not recognised by Berkeley. But these and other matters of biological psychology were for him questions of detail. The distinction between the sensory and motor nerves, important in connexion with the correlative difference between passive and active sense-consciousness, was unknown to Berkeley, to whose philosophy also recent views of the organic unity of conscious life and the nervous system were foreign.

In sect. 29-41, here omitted, Berkeley proceeds to verify his invisible and visible signs, by showing that one class of them can explain a curious optical phenomenon that had baffled Barrow and others.

41. From what hath been premised, it is a manifest consequence, that a man born blind, being made to see, would at first have no idea of Distance by sight: the sun and stars, the remotest objects as well as the nearer, would all seem to be in his eye, or rather in his mind[1]. The objects intromitted by sight would seem to him (as in truth they are) no other than a new set of thoughts or sensations, each whereof is as near to him as the perceptions of pain or pleasure, or the most inward passions of his soul. For, our judging objects perceived by sight to be at any distance, or without the mind, is (vid. sect. 28) entirely the effect of experience, which one in those circumstances could not yet have attained to.

42. It is indeed otherwise upon the common supposition—that men judge of distance by the angle of the optic axes, just as one in the dark, or a blind man by the angle comprehended by two sticks, one whereof he held in each hand. For, if this were true, it would follow that one blind from his birth, being made to see, should stand in need of no new experience, in order to perceive distance by sight. But that this is false has, I think, been sufficiently demonstrated[2].

43. [3]And perhaps, upon a strict inquiry, we shall not find

[1] 'In his eye' and 'in his mind'—i.e. as existing dependently on the organ, or rather on the percipient mind.

[2] He does not here refer as one might expect to experimental verification in actual cases of born-blind persons made to see. Of these afterwards.

[3] Berkeley now advances from his argument that our power to see outward distances is due to 'suggestion,' and proceeds to draw conclusions from the fact that *phenomena of colour* are the only phenomena of which we are originally conscious (percipient) when we see. Having shewn that distances, whether near or remote, are not *seen* but only *suggested by arbitrary signs*, he now proceeds to the more subtle question of the externality or non-externality of the phenomena of colour—externality meaning independence of a percipient.—In what follows he argues that colour cannot be thus external: in the *Principles* he includes in the argument what is perceived in any or all of the five senses, not excepting even touch.

One may here ask, why *touch* is commonly regarded as the test of externality, and why mere visibility without tangibility is supposed to that even those who from their birth have grown up in a continued habit of seeing are irrecoverably prejudiced on the other side, to wit, in thinking what they see to be at a distance from them. For, at this time it seems agreed on all hands, by those who have had any thoughts of that matter, that *colours*, which are the proper and immediate object of sight [1], are not without the mind.—But then, it will be said, by sight we have also the ideas of *extension*, and *figure*, and *motion ;* all which may well be thought without and at some distance from the mind, though colour should not. In answer to this, I appeal to any man's experience, whether the visible extension of any object do not appear as near to him as the colour of that object; nay, whether they do not both seem to be in the very same place. Is not the extension we see coloured, and is it possible for us, so much as in thought, to separate and abstract colour from extension? Now, where the extension is, there surely is the figure, and there the motion too. I speak of those which are perceived by sight [2].

imply that what is seen is illusory? Berkeley. though he argued the purely ideal nature of visible things sooner than the purely ideal nature of tangible things, does not make the distinction between the illusory and the real turn ultimately upon the tangibility of the latter. (See *Principles*, sect. 28-33.) But see Mansel's *Metaphysics*, p. 346; also Brown's *Lectures*, xxiv.

[1] With psychologists generally, since Aristotle (*De Anima*, b. II. ch. 7), he assumes that colour, and whatever colour implies, is the only original datum of sight.

[2] Berkeley started, in sect. 2, with the *assumption* that distance in the line of sight is in its nature invisible; on this foundation he proceeded in the proof, given in sections 3-28, that all outward distances are perceptions of sight only so far as they are 'suggestions' acquired by customary visual signs. He enters here on his second line of proof, which opens the way to his distinctive theory of matter. He argues that *what we see* cannot be independent of perception. This is founded on a second assumption, also sustained by concurrent authority—that *colour* is the only immediate object of sight.—Locke had said that we can see distances between bodies, and between parts of the same body. But can colour involve distance? What Berkeley wants to show is, that distance and extension are ambiguous words— the distances we see being different in *kind* from those of touch. The common doctrine had been, that light or colour is what we see—including

44. But, for a fuller explication of this point, and to shew that the immediate objects of sight are not so much as the ideas or resemblances of things placed at a distance, it is requisite that we look nearer into the matter, and carefully observe what is meant in common discourse when one says, that which he sees is at a distance from him. Suppose, for example, that looking at the moon I should say it were fifty or sixty semidiameters of the earth distant from me. Let us see what moon this is spoken of. It is plain it cannot be the visible moon, or anything like the visible moon, or that which I see—which is only a round luminous plain, of about thirty visible points in diameter. For, in case I am carried from the place where I stand directly towards the moon, it is manifest the object varies still as I go on; and, by the time that I am advanced fifty or sixty semidiameters of the earth, I shall be so far from being near a small, round, luminous flat that I shall perceive nothing like it—this object having long since disappeared, and, if I would recover it, it must be by going back to the earth from whence I set out. Again, suppose I perceive by sight the faint and obscure idea of something, which I doubt whether it be a man, or a tree, or a tower, but judge it to be at the distance of about a mile. It is plain I cannot mean that what I see is a mile off, or that it is the image or likeness of anything which is a mile off; since that every step I take towards it the appearance alters, and from being obscure, small, and faint, grows clear, large, and vigorous. And when I come to the mile's end, that which I saw first is quite lost, neither do I find anything in the likeness of it[1].

whatever extension is necessarily involved in seeing colour; for it was supposed that colour, as originally seen, was in some sort extended, or accompanied by an intuition of extension. The question still unconsidered was the nature of *its* extension. Is it of two dimensions or of three? Is it identical with, or even at all similar to, the extension of touch?

[1] The sceptical objections of the Eleatics and others to the trustworthiness of our senses, referred to by Des Cartes, in his *Meditations*,

45. In these and the like instances, the truth of the matter, I find, stands thus:—Having of a long time experienced certain ideas perceivable by *touch*[1]—as distance, tangible figure, and solidity—to have been connected with certain ideas of sight, I do, upon perceiving these ideas of sight, forthwith conclude what tangible ideas are, by the wonted ordinary course of nature, like to follow. Looking at an object, I perceive a certain visible figure and colour, with some degree of faintness and other circumstances, which, from what I have formerly observed, determine me to think that if I advance forward so many paces, miles, &c., I shall be affected with such and such ideas of touch. So that, in truth and strictness of speech, I neither see distance itself, nor anything that I take to be at a distance. I say, neither distance nor things placed at a distance are themselves, or their ideas, truly perceived by sight. This I am persuaded of, as to what concerns myself. And I believe whoever will look narrowly into his own thoughts, and examine what he means by saying he sees this or that thing at a distance, will agree with me, that what he sees only suggests to his understanding that, after having passed a certain distance, to be

---

and by Malebranche, in the first book of his *Recherche*, may have suggested the illustrations in this section. The sceptical difficulty rises out of the supposition that the extended colour we see, when the tangible object is near, is the *same* extended colour that we see, when the tangible object is more remote. Berkeley insists that what is strictly *seen* in these cases is different, but that what is *signified or suggested by what is seen* may be the same. He does not here pursue the question about the continuous identity of what we touch; or the question what is ultimately meant by sameness in sensible things—foreign to an Essay on Sight, but which he has to meet in defending his conception of Matter as a reality that is necessarily dependent on percipient mind.

[1] This is the first distinct mention of 'touch' in the *Essay*—a term which with Berkeley includes not merely the organic sense of simple *contact*, but also the sense of muscular resistance, and the active sense-consciousness connected with the movements of our bodies or their organs. From this point he begins to unfold the antithesis of the visible and the tangible worlds—of coloured and resistant extension. To explain by suggestion the synthesis of these opposite elements in our acquired perceptions in sight is the aim of his theory of vision.

measured by the *motion of his body*, which is perceivable by touch, he shall come to perceive such and such tangible ideas, which have been usually connected with such and such visible ideas [1]. But, that one might be deceived by these suggestions of sense, and that there is no necessary connexion between visible and tangible ideas suggested by them, we need go no farther than the next looking-glass or picture to be convinced.—Note that, when I speak of tangible ideas, I take the word *idea* for any the immediate object of sense or understanding—in which large signification it is commonly used by the moderns [2].

46. From what we have shewn, it is a manifest consequence that the ideas of Space, Outness, and things placed at a distance are not, strictly speaking, the object of sight; they are not otherwise perceived by the eye than by the ear. Sitting in my study I hear a coach drive along the street; I look through the casement and see it; I walk out and enter into it. Thus, common speech would incline one to think I heard, saw, and touched the same thing, to wit, the coach. It is nevertheless certain the ideas intromitted by each sense are widely different, and distinct from each other; but, having been observed constantly to go together, they are spoken of as one and the same thing. By the variation of the noise, I

---

[1] The important office of our active consciousness of bodily movement, in the development at once of self-consciousness and of the perception of things, might be illustrated in connexion with this sentence. We thus begin to distinguish between 'I can' and 'I cannot;' and the conviction of personality, personal identity, and personal responsibility is gradually drawn out by the antithesis.

[2] 'Moderns'—Locke and Des Cartes for instance. With Locke (*Essay*, Introduction, § 8), 'ideas' mean the phenomena we are conscious of—'whatsoever is the object of the understanding when a man thinks;' and the ideas we are conscious of in sense-perception include those which he says 'resemble' the primary qualities of external things, and also the sensations which the primary qualities produce, referred by him to what he calls secondary qualities in the things. By Des Cartes, 'idea' is sometimes applied to the psychical perception or consciousness, and sometimes to the organic motion or physical impression with which the former is connected by arbitrary divine appointment.

perceive the different distances of the coach, and know that it approaches before I look out. Thus, by the ear I perceive distance just after the same manner as I do by the eye [1].

47. I do not nevertheless say I hear distance, in like manner as I say that I see it—the ideas perceived by hearing not being so apt to be confounded with the ideas of touch as those of sight are. So likewise a man is easily convinced that bodies and external things are not properly the object of hearing, but only sounds, by the mediation whereof the idea of this or that body, or distance, is suggested to his thoughts [2]. But then one is with more difficulty brought to discern the difference there is betwixt the ideas of sight and touch: though it be certain, a man no more sees and feels the same thing, than he hears and feels the same thing.

48. One reason of which seems to be this. It is thought a great absurdity to imagine that one and the same thing should have any more than one extension and one figure. But, the extension and figure of a body being let into the mind two ways, and that indifferently, either by sight or touch, it seems to follow that we see the same extension and the same figure which we feel.

49. But, if we take a close and accurate view of the matter, it must be acknowledged that we never see and feel one and the same object. That which is seen is one thing, and that which is felt is another. If the visible figure and extension be not the same with the tangible figure and extension, we are not to infer that one and the same thing has divers extensions. The true consequence is that the objects of sight and touch are two distinct things. It may perhaps require some thought rightly to conceive this distinction. And the difficulty seems not a little increased, because the combination of visible ideas hath constantly the same name as the com-

---

[1] i.e. the 'perception' in both cases is a suggested expectation.
[2] The original data peculiar to the sense of Hearing might be here analysed by the student, and compared with those of Sight and of Touch.

bination of tangible ideas wherewith it is connected—which doth of necessity arise from the use and end of language.

50. In order, therefore, to treat accurately and unconfusedly of vision, we must bear in mind that there are two sorts of objects apprehended by the eye—the one primarily and immediately, the other secondarily and by intervention of the former. Those of the first sort neither are nor appear to be without the mind, or at any distance off. They may, indeed, grow greater or smaller, more confused, or more clear, or more faint. But they do not, cannot approach or recede from us. Whenever we say an object is at a distance, whenever we say it draws near, or goes farther off, we must always mean it of the latter sort, which properly belong to the touch, and are not so truly perceived as *suggested* by the eye, in like manner as thoughts by the ear [1].

51. No sooner do we hear the words of a familiar language pronounced in our ears but the ideas corresponding thereto present themselves to our minds: in the very same instant the sound and the meaning enter the understanding; so closely are they united that it is not in our power to keep out the one except we exclude the other also. We even act in all respects as if we heard the very thoughts themselves. So likewise the secondary objects, or those which are only suggested by sight, do often more strongly affect us, and are more regarded, than the proper objects of that sense; along with which they enter into the mind, and with which they have a far more strict connexion than ideas have with words. Hence it is we find it so difficult to discriminate between the immediate and mediate objects of sight, and are so prone to attribute to the former what belongs only to the latter. They are, as it were, most closely twisted, blended, and incorporated together. And the prejudice is confirmed and riveted

---

[1] Whether what is perceived in touching is as dependent on a percipient mind as what is perceived in seeing, Berkeley does not discuss in this *Essay*. That, as already noted, is the wider question considered in his *Principles*.

in our thoughts by a long tract of time, by the use of language, and want of reflection. However, I doubt not but any one that shall attentively consider what we have already said, and shall say upon this subject before we have done (especially if he pursue it in his own thoughts), may be able to deliver himself from that prejudice. Sure I am, it is worth some attention to whoever would understand the true nature of vision [1].

52. I have now done with distance, and proceed to shew how it is that we perceive by sight the Magnitude of objects [2]. —It is the opinion of some that we do it by angles, or by angles in conjunction with distance. But, neither angles nor distance being perceivable by sight, and the things we see being in truth at no distance from us, it follows that, as we have shewn lines and angles not to be the medium the mind makes use of in apprehending the apparent place, so neither are they the medium whereby it apprehends the apparent magnitude of objects.

53. It is well known that the same extension at a near distance shall subtend a greater angle, and at a farther distance a lesser angle. And by this principle (we are told) the mind estimates the magnitude of an object, comparing the angle under which it is seen with its distance, and thence inferring the magnitude thereof. What inclines men to this mistake (beside the humour of making one see by geometry) is, that the same perceptions or ideas which suggest distance

[1] The attempt to find the original phenomenal data of any of the senses, taken singly, illustrates this difficulty; but it is more obtrusive in sight and in touch, because the perceptions of extension and its relations (the chief difficulty in the analysis) seem to rise (somehow) in visual and tactual experience exclusively. In his *Commonplace Book* (p. 494) Berkeley well remarks that 'extension is blended with tangible or visible ideas, and by the mind prescinded therefrom.'

[2] Sect. 52–87 treat of the necessary invisibility of the real (tangible) Magnitudes of things—the distances between their parts as data of Touch (in its wide meaning). Cf. *Vindication*, sect. 54–61.

do also suggest magnitude. But, if we examine it, we shall find they suggest the latter as immediately as the former. I say, they do not first suggest distance and then leave it to the judgment to use that as a medium whereby to collect the magnitude; but they have as close and immediate a connexion with the magnitude as with the distance; and suggest magnitude as independently of distance, as they do distance independently of magnitude. All which will be evident to whoever considers what has been already said and what follows.

54. It has been shewn there are two sorts of objects apprehended by sight, each whereof has its distinct magnitude, or extension—the one, properly tangible, *i.e.* to be perceived and measured by touch, and not immediately falling under the sense of seeing; the other, properly and immediately visible, by mediation of which the former is brought in view. Each of these magnitudes are greater or lesser, according as they contain in them more or fewer points, they being made up of points or minimums. For, whatever may be said of extension in abstract, it is certain sensible extension is not infinitely divisible. There is a *minimum tangibile*, and a *minimum visibile*, beyond which sense cannot perceive[1]. This every one's experience will inform him.

55. The magnitude of the object which exists without the mind, and is at a distance, continues always invariably the same: but, the visible object still changing as you approach

---

[1] There is a *minimum visibile* at which we cease to be percipient of colour, and also a *minimum tangibile* at which all sense of resistance and contact disappears from *our* sense-consciousness. This point is, for us, the necessary limit in imagination of (visible or tangible) existence.

Though Berkeley regards visible extension as, in itself, necessarily dependent on a percipient mind, he does not mean that mind, in perceiving extension, itself becomes extended. With him, extension—existing only as a greater or smaller number of coloured or resistant *minima, i.e.* only 'in mind'—nevertheless does not exist in mind *as an attribute*. (Cf. *Principles*, sect. 49.) Mind, he would say, *can* be conscious without being conscious of what is extended: on the other hand, what is extended *cannot* exist without mind.

to or recede from the tangible object, it hath no fixed and determinate greatness. Whenever therefore we speak of the magnitude of any thing, for instance a tree or a house, we must mean the tangible magnitude; otherwise there can be nothing steady and free from ambiguity spoken of it [1]. Now, though the tangible and visible magnitude do in truth belong to two distinct objects, I shall nevertheless (especially since those objects are called by the same name, and are observed to coexist), to avoid tediousness and singularity of speech, sometimes speak of them as belonging to one and the same thing [2].

56. Now, in order to discover by what means the magnitude of tangible objects is perceived by sight, I need only reflect on what passes in my own mind, and observe what those things be which introduce the ideas of greater or lesser, into my thoughts when I look on any object [3]. And these I find to be, *first*, the magnitude or extension of the visible object, which, being immediately perceived by sight, is connected with that other which is tangible and placed at a distance: *secondly*, the confusion or distinctness: and *thirdly*, the vigorousness or faintness of the aforesaid visible appearance. *Cæteris paribus*, by how much the greater or lesser the visible object is, by so much the greater or lesser do

---

[1] But is not this 'unsteadiness' or relativity found in what we touch as well as in what we see—though less obtrusively? A felt thing is felt to be larger or smaller according to the state of the organism of the percipient at the time of the perception. The perception is relative to the state of the sense organ.

[2] Ordinary language identifies what psychological analysis of the original data of the senses seems to Berkeley to distinguish. May language not correspond with a deeper analysis of extension than Berkeley entertains?

[3] The 'signs' which 'suggest,' and so enable us to 'judge' of, the real magnitudes of things are inquired about in the following sections. They are found to be (*a*) the proportion of the field of sight which the object occupies, (*b*) the clearness or indistinctness of its outlines, (*c*) the lightness or faintness of its colours, (*d*) the number of intervening visible objects, and (*e*) the amount of muscular strain in directing both eyes to the object.

I conclude the tangible object to be. But, be the idea immediately perceived by sight never so large, yet, if it be withal confused, I judge the magnitude of the thing to be but small. If it be distinct and clear, I judge it greater. And, if it be faint, I apprehend it to be yet greater. What is here meant by confusion and faintness has been explained in sect. 35[1].

57. Moreover, the judgments we make of greatness do, in like manner as those of distance, depend on the disposition of the eye; also on the figure, number, and situation of intermediate objects, and other circumstances that have been observed to attend great or small tangible magnitudes. Thus, for instance, the very same quantity of visible extension which in the figure of a tower doth suggest the idea of great magnitude shall in the figure of a man suggest the idea of much smaller magnitude. That this is owing to the experience we have had of the usual bigness of a tower and a man, no one, I suppose, need be told.

58. It is also evident that confusion or faintness have no more a *necessary* connexion with little or great magnitude than they have with little or great distance. As they suggest the latter, so they suggest the former to our minds. And, by consequence, if it were not for experience, we should no more judge[2] a faint or confused appearance to be connected with great or little magnitude than we should that it was connected with great or little distance.

59. Nor will it be found that great or small visible magnitude hath any *necessary* relation to great or small tangible magnitude—so that the one may certainly and infallibly be inferred from the other.—But, before we come to the proof of this, it is fit we consider the difference there is betwixt the

---

[1] See Berkeley's *Works*, vol. I. p. 49.
[2] 'Judge,' *i. e. presume as sufficiently proved*—again in Locke's meaning of 'judgment,' in contrast with what is either intuitively or demonstratively 'known.' With Berkeley rational judgments *somehow* rise out of the ' suggestions ' of experience, but he does not explain how or why.

extension and figure which is the proper object of touch, and that other which is termed visible; and how the former is principally, though not immediately, taken notice of when we look at any object.) This has been before mentioned, but we shall here inquire into the cause thereof. We regard the objects that environ us in proportion as they are adapted to benefit or injure our own bodies, and thereby produce in our minds the sensations of pleasure or pain. ⁄Now, bodies operating on our organs by an immediate application, and the hurt and advantage arising therefrom depending altogether on the tangible, and not at all on the visible, qualities of any object)—this is a plain reason why those should be regarded by us much more than these. And for this end the visive sense seems to have been bestowed on animals, to wit, that, by the perception of visible ideas[1] (which in themselves are not capable of affecting or anywise altering the frame of their bodies), they may be able to foresee (from the experience they have had what tangible ideas are connected with such and such visible ideas) the damage or benefit which is like to ensue upon the application of their own bodies to this or that body which is at a distance. Which foresight, how necessary it is for the preservation of an animal, every one's experience can inform him[2]. ⁄Hence it is that, when we look at an object, the tangible figure and extension thereof are principally attended to; whilst there is small heed taken of the visible figure and magnitude, which, though more immediately perceived, do less sensibly affect

[1] 'Perception of visible ideas,' *i.e.* of the phenomena presented to sight. He proceeds to offer reasons for the greater practical importance of touch than of sight (even when we are using the latter sense), and therefore for associating *reality* with the former rather than with the latter.

[2] Much of what is commonly called 'vision' is really *prevision*, and proceeds on an unconscious assumption of law in nature. In all developed visual perception we go beyond present sense, just as we do in all the inferences of physical science, and virtually on the same rational basis; the judgment in science being however conscious of a rational ground, and not the issue of habit only.

us, and are not fitted to produce any alteration in our bodies.

60. That the matter of fact is true will be evident to any one who considers that a man placed at ten foot distance is thought as great as if he were placed at the distance only of five foot; which is true, not with relation to the visible, but tangible greatness of the object: the visible magnitude being far greater at one station than it is at the other.

61. Inches, feet, &c. are settled, stated lengths, whereby we measure objects and estimate their magnitude. We say, for example, an object appears to be six inches, or six foot long. Now, that this cannot be meant of visible inches, &c. is evident, because a visible inch is itself no constant determinate magnitude, and cannot therefore serve to mark out and determine the magnitude of any other thing. Take an inch marked upon a ruler; view it successively, at the distance of half a foot, a foot, a foot and a half, &c. from the eye: at each of which, and at all the intermediate distances, the inch shall have a different visible extension, *i.e.* there shall be more or fewer points discerned in it. Now, I ask which of all these various extensions is that stated determinate one that is agreed on for a common measure of other magnitudes? No reason can be assigned why we should pitch on one more than another. And, except there be some invariable determinate extension fixed on to be marked by the word inch, it is plain it can be used to little purpose; and to say a thing contains this or that number of inches shall imply no more than that it is extended, without bringing any particular idea of that extension into the mind. Farther, an inch and a foot, from different distances, shall both exhibit the same visible magnitude, and yet at the same time you shall say that one seems several times greater than the other. From all which it is manifest, that the judgments we make of the magnitude of objects by sight are altogether in reference to their tangible extension. Whenever we say an object is great or

small, of this or that determinate measure, I say, it must be meant of the tangible and not the visible extension, which, though immediately perceived, is nevertheless little taken notice of[1].

62. Now, that there is no necessary connexion between these two distinct extensions is evident from hence—because our eyes might have been framed in such a manner as to be able to see nothing but what were less than the *minimum tangibile*. In which case it is not impossible we might have perceived all the immediate objects of sight the very same that we do now; but unto those visible appearances there would not be connected those different tangible magnitudes that are now. (Which shews the judgments we make of the magnitude of things placed at a distance, from the various greatness of the immediate objects of sight, do not arise from any essential or necessary, but only a customary[2] tie which has been observed betwixt them.)

63. Moreover, it is not only certain that any idea of sight might not have been connected with this or that idea of touch we now observe to accompany it, but also that the greater visible magnitudes might have been connected with and introduced into our minds lesser tangible magnitudes, and the lesser visible magnitudes greater tangible magnitudes. Nay, that it actually is so, we have daily experience—that object which makes a strong and large appearance not seeming near so great as another the visible magnitude whereof is much less, but more faint, and the appearance upper, or

---

[1] But if the phenomenon of extension is an empirical datum of sense, and if resistant as well as coloured extension fluctuates relatively to the state of the sense organism, we need an objective criterion of the former as well as of the latter. What is it?.

[2] So Hume afterwards, who tried to reduce all so-called 'necessary' connexion in the universe to the physical issue of habit, induced by custom or previous experience. 'All inferences from experience,' he concludes, 'are *effects* of *custom* not (*conclusions*) of *reasoning*. Custom is the great guide of human life.' (*Inquiry*, V. p. 1.) With Bishop Butler, in like manner, 'probability is the guide of life.' (*Analogy*, Introd.) So too Pascal and Locke.

which is the same thing, painted lower on the retina, which faintness and situation suggest both greater magnitude and greater distance.

64. From which, and from sect. 57 and 58, it is manifest that, as we do not perceive the magnitude of objects immediately by sight, so neither do we perceive them by the mediation of anything which has a necessary connexion with them. Those ideas that now suggest unto us the various magnitudes of external objects before we touch them might possibly have suggested no such thing; or they might have signified them in a direct contrary manner, so that the very same ideas on the perception whereof we judge an object to be small might as well have served to make us conclude it great; those ideas being in their own nature equally fitted to bring into our minds the idea of small or great, or no size at all, of outward objects, just as the words of any language are in their own nature indifferent to signify this or that thing, or nothing at all.

65. As we see distance so we see magnitude. And we see both in the same way that we see shame or anger in the looks of a man. Those passions are themselves invisible; they are nevertheless let in by the eye along with colours and alterations of countenance which are the immediate object of vision, and which signify them for no other reason than barely because they have been observed to accompany them. Without which experience we should no more have taken blushing for a sign of shame than of gladness.

66. We are nevertheless exceedingly prone to imagine those things which are perceived only by the mediation of others to be themselves the immediate objects of sight, or at least to have in their own nature a fitness to be suggested by them before ever they had been experienced to coexist with them. From which prejudice every one perhaps will not find it easy to emancipate himself, by any the clearest convictions of reason. And there are some grounds to think that, if there was one only invariable and universal language in the world,

and that men were born with the faculty of speaking it, it would be the opinion of some, that the ideas in other men's minds were properly perceived by the ear, or had at least a necessary and inseparable tie with the sounds that were affixed to them. All which seems to arise from want of a due application of our discerning faculty, thereby to discriminate between the ideas that are in our understandings, and consider them apart from each other; which would preserve us from confounding those that are different, and make us see what ideas do, and what do not, include or imply this or that other idea[1].

* * * * * *

77. For the further clearing up of this point, it is to be observed, that what we immediately and properly see are only lights and colours in sundry situations and shades, and degrees of faintness and clearness, confusion and distinctness. All which visible objects are only in the mind[2]; nor do they suggest aught external[3], whether distance or magnitude, otherwise than by habitual connexion, as words do things. We are also to remark, that beside the straining of the eyes, and beside the vivid and faint, the distinct and confused appearances (which, bearing some proportion to lines and angles,

[1] Mark the stress put in these sections on the *arbitrariness* of the connexion between the visual signs which suggest tangible magnitudes, and that which they signify—a fundamental principle throughout the *Essay*, just as in language any term might *a priori* be made the sign of any meaning. This so far accords with Hume, when he says that 'if we reason *a priori* anything may appear able to produce anything. The falling of a pebble may, for all we know, extinguish the sun; or the wish of a man control the planets in their orbits. It is only experience that teaches us the nature and bounds of cause and effect' (*Inquiry*, ch. XII. pt. 3). Here 'cause' means sign, and physical causation means natural signification.

In sect. 67-77, which are here omitted, Berkeley tries to verify the preceding doctrines, as to the visual signs of Magnitude, by applying them to solve a scientific puzzle of long standing—the fact of the greater visible magnitude of the moon and other heavenly bodies when in the horizon. See Berkeley's *Works*, vol. I.

[2] 'in the mind,' *i.e.* dependent on being perceived.

[3] 'External,' *i. e.* given in touch, the data of which are (meantime) granted to be possibly independent of perception.

have been substituted instead of them in the foregoing part of this Treatise), there are other means which suggest both distance and magnitude—particularly the situation of visible points or objects, as upper or lower; the former suggesting a farther distance and greater magnitude, the latter a nearer distance and lesser magnitude—all which is an effect only of custom and experience, there being really nothing intermediate in the line of distance between the uppermost and the lowermost, which are both equidistant, or rather at no distance from the eye; as there is also nothing in upper or lower which by necessary connexion should suggest greater or lesser magnitude. Now, as these customary experimental means of suggesting distance do likewise suggest magnitude, so they suggest the one as immediately as the other. I say, they do not (vide sect. 53) first suggest distance, and then leave the mind from thence to infer or compute magnitude, but suggest magnitude as immediately and directly as they suggest distance [1].

78. This phenomenon of the horizontal moon is a clear instance of the insufficiency of lines and angles for explaining the way wherein the mind perceives and estimates the magnitude of outward objects. There is, nevertheless, a use of computation by them—in order to determine the apparent magnitude of things, so far as they have a connexion with and are proportional to those other ideas or perceptions which are the true and immediate occasions that suggest to the mind the apparent magnitude of things. But this in general may, I think, be observed concerning mathematical computation in optics—that it can never be very precise and exact, since the judgments we make of the magnitude of external things do often depend on several circumstances which are not proportional to or capable of being defined by lines and angles.

[1] Note the contrast here between 'inference' and 'suggestion.' See *Vindication*, sect. 42.

79. From what has been said, we may safely deduce this consequence, to wit, that a man born blind, and made to see, would, at first opening of his eyes, make a very different judgment of the magnitude of objects intromitted by them from what others do. He would not consider the ideas of sight with reference to, or as having any connexion with the ideas of touch. His view of them being entirely terminated within themselves, he can no otherwise judge them great or small than as they contain a greater or lesser number of visible points. Now, it being certain that any visible point can cover or exclude from view only one other visible point, it follows that whatever object intercepts the view of another hath an equal number of visible points with it; and, consequently, they shall both be thought by him to have the same magnitude. Hence, it is evident one in those circumstances would judge his thumb, with which he might hide a tower, or hinder its being seen, equal to that tower; or his hand, the interposition whereof might conceal the firmament from his view, equal to the firmament: how great an inequality soever there may, in our apprehensions, seem to be betwixt those two things, because of the customary and close connexion that has grown up in our minds between the objects of sight and touch, whereby the very different and distinct ideas of those two senses are so blended and confounded together as to be mistaken for one and the same thing—out of which prejudice we cannot easily extricate ourselves.

80. For the better explaining the nature of vision, and setting the manner wherein we perceive Magnitudes in a due light, I shall proceed to make some observations concerning matters relating thereto, whereof the want of reflection, and duly separating between tangible and visible ideas, is apt to create in us mistaken and confused notions.

And, *first*, I shall observe, that the *minimum visibile* is exactly equal in all beings whatsoever that are endowed with the visive faculty. No exquisite formation of the eye, no peculiar sharpness of sight, can make it less in one creature than in another; for, it not being distinguishable into parts, nor in anywise consisting of them, it must necessarily be the same to all. For, suppose it otherwise, and that the *minimum visibile* of a mite, for instance, be less than the *minimum visibile* of a man; the latter therefore may, by detraction of some part, be made equal to the former. It doth therefore consist of parts, which is inconsistent with the notion of a *minimum visibile* or point[1].

81. It will, perhaps, be objected, that the *minimum visibile* of a man doth really and in itself contain parts whereby it surpasses that of a mite, though they are not perceivable by the man. To which I answer, the *minimum visibile* having (in like manner as all other the proper and immediate objects of sight) been shewn not to have any existence without the mind of him who sees it, it follows there cannot be any part of it that is not actually perceived and therefore visible. Now, for any object to contain several distinct visible parts, and at the same time to be a *minimum visibile*, is a manifest contradiction.

82. Of these visible points we see at all times an equal number. It is every whit as great when our view is contracted and bounded by near objects as when it is extended to larger and remoter ones. For, it being impossible that one *minimum visibile* should obscure or keep out of sight more than one other, it is a plain consequence that, when my view is on all sides bounded by the walls of my study, I see just as many visible points as I could in case that, by the

[1] On Berkeley's principles, there can be no independent visible (or tangible) magnitude—independent, that is, of all percipients, and therefore no absolute *minimum visibile*—the *minimum* being in each case *the least that can be actually perceived*, and thus relative to the percipient and his organ. This abolishes an objective standard of perceived magnitudes, or at least refers the relations of primary quantities with secondary qualities to the voluntary institution by God of the Order of Nature.

removal of the study-walls and all other obstructions, I had a full prospect of the circumjacent fields, mountains, sea, and open firmament. For, so long as I am shut up within the walls, by their interposition every point of the external objects is covered from my view. But, each point that is seen being able to cover or exclude from sight one only other corresponding point, it follows that, whilst my sight is confined to those narrow walls, I see *as many* points or *minima visibilia* as I should were those walls away, by looking on all the external objects whose prospect is intercepted by them. Whenever, therefore, we are said to have a greater prospect at one time than another, this must be understood with relation, not to the proper and immediate, but the secondary and mediate objects of vision—which, as hath been shewn, do properly belong to the touch.

83. The visive faculty, considered with reference to its immediate objects, may be found to labour of two defects. *First,* in respect of the extent or number of visible points that are at once perceivable by it, which is narrow and limited to a certain degree. It can take in at one view but a certain determinate number of *minima visibilia,* beyond which it cannot extend its prospect. *Secondly,* our sight is defective in that its view is not only narrow, but also for the most part confused. Of those things that we take in at one prospect, we can see but a few at once clearly and unconfusedly; and the more we fix our sight on any one object, by so much the darker and more indistinct shall the rest appear [1].

84. Corresponding to these two defects of sight, we may imagine as many perfections, to wit, 1st. That of comprehending in one view a greater number of visible points; 2ndly. of being able to view them all equally and at once, with

[1] This is the natural issue of Attention, which is concentration of consciousness, and hence involves a withdrawal of the consciousness expended in other directions, if each person has only a limited amount of disposable conscious energy.

the utmost clearness and distinction. That those perfections are not actually in some intelligences of a different order and capacity from ours, it is impossible for us to know [1].

85. In neither of those two ways do microscopes contribute to the improvement of sight. For, when we look through a microscope, we neither see more visible points, nor are the collateral points more distinct than when we look with the naked eye at objects placed at a due distance. A microscope brings us, as it were, into a new world. It presents us with a new scene of visible objects, quite different from what we behold with the naked eye. But herein consists the most remarkable difference, to wit, that whereas the objects perceived by the eye alone have a certain connexion with tangible objects, whereby we are taught to foresee what will ensue upon the approach or application of distant objects to the parts of our own body—which much conduceth to its preservation—there is not the like connexion between things tangible and those visible objects that are perceived by help of a fine microscope.

86. Hence, it is evident that, were our eyes turned into the nature of microscopes, we should not be much benefitted by the change. We should be deprived of the forementioned advantage we at present receive by the visive faculty, and have left us only the empty amusement of seeing, without any other benefit arising from it. But, in that case, it will perhaps be said, our sight would be endued with a far greater sharpness and penetration than it now hath. But I would fain know wherein consists that sharpness which is esteemed so great an excellency of sight. It is certain, from what we

---

[1] These defects belong to the intuitive consciousness of a finite being. Cf. Locke's *Essay*, b. II. ch. 10. § 8, on inevitable defects of a finite or human memory.—Hence too the need, in a finite mind, for *inferential* or *ratiocinative* activity—reasoning being a function intermediate between Sense and Omniscience. Our scientific inferences are the results of tentative struggles to reach the laws of the Universal Order, hid beneath the changing phenomena that induce us to search for their causes—or, as Berkeley might say, for their meanings.

have already shewn, that the *minimum visibile* is never greater or lesser, but in all cases constantly the same. And, in the case of microscopical eyes, I see only this difference, to wit, that upon the ceasing of a certain observable connexion betwixt the divers perceptions of sight and touch, which before enabled us to regulate our actions by the eye, it would now be rendered utterly unserviceable to that purpose[1].

87. Upon the whole it seems that, if we consider the use and end of sight, together with the present state and circumstances of our being, we shall not find any great cause to complain of any defect or imperfection in it, or easily conceive how it could be mended. With such admirable wisdom is that faculty contrived, both for the pleasure and convenience of life.

88. Having finished what I intended to say concerning the Distance and Magnitude of objects, I come now to treat of the manner wherein the mind perceives by sight their Situation[2]. Among the discoveries of the last age, it is reputed none of the least, that the manner of vision has been more clearly explained than ever it had been before. There is, at this day, no one ignorant that the pictures of external objects are painted on the retina or fund of the eye; that we can see nothing which is not so painted; and that, according as the picture is more distinct or confused, so also is the perception we have of the object.

[1] Unless indeed the corresponding perceptions of touch were to be changed too, and brought into harmony with this more refined and intensified sight.—The capacity of our present senses singly, and in their co-operative 'suggestions,' for further development; also the possibility of additional senses, each affording data as foreign to our present experience as colours are to the experience of one born blind—and that either in other beings, or in us human beings at some future stage of our existence—all afford interesting scope for imaginative speculation.

[2] Sect. 88-119 refer to the nature, necessary invisibility, and arbitrary visual signs of the actual Situations or Places of the various bodies we see. (Cf. *Vindication*, sect. 48-53.) They contain an ingenious attempt to solve the once famous puzzle—an erect vision of things by means of inverted images on the retina.

But then, in this explication of vision, there occurs one mighty difficulty—The objects are painted in an inverted order on the bottom of the eye: the upper part of any object being painted on the lower part of the eye, and the lower part of the object on the upper part of the eye; and so also as to right and left. Since, therefore, the *pictures* are thus inverted, it is demanded how it comes to pass that we see the *objects* erect and in their natural posture?

89. In answer to this difficulty, we are told that the mind, perceiving an impulse of a ray of light on the upper part of the eye, considers this ray as coming in a direct line from the lower part of the object; and, in like manner, tracing the ray that strikes on the lower part of the eye, it is directed to the upper part of the object. Thus, in the adjacent figure,

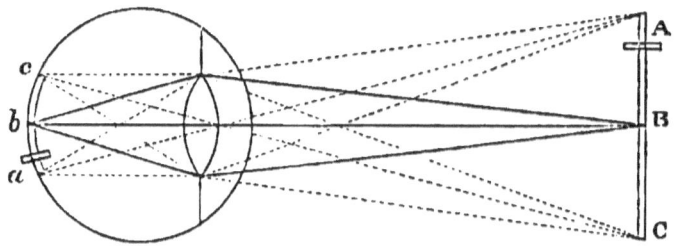

C, the lower point of the object A B C, is projected on c the upper part of the eye. So likewise, the highest point A is projected on a the lowest part of the eye; which makes the representation c b a inverted. But the mind—considering the stroke that is made on c as coming in the straight line C c from the lower end of the object; and the stroke or impulse on a, as coming in the line A a from the upper end of the object—is directed to make a right *judgment* of the *situation* of the object A B C, notwithstanding the picture of it be inverted. Moreover, this is illustrated by conceiving a blind man, who, holding in his hands two sticks that cross each other, doth with them touch the extremities of an object, placed in a perpendicular situation. It is certain this man will judge that to be the upper part of the object which he touches with the stick held in the undermost hand, and that to be the lower part of the object which he touches with the stick in his uppermost hand. This is the common explication of the erect appearance of objects, which is generally received and acquiesced in, being (as Mr. Molyneux tells us, *Diopt.* part ii. ch. vii. p. 289) 'allowed by all men as satisfactory.'

90. But this account to me does not seem in any degree true. Did I perceive those impulses, decussations, and directions of the rays of light, in like manner as hath been set forth, then, indeed, it would not at first view be altogether void of probability. And there might be some pretence for the comparison of the blind man and his cross sticks. But the case is far otherwise. I know very well that I perceive no such thing. And, of consequence, I cannot thereby make an estimate of the situation of objects. Moreover, I appeal to any one's experience, whether he be conscious to himself that he thinks on the intersection made by the radius pencils, or pursues the impulses they give in right lines, whenever he perceives by sight the position of any object? To me it seems evident that crossing and tracing of the rays, &c. is never thought on by children, idiots, or, in truth, by any other, save only those who have applied themselves to the study of Optics. And for the mind to judge of the situation of objects by those things without perceiving them, or to perceive them without knowing it[1], take which you please, it is perfectly beyond my comprehension. Add to this, that the explaining the manner of vision by the example of cross sticks, and hunting for the object along the axes of the radius pencils,

---

[1] 'To perceive them without knowing it.' Berkeley makes nothing here of a rational activity of which the apparent agent is unconscious; nor of the reason that is often latent in habit or suggestion—views which, since Leibnitz, have mixed so much with psychological and physiological speculation. Yet he had afterwards glimpses of this. See *Siris*, sect. 257, and note.

doth suppose the proper objects of sight to be perceived at a distance from us, contrary to what hath been demonstrated.

91. It remains, therefore, that we look for some other explication of this difficulty. And I believe it not impossible to find one, provided we examine it to the bottom, and carefully distinguish between the ideas of Sight and Touch[1]; which cannot be too oft inculcated in treating of vision. But, more especially throughout the consideration of this affair, we ought to carry that distinction in our thoughts, for that from want of a right understanding thereof, the difficulty of explaining erect vision seems chiefly to arise[2].

92. In order to disentangle our minds from whatever prejudices we may entertain with relation to the subject in hand, nothing seems more apposite than the taking into our thoughts the case of one born blind, and afterwards, when grown up, made to see. And—though perhaps it may not be a task altogether easy and familiar to us, to divest ourselves entirely of the experiences received from sight, so as to be able to put our thoughts exactly in the posture of such a one's—we must, nevertheless, as far as possible, endeavour to frame true conceptions of what might reasonably be supposed to pass in his mind.

93. It is certain that a man actually blind, and who had continued so from his birth, would, by the sense of feeling, attain to have ideas of upper and lower. By the motion of his hand, he might discern the situation of any tangible object placed within his reach. That part on which he felt himself supported, or towards which he perceived his body to

---

[1] 'Ideas' of Sight and Touch, *i.e.* the phenomena presented in each of these senses singly, apart from what their data 'suggest,' when one sense does duty for another.

[2] This *contrast* between the data in question is what the analytical part of the *Essay* endeavours to enforce. Its '*theory* of vision,' or constructive part, is the explanation, by 'suggestion,' of our tendency to 'judge' or interpret one class of the contrasted phenomena in terms significant of the other. This in the end becomes an explanation of our inductive interpretation of nature and of the logic of experience.

gravitate, he would term 'lower,' and the contrary to this 'upper;' and accordingly denominate whatsoever objects he touched.

94. But then, whatever judgments he makes concerning the situation of objects are confined to those only that are perceivable by touch. All those things that are intangible, and of a spiritual nature—his thoughts and desires, his passions, and in general all the modifications of his soul—to these he would never apply the terms upper and lower, except only in a metaphorical sense. He may perhaps, by way of allusion, speak of high or low thoughts: but those terms, in their proper signification, would never be applied to anything that was not conceived to exist without the mind. For, a man born blind, and remaining in the same state, could mean nothing else by the words 'higher' and 'lower' than a greater or lesser distance from the earth—which distance he would measure by the motion or application of his hand, or some other part of his body. It is, therefore, evident that all those things which, in respect of each other, would by him be thought higher or lower, must be such as were conceived to exist without his mind, in the ambient space.

95. Whence it plainly follows, that such a one, if we suppose him made to see, would not at first sight think that anything he saw was high or low, erect or inverted. For, it hath been already demonstrated, in sect. 41, that he would not think the things he perceived by sight to be at any distance from him, or without his mind. The objects to which he had hitherto been used to apply the terms 'up' and 'down,' 'high' and 'low,' were such only as affected, or were some way perceived by his touch. But, the proper objects of vision make a new set of ideas, perfectly distinct and different from the former, and which can in no sort make themselves perceived by touch. There is, therefore, nothing at all that could induce him to think those terms applicable to

them. Nor would he ever think it, till such time as he had observed their connexion with tangible objects, and the same prejudice began to insinuate itself into his understanding, which, from their infancy, had grown up in the understandings of other men.

96. To set this matter in a clearer light, I shall make use of an example. Suppose the above-mentioned blind person, by his touch, perceives a man to stand erect. Let us inquire into the manner of this. By the application of his hand to the several parts of a human body, he had perceived different tangible ideas, which being collected into sundry complex ones have distinct names annexed to them. Thus, one combination of a certain tangible figure, bulk, and consistency of parts is called the 'head;' another the 'hand;' a third the 'foot,' and so of the rest—all which complex ideas could, in his understanding, be made up only of ideas perceivable by touch. He had also, by his touch, obtained an idea of 'earth' or 'ground,' towards which he perceives the parts of his body to have a natural tendency. Now—by 'erect' nothing more being meant than that perpendicular position of a man wherein his feet are nearest to the earth—if the blind person, by moving his hand over the parts of the man who stands before him, do perceive the tangible ideas that compose the head to be farthest from, and those that compose the feet to be nearest to, that other combination of tangible ideas which he calls earth, he will denominate that man erect. But, if we suppose him on a sudden to receive his sight, and that he behold a man standing before him, it is evident, in that case, he would neither judge the man he sees to be erect nor inverted; for he, never having known those terms applied to any other save tangible things, or which existed in the space without him, and what he sees neither being tangible, nor perceived as existing without, he could not know that, in propriety of language, they were applicable to it.

97. Afterwards, when, upon turning his head or eyes up

and down to the right and left, he shall observe the visible objects to change, and shall also attain to know that they are called by the same names, and connected with the objects perceived by touch; then, indeed, he will come to speak of them and their situation in the same terms that he has been used to apply to tangible things: and those that he perceives by turning up his eyes he will call 'upper,' and those that by turning down his eyes he will call 'lower.'

98. And this seems to me the true reason why he should think those objects uppermost that are painted on the lower part of his eye. For, by turning the eye up they shall be distinctly seen; as likewise they that are painted on the highest part of the eye shall be distinctly seen by turning the eye down, and are for that reason esteemed lowest. For, we have shewn that to the immediate objects of sight, considered in themselves, he would not attribute the terms high and low. It must therefore be on account of some circumstances which are observed to attend them. And these, it is plain, are the actions of turning the eye up and down, which suggest a very obvious reason why the mind should denominate the objects of sight accordingly high or low. And, without this motion of the eye—this turning it up and down, in order to discern different objects—doubtless 'erect,' 'inverse,' and other the like terms relating to the position of tangible objects, would never have been transferred, or in any degree apprehended to belong to the ideas of sight—the mere act of seeing including nothing in it to that purpose; whereas the different situations of the eye naturally direct the mind to make a suitable judgment of the situation of objects intromitted by it[1].

[1] This briefly is Berkeley's solution of what he calls elsewhere 'the knot about inverted images.' (*Vindication*, sect. 52.) He does not here say whether in seeing we really see the (inverted) images on the retina—whether in short we see our own eyes; or, if not, why the images should be so elaborately delineated although they are invisible to the percipient.

These sections are apt to make the reader ask how space, and objects

99. Farther, when he has by experience learned the connexion there is between the several ideas of sight and touch, he will be able, by the perception he has of the situation of visible things in respect of one another, to make a sudden and true estimate of the situation of outward, tangible things corresponding to them. And thus it is he shall perceive by *sight* the situation of external objects, which do not properly fall under that sense [1].

100. I know we are very prone to think that, if just made to see, we should judge of the situation of visible things as we do now. But we are also as prone to think that, at first sight, we should in the same way apprehend the distance and magnitude of objects, as we do now; which hath been shewn to be a false and groundless persuasion. And, for the like reasons, the same censure may be passed on the positive

placed in it, are actually conceived by persons who have never been able to see. 'Observation of the born-blind,' says Platner, in a well-known passage, 'has convinced me that the sense of Touch, *by itself*, is altogether incompetent to afford us the representation of space, and is not even cognizant of local exteriority; in a word, that a man born destitute of sight has absolutely *no perception of an outer world, beyond the existence of something effective, different from his own feeling of passivity*; and in general only of the *numerical* diversity [i.e. as distinguished from the *partes extra partes* of Outwardness proper]—shall I say of *mental impressions* or of *things?* In fact, to those born blind, time serves instead of space. Vicinity and distance mean in their mouths nothing more than the longer or shorter time—the smaller or greater number of feelings—which they find it necessary to pass through in order to attain from some one feeling to some other. Inasmuch as space and extension are empirically possible *only* through the perceptions of sight, one born blind, after his eyes are freed from cataract, must first *learn to live in space*.'—All this goes to confirm the opinion that the perception of Space is not called forth merely in sensations of felt resistance and bodily movement; that it is only called forth after we have also had sensations of colour, and can interpret these as significant of past and future sensations of touch—that sight in short is somehow indispensable to the development of our perception of Space.—Does this consist with the view of Sir W. Hamilton and others, that the phenomena of which we are conscious in *all* the five senses, being the phenomena of an extended organism, afford us immediately and necessarily an apprehension of extension; or does Hamilton's later view itself agree with his previously (see his *Lectures on Metaphysics*, XXVIII) professed inability to determine whether *sight* may not exclusively give us our empirical knowledge of extension and space?

assurance that most men, before they have thought sufficiently of the matter, might have of their being able to determine by the eye, at first view, whether objects were erect or inverse.

101. It will perhaps be objected to our opinion, that a man, for instance, being thought erect when his feet are next the earth, and inverted when his head is next the earth, it doth hence follow that, by the mere act of vision—without any experience or altering the situation of the eye—we should have determined whether he were erect or inverted. For, both the earth itself, and the limbs of the man who stands thereon, being equally perceived by sight, one cannot choose seeing what part of the man is nearest the earth, and what part farthest from it, *i.e.* whether he be erect or inverted.

102. To which I answer, the ideas which constitute the tangible earth and man are entirely different from those which constitute the visible earth and man. Nor was it possible, by virtue of the visive faculty alone—without superadding any experience of touch, or altering the position of the eye—ever to have known, or so much as suspected, there had been any relation or connexion between them. Hence, a man at first view would not denominate anything he saw, 'earth,' or 'head,' or 'foot;' and consequently, he could not tell, by the mere act of vision, whether the head or feet were nearest the earth. Nor, indeed, would we have thereby any thought of earth or man, erect or inverse, at all—which will be made yet more evident, if we nicely observe, and make a particular comparison between, the ideas of both senses.

103. That which I *see* is only variety of light and colours. That which I *feel* is hard or soft, hot or cold, rough or smooth. What similitude, what connexion, have those ideas with these? Or, how is it possible that any one should see reason to give one and the same name to combinations of ideas so very different, before he had experienced their co-existence? We do

not find there is any *necessary* connexion betwixt this or that tangible quality and any colour whatsoever. And we may sometimes perceive colours, where there is nothing to be felt. All which doth make it manifest that no man, at first receiving of his sight, would know there was any agreement between this or that particular object of his sight and any object of touch he had been already acquainted with. The *colours* therefore of the head would to him no more suggest the idea of head[1] than they would the idea of feet.

104. Farther, we have at large shewn (vid. sect. 63 and 64) there is no discoverable necessary connexion between any given visible magnitude and any one particular tangible magnitude; but that it is entirely the result of custom and experience, and depends on foreign and accidental circumstances, that we can, by the perception of visible extension, inform ourselves what may be the extension of any tangible object connected with it. Hence, it is certain, that neither the visible magnitude of head or foot would bring along with them into the mind, at first opening of the eyes, the respective tangible magnitudes of those parts.

105. By the foregoing section, it is plain the visible figure of any part of the body hath no necessary connexion with the tangible figure thereof, so as at first sight to suggest it to the mind. For, figure is the termination of magnitude. Whence it follows that no visible magnitude having in its own nature an aptness to suggest any one particular tangible magnitude, so neither can any visible figure be inseparably connected with its corresponding tangible figure, so as of itself, and in a way prior to experience, it might suggest it to the understanding. This will be farther evident, if we consider that what seems smooth and round to the touch may to sight, if viewed through a microscope, seem quite otherwise.

106. From all which, laid together and duly considered, we may clearly deduce this inference:—In the first act of

---

[1] 'idea of head,' *i.e.* phenomena of the tangible or real head.

vision, no idea entering by the eye would have a perceivable connexion with the ideas to which the names earth, man, head, foot, &c. were annexed in the understanding of a person blind from his birth; so as in any sort to introduce them into his mind, or make themselves be called by the same names, and reputed the same things with them, as afterwards they come to be.

107. There doth, nevertheless, remain one difficulty, which to some may seem to press hard on our opinion, and deserve not to be passed over. For, though it be granted that neither the colour, size, nor figure of the visible feet have any necessary connexion with the ideas that compose the tangible feet, so as to bring them at first sight into my mind, or make me in danger of confounding them, before I had been used to and for some time experienced their connexion; yet thus much seems undeniable, namely, that the *number* of the visible feet being the same with that of the tangible feet, I may from hence, without any experience of sight, reasonably conclude that they represent or are connected with the feet rather than the head. I say, it seems the idea of two visible feet will sooner suggest to the mind the idea of two tangible feet than of one head—so that the blind man, upon first reception of the visive faculty, might know which were the feet or two, and which the head or one.

108. In order to get clear of this seeming difficulty, we need only observe that diversity of visible objects does not necessarily infer diversity of tangible objects corresponding to them. A picture painted with great variety of colours affects the touch in one uniform manner; it is therefore evident that I do not, by any necessary consecution, independent of experience, judge of the number of things tangible from the number of things visible. I should not therefore at first opening my eyes conclude that because I see two I shall feel two. How, therefore, can I, before experience teaches me, know that the visible legs, because two, are connected with the

tangible legs; or the visible head, because one, is connected with the tangible head? The truth is, the things I see are so very different and heterogeneous from the things I feel that the perception of the one would never have suggested the other to my thoughts, or enabled me to pass the least judgment thereon, until I had experienced their connexion[1].

109. But, for a fuller illustration of this matter, it ought to be considered, that *number* (however some may reckon it amongst the primary qualities) is nothing fixed and settled, really existing in things themselves[2]. It is entirely the creature of the mind, considering either a simple idea by itself, or any combination of simple ideas to which it gives one name, and so makes it pass for a unit. According as the mind variously combines its ideas, the unit varies; and as the unit, so the number, which is only a collection of units, doth also vary. We call a window one, a chimney one; and

[1] A man born blind, it has been objected, 'would, by being accustomed to feel one hand with the other, have learned to perceive that the extremity of the hand was divided into fingers—that the extremities of these fingers were distinguished by certain hard, smooth surfaces, of a different texture from the rest of the fingers—and that each finger had certain joints or flexures. Now, if this man were to receive the sense of seeing, and immediately on getting this sense to look at his hand before he touched it again, it is manifest that the divisions of its extremity into fingers would be visible. He would note too the small spaces at the extremity of each finger, which affected his sight differently from the fingers; upon moving his fingers he would see the joints. Though therefore, by means of this lately acquired sense of *seeing*, the hand affected his mind in a new and different manner from what it did before, yet, as by *touch* he had acquired the knowledge of these several divisions, marks, and distinctions of the hand, and, as the new object of sight appeared to be divided, marked, and distinguished in a similar manner, I think he would certainly conclude, *before he touched his hand*, that the thing which he now *saw* was *the same* which he had *felt* before and called his hand.' The text shows how Berkeley would reply to this.—The dependence on experience of our visual judgments of objects previously familiar to touch is discussed by Reid. See *Inquiry*, ch. VI. § 11.

[2] It must be remembered that the 'primary qualities' of bodies, according to Locke, are *solidity, extension, figure, motion* or *rest*, and *number*. See *Essay*, b. II. ch. 8. § 9. Their dependence, at least so far as they are data of sight, on percipient mind, is what Berkeley here insists on.—On the subjectivity (or at least relativity) of 'number,' cf. *Principles*, sect. 12, 13, 119-122.

yet a house, in which there are many windows and many chimneys, has an equal right to be called one; and many houses go to the making of one city. In these and the like instances, it is evident the *unit* constantly relates to the particular draughts the mind makes of its ideas, to which it affixes names, and wherein it includes more or less, as best suits its own ends and purposes. Whatever therefore the mind considers as one, that is an unit. Every combination of ideas is considered as one thing by the mind, and in token thereof is marked by one name. Now, this naming and combining together of ideas is perfectly arbitrary, and done by the mind in such sort as experience shews it to be most convenient—without which our ideas had never been collected into such sundry distinct combinations as they now are.

110. Hence, it follows that a man born blind, and afterwards, when grown up, made to see, would not, in the first act of vision, parcel out the ideas of sight into the same distinct collections that others do who have experienced which do regularly co-exist and are *proper* to be bundled up together under one name. He would not, for example, make into one complex idea, and thereby esteem and unite all those particular ideas which constitute the visible head or foot. For, there can be no reason assigned why he should do so, barely upon his seeing a man stand upright before him. There crowd into his mind the ideas which compose the visible man, in company with all the other ideas of sight perceived at the same time. But all these ideas offered at once to his view he would not distribute into sundry distinct combinations, till such time as, by observing the motion of the parts of the man and other experiences, he comes to know which are to be separated, and which to be collected together[1].

111. From what hath been premised, it is plain the objects

---

[1] In forming our units of numerable things, the mind, it may be argued, must proceed in conformity with objective relations in nature, and thus found on reason, not on individual caprice.

of sight and touch make, if I may so say, two sets of ideas, which are widely different from each other. To objects of either kind we indifferently attribute the terms high and low, right and left, and such like, denoting the position or situation of things; but then we must well observe that the position of any object is determined with respect only to objects of the same sense. We say any object of touch is high or low, according as it is more or less distant from the tangible earth: and in like manner we denominate any object of sight high or low, in proportion as it is more or less distant from the visible earth. But, to define the situation of visible things with relation to the distance they bear from any tangible thing, or *vice versa*, this were absurd and perfectly unintelligible. For all *visible* things are equally in the mind, and take up no part of the external space; and consequently are equidistant from any *tangible* thing which exists without the mind[1].

112. Or rather, to speak truly, the proper objects of sight are at no distance, neither near nor far from any tangible thing. For, if we inquire narrowly into the matter, we shall find that those things only are compared together in respect of distance which exist after the same manner, or appertain unto the same sense. For by the distance between any two points, nothing more is meant than the number of intermediate points. If the given points are visible, the distance between them is marked out by the number of the interjacent visible points; if they are tangible, the distance between them is a line consisting of tangible points; but, if they are one tangible and the other visible, the distance between them doth neither consist of points perceivable by sight nor by

---

[1] Note Berkeley's continued reticence in this *Essay* as to his 'discovery' of the essential dependence of the material world on percipient and active mind. Meantime he does not deny that 'tangible things' may exist 'without the mind,' *i.e.* unperceived. In the *Principles* he of course maintains that even this is an illegitimate sort of 'externality,' and he tries to determine what *external existence* really means.

touch, *i. e.* it is utterly inconceivable.—This, perhaps, will not find an easy admission into all men's understanding. However, I should gladly be informed whether it be not true, by any one who will be at the pains to reflect a little, and apply it home to his thoughts.

113. The not observing what has been delivered in the two last sections, seems to have occasioned no small part of the difficulty that occurs in the business of erect appearances. The head, which is painted nearest the earth, seems to be farthest from it; and on the other hand, the feet, which are painted farthest from the earth, are thought nearest to it. Herein lies the difficulty, which vanishes if we express the thing more clearly and free from ambiguity, thus :—How comes it that to the eye, the visible head, which is nearest the tangible earth, seems farthest from the earth; and the visible feet, which are farthest from the tangible earth, seem nearest the earth? The question being thus proposed, who sees not the difficulty is founded on a supposition that the eye or visive faculty, or rather the soul by means thereof, should judge of the situation of visible objects with reference to their distance from the tangible earth? Whereas, it is evident the tangible earth is not perceived by sight. And it hath been shewn, in the two last preceding sections, that the location of visible objects is determined only by the distance they bear from one another, and that it is nonsense to talk of distance, far or near, between a *visible* and *tangible* thing.

114. If we confine our thoughts to the proper objects of sight, the whole is plain and easy. The head is painted farthest from, and the feet nearest to, the visible earth; and so they appear to be. What is there strange or unaccountable in this? Let us suppose the pictures in the fund of the eye to be the immediate objects of sight. The consequence is that things should appear in the same posture they are painted in; and is it not so? The head which is seen seems farthest

from the earth which is seen; and the feet which are seen seem nearest to the earth which is seen. And just so they are painted[1].

115. But, say you, the picture of the man is inverted, and yet the appearance is erect. I ask, what mean you by the picture of the man, or, which is the same thing, the visible man's being inverted? You tell me it is inverted, because the heels are uppermost and the head undermost. Explain me this. You say that by the head's being undermost, you mean that it is nearest to the earth; and, by the heels being uppermost, that they are farthest from the earth. I ask again, what earth you mean? You cannot mean the earth that is painted on the eye or the visible earth—for the picture of the head is farthest from the picture of the earth, and the picture of the feet nearest to the picture of the earth; and accordingly the visible head is farthest from the visible earth, and the visible feet nearest to it. It remains, therefore, that you mean the tangible earth; and so determine the situation of visible things with respect to tangible things—contrary to what hath been demonstrated in sect. 111 and 112. The two distinct provinces of sight and touch should be considered apart, and as though their objects had no intercourse, no manner of relation to one another, in point of distance or position.

116. Farther, what greatly contributes to make us mistake in this matter is that, when we think of the pictures in the fund of the eye, we imagine ourselves looking on the fund of another's eye, or another looking on the fund of our own eye, and beholding the pictures painted thereon. Suppose two eyes, A and B. A from some distance looking on the pictures in B sees them inverted, and for that reason concludes they are inverted in B. But this is wrong. There are projected in little on the bottom of A the images of the pictures

---

[1] This almost seems to say that the inverted image on the retina is *itself* seen.

of, suppose, man, earth, &c., which are painted on *B*. And, besides these, the eye *B* itself, and the objects which environ it, together with another earth, are projected in a larger size on *A*. Now, by the eye *A* these larger images are deemed the true objects, and the lesser only pictures in miniature. And it is with respect to those greater images that it determines the situation of the smaller images; so that, comparing the little man with the great earth, *A* judges him inverted, or that the feet are farthest from and the head nearest to the great earth. Whereas, if *A* compare the little man with the little earth, then he will appear erect, *i. e.* his head shall seem farthest from and his feet nearest to the little earth. But we must consider that *B* does not see two earths as *A* does. It sees only what is represented by the little pictures in *A*, and consequently shall judge the man erect. For, in truth, the man in *B* is not inverted, for there the feet are next the earth; but it is the representation of it in *A* which is inverted, for there the head of the representation of the picture of the man in *B* is next the earth, and the feet farthest from the earth—meaning the earth which is without the representation of the pictures in *B*. For, if you take the little images of the pictures in *B*, and consider them by themselves, and with respect only to one another, they are all erect and in their natural posture.

117. Farther, there lies a mistake in our imagining that the pictures of external[1] objects are painted on the bottom of the eye. It has been shown there is no resemblance between the ideas of sight and things tangible. It hath likewise been demonstrated, that the proper objects of sight do not exist without the mind. Whence it clearly follows that the pictures painted on the bottom of the eye are not the pictures of external[1] objects. Let any one consult his own thoughts,

---

[1] 'External,' *i.e.* given phenomenally in touch; but without any inquiry by Berkeley here whether the extension and externality so given does or does not depend on a percipient.

and then tell me, what affinity, what likeness, there is between that certain variety and disposition of colours which constitute the visible man, or picture of a man, and that other combination of far different ideas, sensible by touch, which compose the tangible man. But, if this be the case, how come they to be accounted pictures or images, since that supposes them to copy or represent some originals or other?

118. To which I answer—In the forementioned instance, the eye *A* takes the little images, included within the representation of the other eye *B*, to be pictures or copies, whereof the archetypes are not things existing without, but the larger pictures projected on its own fund; and which by *A* are not thought pictures, but the originals or true things themselves. Though if we suppose a third eye *C*, from a due distance, to behold the fund of *A*, then indeed the things projected thereon shall, to *C*, seem pictures or images, in the same sense that those projected on *B* do to *A*.

119. Rightly to conceive the business in hand, we must carefully distinguish between the ideas of sight and touch, between the visible and tangible eye; for certainly on the tangible eye nothing either is or seems to be painted. Again, the visible eye, as well as all other visible objects, hath been shewn to exist only in the mind; which, perceiving its own ideas, and comparing them together, does call some pictures in respect to others. What hath been said, being rightly comprehended and laid together, does, I think, afford a full and genuine explication of the erect appearance of objects— which phenomenon, I must confess, I do not see how it can be explained by any theories of vision hitherto made public.

120. In treating of these things, the use of language is apt to occasion some obscurity and confusion, and create in us wrong ideas. For, language being accommodated to the common notions and prejudices of men, it is scarce possible to deliver the naked and precise truth, without great circum-

locution, impropriety, and (to an unwary reader) seeming contradictions. I do, therefore, once for all, desire whoever shall think it worth his while to understand what I have written concerning Vision, that he would not stick in this or that phrase or manner of expression, but candidly collect my meaning from the whole sum and tenor of my discourse, and, laying aside the words as much as possible, consider the bare notions[1] themselves, and then judge whether they are agreeable to truth and his own experience or no.

121. We have shewn the way wherein the mind, by mediation of visible ideas[2], doth perceive or apprehend the distance, magnitude, and situation of tangible objects. I come now to inquire more particularly concerning the difference between the ideas of Sight and Touch which are called by the same names, and see whether there be any idea common to both senses. From what we have at large set forth and demonstrated in the foregoing parts of this treatise, it is plain there is no one self-same *numerical* Extension, perceived both by sight and touch; but that the particular figures and extensions perceived by sight, however they may be called by the same names, and reputed the same things with those perceived by touch, are nevertheless different, and have an existence very distinct and separate from them. So that the question is not now concerning the same numerical ideas, but whether there be any one and the same *sort* or *species* of ideas equally perceivable to both senses? or, in other words, whether extension, figure, and motion perceived by sight, are not *specifically* distinct from extension, figure, and motion perceived by touch?

[1] This appeal is in the spirit of Descartes' rule about clear and distinct ideas as the test of truth, and of the logical precept to individualise our concepts.
[2] 'Visible ideas'—say rather *visual* ideas or sensations; for he here includes not only colours which we *see*, but also the invisible 'sensations' in the visual organ—muscular and locomotive—which are *felt* (not seen). Cf. sect. 16-27, 56, 57.

122. But, before I come more particularly to discuss this matter, I find it proper to take into my thoughts extension in abstract. For of this there is much talk; and I am apt to think that when men speak of extension as being an idea common to two senses, it is with a secret supposition that we can single out extension from all other tangible and visible qualities, and form thereof an *abstract idea*, which idea they will have common both to sight and touch. We are therefore to understand by extension in abstract, an *idea* of extension— for instance, a line or surface entirely stripped of all other sensible qualities and circumstances that might determine it to any particular existence; it is neither black, nor white, nor red, nor hath it any colour at all, or any tangible quality whatsoever, and consequently it is of no finite determinate magnitude; for that which bounds or distinguishes one extension from another is some quality or circumstance wherein they disagree [1].

123. Now, I do not find that I can perceive, imagine, or anywise frame in my mind such an abstract idea as is here spoken of. A line or surface which is neither black, nor white, nor blue, nor yellow, &c.; nor long, nor short, nor rough, nor smooth, nor square, nor round, &c.[2] is perfectly incomprehensible. This I am sure of as to myself; how far the faculties of other men may reach they best can tell [3].

124. It is commonly said that the object of Geometry is

[1] This assault on 'abstract ideas' is resumed in the 'Introduction' to the *Principles*, published a year after this *Essay*.

[2] We may, however, make a concept of a 'line,' which concept can be exemplified for the imagination in each of these particular ways, although the attributes which constitute its *content* are not necessarily connected with any one of the individual exemplifications included under its *extent*.

[3] In this reasoning against the possibility of *abstract*, as distinguished from *phenomenal* Extension, Berkeley alleges his usual objections to metaphysical abstractions. That there may be a perception of Space *necessarily* involved, by the very constitution of reason, in all visual and tactual perception, constitutive of its outwardness, and explaining perception in its difference from mere sensation (as afterwards held by Kant), nowhere occurs to him.

abstract extension. But geometry contemplates figures : now, figure is the termination of magnitude; but we have shewn that extension in abstract hath no finite determinate magnitude; whence it clearly follows that it can have no figure, and consequently is not the object of geometry. It is indeed a tenet, as well of the modern as the ancient philosophers, that all general truths are concerning *universal abstract* ideas; without which, we are told, there could be no science, no demonstration of any general proposition in geometry. But it were no hard matter, did I think it necessary to my present purpose, to shew that propositions and demonstrations in geometry might be universal, though they who make them never think of abstract general ideas of triangles or circles [1].

125. After reiterated efforts and pangs of thought to apprehend the general idea of a triangle, I have found it altogether incomprehensible. And surely, if any one were able to let that idea into my mind, it must be the author of the *Essay concerning Human Understanding:* he, who has so far distinguished himself from the generality of writers, by the clearness and significancy of what he says. Let us therefore see how that great man describes the general or abstract idea of a triangle. 'It must be,' says he, 'neither oblique nor rectangle, neither equilateral, equicrural, nor scalenum; but all and none of these at once. In effect it is somewhat imperfect that cannot exist; an idea, wherein some parts of several different and inconsistent ideas are put together.' (*Essay on Human Understanding*, b. IV. ch. 7. s. 9.) This is the idea which he thinks needful for the enlargement of

---

[1] It was the question of 'the possibility of pure mathematics, or a necessary science of the laws of space,' which suggested to Kant the analysis of perception that issued in the theory of space given in his 'Æsthetic.' The need for explaining the existence of mathematics is an obvious difficulty in the way of those who, like Berkeley, dissolving extension in sensible *minima*, have never entertained the perception of space as that on which the successive data of the senses depend for their perceivability, and which explains their transformation out of mere *phenomena that follow one another* into *outward things*.

knowledge, which is the subject of mathematical demonstration, and without which we could never come to know any general proposition concerning triangles. That author acknowledges it doth 'require some pains and skill to form this general idea of a triangle.' (*Ibid.*) But, had he called to mind what he says in another place, to wit, 'that ideas of mixed modes wherein any inconsistent ideas are put together, cannot so much as exist in the mind, *i. e.* be conceived,' (vid. b. III. ch. 10. s. 33, *ibid.*)—I say, had this occurred to his thoughts, it is not improbable he would have owned it above all the pains and skill he was master of to form the above-mentioned idea of a triangle—which is made up of manifest staring contradictions. That a man, who thought so much and so well, and laid so great a stress on clear and determinate ideas, should nevertheless talk at this rate, seems very surprising. But the wonder will lessen, if it be considered that the source whence this opinion flows is the prolific womb which has brought forth innumerable errors and difficulties, in all parts of philosophy, and in all the sciences. But this matter, taken in its full extent, were a subject too vast and comprehensive to be insisted on in this place [1]. And so much for extension in abstract.

126. Some, perhaps, may think *pure space, vacuum,* or *trine dimension,* to be equally the object of sight and touch. But, though we have a very great propension to think the ideas of Outness and Space to be the *immediate* object of sight, yet, if I mistake not, in the foregoing parts of this Essay, that hath been clearly demonstrated to be a mere delusion, arising from the quick and sudden *suggestion of*

---

[1] The question here is as to what the *triangularity* of any 'particular' triangle consists in. Does it consist in transitory phenomena, whether of colour or resistance; or in permanent intelligible relations, the presence of which converts the 'phenomena' into scientific knowledge of a triangle, and also explains the universality of mathematical propositions? Neither Locke nor Berkeley looks at the question in this light, nor inquires into the respective offices of Sense, with its empirical data, and of Reason, with its fixed relations, in the constitution of human knowledge.

fancy, which so closely connects the idea of distance with those of sight, that we are apt to think it is itself a proper and immediate object of that sense, till reason corrects the mistake[1].

127. It having been shewn that there are no abstract ideas of figure, and that it is impossible for us, by any *precision* of thought, to frame an idea of extension separate from all other visible and tangible qualities, which shall be common both to sight and touch—the question now remaining is, Whether the particular extensions, figures, and motions perceived by sight, be of the same kind with the particular extensions, figures, and motions perceived by touch? In answer to which I shall venture to lay down the following proposition:—*The extension, figures, and motions perceived by sight are specifically distinct from the ideas of touch, called by the same names; nor is there any such thing as one idea, or kind of idea, common to both senses*[2]. This proposition may, without much difficulty, be collected from what hath

[1] Does he mean to imply that Outness could be supposed to be the immediate object of either sense, if by this be meant that it is presented as a mere aggregate of *minima visibilia* (sensations of colour) or of *minima tangibilia* (sensations of movement and resistance)? This way of expressing it is surely inadequate to the facts of which we are conscious, when we perceive phenomena as outward objects, whether in seeing or in touching them. But whether the genuine perception of outwardness is *called forth* in touch, in sight, or in comparing the presentations of sight with those of touch, or in each of the five senses, may still be a question.

[2] This implies that there are no 'common sensibles,' as Aristotle called them, and as the primary qualities are by many held to be. That space may be a common and presupposed perception, *necessarily* involved in all perceptions of sense, while *per se* inconceivable apart from these perceptions, does not occur to Berkeley. He rightly insists on the impossibility of perceiving or conceiving space separately from empirical phenomena of sense; but he does not seem to apprehend the counter impossibility of anything external being perceived or conceived *as outward* without space; nor that the perceptions which involve extension may be *occasioned* by sensations in touch or in sight, without space being therefore identified either with feelings or with sensations of colour. Is it not the perception thus occasioned that *gives outness* to what we are conscious of in sense, and enables us to conceive objects as 'outward,' or in space—not merely as unknown powers that are 'external' to, because uncontrollable by, our free agency?

been said in several places of this Essay. But, because it seems so remote from, and contrary to the received notions and settled opinion of mankind, I shall attempt to demonstrate it more particularly and at large by the following arguments :—

128. *First*, When, upon perception of an idea, I range it under this or that sort, it is because it is perceived after the same manner, or because it has a likeness or conformity with or affects me in the same way as the ideas of the sort I rank it under. It short, it must not be entirely new, but have something in it old and already perceived by me. It must, I say, have so much, at least, in common with the ideas I have before known and named, as to make me give it the same name with them. But, it has been, if I mistake not, clearly made out that a man born blind would not, at first reception of his sight, think the things he saw were of the same nature with the objects of touch, or had anything in common with them ; but that they were a new set of ideas, perceived in a new manner, and entirely different from all he had ever perceived before. So that he would not call them by the same name, nor repute them to be of the same sort, with anything he had hitherto known.

129. *Secondly*, Light and colours are allowed by all to constitute a sort or species entirely different from the ideas of touch ; nor will any man, I presume, say they can make themselves perceived by that sense. But there is no other immediate object of sight besides light and colours. It is therefore a direct consequence, that there is no idea common to both senses.

130. It is a prevailing opinion, even amongst those who have thought and writ most accurately concerning our ideas, and the ways whereby they enter into the understanding, that something *more* is perceived by sight than barely light and colours with their variations. Mr. Locke termeth sight 'the most comprehensive of all our senses, conveying to our minds the ideas of light and colours, which are peculiar only to that

sense; and also the far different ideas of space, figure, and motion.' (*Essay on Human Understanding*, b. II. ch. 9. s. 9.) Space or distance, we have shewn, is no otherwise the object of sight than of hearing. (Vid. sect. 46.) And, as for figure and extension, I leave it to any one that shall calmly attend to his own clear and distinct ideas to decide whether he has any idea intromitted immediately and properly by sight save only light and colours: or, whether it be possible for him to frame in his mind a distinct abstract idea of visible extension, or figure, exclusive of all colour; and, on the other hand, whether he can conceive colour without visible extension? For my own part, I must confess, I am not able to attain so great a nicety of abstraction. I know very well that, in a strict sense, I see nothing but light and colours, with their several shades and variations[1]. He who beside these doth also perceive by sight ideas far different and distinct from them, hath that faculty in a degree more perfect and comprehensive than I can pretend to. It must be owned, indeed, that, by the mediation of light and colours, other far different ideas are *suggested* to my mind. But then, upon this score, I see no reason why the sight should be thought more 'comprehensive' than the hearing, which, beside sounds which are peculiar to that sense, doth, by their mediation, suggest not only space, figure, and motion, but also all other ideas whatsoever that can be signified by words.

131. *Thirdly*, It is, I think, an axiom universally received, that 'quantities of the same kind may be added together and make one entire sum.' Mathematicians add lines together; but they do not add a line to a solid, or conceive it as making one sum with a surface. These three kinds of quantity being thought incapable of any such mutual addition, and consequently of being compared together in the several ways of

---

[1] This is consistent with perception of an extension that is visible —the constituent colours being seen 'in sundry institutions' (sect. 77), and composed of a larger or smaller number of coloured points (*minima visibilia*), coexisting each outside of the other.

porportion, are by them for that reason esteemed entirely disparate and heterogeneous. Now let any one try in his thoughts to add a *visible* line or surface to a *tangible* line or surface, so as to conceive them making one continued sum or whole. He that can do this may think them homogeneous; but he that cannot must, by the foregoing axiom, think them heterogeneous. A blue and a red line I can conceive added together into one sum and making one continued line; but, to make, in my thoughts, one continued line of a visible and tangible line added together, is, I find, a task far more difficult, and even insurmountable—and I leave it to the reflection and experience of every particular person to determine for himself.

132. A farther confirmation of our tenet may be drawn from the solution of Mr. Molyneux's problem, published by Mr. Locke in his *Essay:* which I shall set down as it there lies, together with Mr. Locke's opinion of it:—'Suppose a man born blind, and now adult, and taught by his touch to distinguish between a cube and a sphere of the same metal, and nighly of the same bigness, so as to tell when he felt one and the other, which is the cube and which the sphere. Suppose then the cube and sphere placed on a table, and the blind man made to see: Quære, Whether by his sight, before he touched them, he could now distinguish, and tell, which is the globe, which the cube. To which the acute and judicious proposer answers: Not. For, though he has obtained the experience of how a globe, how a cube affects his touch; yet he has not yet attained the experience, that what affects his touch so or so must affect his sight so or so: or that a protuberant angle in the cube, that pressed his hand unequally, shall appear to his eye as it doth in the cube. I agree with this thinking gentleman, whom I am proud to call my friend, in his answer to this his problem; and am of opinion that the blind man, at first sight, would not be able with certainty to say, which was the globe, which the cube,

whilst he only saw them.' (*Essay on Human Understanding*, b. II. ch. 9. s. 8 [1].)

133. Now, if a square surface perceived by touch be of the same *sort* with a square surface perceived by sight, it is certain the blind man here mentioned might know a square surface as soon as he saw it. It is no more but introducing into his mind, by a new inlet, an idea he has been already well acquainted with. Since therefore he is supposed to have known by his touch that a cube is a body terminated by square surfaces; and that a sphere is not terminated by square surfaces—upon the supposition that a visible and tangible square differ only *in numero*, it follows that he might know, by the unerring mark of the square surfaces, which was the cube, and which not, while he only saw them. We must therefore allow, either that visible extension and figures are specifically distinct from tangible extension and figures, or else, that the solution of this problem, given by those two thoughtful and ingenious men, is wrong.

134. Much more might be laid together in proof of the proposition I have advanced. But, what has been said is, if I mistake not, sufficient to convince any one that shall yield a reasonable attention. And, as for those that will not be at the pains of a little thought, no multiplication of words will ever suffice to make them understand the truth, or rightly conceive my meaning.

135. I cannot let go the above-mentioned problem without some reflection on it. It hath been made evident that a man blind from his birth would not, at first sight, denominate anything he saw, by the names he had been used to appropriate to ideas of touch. (Vid. sect. 106.) Cube, sphere, table are words he has known applied to things perceivable by touch, but to things perfectly intangible he never knew them applied. Those words, in their wonted application,

---

[1] See Leibnitz (*Nouveaux Essais*, liv. II. ch. 9), who disputes the alleged heterogeneity.

always marked out to his mind bodies or solid things which were perceived by the resistance they gave. But there is no solidity, no resistance or protrusion, perceived by sight. In short, the ideas of sight are all new perceptions, to which there be no names annexed in his mind; he cannot therefore understand what is said to him concerning them. And, to ask of the two bodies he saw placed on the table, which was the sphere, which the cube, were to him a question downright bantering and unintelligible; nothing he sees being able to suggest to his thoughts the idea of body, distance, or, in general, of anything he had already known.

136. It is a mistake to think the *same* thing affects both sight and touch. If the same angle or square which is the object of touch be also the object of vision, what should hinder the blind man, at first sight, from knowing it? For, though the manner wherein it affects the sight be different from that wherein it affected his touch, yet, there being, beside this manner or circumstance, which is new and unknown, the angle or figure, which is old and known, he cannot choose but discern it.

137. Visible figure and extension having been demonstrated to be of a nature entirely different and heterogeneous from tangible figure and extension, it remains that we inquire concerning *motion*. Now, that visible motion is not of the same sort with tangible motion seems to need no farther proof; it being an evident corollary from what we have shewn concerning the difference there is betwixt visible and tangible extension. But, for a more full and express proof hereof, we need only observe that one who had not yet experienced vision would not at first sight know motion. Whence it clearly follows that motion perceivable by sight is of a sort distinct from motion perceivable by touch. The antecedent I prove thus—By touch he could not perceive any motion but what was up or down, to the right or left, nearer or farther from him; besides these, and their several varieties

or complications, it is impossible he should have any idea of motion. He would not therefore think anything to be motion, or give the name motion to any idea, which he could not range under some or other of those particular kinds thereof. But, from sect. 95, it is plain that, by the mere act of vision, he could not know motion upwards or downwards, to the right or left, or in any other possible direction. From which I conclude, he would not know motion at all at first sight[1].—As for the idea of motion in abstract, I shall not waste paper about it, but leave it to my reader to make the best he can of it. To me it is perfectly unintelligible.

138. The consideration of motion may furnish a new field for inquiry. But, since the manner wherein the mind apprehends by sight the motion of tangible objects, with the various degrees thereof, may be easily collected from what has been said concerning the manner wherein that sense doth suggest their various distances, magnitudes, and situations, I shall not enlarge any farther on this subject, but proceed to inquire what may be alleged, with greatest appearance of reason, against the proposition we have demonstrated to be true; for, where there is so much prejudice to be encountered, a bare and naked demonstration of the truth will scarce suffice. We must also satisfy the scruples that men may start in favour of their preconceived notions, shew whence the mistake arises, how it came to spread, and carefully disclose and root out those false persuasions that an early prejudice might have implanted in the mind.

139. *First*, therefore, it will be demanded how visible ex-

---

[1] We should not, at first, he holds, be able to interpret the visual signs of real movements—organic or extra-organic. On Berkeley's further developed doctrine, real space in its three dimensions consists of tactual sensations and active consciousness of movements; but the sight of coloured extension, and familiarity with the signs of real extensions which it affords, is required as a condition for enabling us distinctly to *image* local exteriority, or an 'ambient space'—very much as artificial language is a condition indispensable to our being able to pursue a train of reasoning.

tension and figures come to be called by the same *name* with tangible extension and figures, if they are not of the same kind with them? It must be something more than humour or accident that could occasion a custom so constant and universal as this, which has obtained in all ages and nations of the world, and amongst all ranks of men, the learned as well as the illiterate.

140. To which I answer, we can no more argue a visible and tangible square to be of the same species, from their being called by the same name, than we can that a tangible square, and the monosyllable consisting of six letters whereby it is marked, are of the same species, because they are both called by the same name. It is customary to call written words, and the things they signify, by the same name: for, words not being regarded in their own nature, or otherwise than as they are marks of things, it had been superfluous, and beside the design of language, to have given them names distinct from those of the things marked by them. The same reason holds here also. Visible figures are the marks of tangible figures; and, from sect. 59, it is plain that in themselves they are little regarded, or upon any other score than for their connexion with tangible figures, which by nature they are ordained to signify. And, because this Language of Nature does not vary in different ages or nations, hence it is that in all times and places visible figures are called by the same names as the respective tangible figures suggested by them; and not because they are alike, or of the same sort with them.

141. But, say you, surely a tangible square is liker to a visible square than to a visible circle: it has four angles, and as many sides; so also has the visible square—but the visible circle has no such thing, being bounded by one uniform curve, without right lines or angles, which makes it unfit to represent the tangible square, but very fit to represent the tangible circle. Whence it clearly follows, that visible figures are

patterns of, or of the same species with, the respective tangible figures represented by them; that they are like unto them, and of their own nature fitted to represent them, as being of the same sort; and that they are in no respect arbitrary signs, as words.

142. I answer, it must be acknowledged the visible square is fitter than the visible circle to represent the tangible square, but then it is not because it is liker, or more of a species with it; but, because the visible square contains in it several distinct parts, whereby to mark the several distinct corresponding parts of a tangible square, whereas the visible circle doth not. The square perceived by touch hath four distinct equal sides, so also hath it four distinct equal angles. It is therefore necessary that the visible figure which shall be most proper to mark it contain four distinct equal parts, corresponding to the four sides of the tangible square; as likewise four other distinct and equal parts, whereby to denote the four equal angles of the tangible square. And accordingly we see the visible figures contain in them distinct visible parts, answering to the distinct tangible parts of the figures signified or suggested by them.

143. But, it will not hence follow that any visible figure is like unto or of the same species with its corresponding tangible figure—unless it be also shewn that not only the number, but also the kind of the parts be the same in both. To illustrate this, I observe that visible figures represent tangible figures much after the same manner that written words do sounds. Now, in this respect, words are not arbitrary; it not being indifferent what written word stands for any sound. But, it is requisite that each word contain in it as many distinct characters as there are variations in the sound it stands for. Thus, the single letter *a* is proper to mark one simple uniform sound; and the word *adultery* is accommodated to represent the sound annexed to it—in the formation whereof there being eight different collisions or modifications of the air by

the organs of speech, each of which produces a difference of sound, it was fit the word representing it should consist of as many distinct characters, thereby to mark each particular difference or part of the whole sound. And yet nobody, I presume, will say the single letter *a*, or the word *adultery*, are alike unto or of the same species with the respective sounds by them represented. It is indeed arbitrary that, in general, letters of any language represent sounds at all; but, when that is once agreed, it is not arbitrary what combination of letters shall represent this or that particular sound. I leave this with the reader to pursue, and apply it in his own thoughts.

144. It must be confessed that we are not so apt to confound other signs with the things signified, or to think them of the same species, as we are visible and tangible ideas. But, a little consideration will shew us how this may well be, without our supposing them of a like nature. These signs are constant and universal; their connexion with tangible ideas has been learnt at our first entrance into the world; and ever since, almost every moment of our lives, it has been occurring to our thoughts, and fastening and striking deeper on our minds. When we observe that signs are variable, and of human institution; when we remember there was a time they were not connected in our minds with those things they now so readily suggest, but that their signification was learned by the slow steps of experience: this preserves us from confounding them. But, when we find the same signs suggest the same things all over the world; when we know they are not of human institution, and cannot remember that we ever learned their signification, but think that at first sight they would have suggested to us the same things they do now: all this persuades us they are of the same species as the things respectively represented by them, and that it is by a natural resemblance they suggest them to our minds.

145. Add to this that whenever we make a nice survey of any object, successively directing the optic axis to each point thereof, there are certain lines and figures, described by the motion of the head or eye, which, being in truth perceived by feeling, do nevertheless so mix themselves, as it were, with the ideas of sight that we can scarce think but they appertain to that sense. Again, the ideas of sight enter into the mind several at once, more distinct and unmingled than is usual in the other senses beside the touch. Sounds, for example, perceived at the same instant, are apt to coalesce, if I may so say, into one sound: but we can perceive, at the same time, great variety of visible objects, very separate and distinct from each other. Now, tangible extension being made up of several distinct coexistent parts, we may hence gather another reason that may dispose us to imagine a likeness or analogy between the immediate objects of sight and touch. But nothing, certainly, does more contribute to blend and confound them together, than the strict and close connexion they have with each other. We cannot open our eyes but the ideas of distance, bodies, and tangible figures are suggested by them. So swift, and sudden, and unperceived is the transit from visible to tangible ideas that we can scarce forbear thinking them *equally* the immediate object of vision.

146. The prejudice which is grounded on these, and whatever other causes may be assigned thereof, sticks so fast on our understandings, that it is impossible, without obstinate striving and labour of the mind, to get entirely clear of it. But then the reluctancy we find in rejecting any opinion can be no argument of its truth, to whoever considers what has been already shewn with regard to the prejudices we entertain concerning the distance, magnitude, and situation of objects; prejudices so familiar to our minds, so confirmed and inveterate, as they will hardly give way to the clearest demonstration.

147 [1]. Upon the whole, I think we may fairly conclude that the proper objects of vision constitute the Universal Language of Nature, whereby we are instructed how to regulate our actions, in order to attain those things that are necessary to the preservation and well-being of our bodies, as also to avoid whatever may be hurtful and destructive of them. It is by their information that we are principally guided in all the transactions and concerns of life. And the manner wherein they signify and mark out unto us the objects which are at a distance is the same with that of languages and signs of human appointment; which do not suggest the things signified by any likeness or identity of nature, but only by an habitual connexion that experience has made us to observe between them.

148. Suppose one who had always continued blind be told by his guide that after he has advanced so many steps he shall come to the brink of a precipice, or be stopped by a wall; must not this to him seem very admirable and surprising? He cannot conceive how it is possible for mortals to frame such predictions as these, which to him would seem as strange and unaccountable as prophecy does to others. Even they who are blessed with the visive faculty may (though familiarity make it less observed) find therein sufficient cause of admiration. The wonderful art and contrivance wherewith it is adjusted to those ends and purposes for which it was apparently designed; the vast extent, number, and variety of

[1] In this and the next section Berkeley sums up the 'theory' which the preceding analyses called for; after having as he believed shewn the complete heterogeneity of the original data in the sense of Sight, and the original data in the sense of Touch. He had been gradually approaching it in the preceding sections, where his favourite metaphor of a 'language' in nature occurs, with the implied *arbitrariness* and *generality* in the signs. When this theory is pushed into its issues, the mathematical as well as physical sciences appear as if based on arbitrary relations among the data of the two senses, all their inferences being sustained by 'suggestions' which are themselves not fully explained, and which yield only *general*, not *necessary* or *universal* conclusions. Compare *Vindication*, sect. 35-47.

objects that are at once, with so much ease, and quickness, and pleasure, suggested by it—all these afford subject for much and pleasing speculation, and may, if anything, give us some glimmering analogous prænotion of things, that are placed beyond the certain discovery and comprehension of our present state [1].

149. I do not design to trouble myself much with drawing corollaries from the doctrine I have hitherto laid down. If it bears the test, others may, so far as they shall think convenient, employ their thoughts in extending it farther, and applying it to whatever purposes it may be subservient to. Only, I cannot forbear making some inquiry concerning the object of Geometry, which the subject we have been upon does naturally lead one to. We have shewn there is no such idea as that of extension in abstract, and that there are two kinds of sensible extension and figures, which are entirely distinct and heterogeneous from each other. Now, it is natural to inquire which of these is the object of geometry [2].

150. Some things there are which, at first sight, incline one to think geometry conversant about *visible* extension. The constant use of the eyes, both in the practical and speculative parts of that science, doth very much induce us thereto. It would, without doubt, seem odd to a mathematician to go about to convince him the diagrams he saw upon paper were not the figures, or even the likeness of the figures, which make the subject of the demonstration—the contrary being held an unquestionable truth, not only by mathematicians, but also by those who apply themselves more particularly to the

[1] Mixed mathematical science is on Berkeley's theory *previsive*. The Book of Vision is throughout a Book of God, which we are really interpreting, when we seem to be seeing, and which we find to be literally a Book of Prophecy.

[2] But it has been held that the 'object of geometry' is neither the phenomena of colour nor the phenomena of resistance, but an extension that is necessarily presupposed in all perception of sensible objects, although not in its intelligible relations an object of any of the senses. This view of space, as somehow universally and necessarily blended with the data of sight and touch, is not entertained in the *Essay*.

study of logic; I mean who consider the nature of science, certainty, and demonstration; it being by them assigned as one reason of the extraordinary clearness and evidence of geometry, that in that science the reasonings are free from those inconveniences which attend the use of arbitrary signs, the very ideas themselves being copied out, and exposed to view upon paper. But, by the bye, how well this agrees with what they likewise assert as abstract ideas being the object of geometrical demonstration I leave to be considered.

151. To come to a resolution in this point, we need only observe what has been said in sect. 59, 60, 61, where it is shewn that visible extensions in themselves are little regarded, and have no settled determinate greatness, and that men measure altogether by the application of tangible extension to tangible extension. All which makes it evident that visible extension and figures are not the object of geometry.

152. It is therefore plain that visible figures are of the same use in geometry that words are. And the one may as well be accounted the object of that science as the other; neither of them being any otherwise concerned therein than as they represent or suggest to the mind the particular tangible figures connected with them. There is, indeed, this difference betwixt the signification of tangible figures by visible figures, and of ideas by words—that whereas the latter is variable and uncertain, depending altogether on the arbitrary appointment of men, the former is fixed, and immutably the same in all times and places. A visible square, for instance, suggests to the mind the same tangible figure in Europe that it doth in America. Hence it is, that the voice of nature, which speaks to our eyes, is not liable to that misinterpretation and ambiguity that languages of human contrivance are unavoidably subject to. From which may, in some measure, be derived that peculiar evidence and clearness of geometrical demonstrations.

153. Though what has been said may suffice to shew what

ought to be determined with relation to the object of geometry, I shall, nevertheless, for the fuller illustration thereof, take into my thoughts the case of an intelligence or unbodied spirit, which is supposed to see perfectly well, *i.e.* to have a clear perception of the proper and immediate objects of sight, but to have no sense of touch. Whether there be any such being in nature or no, is beside my purpose to inquire; it suffices, that the supposition contains no contradiction in it. Let us now examine what proficiency such a one may be able to make in geometry. Which speculation will lead us more clearly to see whether the ideas of sight can possibly be the object of that science[1].

154. *First*, then, it is certain the aforesaid intelligence could have no idea of a solid or quantity of three dimensions, which follows from its not having any idea of distance. We, indeed, are prone to think that we have by sight the ideas of space and solids; which arises from our imagining that we do, strictly speaking, see distance, and some parts of an object at a greater distance than others; which has been demonstrated to be the effect of the experience we have had what ideas of touch are connected with such and such ideas attending vision. But the intelligence here spoken of is supposed to have no experience of touch. He would not, therefore, judge as we do, nor have any idea of distance, outness, or profundity, nor consequently of space or body, either immediately or by suggestion. Whence it is plain he can have no notion of those parts of geometry which relate to the mensuration of solids, and their convex or concave surfaces, and

[1] This is a conjecture, not as to the possible conceptions of the born blind, but as to the conceptions of an 'unbodied' intelligence, capable only of the 'ideas' of pure vision. Compare Reid's speculations on the 'Geometry of Visibles' and the Idomenians, *Inquiry*, ch. vi. s. 9—as to which Priestley remarks, 'I do not remember to have seen a more egregious piece of solemn trifling than the chapter which our author calls the "Geometry of Visibles," and his account of the "Idomenians," as he terms those imaginary beings who have no ideas of substance but from sight.' See Reid's allusion to this passage in his *Essays on the Intellectual Powers*, p. 282, Hamilton's Edition.

contemplate the properties of lines generated by the section of a solid. The conceiving of any part whereof is beyond the reach of his faculties.

155. *Farther*, he cannot comprehend the manner wherein geometers describe a right line or circle; the rule and compass, with their use, being things of which it is impossible he should have any notion. Nor is it an easier matter for him to conceive the placing of one plane or angle on another, in order to prove their equality; since that supposes some idea of distance, or external space. All which makes it evident our pure intelligence could never attain to know so much as the first elements of plain geometry. And perhaps, upon a nice inquiry, it will be found he cannot even have an idea of plain figures any more than he can of solids; since some idea of distance is necessary to form the idea of a geometrical plane, as will appear to whoever shall reflect a little on it.

156. All that is properly perceived by the visive faculty amounts to no more than colours with their variations, and different proportions of light and shade—but the perpetual mutability and fleetingness of those immediate objects of sight render them incapable of being managed after the manner of geometrical figures; nor is it in any degree useful that they should. It is true there be divers of them perceived at once; and more of some, and less of others; but accurately to compute their magnitude, and assign precise determinate proportions between things so variable and inconstant, if we suppose it possible to be done, must yet be a very trifling and insignificant labour.

157. I must confess, it seems to be the opinion of some very ingenious men that flat or plane figures are immediate objects of sight, though they acknowledge solids are not. And this opinion of theirs is grounded on what is observed in painting, wherein (say they) the ideas immediately imprinted in the mind are only of planes variously coloured, which, by a sudden act of the judgment, are changed into solids: but,

with a little attention, we shall find the planes here mentioned as the immediate objects of sight are not visible but tangible planes. For, when we say that pictures are planes, we mean thereby that they appear to the touch smooth and uniform. But then this smoothness and uniformity, or, in other words, this planeness of the picture is not perceived immediately by vision; for it appeareth to the eye various and multiform.

158. From all which we may conclude that planes are no more the immediate object of sight than solids. What we strictly see are not solids, nor yet planes variously coloured— they are only diversity of colours. And some of these suggest to the mind solids, and others plain figures; just as they have been experienced to be connected with the one or the other: so that we see planes in the same way that we see solids—both being equally suggested by the immediate objects of sight, which accordingly are themselves denominated planes and solids. But, though they are called by the same names with the things marked by them, they are, nevertheless, of a nature entirely different, as hath been demonstrated[1].

[1] Does Berkeley mean to hint, in this and the preceding sections, that the only proper object of sight is *unextended* colour—that even superficial extension is invisible—and that, apart from sensations and exertions in the motor organs, all *visibilia* are regarded as unextended points? For, it has since been asked whether even the smallest coloured extension could be seen without an experience of organic movement? Among British writers, Brown (*Lectures*, XXIX), J. S. Mill (*Exam. of Hamilton*, pp. 285-287), and Dr. Bain (*Senses and Intellect*, pp. 366-378), answer this question in the negative. They virtually analyse our perception of extension in length and breadth, as well as in depth, into sensations of impeded and unimpeded organic movement, including muscular expansion and contraction. They deny that *form* can be seen in colour alone, or that what we mean by visible form can be conceived by one who has never been conscious of sensations of locomotion—at least in the eye. They suppose us to understand by a 'round' form something that presupposes a felt sweep of the eye to enable us to apprehend it. We must, it is argued, have experience of movement before we can find *any* extension in our visual perceptions of colour. 'I cannot,' says Mill, 'admit that we could have what is meant by a perception of *superficial* space, unless we conceived it as something which the hand could be moved across.' Yet both Mill and Dr. Bain seem to allow that when the extended area is very small (less than $\frac{1}{10}$ of

159. What has been said is, if I mistake not, sufficient to decide the question we proposed to examine, concerning the ability of a pure spirit, such as we have described, to know geometry. It is, indeed, no easy matter for us to enter precisely into the thoughts of such an intelligence; because we cannot, without great pains, cleverly separate and disentangle in our thoughts the proper objects of sight from those of touch which are connected with them. This, indeed, in a complete degree seems scarce possible to be performed; which will not seem strange to us, if we consider how hard it is for any one to hear the words of his native language, which is familiar to him, pronounced in his ears without understand-

an inch in diameter), it can be seen without any motion even in the visual organ. On this subject see Hamilton's Lectures on Metaphysics, vol. II. p. 165, where a reason is offered for concluding the *necessary* implication of superficial extension in all sense-experience of colours.

As to all this the question arises, whether the very perception of phenomena in motion does not necessarily presuppose that of space or room, as the condition of our having it. If so, the proposed explanation of the latter by the former would involve *petitio principii*. Can the notion of motion be resolved into that of *successive* phenomena of any kind? As a relative question, one might also ask what conception of motion is possible to a person born blind?

Some hold that all sensuous impressions, in all the senses, are originally given as external to one another in place—in short, that we cannot have *any* organic sensation without a corresponding perception of an involved extension—that 'sensation proper [of our organism] and perception proper [of the extended] exist only as they co-exist,' though always in an inverse ratio of intensity—and that we are originally and properly sentient and percipient of our own extended organism and of that only. 'All the senses,' says Hamilton, 'simply or in combination, afford conditions for the perception of the primary qualities' (Reid, *Works*, p. 864). But of what sort of 'extension' is this affirmed: and do we find as a fact in any of the senses that, in any meaning of extension, we perceive the extent of the organ affected?

'Mind *alone*,' says Mansel, 'is not capable of sensation; for it is sentient only so far as it animates a bodily organism. That a disembodied spirit *has consciousness* we must believe;—at least it is impossible to conceive how spiritual existence can be otherwise manifested;—but it is impossible to conceive such consciousness as at all resembling our own, at any rate in the particular phenomena which are conveyed by means of the senses' (*Metaphysics*, p. 91). Compare this assumption with Berkeley, quoted in note 1, p. 132, who assumes, on the contrary, that it is possible to be conscious of seeing colours without our having an eye, and sounds when we are destitute of our present organ of hearing.

ing them. Though he endeavour to disunite the meaning from the sound, it will nevertheless intrude into his thoughts, and he shall find it extreme difficult, if not impossible, to put himself exactly in the posture of a foreigner that never learnt the language, so as to be affected barely with the sounds themselves, and not perceive the signification annexed to them.—By this time, I suppose, it is clear that neither *abstract* nor *visible* extension makes the object of geometry; the not discerning of which may, perhaps, have created some difficulty and useless labour in Mathematics.

⁎ I am informed that, soon after the first edition of this treatise, a man somewhere near London was made to see, who had been born blind and continued so for about twenty years[1]. Such a one may be supposed a proper judge to decide how far some tenets laid down in several places of the foregoing Essay are agreeable to truth; and if any curious person hath the opportunity of making proper interrogatories to him thereon, I should gladly see my notions either amended or confirmed by experience.

[1] This reference (added in the second edition) seems to be to a case, described in the *Tatler* (No. 55) of August 16, 1709, of a young man, William Jones, born blind, who, at the age of twenty, on the 29th of June preceding, had received sight by a surgical operation. The question which these experiments may help to determine is, whether the space perceived in sight and the space perceived in touch are identical; or whether, on the contrary, our tendency to suppose them the same may not be explained by the fact that the data of sight are signs which lead us, through *suggestion* consequent upon custom, to anticipate experiences of tactual extension which the visual signs signify—thus producing an illusion of their sameness.

DIVINE VISUAL LANGUAGE:

A DIALOGUE.

DIVINE VISUAL LANGUAGE:

A DIALOGUE[1].

1. EARLY the next morning, as I looked out of my window, I saw Alciphron walking in the garden with all the

---

[1] This is the Fourth of the Seven Dialogues, published by Berkeley in 1732, under the title of *Alciphron, or the Minute Philosopher*. 'Minute philosophers' were sensationalist sceptics. Alciphron and Lysicles represent minute philosophy—the former in its more intellectual form, and the latter as received by men of pleasure; Euphranor and Crito vindicate religion. The following Dialogue discusses the reason for our faith in the perpetual activity of God in the world to which we are awakened in the Senses. As the Power that regulates the succession of phenomena present in the senses is continually making us percipient in Sight of significant phenomena, which are to all intents and purposes a Universal Language, it is argued that we have the same kind (and a greater amount) of evidence for that Power being an intelligent and intending Spirit as we have for the existence of a human being when one is actually speaking to us. The explanation raises the inquiry, how individual mind communicates with individual mind through the medium of a material world composed of sense phenomena. The lesson is that the world of visible phenomena is a symbolical revelation of God; that nature is significant of a religious meaning; that natural laws are the expression of a constant providence.

The subject is introduced in sect. 1-7. The theory that what is commonly called 'seeing' is to a great degree interpreting what is seen is explained in sect. 8-15; where it is argued that, as the visible world at least has no independent existence, the phenomena presented to Sight, in their orderly and therefore significant relations to those of Touch, must be the expression of Supreme Rational Will.—The remainder of the Dialogue (sect. 16-24) is devoted to a discussion of the nature and limits of human knowledge of the Supreme Power. Crito argues that it cannot be merely negative; for absolute nescience is not consistent with faith. It is a supreme governing Spirit, on whom we all depend; the knowledge or 'notion' we have of our own *ego* being the root of our knowledge of *all* spiritual agency—finite or Divine. God is inferred from the significant phenomena of the visible world in the same sort of way that other human spirits are inferred from their words and actions manifested to our senses.

This Dialogue may be taken as an introduction to Natural Theology, founded on the suggested significance of the data of Sense—especially of sight.

signs of a man in deep thought. Upon which I went down to him.

Alciphron, said I, this early and profound meditation puts me in no small fright.

How so?

Because I should be sorry to be convinced there was no God. The thought of anarchy in Nature is to me more shocking than in civil life: inasmuch as natural concerns are more important than civil, and the basis of all others.

I grant, replied Alciphron, that some inconvenience may possibly follow from disproving a God: but as to what you say of fright and shocking, all that is nothing but mere prejudice. Men frame an idea or chimera in their own minds, and then fall down and worship it. Notions govern mankind: but of all notions that of God's governing the world hath taken the deepest root and spread the farthest: it is therefore in philosophy an heroical achievement to dispossess this imaginary monarch of his government, and banish all those fears and spectres which the light of reason can alone dispel:

Non radii solis, non lucida tela diei
Discutiunt, sed naturae species ratioque [1].

My part, said I, shall be to stand by, as I have hitherto done, and take notes of all that passeth during this memorable event; while a minute philosopher, not six feet high, attempts to dethrone the monarch of the universe.

Alas! replied *Alciphron*, arguments are not to be measured by feet and inches. One man may see more than a million; and a short argument, managed by a free-thinker, may be sufficient to overthrow the most gigantic chimera.

As we were engaged in this discourse, Crito and Euphranor joined us.

I find you have been beforehand with us to-day, said *Crito* to Alciphron, and taken the advantage of solitude and early

[1] Lucretius.

hours, while Euphranor and I were asleep in our beds. We may, therefore, expect to see Atheism placed in the best light, and supported by the strongest arguments.

2. *Alc.* The being of a God is a subject upon which there has been a world of commonplace, which it is needless to repeat. Give me leave therefore to lay down certain rules and limitations, in order to shorten our present conference. For, as the end of debating is to persuade, all those things which are foreign to this end should be left out of our debate.

First then, let me tell you I am not to be persuaded by metaphysical arguments; such, for instance, as are drawn from the idea of an all-perfect being, or the absurdity of an infinite progression of causes. This sort of arguments I have always found dry and jejune; and, as they are not suited to my way of thinking, they may perhaps puzzle, but never will convince me. Secondly, I am not to be persuaded by the authority either of past or present ages, of mankind in general, or of particular wise men, all which passeth for little or nothing with a man of sound argument and free thought. Thirdly, all proofs drawn from utility or convenience are foreign to the purpose. They may prove indeed the usefulness of the notion, but not the existence of the thing. Whatever legislators or statesmen may think, truth and convenience are very different things to the rigorous eye of a philosopher.

And now, that I may not seem partial, I will limit myself also not to object, in the first place, from anything that may seem irregular or unaccountable in the works of nature, against a cause of infinite power and wisdom; because I already know the answer you will make, to wit, that no one can judge of the symmetry and use of the parts of an infinite machine, which are all relative to each other, and to the whole, without being able to comprehend the entire machine, or the whole universe. And, in the second place, I shall engage myself not to object against the justice and providence of a supreme Being from the evil that befalls good men, and the prosperity which is often the portion of wicked men in this life; because I know that, instead of admitting this to be an objection against a Deity, you would make it an argument for a future state, in which there shall be such a retribution of rewards and punishments as may vindicate the Divine attributes, and set all things right in the end. Now, these answers, though they should be admitted for good ones, are in truth no proofs of the being of God, but only solutions of certain difficulties which might be objected, supposing it already proved by proper arguments. Thus much I thought fit to premise, in order to save time and trouble both to you and myself.

Cri. I think that as the proper end of our conference ought to be supposed the discovery and defence of truth, so truth may be justified, not only by persuading its adversaries, but, where that cannot be done, by shewing them to be unreasonable. Arguments, therefore, which carry light have their effect, even against an opponent who shuts his eyes, because they shew him to be obstinate and prejudiced. Besides, this distinction between arguments that puzzle and that convince, is least of all observed by minute philosophers, and need not therefore be observed by others in their favour. — But, perhaps, Euphranor may be willing to encounter you on your own terms, in which case I have nothing further to say.

3. *Euph.* Alciphron acts like a skilful general, who is bent upon gaining the advantage of the ground, and alluring the enemy out of their trenches. We who believe a God are entrenched within tradition, custom, authority, and law. And, nevertheless, instead of attempting to force us, he proposes that we should voluntarily abandon these intrenchments, and make the attack; when we may act on the defensive with much security and ease, leaving him the trouble to dispossess us of what we need not resign. Those reasons (continued he, addressing himself to Alciphron) which you have mustered up in this morning's meditation, if they do not weaken, must

establish our belief of a God; for the utmost is to be expected from so great a master in his profession, when he sets his strength to a point.

Alc. I hold the confused notion of a Deity, or some invisible power, to be of all prejudices the most unconquerable. When half-a-dozen ingenious men are got together over a glass of wine, by a cheerful fire, in a room well lighted, we banish with ease all the spectres of fancy and education, and are very clear in our decisions. But, as I was taking a solitary walk before it was broad daylight in yonder grove, methought the point was not quite so clear; nor could I readily recollect the force of those arguments which used to appear so conclusive at other times. I had I know not what awe upon my mind, and seemed haunted by a sort of panic, which I cannot otherwise account for than by supposing it the effect of prejudice: for, you must know, that I, like the rest of the world, was once upon a time catechised and tutored into the belief of a God or Spirit. There is no surer mark of prejudice than the believing a thing without reason. What necessity then can there be that I should set myself the difficult task of proving a negative, when it is sufficient to observe that there is no proof of the affirmative, and that the admitting it without proof is unreasonable? Prove therefore your opinion; or, if you cannot, you may indeed remain in possession of it, but you will only be possessed of a prejudice.

Euph. O Alciphron, to content you we must prove, it seems, and we must prove upon your own terms. But, in the first place, let us see what sort of proof you expect.

Alc. Perhaps I may not expect it, but I will tell you what sort of proof I would have: and that is, in short—such proof as every man of sense requires of a matter of fact, or the existence of any other particular thing. For instance, should a man ask why I believe there is a king of Great Britain? I might answer—Because I had seen him. Or a king of Spain?

Because I had seen those who saw him. But as for this King of kings, I neither saw him myself, or any one else that ever did see Him. Surely, if there be such a thing as God, it is very strange that He should leave Himself without a witness; that men should still dispute His being; and that there should be no one evident, sensible, plain proof of it, without recourse to philosophy or metaphysics. A matter of fact is not to be proved by notions, but by facts[1]. This is clear and full to the point. You see what I would be at. Upon these principles I defy superstition.

Euph. You believe then as far as you can see?

Alc. That is my rule of faith.

Euph. How! will you not believe the existence of things which you hear, unless you also see them?

Alc. I will not say so neither. When I insisted on *seeing*, I would be understood to mean perceiving in general. Outward objects make very different impressions upon the animal spirits, all of which are comprised under the common name of *sense*. And whatever we can perceive by *any* sense we may be sure of.

---

[1] So Hume in *Inquiry concerning Understanding*, sect. 4, pt. 1. Those matters of fact for which we have not the direct evidence of sense cannot be ascertained in the same way as abstract conclusions, which are demonstratively certain. 'The contrary of every matter of fact,' he points out, 'is still possible, because it can never imply a contradiction . . . That the sun will not rise to-morrow is no less intelligible a proposition, and implies no more contradiction, than the affirmation, that it will rise . . . All reasonings concerning matters of fact seem to be founded on the relation of cause and effect. [This relation with Hume, as with Berkeley, is virtually that of sign and thing signified.] If you ask a man why he believes *any matter of fact which is absent*, he would give you a reason; and this reason would be *some other fact*' [which is present].—But is God in this respect like ordinary matters of fact, as Berkeley tries to make out? His existence is the fact of the absolute supremacy of reason and moral government in the universe? 'The existence and nature of the Supreme Being,' says Reid (so far recognising the peculiarity), 'is the only *real fact* that is *necessary*. Other real existences are the effects of will and power. They had a beginning and are mutable.' (Hamilton's Reid, p. 442.) In this respect the existence of God is unique, and thus out of analogy with the existence of an embodied human spirit external to me.

4. *Euph.* What! do you believe then that there are such things as animal spirits?

Alc. Doubtless.

Euph. By what sense do you perceive them?

Alc. I do not perceive them immediately by any of my senses. I am nevertheless persuaded of their existence, because I can collect it from their effects and operations. They are the messengers which, running to and fro in the nerves, preserve a communication between the soul and outward objects.

Euph. You admit then the being of a soul?

Alc. Provided I do not admit an immaterial substance, I see no inconvenience in admitting there may be such a thing as a soul. And this may be no more than a thin fine texture of subtle parts or spirits residing in the brain.

Euph. I do not ask about its nature. I only ask whether you admit that there is a principle of thought and action, and whether it be perceivable by sense.

Alc. I grant that there is such a principle, and that it is not the object of sense itself, but inferred from appearances which are perceived by sense.

Euph. If I understand you rightly, from animal functions and motions you infer the existence of animal spirits, and from reasonable acts you infer the existence of a reasonable soul. Is is not so?

Alc. It is.

Euph. It should seem, therefore, that the being of things imperceptible to sense may be collected from effects and signs, or sensible tokens.

Alc. It may.

Euph. Tell me, Alciphron, is not the soul that which makes the principal distinction between a real person and a shadow, a living man and a carcass?

Alc. I grant it is.

Euph. I cannot, therefore, know that *you*, for instance, are a distinct thinking individual, or a living real man, by surer or other signs than those from which it can be inferred that you have a soul?

Alc. You cannot.

Euph. Pray tell me, are not all acts immediately and properly perceived by sense reducible to motion?

Alc. They are.

Euph. From motions, therefore, you infer a mover or cause; and from reasonable motions (or such as appear calculated for a reasonable end) a rational cause, soul or spirit?

Alc. Even so.

5. *Euph.* The soul of man actuates but a small body, an insignificant particle, in respect of the great masses of Nature, the elements, and heavenly bodies, and System of the World. And the wisdom that appears in those motions which are the effect of human reason is incomparably less than that which discovers itself in the structure and use of organised natural bodies, animal or vegetable. A man with his hand can make no machine so admirable as the hand itself; nor can any of those motions by which we trace out human reason approach the skill and contrivance of those wonderful motions of the heart, and brain, and other vital parts, which do not depend on the will of man.

Alc. All this is true.

Euph. Doth it not follow, then, that from natural motions, independent of man's will, may be inferred both power and wisdom incomparably greater than that of the human soul?

Alc. It should seem so.

Euph. Further, is there not in natural productions and effects a visible unity of counsel and design? Are not the rules fixed and immoveable? Do not the same laws of motion obtain throughout? The same in China and here, the same two thousand years ago and at this day?

Alc. All this I do not deny.

Euph. Is there not also a connexion or relation between

animals and vegetables, between both and the elements, between the elements and heavenly bodies; so that, from their mutual respects, influences, subordinations, and uses, they may be collected to be parts of one whole, conspiring to one and the same end, and fulfilling the same design?

Alc. Supposing all this to be true.

Euph. Will it not then follow that this vastly great, or infinite, power and wisdom must be supposed in one and the same Agent, Spirit, or Mind; and that we have at least as clear, full, and immediate certainty of the being of this infinitely wise and powerful Spirit, as of any one human soul whatsoever besides our own?

Alc. Let me consider: I suspect we proceed too hastily. What! Do you pretend you can have the same assurance of the being of a God that you can have of mine, whom you actually *see* stand before you and talk to you?

Euph. The very same, if not greater.

Alc. How do you make this appear?

Euph. By the person Alciphron is meant an individual thinking thing, and not the hair, skin, or visible surface, or any part of the outward form, colour, or shape of Alciphron.

Alc. This I grant[1].

Euph. And, in granting this, you grant that, in a strict sense, I do not see Alciphron, *i.e.* that individual thinking thing, but only such visible signs and tokens as suggest and infer[2] the being of that invisible thinking principle or soul. Even so, in the self-same manner, it seems to me that, though I cannot with eyes of flesh behold the invisible God, yet I do

---

[1] Later theological scepticism would object to this separate unbodied individuality, as an abstraction foreign to our whole experience of self-conscious personality and agency, which we always find embodied in an organism. It concludes, accordingly, that self-conscious persons and all their states ultimately depend on organised matter, and would accept the organism as the 'individual.'

[2] Here 'suggestion' and 'inference' are both included in the process which conducts to our belief in the existence of other persons—or, as Berkeley calls them, other 'thinking *things.*'

in the strictest sense behold and perceive by all my senses such signs and tokens, such effects and operations, as suggest, indicate, and demonstrate an invisible God—as certainly, and with the same evidence, at least, as any other signs, perceived by sense, do suggest to me the existence of your soul, spirit, or thinking principle; which I am convinced of only by a few signs or effects, and the motions of one small organised body: whereas I do at all times and in all places perceive sensible signs which evince the being of God. The point, therefore, doubted or denied by you at the beginning, now seems manifestly to follow from the premises. Throughout this whole enquiry, have we not considered every step with care, and made not the least advance without clear evidence? You and I examined and assented singly to each foregoing proposition: what shall we do then with the conclusion? For my part, if you do not help me out, I find myself under an absolute necessity of admitting it for true. You must therefore be content henceforward to bear the blame, if I live and die in the belief of a God [1].

6. *Alc.* It must be confessed, I do not readily find an answer. There seems to be some foundation for what you say. But, on the other-hand, if the point was so clear as you pretend, I cannot conceive how so many sagacious men of our sect should be so much in the dark as not to know or believe one syllable of it.

Euph. O Alciphron, it is not our present business to account for the oversights, or vindicate the honour, of those great men the free-thinkers, when their very existence is in danger of being called in question.

Alc. How so?

Euph. Be pleased to recollect the concessions you have

---

[1] The argument here ascends from facts that are given in sense to a transcendent Fact. It is based on the analogy of the sensible facts which are accepted as a proof of the existence of our fellow-men. But if *their* existence is only as organised spirits, are we to transfer this analogy too to God?

God speaks to Man through the Senses.

made, and then shew me, if the arguments for a Deity be not conclusive, by what better arguments you can prove the existence of that thinking thing[1] which in strictness constitutes the free-thinker.

As soon as Euphranor had uttered these words, Alciphron stopped short, and stood in a posture of meditation, while the rest of us continued our walk and took two or three turns, after which he joined us again with a smiling countenance, like one who had made some discovery.

I have found, said he, what may clear up the point in dispute, and give Euphranor entire satisfaction; I would say an argument which will prove the existence of a free-thinker, the like whereof cannot be applied to prove the existence of God. You must know then that your notion of our perceiving the existence of God, as certainly and immediately as we do that of a human person, I could by no means digest, though I must own it puzzled me, till I had considered the matter. At first methought a particular structure, shape, or motion was a most certain proof of a thinking reasonable soul. But a little attention satisfied me that these things have no necessary connexion with reason, knowledge, and wisdom; and that, allowing them to be certain proofs of a living soul, they cannot be so of a thinking and reasonable one. Upon second thoughts, therefore, and a minute examination of this point, I have found that nothing so much convinces me of the existence of another person as *his speaking to me*. It is my hearing you talk that, in strict and philosophical truth, is to me the best argument for your being. And this is a peculiar argument, inapplicable to your purpose; for, you will not, I suppose, pretend that God speaks to man in the same clear and sensible manner as one man doth to another?

7. *Euph.* How! is then the impression of sound so much more evident than that of other senses? Or, if it be, is the voice of man louder than that of thunder?

[1] See the two preceding notes.

Alc. Alas! you mistake the point. What I mean is not the sound of speech merely as such, but the *arbitrary* use of sensible signs, which have no similitude or necessary connexion with the things signified; so as by the apposite management of them to suggest and exhibit to my mind an endless variety of things, differing in nature, time, and place; thereby informing me, entertaining me, and directing me how to act, not only with regard to things near and present, but also with regard to things distant and future. No matter whether these signs are pronounced or written; whether they enter by the eye or ear: they have the same use, and are equally proofs of an intelligent, thinking, designing cause.

Euph. But what if it should appear that God really speaks to man; would this content you?

Alc. I am for admitting no inward speech, no holy instincts, or suggestions of light or spirit. All that, you must know, passeth with men of sense for nothing[1]. If you do not make it plain to me that God speaks to men by outward sensible signs, of such sort and in such manner as I have defined, you do nothing.

Euph. But if it shall appear plainly that God speaks to men by the intervention and use of arbitrary,. outward, sensible signs, having no resemblance or necessary connexion with the things they stand for and suggest: if it shall appear that, by innumerable combinations of these signs, an endless variety of things is discovered and made known to us; and that we are thereby instructed or informed in their different natures; that we are taught and admonished what to shun,

---

[1] If 'men of sense' could mean *mere sensationalists* this might pass. But what if universally valid evidence of the supremacy in the universe of moral reason can be found in our moral and spiritual experience— evidence which if rejected would oblige us in consistency to disallow in external perception all that gives permanence and objectivity to what otherwise is a mere flux of unconnected phenomena? What if the elevation of sensation into perception is itself indefensible, except on grounds which require us to interpret our moral experience into a rational conviction that the universe is morally governed, and that *what ought to be is the deepest and truest reality?*

and what to pursue ; and are directed how to regulate our motions, and how to act with respect to things distant from us, as well in time as place, will this content you ?

Alc. It is the very thing I would have you make out; for therein consists the force, and use, and nature of language.

8. *Euph.* Look, Alciphron, do you not see the castle upon yonder hill ?

Alc. I do.

Euph. Is it not at a great distance from you ?

Alc. It is.

Euph. Tell me, Alciphron, is not distance [1] a line turned endwise to the eye ?

Alc. Doubtless.

Euph. And can a line, in that situation, project more than one single point on the bottom of the eye ?

Alc. It cannot.

Euph. Therefore the appearance [2] of a long and of a short distance is of the same magnitude, or rather of no magnitude at all—being in all cases one single point.

Alc. It seems so.

Euph. Should it not follow from hence that distance is not immediately perceived by the eye ?

Alc. It should [3].

[1] *i. e.* distance outwards or in the line of sight.

[2] 'Appearance.' Does he mean here the *visible* appearance, and that we actually see the single point in the retina, which, as always of the same size, or rather of no size, cannot be a visible sign of distances that are of various degrees ; or does he mean that, being of 'no magnitude,' the appearance cannot be either a visible or invisible sign ? In what follows, as in the *Essay*, he makes nothing of instinct—which is a name for the unexplained—in his account of the way we learn to see things existing under space relations. To allege 'instinct' would be to grant that the visual perception of placed things is an inexplicable fact. If Berkeley can explain it, as he professes to do, by means of 'suggestion,' he might argue against its instinctive character, on the principle, *entia non sunt multiplicanda praeter necessitatem.*

[3] How could it be *immediately* perceived in seeing, even if the 'appearance'—the point in the bottom of the eye—*did* vary according to the distance of the object seen ?

Euph. Must it not then be perceived by the mediation of some other thing?

Alc. It must.

Euph. To discover what this is, let us examine what alteration there may be in the appearance of the same object placed at different distances from the eye. Now, I find by experience that when an object is removed still farther and farther off in a direct line from the eye, its visible appearance still grows lesser and fainter; and this change of appearance, being proportional and universal, seems to me to be that by which we apprehend the various degrees of distance.

Alc. I have nothing to object to this.

Euph. But littleness or faintness, in their own nature, seem to have no necessary connexion with greater length of distance?

Alc. I admit this to be true.

Euph. Will it not follow then that they could never suggest it but from experience?

Alc. It will.

Euph. That is to say—we perceive distance, not immediately, but by mediation of a sign, which hath no likeness to it, or necessary connexion with it, but only suggests it from repeated experience—as words do things.

Alc. Hold, Euphranor: now I think of it, the writers in optics tell us of an angle made by the two optic axes, where they meet in the visible point or object; which angle, the obtuser it is the nearer it shews the object to be, and by how much the acuter, by so much the farther off; and this from a necessary demonstrable connexion.

Euph. The mind then finds out the distance of things by geometry?

Alc. It doth.

Euph. Should it not follow, therefore, that nobody could see but those who had learned geometry, and knew something of lines and angles?

Alc. There is a sort of natural geometry which is got without learning.

Euph. Pray inform me, Alciphron, in order to frame a proof of any kind, or deduce one point from another, is it not necessary that I perceive the connexion of the terms in the premises, and the connexion of the premises with the conclusion; and, in general, to know one thing by means of another, must I not first know that other thing? When I perceive your meaning by your words, must I not first perceive the words themselves? and must I not know the premises before I infer the conclusion?

Alc. All this is true.

Euph. Whoever, therefore, collects a nearer distance from a wider angle, or a farther distance from an acuter angle, must first perceive the angles themselves. And he who doth not perceive those angles can infer nothing from them. Is it so or not?

Alc. It is as you say.

Euph. Ask now the first man you meet whether he perceives or knows anything of those optic angles? or whether he ever thinks about them, or makes any inferences from them, either by natural or artificial geometry? What answer do you think he would make?

Alc. To speak the truth, I believe his answer would be, that he knew nothing of these matters.

Euph. It cannot therefore be that men judge[1] of distance by angles: nor, consequently, can there be any force in the argument you drew from thence, to prove that distance is perceived by means of something which hath a necessary connexion with it.

Alc. I agree with you.

---

[1] 'Judge' here seems equivalent to demonstration founded on necessary relations of thought, and so is different from Locke's 'judgment,' which is probable presumption based on analogy—understanding judging according to the custom of sense.

9. *Euph.* To me it seems that a man may know whether he perceives a thing or no; and, if he perceives it, whether it be immediately or mediately: and, if mediately, whether by means of something like or unlike, necessarily or arbitrarily connected with it.

Alc. It seems so.

Euph. And is it not certain that distance is perceived only by experience[1], if it be neither perceived immediately by itself, nor by means of any image, nor of any lines and angles which are like it, or have a necessary connexion with it?

Alc. It is.

Euph. Doth it not seem to follow, from what hath been said and allowed by you, that before all experience a man would not imagine the things he saw were at any distance from him?

Alc. How! let me see.

Euph. The littleness or faintness of appearance, or any other idea or sensation not necessarily connected with or resembling distance, can no more suggest different degrees of distance, or any distance at all, to the mind which hath not experienced a connexion of the things signifying and signified, than words can suggest notions before a man hath learned the language.

Alc. I allow this to be true.

Euph. Will it not thence follow that a man born blind, and made to see, would, upon first receiving his sight, take the things he saw not to be at any distance from him, but in his eye, or rather in his mind?

Alc. I must own it seems so. And yet, on the other hand,

---

[1] 'Experience,' namely, of the connexion, established independently of our will, between what we see and our past experience of movement among (what we have found to be) extra-organic bodies. But more than mere phenomena and blind suggestion is surely involved (tacitly) in this account of the constitution of perception. Is not reason latent in *such* 'suggestions'?

I can hardly persuade myself that, if I were in such a state, I should think those objects which I *now* see at so great distance to be at no distance at all.

Euph. It seems, then, that you now think[1] the objects of sight are at a distance from you?

Alc. Doubtless I do. Can any one question but yonder castle is at a great distance?

Euph. Tell me, Alciphron, can you discern the doors, windows, and battlements of that same castle?

Alc. I cannot. At this distance it seems only a small round tower.

Euph. But I, who have been at it, know that it is no small round tower, but a large square building with battlements and turrets, which it seems you do not see.

Alc. What will you infer from thence?

Euph. I would infer that the very object which you strictly and properly perceive by sight is not that thing which is several miles distant.

Alc. Why so?

Euph. Because a little round object is one thing, and a great square object is another. Is it not?

Alc. I cannot deny it.

Euph. Tell me, is not the visible appearance alone the proper object of sight?

Alc. It is.

What think you now (said Euphranor, pointing towards the heavens) of the visible appearance of yonder planet? Is it not a round luminous flat, no bigger than a sixpence?

Alc. What then?

Euph. Tell me then, what you think of the planet itself. Do you not conceive it to be a vast opaque globe, with several unequal risings and valleys?

Alc. I do.

---

[1] Think, *i. e.* judge—the judgment somehow emerging in the suggestion. Berkeley does not explain its appearance.

Euph. How can you therefore conclude that the proper object of your sight[1] exists at a distance?

Alc. I confess I know not.

Euph. For your further conviction, do but consider that crimson cloud. Think you that, if you were in the very place where it is, you would perceive anything like what you now see?

Alc. By no means. I should perceive only a dark mist.

Euph. Is it not plain, therefore, that neither the castle, the planet, nor the cloud, which you see here, are those real ones which you suppose exist at a distance?

10. *Alc.* What am I to think then? Do we see anything at all, or is it altogether fancy and illusion?

Euph. Upon the whole, it seems the proper objects of sight are light and colours, with their several shades and degrees; all which, being infinitely diversified and combined, do form a language wonderfully adapted to suggest and exhibit to us the distances, figures, situations, dimensions, and various qualities of tangible objects—not by similitude, nor yet by inference of necessary connexion, but by the arbitrary imposition of Providence[2], just as words suggest the things signified by them.

Alc. How! Do we not, strictly speaking, perceive by sight such things as trees, houses, men, rivers, and the like?

Euph. We do, indeed, perceive or apprehend[3] those things

---

[1] 'The proper object of sight,' i. e. the data due exclusively to sight, before we have learned, in the way supposed, to read into them the data of our experience of things in touch. This primary consciousness cannot now be revived by us. And could we, one may ask, have read extension and space, with their objective relations, into the sense phenomena either of touch or sight, unless extension and space had been already somehow latent in them?

[2] Modern doubt would not be satisfied by so rapid a reference of interpretable nature to a supreme intending Agency like our own. Moreover he takes no account of the supremacy of conscience, and the correlative supremacy of moral government in the universe—the essence of practical Theism.—'It is the heart and conscience, and not the understanding,' says Pascal, 'that has properly the perception of God.'

[3] 'Perceive or apprehend'—through suggestion, or judgment according

by the faculty of sight. But will it follow from thence that they are the proper and immediate objects of sight, any more than that all those things are the proper and immediate objects of hearing which are signified by the help of words or sounds?

Alc. You would have us think, then, that light, shades, and colours, variously combined, answer to the several articulations of sound in language; and that, by means thereof, all sorts of objects are suggested to the mind through the eye, in the same manner as they are suggested by words or sounds through the ear: that is, neither from necessary deduction to the judgment, nor from similitude to the fancy, but purely and solely from experience, custom, and habit.

Euph. I would not have you think anything more than the nature of things obligeth you to think, nor submit in the least to my judgment, but only to the force of truth: which is an imposition that I suppose the freest thinkers will not pretend to be exempt from.

Alc. You have led me, it seems, step by step, till I am got I know not where. But I shall try to get out again, if not by the way I came, yet by some other of my own finding.

Here *Alciphron,* having made a short pause, proceeded as follows—

11. Answer me, Euphranor, should it not follow from these principles that a man born blind, and made to see, would, at first sight, not only not perceive their distance, but also not so much as know the very things themselves which he saw, for instance, men or trees? which surely to suppose must be absurd.

Euph. I grant, in consequence of those principles, which both you and I have admitted, that such a one would never

to sense, as distinguished by Berkeley from the mere *consciousness* of phenomena—which also he calls 'perception'—both falling short of the scientific, and still more of the philosophic understanding of things.

think of men, trees, or any other objects that he had been accustomed to perceive by touch, upon having his mind filled with new sensations of light and colours[1], whose various combinations he doth not yet understand, or know the meaning of; no more than a Chinese, upon first hearing the words *man* and *tree* would think of the things signified by them. In both cases, there must be time and experience, by repeated acts, to acquire a habit of knowing[2] the connexion between the signs and things signified; that is to say, of understanding the language, whether of the eyes or of the ears. And I conceive no absurdity in all this.

Alc. I see, therefore, in strict philosophical truth, that rock only in the same sense that I may be said to hear it, when the word *rock* is pronounced.

Euph. In the very same.

Alc. How comes it to pass then that every one shall say he sees, for instance, a rock or a house, when those things are before his eyes; but nobody will say he hears a rock or a house, but only the words or sounds themselves by which those things are said to be signified or suggested but not heard? Besides, if vision be only a language speaking to the eyes, it may be asked, when did men learn this language? To acquire the knowledge of so many signs as go to the making up a language is a work of some difficulty. But, will any man say he hath spent time, or been at pains, to learn this Language of Vision?

---

[1] Here throughout he speaks of 'sensations of light and colours' as the language of vision, making no account of the visual but invisible signs *felt* in the organ of seeing.

[2] A 'habit of knowing.' Is knowledge *ultimately* constituted only by habit and suggestion? if not, what higher elements are needed to constitute it?—The function of custom must be recognised. It is a stage on the way to rational knowledge, and in the development of the thinker. 'Custom,' says Pascal, 'may be conceived as a secondary nature, and nature as a primary custom.' 'What,' he even asks, 'are all our natural principles but principles of custom, derived by hereditary descent from parents to children, as fear and flight in beasts of sport?' So too Wordsworth—

'And custom lie upon thee with a weight
. . . . deep almost as life.'

Euph. No wonder; we cannot assign a time beyond our remotest memory. If we have been all practising this language, ever since our first entrance into the world: if the Author of Nature constantly speaks to the eyes of all mankind, even in their earliest infancy, whenever the eyes are open in the light, whether alone or in company: it doth not seem to me at all strange that men should not be aware they had ever learned a language begun so early, and practised so constantly, as this of Vision. And, if we also consider that it is the same throughout the whole world, and not, like other languages, differing in different places, it will not seem unaccountable that men should mistake the connexion between the proper objects of sight and the things signified by them to be founded in necessary relation or likeness; or, that they should even take them for the same things. Hence it seems easy to conceive why men who do not think should confound in this language of vision the signs with the things signified, otherwise than they are wont to do in the various particular languages formed by the several nations of men.

12. It may be also worth while to observe that signs, being little considered in themselves, or for their own sake, but only in their relative capacity, and for the sake of those things whereof they are signs, it comes to pass that the mind overlooks them, so as to carry its attention immediately on to the things signified. Thus, for example, in reading we run over the characters with the slightest regard, and pass on to the meaning. Hence it is frequent for men to say, they see words, and notions, and things in reading of a book; whereas in strictness they see only the characters which suggest words, notions, and things. And, by parity of reason, may we not suppose that men, not resting in, but overlooking the immediate and proper objects of sight, as in their own nature of small moment, carry their attention onward to the very things signified, and talk as if they saw the secondary objects? which, in truth and strictness, are not *seen*, but only

suggested and *apprehended* by means of the proper objects of sight, which alone are seen.

Alc. To speak my mind freely, this dissertation grows tedious, and runs into points too dry and minute for a gentleman's attention.

I thought, said *Crito*, we had been told that minute philosophers loved to consider things closely and minutely.

Alc. That is true, but in so polite an age who would be a mere philosopher? There is a certain scholastic accuracy which ill suits the freedom and ease of a well-bred man. But, to cut short this chicane, I propound it fairly to your own conscience, whether you really think that God Himself speaks every day and in every place to the eyes of all men.

Euph. That is really and in truth my opinion; and it should be yours too, if you are consistent with yourself, and abide by your own definition of language. Since you cannot deny that the great Mover and Author of nature constantly explaineth Himself to the eyes of men by the sensible intervention of arbitrary signs, which have no. similitude or connexion with the things signified; so as, by compounding and disposing them, to suggest and exhibit an endless variety of objects, differing in nature, time, and place; thereby informing and directing men how to act with respect to things distant and future, as well as near and present. In consequence, I say, of your own sentiments and concessions, you have as much reason to think the Universal Agent or God speaks to your eyes, as you can have for thinking any particular person speaks to your ears [1].

---

[1] This argument virtually *universalises* the fact of continuous personal existence, assumed to be given in our primary consciousness (*Principles*, § 2), and of which in Berkeley's language we have a 'notion.' It is here converted, by analogy, into the ultimate principle of the universe. The argument is an application of the analogy between the visible signs of the existence of a fellow-man, on the one hand, and the whole symbolism of the sensible world, on the other hand, in the conclusion that both are the organised manifestation of a spiritual agent. It implies too that our causal tendency can find rest only in an *uncaused* Cause.

Alc. I cannot help thinking that some fallacy runs throughout this whole ratiocination, though perhaps I may not readily point it out. Hold! let me see. In language the signs are arbitrary, are they not?

Euph. They are.

Alc. And, consequently, they do not always suggest real matters of fact. Whereas this Natural Language, as you call it, or these visible signs, do always suggest things in the same uniform way, and have the same constant regular connexion with matters of fact: whence it should seem the connexion was necessary; and, therefore, according to the definition premised, it can be no language. How do you solve this objection?

Euph. You may solve it yourself by the help of a picture or looking-glass.

Alc. You are in the right. I see there is nothing in it. I know not what else to say to this opinion, more than that it is so odd and contrary to my way of thinking that I shall never assent to it.

13. *Euph.* Be pleased to recollect your own lectures upon prejudice, and apply them in the present case. Perhaps they may help you to follow where reason leads, and to suspect notions which are strongly rivetted, without having been ever examined.

Alc. I disdain the suspicion of prejudice. And I do not speak only for myself. I know a club of most ingenious men, the freest from prejudice of any men alive, who abhor the notion of a God, and I doubt not would be very able to untie this knot.

Upon which words of Alciphron, I, who had acted the part of an indifferent stander-by, observed to him—That it

But the alleged analogy does not fully meet the position of those who find in signs of human agency signs not of a pure unbodied spirit, but of a conscious and active organism—unless indeed the sensible world is to be viewed as the Divine organism, or the natural incarnation of God.

misbecame his character and repeated professions, to own an attachment to the judgment, or build upon the presumed abilities of other men, how ingenious soever; and that this proceeding might encourage his adversaries to have recourse to authority [1], in which perhaps they would find their account more than he.

Oh! said *Crito*, I have often observed the conduct of minute philosophers. When one of them has got a ring of disciples round him, his method is to exclaim against prejudice, and recommend thinking and reasoning, giving to understand that himself is a man of deep researches and close argument, one who examines impartially, and concludes warily. The same man, in other company, if he chance to be pressed with reason, shall laugh at logic, and assume the lazy supine airs of a fine gentleman, a wit, a *railleur*, to avoid the dryness of a regular and exact inquiry. This double face of the minute philosopher is of no small use to propagate and maintain his notions. Though to me it seems a plain case that if a fine gentleman will shake off authority, and appeal from religion to reason, unto reason he must go: and, if he cannot go without leading-strings, surely he had better be led by the authority of the public than by that of any knot of minute philosophers.

Alc. Gentlemen, this discourse is very irksome, and needless. For my part, I am a friend to inquiry. I am willing reason should have its full and free scope. I build on no man's authority. For my part, I have no interest in denying a God. Any man may believe or not believe a God, as he pleases, for me. But, after all, Euphranor must allow me to stare a little at his conclusions.

---

[1] 'Authority,' *i. e.* the authority of trusted men—faith in the insight of other persons, as distinguished from our own. But with Berkeley's view of 'language' in Nature, all reasonings about natural laws are, in their ultimate ground, matter-of-fact reasonings, based at last on faith in the ever-active Divine Person, and are in that respect reasonings grounded on authority.

Euph. The conclusions are yours as much as mine, for you were led to them by your own concessions.

14. You, it seems, stare to find that God is not far from every one of us; and that in Him we live, and move, and have our being[1]. You, who, in the beginning of this morning's conference, thought it strange that God should leave Himself without a witness, do now think it strange the witness should be so full and clear.

Alc. I must own I do. I was aware, indeed, of a certain metaphysical hypothesis of our seeing all things in God by the union of the human soul with the intelligible substance of the Deity, which neither I nor any one else could make sense of[2]. But I never imagined it could be pretended that we saw God with our fleshly eyes as plain as we see any human person whatsoever, and that He daily speaks to our senses in a manifest and clear dialect.

Cri. As for that metaphysical hypothesis, I can make no more of it than you. But I think it plain this Optic Language hath a necessary connexion[3] with knowledge, wisdom, and goodness. It is equivalent to a constant creation, betokening an immediate act of power and providence. It cannot be accounted for by mechanical principles, by atoms, attractions, or effluvia. The instantaneous production and reproduction of so many signs, combined, dissolved, transposed, diversified, and adapted to such an endless variety of purposes, ever shifting with the occasions and suited to them,

[1] Because, on the view of things here maintained, God really animates the whole sensible universe in the same sort of way as a man animates the movements of his own body; and uses the physical system too as the subordinate symbol or sacrament of the spiritual agency that is externalised in it, all its changes being resolved into the direct will of God.

[2] This refers to Malebranche's hypothesis, which Berkeley here and elsewhere disclaims, for reasons which should be studied. It is perhaps less remote from his own philosophy, as developed in *Siris*, than he here supposes it to be.

[3] He thus presumes a *necessary connexion* between the physical and the spiritual or moral government of the universe—without explaining the 'necessity.' He implies that the former is in a subordinate relation to the latter.

being utterly inexplicable and unaccountable by the laws of motion, by chance, by fate, or the like blind principles, doth set forth and testify the immediate operation of a spirit or thinking being; and not merely of a spirit, which every motion or gravitation may possibly infer, but of one wise, good, and provident Spirit, which directs and rules and governs the world. Some philosophers, being convinced of the wisdom and power of the Creator, from the make and contrivance of organised bodies and orderly system of the world, did nevertheless imagine that he left this system with all its parts and contents well adjusted and put in motion, as an artist leaves a clock, to go thenceforward of itself for a certain period[1]. But this Visual Language proves, not a Creator merely, but a provident Governor, actually and intimately present, and attentive to all our interests and motions, who watches over our conduct, and takes care of our minutest actions and designs throughout the whole course of our lives, informing, admonishing, and directing incessantly, in a most evident and sensible manner. This is truly wonderful.

Euph. And is it not so, that men should be encompassed by such a wonder, without reflecting on it?

15. Something there is of Divine and admirable in this Language, addressed to our eyes, that may well awaken the mind, and deserve its utmost attention:—it is learned with so little pains: it expresseth the differences of things so clearly and aptly: it instructs with such facility and despatch, by one glance of the eye conveying a greater variety of advices, and a more distinct knowledge of things, than could be got

[1] This is the philosophical theory of a pre-established Causal Harmony (instead of the Cartesian constant Occasional Causation), by which Leibnitz sought to explain the consistent, yet mutually independent, agency of conscious persons and unconscious things. Leibnitz uses the analogy of the watch in his correspondence with Clarke. See *Collection of Papers between Leibnitz and Clarke, relating to the Principles of Natural Philosophy and Religion* (1717), pp. 2-6, 12-16, 28-34.&c. On Berkeley's conception of what the real existence of the material world means, the Cosmos must relapse into a meaningless abstraction, if the Divine perception of it, and providential action in it, is for a moment withdrawn.

by a discourse of several hours. And, while it informs, it amuses and entertains the mind with such singular pleasure and delight. It is of such excellent use in giving a stability and permanency to human discourse, in recording sounds and bestowing life on dead languages, enabling us to converse with men of remote ages and countries. And it answers so apposite to the uses and necessities of mankind, informing us more distinctly of those objects whose nearness and magnitude qualify them to be of greatest detriment or benefit to our bodies, and less exactly in proportion as their littleness or distance makes them of less concern to us [1].

Alc. And yet these strange things affect men but little.

Euph. But they are not strange, they are familiar; and that makes them be overlooked. Things which rarely happen strike; whereas frequency lessens the admiration of things, though in themselves ever so admirable. Hence, a common man, who is not used to think and make reflections, would probably be more convinced of the being of a God by one single sentence heard once in his life from the sky than by all the experience he has had of this Visual Language, contrived with such exquisite skill, so constantly addressed to his eyes, and so plainly declaring the nearness, wisdom, and providence of Him with whom we have to do [2].

Alc. After all, I cannot satisfy myself how men should be so little surprised or amazed about this visive faculty, if it was really of a nature so surprising and amazing.

Euph. But let us suppose a nation of men blind from their infancy, among whom a stranger arrives, the only man who can see in all the country; let us suppose this stranger

---

[1] Berkeley makes much of the sensible evidence of God being such that we may be said to *see* Him as we see a fellow-man; not much of our finding God, still more nearly, in our own heart and conscience.

[2] 'In philosophy equally as in poetry,' says Coleridge, 'it is the highest and most useful prerogative of genius to produce the strongest impressions of novelty, while it rescues admitted truths from the neglect caused by the very circumstance of their universal admission.'

travelling with some of the natives, and that one while he foretells to them that, in case they walk straight forward, in half an hour they shall meet men or cattle, or come to a house; that, if they turn to the right and proceed, they shall in a few minutes be in danger of falling down a precipice; that, shaping their course to the left, they will in such a time arrive at a river, a wood, or a mountain. What think you? Must they not be infinitely surprised that one who had never been in their country before should know it so much better than themselves? And would not those predictions seem to them as unaccountable and incredible as Prophecy to a minute philosopher?

Alc. I cannot deny it.

Euph. But it seems to require intense thought to be able to unravel a prejudice that has been so long forming; to get over the vulgar errors or ideas common to both senses; and so to distinguish between the objects of Sight and Touch, which have grown (if I may so say), blended together[1] in our fancy, as to be able to suppose ourselves exactly in the state that one of those men would be in, if he were made to see. And yet this I believe is possible, and might seem worth the pains of a little thinking, especially to those men whose proper employment and profession it is to think, and unravel prejudices, and confute mistakes.

Alc. I frankly own I cannot find my way out of this maze, and should gladly be set right by those who see better than myself.

Cri. The pursuing this subject in their own thoughts would possibly open a new scene to those speculative gentlemen of the minute philosophy. It puts me in mind of a passage in the Psalmist, where he represents God to be covered with light as with a garment, and would methinks be no ill comment on that ancient notion of some eastern sages

---

[1] 'Blended together.' So in his Commonplace Book (*Life*, p. 494) he says that 'extension is *blended with* tangible or visible ideas.'

—that God had light for His body, and truth for His soul[1].

This conversation lasted till a servant came to tell us the tea was ready: upon which we walked in, and found Lysicles at the tea-table.

16. As soon as we sat down, I am glad, said *Alciphron*, that I have here found my second, a fresh man to maintain our common cause, which, I doubt, Lysicles will think hath suffered by his absence.

Lys. Why so?

Alc. I have been drawn into some concessions you will not like.

Lys. Let me know what they are.

Alc. Why, that there is such a thing as a God, and that His existence is very certain.

Lys. Bless me! How came you to entertain so wild a notion?

Alc. You know we profess to follow reason wherever it leads. And in short I have been reasoned into it.

Lys. Reasoned! You should say, amused with words, bewildered with sophistry.

Euph. Have you a mind to hear the same reasoning that led Alciphron and me step by step, that we may examine whether it be sophistry or no?

Lys. As to that I am very easy. I guess all that can be said on that head. It shall be my business to help my friend out, whatever arguments drew him in.

[1] According to this philosophy, the phenomena presented in the senses, conspicuously those given in sight, are types or symbols of spiritual and unseen realities: physical is the instrument of moral government. The supporting argument for this might be, that the theistic explanation of what we 'experience,' and that alone, fully satisfies the entire cognitive, sensitive, and moral constitution of man; though Berkeley relies too exclusively on sense, scientific prevision, and conclusions that are conceivable by the understanding judging according to the suggestions of sense, and here takes little account of conscience and our moral experience.

Euph. Will you admit the premises and deny the conclusions?

Lys. What if I admit the conclusion?

Euph. How! will you grant there is a God?

Lys. Perhaps I may.

Euph. Then we are agreed.

Lys. Perhaps not.

Euph. O Lysicles, you are a subtle adversary. I know not what you would be at.

Lys. You must know then that at bottom the being of a God is a point in itself of small consequence, and a man may make this concession without yielding much. The great point is what sense the word *God* is to be taken in [1]. The very Epicureans allowed the being of gods; but then they were indolent gods, unconcerned with human affairs. Hobbes allowed a corporeal god: and Spinosa held the universe to be God. And yet nobody doubts they were staunch freethinkers. I could wish indeed the word God were quite omitted; because in most minds it is coupled with a sort of superstitious awe, the very root of all religion. I shall not, nevertheless, be much disturbed, though the *name* be retained, and the being of a God allowed in any sense but in that of a Mind, which knows all things, and beholds human actions, like some judge or magistrate, with infinite observation and intelligence. The belief of a God in this sense fills a man's mind with scruples, lays him under constraints, and embitters his very being: but in another sense it may be attended with no great ill consequence. This I know was the opinion of our great Diagoras, who told me he would never have been at the pains to find out a demonstration that there was no

---

[1] This is still the 'great point' in the philosophy of religion. Is God a conscious Person—the ultimate Principle of the moral government of the universe, and therefore incognisable by *us* otherwise than as a self-conscious intending agent;—or is 'God' merely a name for the universal relations of thought presupposed in science; or even for the unknowable 'cause' of nature?

God[1], if the received notion of God had been the same with that of some Fathers and Schoolmen.

Euph. Pray what was that?

17. *Lys.* You must know, Diagoras, a man of much reading and inquiry, had discovered that once upon a time the most profound and speculative divines, finding it impossible to reconcile the attributes of God—taken in the common sense, or in any known sense—with human reason, and the appearances of things, taught that the words *knowledge, wisdom, goodness*, and such like, when spoken of the Deity, must be understood in quite a different sense from what they signify in the vulgar acceptation, or from anything that we can form a notion of or conceive. Hence, whatever objections might be made against the attributes of God they easily solved—by denying those attributes belonged to God, in this, or that, or any known particular sense or notion; which was the same thing as to deny they belonged to Him at all. And, thus denying the attributes of God, they in effect denied His being, though perhaps they were not aware of it.

Suppose, for instance, a man should object that future contingencies were inconsistent with the Foreknowledge of God, because it is repugnant that certain knowledge should be of an uncertain thing: it was a ready and an easy answer to say that this may be true with respect to knowledge taken in the common sense, or in any sense that we can possibly form any notion of; but that there would not appear the same inconsistency between the contingent nature of things and Divine Foreknowledge, taken to signify somewhat that we know nothing of, which in God supplies the place of what we understand by knowledge; from which it differs not in

---

[1] The most plausible objections to Theism in this age are founded on the supposition of the proved insolubility of the whole problem. Agnosticism is offered as the alternative to either Theism or dogmatic Atheism, and 'suspense of judgment' as the only possible issue of utmost rational reflection. But there are facts of our experience in our moral consciousness which forbid practical Agnosticism.

quantity or degree of perfection, but altogether, and in kind, as light doth from sound;—and even more, since these agree in that they are both sensations; whereas knowledge in God hath no sort of resemblance or agreement with any notion that man can frame of knowledge. The like may be said of all the other attributes, which indeed may by this means be equally reconciled with everything or with nothing. But all men who think must needs see this is cutting knots and not untying them. For, how are things reconciled with the Divine attributes when these attributes themselves are in every intelligible sense denied; and, consequently, the very notion of God taken away, and nothing left but the name, without any meaning annexed to it? In short, the belief that there is an unknown subject of attributes absolutely unknown is a very innocent doctrine; which the acute Diagoras well saw, and was therefore wonderfully delighted with this system.

18. For, said he, if this could once make its way and obtain in the world, there would be an end to all natural or rational religion, which is the basis both of the Jewish and the Christian: for he who comes to God, or enters himself in the church of God, must first believe that there is a *God in some intelligible sense;* and not only that there is *Something in general, without any proper notion, though never so inadequate, of any of its qualities or attributes:* for this may be fate, or chaos, or plastic nature, or anything else as well as God.—Nor will it avail to say:—There is something in this unknown being *analogous* to knowledge and goodness; that is to say, which produceth those effects which we could not conceive to be produced by men, in any degree, without knowledge and goodness. For, this is in fact to give up the point in dispute between theists and atheists—the question having always been, not whether there was a Principle (which point was allowed by all philosophers, as well before as since Anaxagoras), but whether this principle was a νοῦς, a

thinking intelligent being: that is to say, whether that order, and beauty, and use, visible in natural effects, could be produced by anything but a Mind or Intelligence, in the proper sense of the word? And whether there must not be true, real, and proper knowledge, in the First Cause? We will, therefore, acknowledge that all those natural effects which are vulgarly ascribed to knowledge and wisdom proceed from a being in which there is, properly speaking, no knowledge or wisdom at all, but only something else, which in reality is the cause of those things which men, for want of knowing better, ascribe to what they call knowledge and wisdom and understanding. You wonder perhaps to hear a man of pleasure, who diverts himself as I do, philosophize at this rate. But you should consider that much is to be got by conversing with ingenious men, which is a short way to knowledge, that saves a man the drudgery of reading and thinking.

And, now we have granted to you that there is a God in this indefinite sense, I would fain see what use you can make of this concession. You cannot argue from unknown attributes, or, which is the same thing, from attributes in an unknown sense. You cannot prove that God is to be loved for His goodness, or feared for His justice, or respected for His knowledge: all which consequences, we own, would follow from those attributes admitted in an intelligible sense. But we deny that those or any other consequences can be drawn from attributes admitted in no particular sense, or in a sense which none of us understand. Since, therefore, nothing can be inferred from such an account of God, about conscience, or worship, or religion, you may even make the best of it. And, not to be singular, we will use the name too, and so at once there is an end of atheism.

Euph. This account of a Deity is new to me. I do not like it, and therefore shall leave it to be maintained by those who do.

19. *Cri.* It is not new to me. I remember not long since to have heard a minute philosopher triumph upon this very point; which put me on inquiring what foundation there was for it in the Fathers or Schoolmen. And, for aught that I can find, it owes its original to those writings which have been published under the name of Dionysius the Areopagite[1]. The author of which, it must be owned, hath written upon the Divine attributes in a very singular style. In his treatise *De Hierarchia Cœlesti*, he saith that God is something above all essence and life, ὑπὲρ πᾶσαν οὐσίαν καὶ ζωήν; and again, in his treatise *De Divinis Nominibus*, that He is above all wisdom and understanding, ὑπὲρ πᾶσαν σοφίαν καὶ σύνεσιν, ineffable and innominable, ἄρρητος καὶ ἀνώνυμος; the wisdom of God he terms an unreasonable, unintelligent, and foolish wisdom, τὴν ἄλογον, καὶ ἄνουν, καὶ μωρὰν σοφίαν. But then the reason he gives for expressing himself in this strange manner is, that the Divine wisdom is the cause of all reason, wisdom, and understanding, and therein are contained the treasures of all wisdom and knowledge. He calls God ὑπέρσοφος and ὑπέρζως; as if wisdom and life were words not worthy to express the Divine perfections: and he adds that the attributes unintelligent and unperceiving must be ascribed to the Divinity, not κατ' ἔλλειψιν, by way of defect, but καθ' ὑπεροχήν, by way of eminency; which he explains by our giving the name of darkness to light inaccessible. And, notwithstanding

---

[1] May we not say that our metaphysical understanding of the universe at last necessarily merges in theological faith, in the attempt to comprehend the Power at work in the physical and spiritual government in which, in our bodily and moral experience, we find ourselves included? May not the historical fact of Divine Incarnation, with its background of mystery, satisfy this sense of intellectual inadequacy in the only way possible; in making God practically comprehended, while still scientifically incomprehensible? Does not Berkeley incline too much to the anthropomorphic Theism that is content to think that God is absolutely *only* what man is able to conceive? 'Knowledge,' 'wisdom,' and 'goodness,' as we experience them, may be inadequate terms when applied to Deity; not because the Supreme Being includes less, but because the Supreme Being includes more than even our highest spiritual experience enables us to connote by these terms.

the harshness of his expressions in some places, he affirms over and over in others—that God knows all things; not that He is beholden to the creatures for His knowledge, but by knowing Himself, from whom they all derive their being, and in whom they are contained as in their cause. It was late before these writings appear to have been known in the world; and, although they obtained credit during the age of the Schoolmen, yet, since critical learning hath been cultivated, they have lost that credit, and are at this day given up for spurious, as containing several evident marks of a much later date than the age of Dionysius.—Upon the whole, although this method of growing in expression and dwindling in notion, of clearing up doubts by nonsense, and avoiding difficulties by running into affected contradictions, may perhaps proceed from a well-meant zeal, yet it appears not to be according to knowledge; and, instead of reconciling atheists to the truth, hath, I doubt, a tendency to confirm them in their own persuasion. It should seem, therefore, very weak and rash in a Christian to adopt this harsh language of an apocryphal writer preferably to that of the Holy Scriptures. I remember, indeed, to have read of a certain philosopher, who lived some centuries ago, that used to say—if these supposed works of Dionysius had been known to the primitive Fathers, they would have furnished them admirable weapons against the heretics, and would have saved a world of pains. But the event since their discovery hath by no means confirmed his opinion [1].

[1] The books attributed to Dionysius the Areopagite (*Acts* xvii. 34), who was said to be a contemporary of the Apostles and first Bishop of Athens. They belong probably to the fourth century after Christ, if not to a later period, and to the New Platonic school. They are entitled *De Hierarchia Cœlesti*, *De Nominibus Divinis*, *De Hierarchia Ecclesiastica*, and *De Theologia Mystica*. Various editions appeared in the sixteenth and seventeenth centuries. In common with some Fathers of the Church, the pseudo-Dionysius expresses, in paradoxical language, the ontological incomprehensibility of God, unbalanced by the counter truth that God may be practically known, i. e. relatively to the ends of human life. He ascends (or descends) to a point at which,

It must be owned, the celebrated Picus of Mirandula[1], among his nine hundred conclusions (which that prince, being very young, proposed to maintain by public disputation at Rome), hath this for one—to wit, that it is more improper to say of God, He is an intellect or intelligent Being, than to say of a reasonable soul that it is an angel : which doctrine it seems was not relished. And Picus, when he comes to defend it, supports himself altogether by the example and authority of Dionysius, and in effect explains it away into a mere verbal difference—affirming that neither Dionysius nor himself ever meant to deprive God of knowledge, or to deny that He knows all things; but that, as reason is of kind peculiar to man, so by intellection he understands a kind or manner of knowing peculiar to angels ; and that the knowledge which is in God is more above the intellection of angels than angel is above man. He adds that, as his tenet consists with admitting the most perfect knowledge in God, so he would by no means be understood to exclude from the Deity intellection itself, taken in the common or general sense, but only that peculiar sort of intellection proper to angels, which he thinks ought not to be attributed to God any more than human reason. Picus, therefore, though he speaks as the apocryphal Dionysius, yet, when he explains himself, it is evident he speaks like other men. And, although the forementioned books of the Celestial Hierarchy and of the Divine Names, being attributed to a saint and martyr of the apostolical age, were respected by the Schoolmen, yet it is certain they rejected or softened his harsh expressions, and explained away or reduced his doctrine to the received notions taken from Holy Scripture and the light of nature.

by elimination of all positive and even negative attributes, the Supreme Principle in the universe becomes inexpressible. The subject invites to the study of Kant's 'Dialectic,' B. II. ch. 3, especially § 7—in his *Critick of Pure Reason.*

[1] John Picus, Count of Mirandula, lived in the fifteenth century. The disputation in which he proposed to defend his famous nine hundred theses never took place.

20. Thomas Aquinas[1] expresseth his sense of this point in the following manner. All perfections, saith he, derived from God to the creatures are in a certain higher sense, or (as the Schoolmen term it) *eminently* in God. Whenever, therefore, a name borrowed from any perfection in the creature is attributed to God, we must exclude from its signification everything that belongs to the imperfect manner wherein that attribute is found in the creature. Whence he concludes that knowledge in God is not a habit but a pure act. And again, the same Doctor observes that our intellect gets its notions of all sorts of perfections from the creatures, and that as it apprehends those perfections so it signifies them by names. Therefore, saith he, in attributing these names to God we are to consider two things: first the perfections themselves, as goodness, life, and the like, which are properly in God; and secondly, the manner which is peculiar to the creature, and cannot, strictly and properly speaking, be said to agree to the Creator.

And although Suarez[2], with other Schoolmen, teacheth that the mind of man conceiveth knowledge and will to be in God as faculties or operations, by analogy only to created beings, yet he gives it plainly as his opinion that when knowledge is said not to be properly in God it must be understood in a sense including imperfection, such as discursive knowledge[3], or the like imperfect kind found in the creatures:

[1] Thomas of Aquino, in the territory of Naples (1225-74), in whose works the philosophy called Scholastic reached its highest point, accommodating Aristotle to the doctrine of the Catholic Church. His philosophical theology, or theological philosophy, is contained in his *Summa Theologiae*. In the present connexion see especially I. qu. 2, 13, 14.
[2] Suarez, the Spanish Thomist, who died in 1617. What follows is related in his *Disputationes Metaphysicae*, XXX. 'Quid Deus sit.'
[3] Knowledge reached only through the intervention of what is supposed to be already known, i. e. by means of reasoning, is called 'discursive.' Ratiocinative activity may be regarded as a mark of the finitude of the mind that is obliged to have recourse to it. 'Were we capable,' it has been well said, 'of a knowledge of things and their relations at a single view, discursive thought would be a superfluous act. It is by such an intuition that we must suppose that the Supreme

and that, none of those imperfections in the knowledge of men or angels belonging to the formal notion of knowledge, or to knowledge as such, it will not thence follow that knowledge, in its proper formal sense, may not be attributed to God. And of knowledge taken in general for the clear evident understanding of all truth, he expressly affirms that it is in God, and that this was never denied by any philosopher who believed a God[1]. It was, indeed, a current opinion in the schools that even *being* itself should be attributed *analogically* to God and the creatures. That is, they held that God, the supreme, independent, self-originate cause and source of all beings, must not be supposed to *exist* in the same sense with created beings; not that he exists less truly, properly, or formally than they, but only because he exists in a more eminent and perfect manner[2].

21. But, to prevent any man's being led, by mistaking the scholastic use of the terms *analogy* and *analogical*, into an opinion that we cannot frame in any degree a true and proper notion of attributes applied by analogy, or, in the school phrase, predicated analogically, it may not be amiss to inquire into the true sense and meaning of those words. Every one knows that *analogy* is a Greek word used by mathematicians to signify a similitude of proportions. For instance, when we observe that two is to six as three is to nine, this similitude or equality of proportion is termed analogy. And, although proportion strictly signifies the habitude or relation

Intelligence knows all things at once.' So too Pascal, in his *Pensées*, and others.

[1] But if Divine ' knowledge' does not, like ours, presuppose a succession of self-conscious acts going on in God, contemporaneously with our own conscious experience—in the same way as we represent to ourselves that the conscious experience of our fellow-men is going on— we then cannot represent to ourselves, as an act, the 'clear evident understanding of all truth' by God ; for any act that is representable by us must be part of a succession.

[2] All this is very different from the materialistic hypothesis that the Supreme Power in the universe is *below*, instead of including and rising *above*, the personal consciousness which we each have experience of in ourselves.

of one quantity to another, yet, in a looser and translated sense, it hath been applied to signify every other habitude; and, consequently, the term analogy comes to signify all similitude of relations or habitudes whatsoever. Hence the Schoolmen tell us there is analogy between intellect and sight; forasmuch as intellect is to the mind what sight is to the body, and that he who governs the state is analogous to him who steers a ship. Hence a prince is analogically styled a pilot, being to the state as a pilot is to his vessel.

For the further clearing of this point, it is to be observed that a twofold analogy is distinguished by the schoolmen—metaphorical and proper.—Of the first kind there are frequent instances in Holy Scripture, attributing human parts and passions to God. When He is represented as having a finger, an eye, or an ear; when He is said to repent, to be angry, or grieved; every one sees that analogy is metaphorical. Because those parts and passions, taken in the proper signification, must, in every degree, necessarily and from the formal nature of the thing, include imperfection. When, therefore, it is said—the finger of God appears in this or that event, men of common sense mean no more but that it is as truly ascribed to God as the works wrought by human fingers are to man: and so of the rest.—But the case is different when wisdom and knowledge are attributed to God. Passions and senses, as such, imply defect; but in knowledge simply, or as such, there is no defect[1]. Knowledge, therefore, in the proper formal meaning of the word, may be attributed to God proportionably, that is preserving a proportion to the

[1] But what if there is that in the elements of our knowledge, analysed in philosophy, which forbids the ultimate resolution of what really exists into an intelligible unity; and which—whether under the name of an unresolvable 'duality' or any other—obliges us, if we have due regard to the facts of experience, to 'leave many things abrupt,' as Bacon says the philosophical theologian must at last do? The fate of all Monist systems, as contrasted with the unsystematic philosophies, seems to point to this. In a finite knowledge—the only sort we have any experience of—the facts refuse to be fully explained in our 'little systems.'

infinite nature of God[1]. We may say, therefore, that as God is infinitely above man, so is the knowledge of God infinitely above the knowledge of man, and this is what Cajetan calls *analogia proprie facta*. And after this same analogy we must understand all those attributes to belong to the Deity which in themselves simply, and as such, denote perfection. We may, therefore, consistently with what hath been premised, affirm that all sorts of perfection which we can conceive in a finite spirit are in God, but without any of that allay[2] which is found in the creatures. This doctrine, therefore, of analogical perfections in God, or our knowing God by analogy, seems very much misunderstood and misapplied by those who would infer from thence that we cannot frame any direct or proper notion, though never so inadequate, of knowledge or wisdom, as they are in the Deity; or understand any more of them than one born blind can of light and colours[3].

22. And now, gentlemen, it may be expected I should ask your pardon for having dwelt so long on a point of metaphysics, and introduced such unpolished and unfashionable

---

[1] What does this important qualification include?
[2] Alloy. 'Allay' in Bacon and other early writers.
[3] In what he says about an *analogical* knowledge of God, Berkeley had partly in view two contemporary theologians—both Irish bishops. Among other replies to Toland's *Christianity not Mysterious* (1696) was a *Letter* by Peter Browne, afterwards Bishop of Cork and Ross, which appeared in 1699. Browne maintains (so far in verbal agreement with Berkeley) that we have no *idea* of spirit; and further that our knowledge of the spiritual world is gained by 'analogy' from our knowledge of the operations of embodied human spirit. In 1709, Archbishop King published a Sermon on the *Consistency of Predestination and Foreknowledge with the Freedom of Man's Will*, which he defended on the same foundation of analogy, in a way that seemed to imply that our highest conceptions of God are mere metaphors, which mean nothing real. Browne's view of human theological knowledge is fully stated in his *Procedure, Extent, and Limits of Human Understanding* (1728), and in *Things Divine and Supernatural conceived by Analogy with Things Natural and Human* (1733).—Butler's 'analogy' between the visible constitution of things experienced on this side of death, and that larger constitution that is put before us in conscience and Christianity, justifying expectations of a life beyond death, is not to be confounded with Browne's 'analogical interpretation' of the attributes of God.

writers as the Schoolmen into good company; but, as Lysicles gave the occasion, I leave him to answer for it.

Lys. I never dreamt of this dry dissertation. But, if I have been the occasion of discussing these scholastic points, by my unluckily mentioning the Schoolmen, it was my first fault of the kind, and I promise it shall be the last. The meddling with crabbed authors of any sort is none of my taste. I grant one meets now and then with a good notion in what we call dry writers, such a one for example as this I was speaking of, which I must own struck my fancy. But then, for these we have such as Prodicus or Diagoras, who look into obsolete books, and save the rest of us that trouble.

Cri. So you pin your faith upon them?

Lys. It is only for some odd opinions, and matters of fact, and critical points. Besides, we know the men to whom we give credit: they are judicious and honest, and have no end to serve but truth. And I am confident some author or other has maintained the forementioned notion in the same sense as Diagoras related it.

Cri. That may be. But it never was a received notion, and never will, so long as men believe a God: the same arguments that prove a first cause proving an intelligent cause;— intelligent, I say, in the proper sense; wise and good in the true and formal acceptation of the words. Otherwise, it is evident that every syllogism brought to prove those attributes, or, which is the same thing, to prove the being of a God, will be found to consist of four terms, and consequently can conclude nothing[1]. But for your part, Alciphron, you have been fully convinced that God is a thinking intelligent

[1] 'Four terms'—one of the commonest of fallacies, due to the ambiguity, and therefore imperfection, of language. This supposed syllogism does not exemplify it, however, if the terms 'knowledge,' 'wisdom,' 'goodness,' &c.—in their application to God involving an incomprehensibility not found in their application to human agents—are yet sufficiently near their ordinary connotation when they express the practical knowledge of God which we *may* reach.

being, in the same sense with other spirits; though not in the same imperfect manner or degree.

23. *Alc.* And yet I am not without my scruples: for, with knowledge you infer wisdom, and with wisdom goodness. But how is it possible to conceive God so good and man so wicked? It may, perhaps, with some colour be alleged that a little soft shadowing of evil sets off the bright and luminous parts of the creation, and so contributes to the beauty of the whole piece; but for blots so large and so black it is impossible to account by that principle. That there should be so much vice, and so little virtue upon earth, and that the laws of God's kingdom should be so ill observed by His subjects, is what can never be reconciled with that surpassing wisdom and goodness of the supreme Monarch[1].

Euph. Tell me, Alciphron, would you argue that a state was ill administered, or judge of the manners of its citizens, by the disorders committed in the jail or dungeon?

Alc. I would not.

Euph. And, for aught we know, this spot, with the few sinners on it, bears no greater proportion to the universe of intelligences than a dungeon doth to a kingdom. It seems we are led not only by revelation, but by common sense, observing and inferring from the analogy of visible things, to conclude there are innumerable orders of intelligent beings more happy and more perfect than man; whose life is but a span, and whose place, this earthly globe, is but a point, in respect of the whole system of God's creation. We are dazzled, indeed, with the glory and grandeur of things here below, because we know no better. But, I am apt to think, if we knew what it was to be an angel for one hour, we should return to this world, though it were to sit on the

[1] This familiar theological difficulty does not rise, like that which occasioned the analogical hypothesis, from the need for infinite intelligence in order to comprehend Infinite Quantity. It is occasioned by the moral disorder in which we find ourselves, and in which we seem to find the universe.

brightest throne in it, with vastly more loathing and reluctance than we would now descend into a loathsome dungeon or sepulchre[1].

24. *Cri.* To me it seems natural that such a weak, passionate, and short-sighted creature as man should be ever liable to scruples of one kind or other. But, as this same creature is apt to be over-positive in judging, and over-hasty in concluding[2], it falls out that these difficulties and scruples about God's conduct are made objections to His being. And so men come to argue from their own defects against the Divine perfections. And, as the views and humours of men are different and often opposite, you may sometimes see them deduce the same atheistical conclusions from contrary premises. I knew an instance of this in two minute philosophers of my acquaintance, who used to argue each from his own temper against a Providence. One of them, a man of a choleric and vindictive spirit, said he could not believe a Providence, because London was not swallowed up or consumed by fire from heaven; the streets being, as he said, full of people who shew no other belief or worship of God but perpetually praying that He would damn, rot, sink, and confound them. The other, being of an indolent easy temper, concluded there could be no such thing as Providence; for that a being of consummate wisdom must needs employ himself better than in minding the prayers and actions and little interests of mankind.

Alc. After all, if God have no passions, how can it be true that vengeance is His? Or how can He be said to be jealous of His glory?

[1] This solution of the difficulty of the physical and moral evil is in the spirit of Butler's 'Analogy' rather than of Browne's, and especially of Butler's Sermon on the 'Ignorance of Man.'

[2] 'Thus much at least,' says Butler, 'will be found, not taken for granted but *proved* [i. e. by the analogy of the supernatural to the natural], that any reasonable man, who will thoroughly consider the matter, may be as much assured as he is of his own being, that it is not so clear a case that there is a nothing'—in the religious views e. g. of the supremacy of moral government in the universe, and of our conscious life, and continued moral agency, after death.

Cri. We believe that God executes vengeance without revenge, and is jealous without weakness, just as the mind of man sees without eyes, and apprehends without hands.

25. *Alc.* To put a period to this discourse, we will grant there is a God in this dispassionate sense: but what then? What hath this to do with Religion or Divine worship? To what purpose are all these prayers, and praises, and thanksgivings, and singing of praises, which the foolish vulgar call serving God? What sense, or use, or end is there in all these things?

Cri. We worship God, we praise and pray to Him: not because we think that He is proud of our worship, or fond of our praise or prayers, and affected with them as mankind are; or that all our service can contribute in the least degree to His happiness or good: but because it is good for us to be so disposed towards God: because it is just and right, and suitable to the nature of things, and becoming the relation we stand in to our supreme Lord and Governor.

Alc. If it be good for us to worship God, it should seem that the Christian Religion, which pretends to teach men the knowledge and worship of God, was of some use and benefit to mankind.

Cri. Doubtless.

Alc. If this can be made appear, I shall own myself very much mistaken.

Cri. It is now near dinner-time. Wherefore, if you please, we will put an end to this conversation for the present[1].

---

[1] Berkeley, in the preceding Dialogue, argues that our knowledge of God may be explained in the same way as the knowledge we have of our fellow-men. He makes it a suggested judgment, which presupposes a consciousness of ourselves, and which also presupposes a tendency to suggest what has been previously experienced by us. He realises the universe as consisting in the mental experience of a hierarchy of intercommunicating spirits—intercommunicating by means of the phenomena given in sense, and all in communion with the Divine Spirit Supreme. With his aversion to metaphysical abstractions, he never raises the antinomies of Kant, and he ignores the *unica substantia* of Spinoza.

God is with him the self-conscious Spirit, Supreme in the hierarchy, on whom all other conscious spirits depend.

But one may well ask whether this conception enough recognises that ineffable mysteriousness of God and the Infinite which nourishes the sentiment of reverence, so efficacious in our spiritual life ?

At the opposite extreme God disappears in the Unknowable.

The difficulty of an intermediate between these extremes of *anthropomorphism* and *theological nescience* perplexes modern thought. A comprehensible God is no God: an entirely unknown God cannot even engage faith. Berkeley seems unconscious of the difficulty. Out of it has arisen the theological agnosticism of modern physical science, and its counterpart gnosticism in Absolute Thought—personified in finite spirits. *Siris* carries us deeper into this subject.

The preceding Dialogue hardly recognises the difficulties which in these days are most apt to beset the philosophical inquirer in theology; for it countenances the assumption that there is no alternative intermediate between Theism (in a somewhat anthropomorphic form of it too) and dogmatic Atheism. Nothing is said about those who pronounce the whole problem insoluble—in Hume's words, 'a riddle, an aenigma, an inexplicable mystery'; with 'doubt, uncertainty, and suspense of judgment,' as 'the only result of our most accurate scrutiny into it'—and who thus hold themselves absolved from offering any ultimate explanation at all. Thanks indirectly to Hume and Kant, perhaps we are learning that if the ultimate problem is practically insoluble, then even the working principles of life must, on the same ground, be unworthy of trust.

ANONYMOUS LETTER.

In September, 1732, a few months after the preceding Dialogue was published, the following anonymous Letter to its author appeared in the *Daily Post Boy* :—

Reverend Sir,

I have read over your treatise called *Alciphron*, in which the Free-thinkers of the present age, in their various shifted tenets, are pleasantly, elegantly, and solidly confuted. The style is easy, the language plain, and the arguments are nervous. But upon the Treatise annexed thereto, and upon that part where you seem to intimate that Vision is the sole Language of God, I beg leave to make these few observations, and offer them to your's and your readers' consideration [1]:—

1. Whatever it is without that is the cause of any idea within, I call the *object* of sense : the sensations arising from such objects, I call *ideas*. The 'objects,' therefore, that cause such sensations are without us, and the 'ideas' within.

2. Had we but one sense, we might be apt to conclude that there were no objects at all without us, but that the whole scene of ideas which passed through the mind arose from its internal operations ; but since the same object is the cause of ideas by different senses, thence we infer its existence. But, though the object be one and the same, the ideas that it pro-

---

[1] The original *Essay on Vision*, published in 1709, was 'annexed' to *Alciphron*. The preceding Dialogue is the portion of *Alciphron* to which this Letter refers as that in which Berkeley 'intimates that Vision is the sole (?) language of God.'

duces in different senses have no manner of similitude with one another. Because,

3. Whatever connexion there is betwixt the idea of one sense and the idea of another, produced by the same object, arises only from experience. To explain this a little familiarly, let us suppose a man to have such an exquisite sense of feeling given him that he could perceive plainly and distinctly the inequality of the surface of two objects, which, by its reflecting and refracting the rays of light, produces the ideas of colours. At first, in the dark, though he plainly perceived a difference by his touch, yet he could not possibly tell which was red and which was white, whereas a little experience would make him feel a colour in the dark, as well as see it in the light.

4. The same word in languages stands very often for the object without, and the ideas it produces within, in the several senses. When it stands for any object without, it is the representative of no manner of idea; neither can we possibly have any idea of what is solely without us. Because,

5. Ideas within have no other connexion with the objects without than from the frame and make of our bodies, which is by the arbitrary appointment of God; and, though we cannot well help imagining that the objects without are something like our ideas within, yet a new set of senses, or the alteration of the old ones, would soon convince us of our mistake; and, though our ideas would then be never so different, yet the objects might be the same.

6. However, in the present situation of affairs, there is an infallible certain connexion betwixt the idea and the object; and, therefore, when an object produces an idea in one sense,

we know, but from experience only, what idea it will produce in another sense.

7. The alteration of an object may produce a different idea in one sense from what it did before, which may not be distinguished by another sense. But, where the alteration occasions different ideas in different senses, we may, from our infallible experience, argue from the idea of one sense to that of the other; so that, if a different idea arises in two senses from the alteration of an object, either in situation or distance, or any other way, when we have the idea in one sense, we know from use what idea the object so situated will produce in the other.

8. Hence, as the operations of Nature are always regular and uniform, where the same alteration of the object occasions a smaller difference in the ideas of one sense, and a greater in the other, a curious observer may argue as well from exact observations as if the difference in the ideas was equal; since experience plainly teaches us that a just proportion is observed in the alteration of the ideas of each sense, from the alteration of the object. Within this sphere is confined all the judicious observations and knowledge of mankind.

Now, from these observations, rightly understood and considered, your *New Theory of Vision* must in a great measure fall to the ground, and the laws of Optics will be found to stand upon the old unshaken bottom. For, though our ideas of magnitude and distance in one sense are entirely different from our ideas of magnitude and distance in another, yet we may justly argue from one to the other, *as they have one common cause without*, of which, as without, we cannot possibly have the faintest idea. The ideas I have of distance and magnitude by feeling are widely different from the ideas

I have of them by seeing; but that *something without* which is the cause of all the variety of the ideas within, in one sense, is the cause also of the variety in the other; and, as they have a *necessary* connexion with *it*, we may very justly demonstrate from our ideas of feeling of the same object what will be our ideas in seeing. And, though to talk of seeing by tangible angles and tangible lines be, I agree with you, direct nonsense, yet to demonstrate from angles and lines in feelings, to the ideas in seeing that arise from the same common object, is very good sense, and so *vice versâ.*

From these observations, thus hastily laid together, and a thorough digestion thereof, a great many useful corollaries in all philosophical disputes might be collected.

I am,
your humble servant, &c.

This anonymous Letter was the occasion of the following *Vindication of the Theory of Visual Language*, by Berkeley, which appeared in March, 1733.

The *Vindication* contributes to his previous reasonings—

(*a*) Important explanations of his original theory of the development of the power of Seeing through suggestion. In so doing he points to lines of thought which may be run deeper, especially the distinction between the *suggested objects of sense* and their *ultimate or rational cause* (sect 9-18).

(*b*) Answers to the eight objections of the preceding Letter to the Theory of a Divine Visual Language (sect. 19-34).

(*c*) A deductive or synthetical exposition and application of the theory of how we learn to See,—the analytical order of exposition adopted in the original *Essay on Vision* being reversed. At the close there is an allusion to Cheselden's since celebrated case.

The psychological inquiry into the philosophy of Perception leads in this *Vindication* to a consideration of our judgment of Causality. It is argued that causation involves more than the natural succession and metamorphosis of phenomena, seeing that reason cannot be satisfied with a *caused* cause; that we find ourselves obliged to interpret the events of sense as ultimately the expression of Rational Will; and that we are led, by sustained reflection, to transform the visible, and indeed the whole sensible world, into a perpetual Divine Government—physical and at last moral.

A. C. F.

THE
THEORY OF VISUAL LANGUAGE

VINDICATED AND EXPLAINED.

EXTRACTS FROM

THE THEORY OF VISUAL LANGUAGE

VINDICATED AND EXPLAINED.

* * * * *

9. By a *sensible object* I understand that which is properly perceived by sense. Things properly perceived by sense are *immediately* perceived [1].—Besides things properly and immediately *perceived* by any sense, there may be also other things *suggested* to the mind by means of those proper and immediate objects;—which things so suggested are not objects of that sense, being in truth only objects of the imagination [2], and originally belonging to some other sense or faculty. Thus, sounds are the proper object of hearing, being properly and immediately perceived by that, and by no other sense. But, by the mediation of sounds or words, all other things may be suggested to the mind; and yet things so suggested are not thought the object of hearing.

10. The peculiar objects of each sense, although they are truly or strictly perceived by that sense alone, may yet be suggested to the imagination by some other sense. The objects therefore of all the senses may become objects of imagination —which faculty represents all sensible things. A colour, there-

---

[1] Do we become at all percipient—meaning by that cognisant of something that is independent of transient phenomena—in any one of our five senses, taken singly? Does externality so belong to any one of them that, in that one, we have not only sensations, but also apprehend a real object—and an object that is distinguished (not necessarily as something extended) from the percipient? If so, on what rational principle is the distinction made? These questions are scarcely touched by Berkeley.

[2] 'Imagination,' i.e. expectant imagination, or rather expectant conception, discursive thought and rational common sense being latent in the 'suggestion.'

fore, which is truly perceived by sight alone, may, nevertheless, upon hearing the words blue or red, be apprehended by the imagination. It is in a primary and peculiar manner the object of sight; in a secondary manner it is the object of imagination: but cannot properly be supposed the object of hearing[1].

11. The objects of sense, being things immediately perceived, are otherwise called *ideas*[2].

The *cause*[3] of these ideas, or the power of producing them, is not the object of sense—not being itself perceived, but only inferred by reason from its effects, to wit, those objects or ideas which are perceived by sense. From our ideas of sense the inference of reason is good to Power, Cause, Agent. But we may not therefore infer that our ideas are *like* unto this Power, Cause, or Active Being. On the contrary, it seems evident that an idea can be only like another idea, and that in our ideas or immediate objects of sense, there is nothing of Power, Causality, or Agency included.

12. Hence it follows that the power or cause of ideas is not an object of sense, but of *reason*. Our knowledge of the cause is measured by the effect; of the power, by our idea. To the absolute nature, therefore, of outward causes or

[1] In this and the preceding section he distinguishes the *perception* that is immediate and original, given in the senses singly—in each of which he assumes that we are conscious of phenomena appropriate to the sense—from *suggestion*, in which a plurality of the senses is involved, and by which our developed perception of extra-organic things is held by him to be constituted. Berkeley's 'immediate perception' is simply consciousness of phenomena of sense; his suggestion—developed or acquired perception—is the *interpretation* of the significant phenomena of sense that is occasioned by custom or experience.

[2] Elsewhere called also 'sensations' and 'real ideas' (in contrast with 'chimeras' of mere imagination), and afterwards in *Siris* called 'phenomena.' To 'phenomenon,' as on the whole the most convenient term, I have usually adhered in these annotations.

[3] 'Cause' here is not the phenomenal sign, but the efficient and primary productive cause; and that with Berkeley must be (unphenomenal) spirit—cannot be phenomena of which we are percipient in sense.

powers, we have nothing to say: they are no objects of our sense or perception. Whenever, therefore, the appellation of *sensible object* is used in a determined intelligible sense, it is not applied to signify the absolutely existing outward cause or power, but the ideas themselves produced thereby[1].

13. Ideas which are observed to be connected together are vulgarly considered under the relation of cause and effect, whereas, in strict and philosophic truth, they are only related as the sign to the thing signified[2]. For, we know our ideas, and therefore know that one idea cannot be the cause of another. We know that our ideas of sense are not the cause of themselves. We know also that *we* do not cause them. Hence we know they *must* have some other efficient cause, distinct from *them* and *us*.

14. In treating of Vision, it was my purpose to consider the *effects* and *appearances*—the objects perceived by my senses—the ideas of sight as connected with those of touch; to inquire how one idea comes to suggest another belonging to a different sense; how things visible suggest things tangible; how present things suggest things more remote and future—whether by likeness, by necessary connexion, by geometrical inference, or by arbitrary institution.

15. It hath indeed been a prevailing opinion and un-

[1] This seems to say that the 'objects' of Sense are subjective phenomena, given in each of our senses; or suggested, when the data of one sense are interpreted as evidence of sensations to be expected in another of our senses. The relations of Reason on the other hand transcend phenomena. He neither analyses the rational constitution of objectivity, in the localising of our sensations, nor shows, on the other hand, that the merely phenomenal data of sense *can* be 'objects,' in any proper meaning of objectivity.

[2] He does not show what is involved in our being intellectually obliged to refer phenomena to unphenomenal power; nor *why* (which is a very different thing) we connect them, through sense suggestions, as sign and thing signified, i.e. under laws of nature. Mere sense cannot give universality, nor indeed more than the present, but transient, phenomenon. Of suggestion he only says that it is based on 'arbitrary institution,' and he implies that reason involves ' necessary connexion.'

doubted principle among mathematicians and philosophers that there were certain ideas common to both senses: whence arose the distinction of primary and secondary qualities. But, I think it hath been demonstrated that there is no such thing as *a common object*—as an idea, or kind of idea, perceived both by sight and touch.

16. In order to treat with due exactness on the nature of Vision, it is necessary in the first place accurately to consider our own ideas; to distinguish where there is a difference; to call things by their right names; to define terms, and not confound ourselves and others by their ambiguous use; the want or neglect whereof hath so often produced mistakes. Hence it is that men talk as if one idea was the efficient cause of another; hence they mistake *inferences of reason* for *perceptions of sense;* hence they confound *the power residing in somewhat external*[1] with the *proper object of sense*—which is in truth no more than our own idea.

17. When we have well understood and considered the nature of Vision, we may, by reasoning from thence, be better able to collect some knowledge of the *external unseen cause* of our ideas;—whether it be one or many, intelligent or unintelligent, active or inert, body or spirit. But, in order to understand and comprehend this theory[2], and discover the true principles thereof, we should consider the likeliest way is not to attend to unknown substances, external causes, agents, or powers; nor to reason or infer anything about or from things obscure, unperceived, and altogether unknown[3].

18. As in this inquiry we are concerned with what objects we perceive, or our own ideas, so, upon them our reasonings must proceed. To treat of things utterly unknown as if we knew them, and so lay our beginning in obscurity, would not

---

[1] This 'power' is, with Berkeley, Mind or Spirit—not perceived by sense, but found by 'inference.'

[2] i.e. the theory of our power of interpreting the meaning of visual phenomena.

[3] 'Unknown'—so far as mere sense is concerned.

surely seem the properest means for the discovering of truth. Hence it follows, that it would be wrong if one about to treat of the nature of Vision should, instead of attending to visible ideas, define the *object* of sight to be *that obscure cause, that invisible power or agent, which produced visible ideas in our minds*. Certainly such cause or power does not seem to be the object either of the sense or the science of Vision, inasmuch as what we know thereby we know only of the effects [1].

[1] The foregoing sections confine the present question to the *objects* we are immediately percipient of—namely, 'sensations,' 'real ideas,' the 'phenomena' present to our senses—and their *suggested* connexion with one another. The *power* that presents phenomena to our senses in a rational and interpretable order, being a power 'external' and 'unseen,' cannot *itself* be an 'object' of sense: it is rationally inferred from the phenomena. This inference he might justify on the ground that we distinguish what *we can* produce from visible and tangible phenomena which *we cannot* produce, and which therefore we find ourselves in reason obliged to refer to a cause 'distinct from them and us' (sect. 13). Causality, as the fundamental principle of Reason, is thus, as it were, proposed here for philosophical analysis to any student who is so inclined.

The *causal principle* has been often used by philosophers as a premiss in reasonings for the existence of impercipient Matter. The phenomena of sense, they argue, must be caused: *I* am not their cause (although they are perceived by me): they must therefore be effects of an extended and solid substance; or at least of an 'unknown Something,' called Matter.—Unable to accept this abstraction, Berkeley had asked, Must not the *power* of which the phenomena presented to our senses are effects—at least if the word 'power' is to have a meaning— be Mind or Spirit—like our own in kind, but not necessarily in degree —and therefore not a mere abstraction like unphenomenal Matter?— Others, Reid and Hamilton for instance, deny that Matter is *inferred*. Body and mind, in their view, exist as it were face to face in perception—in the *sui generis* relation of *percipient act* and *perceived object*— each equally known to the perceiving mind as phenomenal subject and object, in the irreducible act; neither known as absolute and independent being.—Berkeley argues that we *may* infer that another active Spirit is the cause of our 'sensations,' although we cannot infer that abstract or unphenomenal Matter is. And his implied reason seems to be, that we have had experience of what power means—in the free personal acts of which we recognise ourselves the responsible causes— while we cannot connect any meaning with the term when applied to 'matter': there is meaning in *spiritual power; power in matter* is a meaningless abstraction.

A *representative* perception (after a sort) of sensible things is implied in Berkeley's 'suggestion,' or developed perception, in which 'things'

Having premised thus much, I now proceed to consider the principles laid down in your Letter, which I shall take in order as they lie.

19. In your *first paragraph* or *section*, you say that 'whatever it is without which is the cause of any idea within, you call the object of sense;' and you tell us soon after this, 'that we cannot possibly have an idea of any object without.'—Hence it follows that by an *object of sense* you mean something that we can have no manner of idea of. This making the objects of sense to be things utterly insensible seems to me contrary to common sense and the use of language. That there is nothing in the reason of things to justify such a definition is, I think, plain from what has been premised. And that it is contrary to received custom and opinion, I appeal to the experience of the first man you meet, who I suppose will tell you that by an 'object of sense' he means that which is perceived by sense, and not a thing utterly unperceivable and unknown. The beings, substances, powers which exist without, may indeed concern a treatise on some other science, and may there become a proper subject of inquiry. But why they should be considered as objects of the visive faculty, in a treatise of Optics[1], I do not comprehend.

20. The real 'objects of sight' we see; and what we see we know. And these true objects of sense and knowledge—to wit, *our own ideas*[2]—are to be considered, compared, distinguished, in order to understand the true Theory of Vision.—As to the *outward cause* of these ideas, whether it be one and the same, or various and manifold, whether it be thinking or unthinking, spirit or body, or whatever else we conceive or determine about it, the visible appearances do not alter

---

consist of phenomena that are significant of (and that thus represent) other phenomena, by natural law, which means by Divine appointment.

[1] 'Optics' here includes introspective psychology of the sensations proper to the optic nerve, and of visual perception. Cf. sect. 37.

[2] 'Our own ideas,' i.e. the phenomena of which we are conscious in the five senses.

their nature—our ideas are still the same. Though I may have an erroneous notion of the cause, or though I may be utterly ignorant of its nature, yet this does not hinder my making true and certain judgments about my ideas :—my knowing which are the same, and which different; wherein they agree, and wherein they disagree; which are connected together, and wherein this connexion consists; whether it be founded in a likeness of nature, in a geometrical necessity, or merely in experience and custom[1].

21. In your *second section*, you say 'that if we had but one sense, we might be apt to conclude there were no objects at all without us; but that, since the same object is the cause of ideas by different senses, thence we infer its existence.'—Now, in the first place, I observe, that I am at a loss concerning the point which is here assumed, and would fain be informed how we come to know that the *same* object causeth ideas by different senses. In the next place, I must observe that, if I had only one sense, I should nevertheless infer and conclude there was *some* cause without me (which you, it seems, define to be an *object*), producing the sensations or ideas perceived by that sense. For, if I am conscious that *I* do not cause them, and know that *they* are not the cause of themselves— both which points seem very clear—it plainly follows that there must be *some other third cause* distinct from me and them[2].

22. In your *third section*, you acknowledge with me 'that

---

[1] Berkeley and his critic are at cross purposes about the word 'object.' With the former it is confined to the transitory phenomena of which we are conscious or immediately percipient, or which are suggested in developed perception; with the latter it is applied to their (supposed) external cause, which the critic seems to take for granted is 'abstract' or unphenomenal Matter.—Berkeley does not ask whether, by a merely empirical comparison of phenomena, we can form judgments about their actual relations to one another.

[2] Berkeley proceeds everywhere upon the assumption, that we are intellectually obliged to refer what we perceive by our senses to a spiritual or intending agent, as their proper determining cause, but he does not pause to explain the universality and necessity of this intellectual obligation.

the connexion between ideas of different senses ariseth only from experience.'—Herein we are agreed [1].

In your *fourth section* you say 'that a word denoting an external object is the representative of no manner of idea. Neither can we possibly have an idea of what is solely without us.'—What is here said of an external unknown object hath been already considered (sect. 19).

23. In the *following section* of your Letter, you declare 'that our ideas have only an arbitrary connexion with outward objects, that they are nothing like the outward objects, and that a variation in our ideas doth not imply or infer a change in the objects, which may still remain the same.'— Now, to say nothing about the confused use of the word 'object,' which hath been more than once already observed, I shall only remark that the points asserted in this section do not seem to consist with some others that follow.

24. For, in the *sixth section*, you say 'that in the present situation of things, there is an infallible certain connexion between the idea and the object.'—But how can we perceive this connexion, since, according to you, we never perceive such object, nor can have any idea of it? or, not perceiving it, how can we know this connexion to be infallibly certain?

25. In the *seventh section*, it is said 'that we may, from our infallible experience, argue from our idea of one sense to that of another.'—But, I think it is plain that our experience of the connexion between ideas of sight and touch is not infallible; since, if it were, there could be no *deceptio visus*, neither in painting, perspective, dioptrics, nor any otherwise.

26. In the *last section*, you affirm 'that experience plainly teaches us that a just proportion is observed in the alteration of the ideas of each sense, from the alteration of

---

[1] 'Experience'—elsewhere 'custom' or 'suggestion'—by which he throughout (so far) explains our tendency to make actual data of sense signs or evidence of other data of sense, not actual but expected. In Hume's 'explanation' of our belief in 'necessary connexion' in nature, this hint is worked out. (See Hume's *Inquiry*, ch. vii.)

the object.'—Now, I cannot possibly reconcile this section with the fifth, or comprehend how experience should shew us that the alteration of the project produceth a proportionable alteration in the ideas of different senses; or how indeed it should shew us anything at all either from or about the alteration of an object utterly unknown, of which we neither have nor can have any manner of idea. What I do not perceive or know, how can I perceive or know to be altered? And, knowing nothing of its alterations, how can I compute anything by them, deduce anything from them, or be said to have any experience about them [1]?

27. From the observations you have premised, rightly understood and considered, you say it follows 'that my *New Theory of Vision* must in great measure fall to the ground; and the laws of Optics will be found to stand upon the old unshaken bottom.'—But, though I have considered and endeavoured to understand your remarks, yet I do not in the least comprehend how this conclusion can be inferred from them. The reason you assign for such inference is, 'because, although our ideas in one sense are entirely different from our ideas in another, yet we may justly argue from one to the other, as they have one common cause without; of which, you say, we cannot possibly have even the faintest idea.'—Now, my theory nowhere supposeth that we may not justly argue from the ideas of one sense to those of another, by analogy and by experience [2]; on the contrary, this very point

[1] In the preceding sections Berkeley may be said to be arguing against the possibility of even a *mediate* perception of the supposed abstract Cause of the phenomena presented in sense—the 'external object' of his critic. We *can* think and draw inferences, he implies, either about that whose *esse* is *percipi*, or about that whose *esse* is *percipere;* but not about that which must be meaningless.—Here and elsewhere he, in his own way, presses objections like those of Hamilton and Mansel to the possibility of a *representative* knowledge of *what is absolutely foreign to all our previous presentative experience.*

[2] 'By analogy and by experience,' *i.e.* inductively; for the expectant judgment which emerges from 'suggestion' is virtually an inductive generalisation, the presence of which, involving as it does reason latent in sense suggestion, Berkeley fails to explain.

is affirmed, proved, or supported throughout. (*Essay on Vision*, §§ 38 and 78.)

28. Indeed I do not see how the inferences which we make from visible to tangible ideas include any consideration of one common unknown external cause, or depend thereon, but only on mere custom or habit. The experience which I have had that certain ideas of one sense are [1] attended or connected with certain ideas of a different sense is, I think, a sufficient reason why the one may suggest the other.

29. In the next place, you affirm 'that something without, which is the cause of all the variety of ideas within in one sense, is the cause also of the variety in another: and, as they have a necessary connexion with it, we very justly demonstrate, from our ideas of feeling of the same object, what will be our ideas of seeing.'—As to which, give me leave to remark that to inquire whether that *unknown something* be the same in both cases, or different, is a point foreign to Optics; inasmuch as our perceptions by the visive faculty will be the very same, however we determine that point. Perhaps I think that the same Being which causeth our ideas of sight doth cause not only our ideas of touch likewise, but also all our ideas of all the other senses, with all the varieties thereof. But this, I say, is foreign to the purpose [2].

30. As to what you advance, that our ideas have a *necessary* connexion with such cause, it seems to me *gratis dictum :* no reason is produced for this assertion; and I cannot assent

---

[1] 'Are'—rather *have been*. On what *principle* do we translate the past into the future? He does not pause to ask this; nor to show the rationality of the translation, though he says it involves 'sufficient reason.'

[2] The present 'purpose' is to explain (by 'suggestion') the transformation of phenomena of sense into external things, and thus to explain perception and induction.—Does 'perhaps,' in the preceding sentence, hint any hesitation on Berkeley's part as to the distinctive metaphysical principle of his earlier works—the substantial and causal existence of the whole material world in God and finite spirits, in contrast to the ontology which supposes also 'abstract' material substance and power, 'out of Mind'?

to it without a reason. The ideas or effects I grant are evidently perceived: but the cause you say is utterly unknown. How then can you tell whether such unknown cause acts arbitrarily or necessarily? I *see* the effects or appearances: and I *know* that effects must have a cause: but I neither see nor know that their connexion with that cause is necessary[1]. Whatever there may be, I am sure I see no such necessary connexion, nor, consequently, can demonstrate by means thereof from ideas of one sense to those of another[2].

31. You add that although to talk of seeing by tangible angles and lines be direct nonsense, yet, to demonstrate from angles and lines in feeling to the ideas in seeing that arise from the same common object is very good sense. If by this no more is meant than that men might argue and compute geometrically by lines and angles in Optics, it is so far from carrying in it any opposition to my Theory that I have expressly declared the same thing. (*Essay on Vision*, sect. 78.) This doctrine, as admitted by me, is indeed subject to certain limitations; there being divers cases wherein the writers on Optics thought we judged by lines and angles, or by a sort of natural geometry, with regard to which I think they were mistaken, and I have given my reasons for it. And those reasons, as they are untouched in your letter, retain their force with me.

32. I have now gone through your reflexions, which the

[1] Does this mean that, for aught we can tell, apart from our experience, 'any thing may be the cause of any thing'? So Hume in his doctrine of 'Necessary Connexion.'—With Berkeley, however, it is merely equivalent to saying that any sense-phenomenon might be made the *sign* of any other, the establishment and maintenance of its *significance* (*i. e.* the establishment and maintenance of *law* in nature) being the issue of the rational will of the Supreme Mind; and in subordination, it might be added, to 'laws' still more comprehensive than those of the visible world—the physical symbolism of sense being causally subordinate to the laws of the spiritual world.

[2] He here disclaims the abstract necessity and universality of merely physical law. Thus even a complete knowledge of external nature and its physical laws, apart from the facts and laws of moral government, would still leave the ultimate problem raised by philosophy unsolved.

conclusion intimates to have been written in haste, and, having considered them with all the attention I am master of, must now leave it to the thinking reader to judge whether they contain anything that should oblige me to depart from what I have advanced in my *Theory of Vision*. For my own part, if I were ever so willing, it is not on this occasion in my power to indulge myself in the honest satisfaction it would be frankly to give up a known error; a thing so much more right and reputable to denounce than to defend. On the contrary, it should seem that the Theory will stand secure;— since you agree with me that men do not see by lines and angles; since I, on the other hand, agree with you that we may nevertheless compute in Optics by lines and angles, as I have expressly shewed; since all that is said in your Letter about the 'object,' the 'same' object, the 'alteration' of the object, is quite foreign to the theory, which considereth *our ideas* as *the object of sense*, and hath nothing to do with that unknown, unperceived, unintelligible thing which you signify by the word *object*. Certainly the laws of Optics will not stand on the old, unshaken bottom, if it be allowed that we do not see by geometry; if it be evident that explications of phenomena given by the received theories in Optics are insufficient and faulty; if other principles are found necessary for explaining the nature of vision; if there be no idea, nor kind of idea, common to both senses, contrary to the old received universal supposition of optic writers.

33. We not only impose on others but often on ourselves, by the unsteady or ambiguous use of terms. One would imagine that an *object* should be *perceived*[1]. I must own, when that word is employed in a different sense, that I am at a loss for its meaning, and consequently cannot comprehend

---

[1] Berkeley's *suggested* 'objects of sense' consist of actual and expected phenomena of sense; the former signs of the latter, and the latter not actually perceived. (Cf. sect. 39.) He regards what is suggested as (mediately) perceived, and so resolves *developed* or *acquired* perception into what he calls suggestion.

Vindicated and Explained. 295

any arguments or conclusions about it. And I am not sure that, on my own part, some inaccuracy of expression, as well as the peculiar nature of the subject, not always easy either to explain or conceive, may not have rendered my Treatise concerning Vision difficult to a cursory reader. But, to one of due attention, and who makes my words an occasion of his own thinking, I conceive the whole to be very intelligible : and, when it is rightly understood, I scarce doubt but it will be assented to. One thing at least I can affirm, that, if I am mistaken, I can plead neither haste nor inattention, having taken true pains and much thought about it.

34. And had you, Sir, thought it worth while to have dwelt more particularly on the subject, to have pointed out distinct passages in my Treatise, to have answered any of my objections to the received notions, refuted any of my arguments in behalf of mine, or made a particular application of your own; I might without doubt have profited by your reflexions. But it seems to me we have been considering, either different things, or else the same things in such different views as the one can cast no light on the other. I shall, nevertheless, take this opportunity to make a review of my Theory, in order to render it more easy and clear; and the rather because, as I had applied myself betimes to this subject, it became familiar—and in treating of things familiar to ourselves, we are too apt to think them so to others.

35[1]. It seemed proper, if not unavoidable, to begin in the

---

[1] Sect. 35-47 contain a restatement of the Theory that developed visual perception is the power we acquire of interpreting the divinely ordered phenomena of which we are originally conscious in sight. It was given less fully in the *Essay on Vision*, sect. 147, 148, and there gathered *inductively* from a previous survey of what we are conscious of in visual 'perception' of the distances, sizes, and places of things. This Theory is now assumed provisionally, in order to be applied *deductively*, in sect. 48-70, to explain our developed visual perceptions of real places, sizes, and distances.—The reverse but correlative methods of the *Essay* and the *Vindication* illustrate to the student the contrast

accustomed style of optic writers—admitting divers things as true, which, in a rigorous sense, are not such, but only received by the vulgar and admitted as such. There hath been a long and close connexion in our minds between the ideas of sight and touch. Hence they are considered as *one thing*—which prejudice suiteth well enough with the purpose of life; and language is suited to this prejudice. The work of science and speculation is to unravel our prejudices and mistakes, untwisting the closest connexions, distinguishing things that are different; instead of confused or perplexed, giving us distinct views; gradually correcting our judgment, and reducing it to a philosophical exactness. And, as this work is the work of time, and done by degrees, it is extremely difficult, if at all possible, to escape the snares of popular language, and the being betrayed thereby to say things strictly speaking neither true nor consistent. This makes thought and candour more especially necessary in the reader. For, language being accommodated to the prænotions of men and use of life, it is difficult to express therein the precise truth of things, which is so distant from their use, and so contrary to our prænotions.

36. In the contrivance of Vision, as that of other things, the wisdom of Providence seemeth to have consulted the operation rather than the theory of man: to the former things are admirably fitted, but, by that very means, the latter is often perplexed. For, as useful as these immediate suggestions and constant connexions are to direct our actions; so is our distinguishing between things confounded and as it were blended together no less necessary to the speculation and knowledge of truth.

37. The knowledge of these connexions, relations, and dif-

yet connexion of analytical and synthetical procedure. In the *Essay* Berkeley advances analytically towards his Theory: in the *Vindication* he first (hypothetically) assumes the Theory, and then proceeds to verify it, by showing how it accounts for our visual knowledge of situations, sizes, and distances.

ferences of things visible and tangible, their nature, force, and significancy hath not been duly considered by former writers on Optics, and seems to have been the great *desideratum* in that science, which for want thereof was confused and imperfect. A Treatise, therefore, of this *philosophical* kind[1], for the understanding of Vision, is at least as necessary as the *physical* consideration of the eye, nerve, coats, humours, refractions, bodily nature, and motion of light; or the *geometrical* application of lines and angles for *praxis* or theory, in dioptric glasses and mirrors, for computing and reducing to some rule and measure our judgments, so far as they are proportional to the objects of geometry. In these three lights Vision should be considered, in order to a complete Theory of Optics.

38. It is to be noted that, in considering the Theory of Vision, I observed[2] a certain known method wherein, from false and popular suppositions, men do often arrive at truth. Whereas in the synthetical method of delivering science or truth already found, we proceed in an inverted order, the conclusions in the analysis being assumed as principles in the synthesis. I shall therefore now begin with that conclusion— *That Vision is the Language of the Author of Nature;* from thence deducing theorems and solutions of phenomena, and explaining the nature of visible things and the visive faculty.

39. Ideas which are observed to be connected with other ideas come to be considered as signs[3], by means whereof things not actually perceived by *sense* are signified or suggested

---

[1] Founded, that is, on a philosophical and not on a merely scientific and physiological analysis of developed or acquired perception.
[2] The *Essay on Vision* proceeds from particular facts to the general principle which they exemplify.
[3] How do they so 'come to be considered'? Berkeley says through 'experience' or 'custom.' The customs of external nature presuppose, he thinks, an 'arbitrary (not capricious) institution' of them (sect. 14) by God.

to the *imagination;* whose objects they are, and which alone perceives them. And, as sounds suggest other things, so characters suggest other sounds; and, in general, all signs suggest the things signified, there being no idea which may not offer to the mind another idea which hath been frequently joined with it. In certain cases a sign may suggest its correlate as an image, in others as an effect, in others as a cause [1]. But, where there is no such relation of similitude or causality, nor any necessary connexion whatsoever, two things, by their mere co-existence, or two ideas, merely by being perceived together, may suggest or signify one the other—their connexion being all the while arbitrary; for it is the connexion only, as such, that causeth this effect [2].

40. A great number of *arbitrary* signs, various and opposite, do constitute a Language. If such arbitrary connexion be instituted by men, it is an artificial Language; if by the Author of Nature, it is a Natural Language. Infinitely various are the modifications of light and sound, whence they are each capable of supplying an endless variety of signs, and, accordingly, have been each employed to form languages; the one by the arbitrary appointment of mankind, the other by that of God Himself. A connexion established by the Author of Nature, in the ordinary course of things, may surely be called natural, as that made by men will be named artificial.

---

[1] Does this imply that causes strictly so called—free spiritual causes—may be 'suggested,' instead of being 'inferred by reason'?

[2] *Mental association* seems here taken as the explanation of our belief in objective order in nature; and not only of that, but of our translation of the transitory phenomena of the senses into perceptions of extended objects. This might be compared with Kant's theory of perception, according to which sensations, received in the rationally necessary forms of *space*, are made intelligible by the *categories of understanding.* The modern philosopher has to determine between the two explanations. Berkeley assumes that each human being begins his conscious life with perception of phenomena presented to his senses and recognised by him as his personal experience; he then tries to account, by 'suggestion'—which here seems to mean little more than invariable association—for the externality of this experience, and for inductive science.

And yet this doth not hinder but the one may be as arbitrary as the other. And, in fact, there is no more likeness to exhibit, or necessity to infer, things tangible from the modifications of light, than there is in language to collect the meaning from the sound. (*Essay on Vision*, sect. 144, 147.) But, such as the connexion is of the various tones and articulations of voice with their several meanings, the same is it between the various modes of light and their respective correlates, or, in other words, between the ideas of sight and touch.

41. As to light, and its several modes or colours, all thinking men are agreed that they are ideas peculiar only to sight; neither common to the touch, nor of the same kind with any that are perceived by that sense. But herein lies the mistake, that, beside these, there are supposed other ideas common to both senses, being equally perceived by sight and touch—such as Extension, Size, Figure, and Motion. But that there are in reality no such common ideas, and that the objects of sight, marked by these words, are entirely different and heterogeneous from whatever is the object of feeling, marked by the same names, hath been proved in the *Theory* (*Essay on Vision*, sect. 127), and seems by you admitted; though I cannot conceive how you should in reason admit this, and at the same time contend for the received theories, which are so much ruined as mine is established by this main part and pillar thereof.

42. To *perceive* is one thing: to *judge* is another. So likewise, to be *suggested* is one thing, and to be *inferred* another. Things are suggested and perceived by Sense. We make judgments and inferences by the Understanding. What we immediately and properly perceive by sight is its primary object—light and colours. What is suggested, or perceived by mediation thereof, are tangible ideas—which may be considered as secondary and improper objects of sight. We infer causes from effects, effects from causes,

and properties one from another, where the connexion is necessary[1].

But, how comes it to pass that we apprehend by the ideas of sight certain other ideas, which neither resemble them, nor cause them, nor are caused by them, nor have any necessary connexion with them? The solution of this Problem, in its full extent, doth comprehend the whole Theory of Vision. This stating of the matter placeth it on a new foot, and in a different light from all preceding theories.

43. To explain how the mind or soul of man simply sees is one thing, and belongs to Philosophy[2]. To consider particles as moving in certain lines, rays of light as refracted or reflected, or crossing, or including angles, is quite another thing, and appertaineth to Geometry. To account for the sense of vision by the mechanism of the eye is a third thing, which appertaineth to Anatomy and experiments. These two latter speculations are of use in practice, to assist the defects and remedy the distempers of sight, agreeably to the natural laws contained in this mundane system. But the former Theory is that which makes us understand the true nature of Vision *considered as a faculty of the soul*. Which Theory, as I have already observed, may be reduced to this simple question, to wit, How comes it to pass that a set of ideas, altogether different from tangible ideas, should never-

---

[1] According to Berkeley, the explanation of our ability to read into what we see more than is originally seen (especially to read into it the data of touch—the fundamental sense) implies two faculties—(*a*) immediate perception of phenomena, and (*b*) suggestion in imagination, under associative laws, of phenomena previously perceived. Judgment and inference, on the other hand, involve rational understanding, conversant with necessary relations—in particular that of causation, which with him is the necessary connexion of phenomena, not with other phenomena, but with active and intending mind. What does Berkeley here and elsewhere mean by *necessity* of connexion, and how, on his theory of knowledge, does he account for the 'necessity'? Withal he finds 'judgments' rising out of our suggestions (*Essay on Vision*, sect. 3), but he does not ask why they do so. One again regrets the indistinctness of his account of knowledge.

[2] Philosophy is here equivalent to psychology.

theless suggest them to us—there being no necessary connexion between them? To which the proper answer is—*That this is done in virtue of an arbitrary connexion, instituted by the Author of Nature*[1].

44. The proper, immediate object of vision is light, in all its modes and variations, various colours in kind, in degree, in quantity; some lively, others faint; more of some and less of others; various in their bounds or limits; various in their order and situation. A blind man, when first made to see, might perceive these objects, in which there is an endless variety; but he would neither perceive nor imagine any resemblance or connexion between these visible objects and those perceived by feeling[2]. Lights, shades, and colours would suggest nothing to him about bodies, hard or soft, rough or smooth: nor would their quantities, limits, or order suggest to him geometrical figures, or extension, or situation—which they must do upon the received supposition, that these objects are common to sight and touch.

45. All the various sorts, combinations, quantities, degrees, and dispositions of light and colours, would, upon the first perception thereof, be considered in themselves only as a new set of sensations and ideas. As they are wholly new and unknown, a man born blind would not, at first sight, give them the names of things formerly known and perceived by his touch. But, after some experience, he would perceive their connexion with tangible things, and would, therefore, consider them as signs, and give them (as is usual in other cases) the same names with the things signified.

---

[1] The philosophical inquirer still asks on what *ultimate* ground of evidence we in any case proceed from the known to the unknown—from the *perceived sign* to the *suggested thing signified*. More than the merely empirical data of sense is needed to explain this; and especially to explain that assumption of a steady order among the changes of the phenomena of sense which is involved in suggested expectation and inductive inference.

[2] 'Feeling,' i.e. touch, inclusive of muscular sense and locomotive conscious energy.

46. More and less, greater and smaller, extent, proportion, interval are all found in Time as in Space; but it will not therefore follow that these are homogeneous quantities. No more will it follow, from the attribution of common names, that visible ideas are homogeneous with those of feeling. It is true that *terms* denoting tangible extension, figure, location, motion, and the like, are also applied to denote the quantity, relation, and order of the proper visible objects, or ideas of sight. But this proceeds only from experience and analogy. There is a *higher* and *lower* in the notes of music; men speak in a high or a low key. And this, it is plain, is no more than metaphor or analogy. So, likewise, to express the order of visible ideas, the words *situation*, *high* and *low*, *up* and *down*, are made use of; and their sense, when so applied, is analogical.

47. But, in the case of Vision we do not rest in a supposed *analogy* between different and heterogeneous natures. We suppose an *identity of nature*, or one and the same object common to both senses. And this mistake we are led into; forasmuch as the various motions of the head, upward and downward, to the right and to the left, being attended with a diversity in the visible ideas, it cometh to pass that those motions and situations of the head, which in truth are tangible, do confer their own attributes and appellations on visible ideas wherewith they are connected, and which by that means come to be termed *high* and *low*, *right* and *left*, and to be marked by other names betokening the modes of position; which, antecedently to such experienced connexion, would not have been attributed to them, at least not in the primary and literal sense [1].

[1] Sect. 48-53 treat of the visual 'suggestion' or developed perception, of the Situations of sensible things, and may be compared with sect. 88-119 in the *Essay on Vision*; sect. 54-61 of the 'suggestion' of Magnitudes, and may be compared with sect. 52-87 of the *Essay*; and sect. 62-69 of the 'suggestion' of Distances, and may be compared with sect. 2-51 of the *Essay*. They are here omitted, and the reader is referred to Berkeley's *Works*, vol. I. pp. 391-399.

*   *   *   *   *   *

70. What I have here written may serve as a commentary on my *Essay towards a New Theory of Vision;* and, I believe, will make it plain to thinking men [1]. In an age wherein we hear so much of thinking and reasoning, it may seem needless to observe how useful and necessary it is to think, in order to obtain just and accurate notions, to distinguish things that are different, to speak consistently, to know even our own meaning. And yet, for want of this, we may see many, even in these days, run into perpetual blunders and paralogisms. No friend, therefore, to truth and knowledge would lay any restraint or discouragement on thinking. There are, it must be owned, certain general maxims, the result of ages, and the collected sense of thinking persons, which serve instead of thinking, for a guide or rule to the multitude, who, not caring to think for themselves, it is fit they should be conducted by the thoughts of others. But those who set up for themselves, those who depart from the public rule, or those who would reduce them to it, if they

[1] Objections to the conclusion, that the optic nerve is originally sentient only to light, and that we do not originally see Distance, were offered in Mr. Bailey's *Review of Berkeley's Theory of Vision* (1842). This work was the subject of two interesting critical essays—one by Mr. J. S. Mill, in the *Westminster Review*, republished in his *Discussions;* and another by Prof. Ferrier, in *Blackwood's Magazine*, republished in his *Remains*. These led to some further controversy at the time.— Other objections have since been proposed by Mr. Abbott, of Trinity College, Dublin. His *Sight and Touch* (1864), criticised by me in the *North British Review*, August, 1864, to which he has issued a rejoinder in *Hermathena*, No. 5, Dublin, 1877, is a professed attempt to disprove the 'received (or Berkeleian) Theory of Vision.' Mr. Abbott may have improved our knowledge of what the suggesting signs are, in his proof that certain visual sensations of convergence and adjustment in the eye, for instance, are connected with the perception of distance, rather than those enlarged upon by Berkeley. This, however, is only substituting one set of organic signs for another,. not disproving the theory that educated vision, as we are now conscious of it, is interpretation of arbitrary signs—an interpretation that may be either instinctive (*i.e.* inexplicable) or (as Berkeley holds) suggested by experience. At the same time, Berkeley's 'explanation' may be regarded as inadequate to account for the judgments of which we are necessarily conscious when we contemplate the mathematical relations, sublime boundlessness, and unfathomable mystery of space.

do not think, what will men think of them? As I pretend not to make any discoveries which another might not as well have made, who should have thought it worth his pains: so I must needs say that without pains and thought no man will ever understand the true nature of Vision, or comprehend what I have wrote concerning it.

71. Before I conclude, it may not be amiss to add the following extract from the *Philosophical Transactions* (No. 400), relating to a person blind from his infancy, and long after made to see: 'When he first saw, he was so far from making any judgment about distances that he thought all objects whatever touched his eyes (as he expressed it) as what he felt did his skin, and thought no objects so agreeable as those which were smooth and regular, though he could form no judgment of their shape, or guess what it was in any object that was pleasing to him. He knew not the shape of anything, nor any one thing from another, however different in shape or magnitude: but upon being told what things were, whose form he before knew from Feeling, he would carefully observe them that he might know them again; but having too many objects to learn at once, he forgot many of them; and (as he said) at first he learned to know, and again forgot, a thousand things in a day. Several weeks after he was couched, being deceived by pictures, he asked which was the lying sense—Feeling or Seeing? He was never able to imagine any lines beyond the bounds he saw. The room he was in, he said, he knew to be part of the house, yet he could not conceive that the whole house could look bigger. He said every new object was a new delight, and the pleasure was so great that he wanted ways to express it [1].'—Thus, by

---

[1] Berkeley here quotes the famous experiment of Cheselden, recorded in the *Philosophical Transactions* for 1728. It is offered as evidence that our power of interpreting visual signs is neither (*a*) an instinct nor (*b*) a necessary inference, but (*c*) an expectation suggested by custom or 'experience.'—Cheselden's is among the first of several examples of

fact and experiment, those points of the theory which seem the most remote from common apprehension were not a little confirmed, many years after I had been led into the discovery of them by reasoning.

persons born blind who have been made to see, whose mental experience, immediately consequent upon the change, has been (more or less accurately) recorded. (See *Berkeley's Works*, vol. I. Appendix C, pp. 444-448, where other cases are mentioned. See also Dr. Franz's case in *Philos. Trans.* for 1841, pt. I.) Berkeley's comparative indifference to experiments of the sort, and to the relative physiology of the senses, is not difficult to understand. His introspective appeal to consciousness, to shew that we cannot touch what is visible nor see what is tangible, along with the evidence he offers that our tendency to unite visible and tangible phenomena, as 'qualities' of the same 'substance,' may be explained by the constant association of the latter with the former—the issue of all this seemed to him to make other evidence unnecessary. The results hitherto of experiments like Cheselden's, as tests of our original visual perception, illustrate the remark of Diderot, that an adequate cross-examination of persons born blind would be employment enough for the combined powers of Newton, Descartes, Locke, and Leibnitz.

III.

The Universe and the Universal Mind.

EXTRACTS

FROM

SIRIS:

A CHAIN OF PHILOSOPHICAL REFLEXIONS.

Mens agitat molem, et magno se corpore miscet.—*Virgil.*

Τὸ αὐτὸ νοεῖν τε καὶ εἶναι.—*Parmenides.*

PREFATORY NOTE.

Siris (σειρὰ, a chain) appeared when Berkeley was about sixty, and contains the metaphysics of his later life. Rising from certain supposed medicinal virtues of tar-water, we are here invited to follow the ascending links of a chain, which connects these and all other qualities of sensible things with one another, in and through supreme and pervading Causal Intelligence. In *Siris* too we are brought into connexion with the metaphysics of antiquity: on this historical basis Berkeley here revels in his favourite thought of the whole world of transitory sense-phenomena sustaining its intelligently ordered combinations and sequences in necessary dependence on active Mind.

English metaphysical literature in the eighteenth century contains no work more curiously abundant in seeds of thought than *Siris*. Its immediate practical and benevolent purpose was to confirm the conjecture that tar yields a 'water of health' for the relief of diseases, from which the whole animal creation might draw fresh supplies of the vital essence. It is a series of aphorisms, connected by quaint and subtle associations, the thoughts of ancient and medieval philosophers being interwoven, and the whole forming a study in medical science and in metaphysical philosophy. The work breathes the spirit of Plato and the Neoplatonists, and that in the least Platonic generation in England since the rise of modern philosophy, while it draws this Platonic spirit with the unexpectedness of genius from a thing of sense so commonplace as tar.

More than half of the 368 sections which compose *Siris* are occupied with physical facts and conjectures. The others are adapted to deepen our thought of the dependence of the universe of experience upon Mind, and to enlighten as well as satisfy the philosophical desire for ultimate rational unity. The Selections which follow comprehend the most important of the metaphysical aphorisms. They may be studied apart from Berkeley's medicinal hypothesis about tar-water, and read simply as meditations upon the material world viewed under its constitutive relations to Supreme Intelligence. The conception of passive Nature pervaded by spiritual power is expressed in *Siris* in many ways, and then defended and further unfolded by help of the ancient sages.

Thus in this curious work medicine passes into metaphysics. Doubt regarding the author's hypothesis as to the medicinal virtues of tar-water need not disturb our enjoyment of its philosophical speculations about the rational concatenation of the universe. The medical aphorisms may misinterpret the meaning that is latent in tar; this need not hinder us from learning through *Siris* to see, in an unsubstantial and impotent material world, the constant manifestation of Divine power. The metaphysical aphorisms may be used as aids to reflection upon the interpretability of nature—space and time—free-will and necessity—matter and form—the soul or essence of things—the absolute personality and ineffable mystery of God.

When we compare *Siris* with the *Principles* we find important differences between Berkeley's philosophy when he was sixty and when he was twenty-five. The universals of Reason here overshadow the perishable phenomena of Sense and its Suggestions. Sensible things are looked at as adumbrations of a reality above and beyond Nature, which philosophy helps us to find. The objects of perception are here called *phenomena*, instead of 'ideas' or 'sensations;' while Ideas (not in Locke's meaning, and in Berkeley's early meaning of the term *idea*, but in Plato's) are recognised in the ultimate explanation of things.

An increase of intellectual tolerance and of eclecticism appear in *Siris*, with less disposition to insist upon the dependence of the sensible world on sentient mind as a final settlement of all difficulties. That *esse* is *percipi*, in the sensuous reference of the latter term, is felt more to be the beginning than the completion of a philosophical solution of metaphysical problems. Recluse meditation, with a wider study of the meditation of the past, have given Berkeley a more mystical conception of the universe, and a feeling that it is neither so easily nor so perfectly intelligible under his old formula as it seemed in his ardent and less considerate youth. His awe of its mysteriousness is increased, and also his readiness to allow different ages and countries, each in its own philosophical form, to recognise Reason rather than the phenomena of Sense as the fixed element in existence,— with irreducible data too in the incomplete explanation thus offered. He now welcomes an acknowledgment of God in any intellectual form of faith that consists with this supremacy of Reason in the universe. His last work in philosophy more than any of his former ones breathes and helps to educate the philosophic spirit, which, as it begins in wonder and the sense of mystery, is found at the end to issue in the same, deepened and enlightened by reflexion. Some of its concluding sentences express, with exquisite literary grace, his own spiritual growth in later life. We find him intellectually broader, more modest, and more liberal; more ready to accept with reverence the 'broken' philosophy to which deep and patient insight, with its sense of mystery, seems at last to conduct us all; more aware that in this mortal state, under the present limitations of sense, we must be satisfied to make the best of any openings which occur; yet not without hope— there being 'no subject so obscure but we may discern some glimpse of truth by long poring on it,' if we cultivate love for 'truth, the cry of all,' while it is really 'the game of a few.'

A philosophical analysis of human knowledge naturally begins with Sense and ends with causality and the constitution of Reason. Reason is latent in any knowledge, even through the senses, of the external world; the phenomena of the external world find their ultimate explanation in the reason which gives them intelligibility. Perception involves the contrast between the conscious spirit and the unconscious world, with the unfathomable mysteries of Space and Time which both disclose; Reason involves the ultimate meaning of what in Sense is phenomenally revealed in antithesis, under the mysterious conditions of co-existence and succession. Here are the three great objects of meditative thought—Self—in contrast to the world of Nature—both mutually related in and through God. The antithesis of Self and the phenomena present in Sense is prominent in Berkeley's *Principles of Human Knowledge;* the ultimate unity in Reason is prominent in *Siris*.

A. C. F.

EXTRACTS FROM

SIRIS:

A CHAIN OF PHILOSOPHICAL REFLEXIONS.

For Introduction to the following piece, I assure the reader that nothing could, in my present situation, have induced me to be at the pains of writing it, but a firm belief that it would prove a valuable present to the public. What entertainment soever the reasoning or notional part may afford the Mind, I will venture to say, the other part seemeth so surely calculated to do good to the Body that both must be gainers. For, if the lute be not well tuned, the musician fails of his harmony. And, in our present state, the operations of the mind so far depend on the right tone or good condition of its instrument, that anything which greatly contributes to preserve or recover the health of the Body is well worth the attention of the Mind[1]. These considerations have moved me to communicate to the public the salutary virtues of Tar-water; to which I thought myself indispensably obliged by the duty every man owes to mankind. And, as effects are linked with their causes, my thoughts on this low but useful theme led to farther inquiries, and those on to others, remote perhaps and speculative, but I hope not altogether useless or unentertaining[2].

*　　*　　*　　*　　*　　*

[1] Berkeley in all this recognises more than in his early writings that we are embodied spirits, although his philosophy has become less empirical. He recognises the established interdependence in us of organic and conscious life, but always with the reserve that reason is at last the cause of organisation, not organisation the cause of reason.

[2] What relates to Tar-water and its supposed medicinal effects may be studied in *Siris* (*Works*, vol. II.) by those fond of experimenting on the connexion of our organism with animal and mental health.

154. [1] The order and course of things, and the experiments we daily make, shew there is a Mind that governs and actuates this mundane system, as the proper real agent and cause. * * * We have no proof, either from experiment or reason, of any other agent or efficient cause than Mind or Spirit. When, therefore, we speak of corporeal agents or corporeal causes, this is to be understood in a different, subordinate, and improper sense.

155. The *principles* whereof a thing is compounded, the *instrument* used in its production, and the *end* for which it was intended, are all in vulgar use termed 'causes,'—though none of them be, strictly speaking, agent or efficient. There is not any proof that an extended corporeal or mechanical cause doth really and properly *act*—even motion itself being in truth a passion. * * * They are, nevertheless, sometimes termed 'agents' and 'causes,' although they are by no means active in a strict and proper signification. When therefore force, power, virtue, or action is mentioned as subsisting in an extended and corporeal or mechanical being, this is not to be taken in a true, genuine, and real, but only in a gross and popular sense, which sticks in appearances, and doth not analyse things to their first principles[2]. In compliance with established language and the use of the world, we must employ the popular current phrase. But then in regard to truth we ought to distinguish its meaning.

*   *   *   *   *   *

160. The mind of man acts by an instrument necessarily[3].

---

[1] The following sections express Berkeley's later thoughts about active Reason as the Supreme Power in the universe; also as to the insufficiency of the atomic hypothesis as the ultimate explanation of things. The implied premiss is. that every change must have a *sufficient* cause, and that the only sufficient uncaused cause must be Mind; but that in nature, *a priori, anything* may be the sign, *i.e.* physical cause, of a change.

[2] This view is urged and illustrated in Dr. Thomas Brown's *Inquiry into the Relation of Cause and Effect*. See especially Part I.

[3] This is in the spirit of the opening aphorisms of the *Novum Organum*, which teach that, in order to be able to produce phenomenal changes,

The τὸ ἡγεμονικὸν, or Mind presiding in the world, acts by an instrument freely[1]. Without instrumental and second causes, there could be no regular course of nature. And without a regular course, nature could never be understood; mankind must always be at a loss, not knowing what to expect, or how to govern themselves, or direct their actions for the obtaining of any end. Therefore in the government of the world physical agents—improperly so called—or mechanical or second causes, or natural causes or instruments, are necessary to assist, not the governor, but the governed[2].

* * * * * *

231. The laws of attraction and repulsion are to be regarded as laws of motion; and these only as rules or methods observed in the productions of natural effects,—the efficient and final causes whereof are not of mechanical consideration. Certainly, if the *explaining* a phænomenon be to assign its proper efficient and final cause, it should seem that Mechanical Philosophers never explained any thing; their province being only to discover the laws of nature, that is, the general rules and methods of motion, and to account for particular phænomena by reducing them under, or shewing their conformity to, such general rules.

232. Some corpuscularian philosophers of the last age have indeed attempted to explain the formation of this world and its phænomena by a few simple laws of mechanism. But, if we consider the various productions of nature, in the mineral, vegetable, and animal parts of the creation, I believe we shall see cause to affirm, that not any one of them has

man must observe and understand the established connexions, or sense significance, in nature.

[1] The 'laws of nature,' in obedience to which man must conform his overt actions, are here assumed to be the issue of the free will of God, and constantly dependent on this as their uncaused cause—so that nature is essentially supernatural.

[2] Cf. *Principles*, sect. 60–66, in which Berkeley reconciles the utility to man of an order in nature, and of the interpretation of that order in science, with his theory of the ultimate dependence of phænomena and their changes upon a percipient, and therefore upon reason and will.

hitherto been, or can be, accounted for on principles merely mechanical; and that nothing could be more vain and imaginary than to suppose with Descartes, that merely from a circular motion's being impressed by the supreme Agent on the particles of extended substance, the whole world, with all its several parts, appurtenances, and phænomena, might be produced, by a necessary consequence, from the laws of motion [1].

233. Others suppose that God did more at the beginning, having then made the seeds of all vegetables and animals, containing their solid organical parts in miniature, the gradual filling and evolution of which, by the influx of proper juices, doth constitute the generation and growth of a living body. So that the artificial structure of plants and animals daily generated requires no *present* exercise of art to produce it, having been already framed at the origin of the world, which with all its parts hath ever since subsisted;—going like a clock or machine by itself, according to the laws of nature, without the immediate hand of the artist [2]. But how can this hypothesis explain the blended features of different species in

---

[1] This is part of the scientific cosmogony of Descartes, and inadequately represents his philosophy. He explained the stars and planetary bodies as the issue of vortical motions, in an originally chaotic material mass coextensive with space. But all this must be taken in connexion with what he taught about the apparent interaction of mind and body being really the constant efficient agency of God. This notion of constant Divine agency was brought out further by Geulinx, Malebranche, and other Cartesians, in their theory of 'occasional' causes which culminated in Spinozism.

[2] This is the theory of Leibnitz, already referred to, according to which the force or energy originally infused into the universe remains the same, only passing through phenomenal transformations, agreeably to the laws of nature, in a harmony between *thoughts* and *motions* that has been pre-established by God. Mind and body in man thus agree in a conscious automatism, like two clocks, originally in harmony and moving in concert ever after. And thus the whole material world, without immediate Divine agency, is always in harmony with the moral or spiritual world. — With Cartesians and with Leibnitz, matter is neither that of which we are actually conscious in perception, nor is it the efficient cause of our being percipient: it is made known by present (Cartesians) or previous (Leibnitzians) agency of God.

mules and other mongrels? or the parts added or changed, and sometimes whole limbs lost, by marking in the womb? or how can it account for the resurrection of a tree from its stump, or the vegetative power in its cuttings? in which cases we must necessarily conceive something more than the mere evolution of a seed[1].

234. Mechanical laws of nature or motion direct us how to act, and teach us what to expect. Where Intellect presides there will be method and order, and therefore rules, which if not stated and constant, would cease to be rules. There is therefore a constancy in things, which is styled the Course of Nature[2]. All the phænomena in nature are produced by motion. There appears an uniform working in things great and small, by attracting and repelling forces. But the particular laws of attraction and repulsion are various. Nor are we concerned at all about the forces, neither can we know or measure them otherwise than by their effects, that is to say, the motions; which motions only, and not the forces, are indeed in the bodies. Bodies are moved to or from each other, and this is performed according to different laws. The natural or mechanic philosopher endeavours to discover those laws by experiment and reasoning. But what is said of *forces residing in bodies*, whether attracting or repelling, is to be regarded only as a mathematical hypothesis, and not as any thing really existing in nature[3].

235. We are not therefore seriously to suppose, with certain mechanic philosophers, that the minute particles of

---

[1] We cannot, he argues, find the observed effects in the merely phenomenal data of sense, so that there must be more than an evolution of these data to explain the issue. .The issue presupposes the constant orderly agency of evolving Mind.
[2] The rational presumption of the ultimate supremacy of Mind in the universe is given as the explanation of our inductive assumption of physical law, and of ideals in nature.
[3] That is to say, even if all changes in natural phenomena could be resolved by the laws of motion, motions would be themselves only phenomenal effects, not really efficient or uncaused causes.

bodies have *real* forces or powers, by which they act on each other, to produce the various phenomena in nature. The minute corpuscles are impelled and directed, that is to say, moved to and from each other, according to various rules or laws of motion. The laws of gravity, magnetism, and electricity are divers. And it is not known what other different rules or laws of motion might be established by the Author of Nature [1].

* * * * * *

237. These and numberless other effects seem inexplicable on mechanical principles; or otherwise than by recourse to a Mind or Spiritual Agent. Nor will it suffice from present phænomena and effects, through a chain of natural causes and subordinate blind agents, to trace a Divine Intellect as the remote original cause, that first created the world, and then set it a going. We cannot make even one single step in accounting for the phænomena, without admitting the immediate presence and immediate action of an incorporeal Agent, who connects, moves, and disposes all things, according to such rules, and for such purposes, as seem good to Him [2].

* * * * * *

240. The words attraction and repulsion may, in compliance with custom, be used where, accurately speaking, motion alone is meant. And in that sense it may be said that peculiar attractions or repulsions in the parts are at-

---

[1] The arbitrariness of the existing constitution of nature, meaning by that the dependence of the actual laws of nature on reasonable will. The dependence of the government of the physical world on the still higher laws of the moral world is suggested by this.

[2] In short, there are not even *secondary* causes in the material world, if by that be meant bodily *agents*. There is simply the agency of Supreme Mind; which Berkeley, like Descartes, asserts must be constant, and not, as with Leibnitz, remote. But perhaps the alternative here is one which we cannot settle; nor the involved question of time and succession in relation to Divine Mind. He cannot mean to exclude human volitions as efficient causes, though he leaves in obscurity their ultimate relation to the supreme volition.

tended with specific properties in the whole. The particles of light are vehemently moved to or from, retained, or rejected by, objects: which is the same thing as to say, with Sir Isaac Newton, that the particles of acids are endued with great attractive force, wherein their activity consists; whence fermentation and dissolution; and that the most repellent are, upon contact, the most attracting particles.

241. Gravity and fermentation are received for two most extensive principles. From fermentation are derived the motion and warmth of the heart and blood in animals, subterraneous heat, fires, and earthquakes, meteors, and changes in the atmosphere. And that attracting and repelling forces operate in the nutrition and dissolution of animal and vegetable bodies is the doctrine both of Hippocrates and Sir Isaac Newton. The former of these celebrated authors, in his Treatise concerning Diet or Regimen, observes that in the nourishment of man, one part repels and another attracts. And again in the same Treatise, two carpenters, saith he, saw a piece of timber: one draws, the other pushes: these two actions tend to one and the same end, though in a contrary direction, one up, the other down: this imitates the nature of man : πνεῦμα τὸ μὲν ἕλκει τὸ δὲ ὠθέει.

242. It is the general maxim of Hippocrates, that the manner wherein *nature* acts consisteth in attracting what is meet and good, and in repelling what is disagreeable or hurtful. He makes the whole of the animal economy to be administered by the faculties or powers of nature. Nature alone, saith he, sufficeth for all things to animals. She knows of herself what is necessary for them. Whence it is plain he means a conscious intelligent nature. And though he declares all things are accomplished on man by necessity, yet it is not a blind fate or chain of mere corporeal causes, but a Divine Necessity, as he himself expressly calls it. And what is this

but an overruling intelligent power that disposeth of all things[1]?

243. Attraction cannot produce, and in that sense account for, the phænomena—being itself one of the phænomena produced and to be accounted for. Attraction is performed by different laws, and cannot therefore in all cases be the effect of the elasticity of one uniform medium. The phænomena of electrical bodies, the laws and variations of magnetism, and, not to mention other kinds, even gravity, are not *explained* by elasticity—a phænomenon not less obscure than itself[2]. But then, although it shew not the *agent*, yet it sheweth a *rule* and *analogy* in nature, to say, that the solid parts of animals are endued with attractive powers[3] whereby from contiguous fluids they draw like to like; and that glands have peculiar powers[3] attractive of peculiar juices. Nature seems better known and explained by attractions and repulsions, than by those other mechanical principles of size, figure, and the like; that is, by Sir Isaac Newton, than Descartes. And natural philosophers excel, as they are more or less acquainted with the laws and methods observed by the Author of Nature.

* * * * * *

247. Though it be supposed the chief business of a natural philosopher to trace out causes from the effects, yet this is to be understood not of agents, but of principles;—that is, of component parts, in one sense, or of laws or rules, in another.

---

[1] This notion of a Divine necessity (ἀνάγκη θεία), distinguished from blind materialistic fate, was common among the Greeks. The contemplative spirit found repose in a necessity which resolved into God, and in which man was, therefore, not the sport of a cruel and purposeless force that might at any time convert the universe into physical and moral chaos, our conscious lives too, for aught we can predict, being prolonged without end in this chaos.

[2] He means to say that phenomenal changes cannot be really caused by what is merely phenomenal—as all that is present in the senses *per se* must be.

[3] The term 'power' is used by him metaphorically when applied to the 'solid parts' and 'glands,' because regarded as really inherent only in Mind.

In strict truth, *all agents are incorporeal*, and as such are not properly of physical consideration. The astronomer, therefore, the mechanic, or the chemist, not as such, but by accident only, treat of real causes, agents, or efficients. Neither doth it seem, as is supposed by the greatest of mechanical philosophers, that the true way of proceeding in their science is, from known notions in nature to investigate the moving forces. Forasmuch as *force* is neither corporeal, nor belongs to any corporeal thing; nor yet to be discovered by experiments or mathematical reasonings, which reach no farther than discernible effects, and motions in things passive and moved.

248. *Vis* or force is to the soul what extension is to the body, saith St. Augustin, in his tract concerning the Quantity of the Soul; and without force there is nothing done or made, and consequently there can be no agent. Authority is not to decide in this case. Let any one consult his own notions and reason, as well as experience, concerning the origin of motion, and the respective natures, properties, and differences of soul and body, and he will, if I mistake not, evidently perceive, that there is nothing active in the latter. Nor are they natural agents or corporeal forces which make the particles of bodies to cohere. Nor is it the business of experimental philosophers to find them out.

249. The mechanical philosopher, as hath been already observed, inquires properly concerning the rules and modes of operation alone, and not concerning the cause; forasmuch as nothing mechanical is or really can be a *cause*. And although a mechanical or mathematical philosopher may speak of absolute space, absolute motion, and of force, as existing in bodies, causing such motion and proportional thereto; yet *what* these 'forces' are, which are supposed to be lodged in bodies, to be impressed on bodies, to be multiplied, divided, and communicated from one body to another, and which seem to animate bodies like abstract spirits, or souls, hath been

found very difficult, not to say impossible, for thinking men to conceive and explain.

250. Nor, if we consider the proclivity of mankind to realise their notions[1], will it seem strange that mechanic philosophers and geometricians should, like other men, be misled by prejudice, and take mathematical hypotheses for real beings existing in bodies, so far as even to make it the very aim and end of their science to compute or measure those phantoms; whereas it is very certain that nothing in truth can be measured or computed, besides the very effects or motions themselves. Sir Isaac Newton asks, Have not the minute particles of bodies certain forces or powers by which *they* act on one another, as well as on the particles of light, for producing most of the phænomena in nature? But, in reality, those minute particles are only agitated, according to certain laws of nature, *by some other agent*, wherein the force exists, and not in them, which have only the motion; which motion in the body moved, the Peripatetics rightly judge to be a mere passion, but in the mover to be ἐνέργεια or act[2].

251. It passeth with many, I know not how, that mechanical principles give a clear solution of the phænomena. The Democritic hypothesis, saith Dr. Cudworth, doth much more handsomely and intelligibly solve the phænomena, than that of Aristotle and Plato[3]. But, things rightly considered, per-

---

[1] 'Realise their notions,' by assuming for instance that abstractions of natural philosophy such as 'force' or 'power,' stand for something which may be phenomenalised.

[2] The relation of *motion* (a visible phenomenon) to *power* or *force* (a 'notion' to which no phenomenon corresponds) is the subject of Berkeley's tract *De Motu* (*Works*, vol. III. pp. 75-100).

[3] The passage in Cudworth (1619-1688) is as follows:—'The whole Aristotelical system of philosophy is infinitely to be preferred before the whole Democritical; though the former hath been so much disparaged, and the other cried up of late amongst us. Because, though it cannot be denied but that the Democritic hypothesis doth much more handsomely and intelligibly solve the *corporeal* phænomena, yet *in all other things which are of far the greater moment*, it is rather a madness than a Philosophy,'—*Intellectual System*, b. I. ch. 1. sect. 45. The

haps it will be found not to solve any phænomenon at all: for all *phænomena* are, to speak truly, *appearances in the soul or mind*[1]; and it hath never been explained, nor can it be explained, how external bodies, figures, and motions, should produce an appearance in the mind. These principles, therefore, do not solve—if by solving is meant assigning the real, either efficient or final, cause of appearances—but only reduce them to general rules.

252. [2] There is a certain *analogy, constancy,* and *uniformity* in the phænomena or appearances of nature, which are a foundation for general rules: and these are a Grammar for the understanding of Nature, or that series of effects in the Visible World whereby we are enabled to *foresee* what will come to pass in the natural course of things. Plotinus observes, in his third Ennead, that the art of presaging is in some sort the reading of natural letters denoting order, and that so far forth as analogy obtains in the universe, there may be vaticination. And in reality, he that foretels the motions of the planets, or the effects of medicines, or the results of chemical or mechanical experiments, may be said to do it by natural vaticination[3].

philosophies of Plato (B.C. 427-347) and Aristotle (B.C. 384-322), in contrast to the atomism of Democritus (B.C. 460-370), occupy many of the sections which follow. Bacon and others in the seventeenth century had extolled Democritus and the pre-Socratics, in comparison with Socrates and his school.

[1] 'Phenomena,' I may say again, here corresponds to the 'sensations' or 'ideas of sense' of Berkeley's earlier works. Their actual existence depends upon being perceived. In order to become objects a mind must be percipient of them, but they do not depend on any one individual mind.

[2] The following sections place in some new lights Berkeley's conception of the interpretable and prophetic Language of Nature, that constant expression of Reason and Will; *i.e.* of the Supernatural.

[3] This remarkable passage in Plotinus (A.D. 204-270) in a manner anticipates the modern conception of a scientific *prevision*. Plotinus refers to perception in sense as the obscure thought of that Intelligible World, which discloses itself when we emerge from our struggles to interpret phenomena only dimly intelligible in sense, and reach the rational understanding of things.

253. We know a thing when we understand it; and we understand it when we can interpret or tell what it signifies. Strictly, the Sense knows nothing. We perceive indeed sounds by hearing, and characters by sight. But we are not therefore said to understand them. After the same manner, the phænomena of nature are alike visible to all: but all have not alike learned the connexion of natural things, or understand what they signify, or know how to vaticinate by them. —There is no question, saith Socrates in Theæteto, concerning that which is agreeable to each person; but concerning what will in time to come be agreeable, of which all men are not equally judges. He who *foreknoweth what will be* in every kind is the wisest. According to Socrates, you and the cook may judge of a dish on the table equally well; but while the dish is making, the cook can better foretel what will ensue from this or that manner of composing it. Nor is this manner of reasoning confined only to morals or politics; but extends also to natural science [1].

254. As the natural connexion of *signs* with the *things signified* is regular and constant, it forms a sort of Rational Discourse, and is therefore the immediate effect of an intelligent Cause. This is agreeable to the philosophy of Plato, and other ancients. Plotinus indeed saith, that which acts naturally is not intellection, but a certain power of moving matter, which doth not know but only do.—And it must be owned that, as faculties are multiplied by philosophers according to their operations, the *will* may be distinguished from the *intellect*. But it will not therefore follow that the Will which operates in the course of nature is not conducted and applied by intellect [2], although it be granted that neither

[1] We see in these examples the distinction between the particular and the universal—between *feeling*, which is subjective or private, and *knowledge*, which is objective or universal. The discovery of a sequence in physical causation is as it were the thinking of a portion of the creative thought on which the unity and intelligibility of nature continually depends.

[2] It is not a capricious Will.

will understands, nor intellect wills. Therefore, the phænomena of nature, which strike on the senses and are understood by the mind, do form not only a magnificent spectacle, but also a most coherent, entertaining, and instructive Discourse; and to effect this, they are conducted, adjusted, and ranged by the greatest wisdom. This Language or Discourse is studied with different attention, and interpreted with different degrees of skill. But so far as men have studied and remarked its rules, and can interpret right, so far they may be said to be knowing in nature. A beast is like a man who hears a strange tongue but understands nothing[1].

255. Nature, saith the learned Doctor Cudworth, is not master of art or wisdom: nature is *ratio mersa et confusa*—reason immersed and plunged into matter, and as it were fuddled in it and confounded with it. But the formation of plants and animals, the motions of natural bodies, their various properties, appearances, and vicissitudes, in a word, the whole series of things in this visible world, which we call the Course of Nature, is so wisely managed and carried on that the most improved human reason cannot *thoroughly* comprehend even the least particle thereof;—so far is it from seeming to be produced by fuddled or confounded reason [2].

256. Natural productions, it is true, are not all equally perfect. But neither doth it suit with the order of things, the structure of the universe, or the ends of Providence, that they should be so. General rules are necessary to make the world intelligible: and from the constant observations of such rules, natural evils will sometimes unavoidably ensue:

[1] This section applies to external nature generally the theory that what we see is to all intents a Language. Bacon's favourite conception of the *interpretability* of Nature is in harmony with this. Physical science is the discovery by the human mind of thoughts that are objective in sensible things, and unconsciously presupposed even in our sense-perceptions.

[2] If we cannot know any one thing 'thoroughly' without knowing all its relations to all other things, the only knowledge proper is Omniscience.

things will be produced in a slow length of time, and arrive at different degrees of perfection.

257. It must be owned, we are not conscious of the systole and diastole of the heart, or the motion of the diaphragm. It may not nevertheless be thence inferred, that *unknowing nature* can act regularly, as well as ourselves. The true inference is—that the self-thinking individual, or human person, is not the real author of those natural motions. And, in fact, no man blames himself if they are wrong, or values himself if they are right[1].—The same may be said of the fingers of a musician, which some object to be moved by habit which understands not; it being evident that what is done by rule must proceed from something that understands the rule; therefore, if not from the musician himself, from some other active Intelligence, the same perhaps which governs bees and spiders, and moves the limbs of those who walk in their sleep[2].

258. *Instruments, occasions*, and *signs* (sect. 160) occur in, or rather make up, the whole visible Course of Nature. These, being no agents themselves, are under the direction of One Agent concerting all for one end, the supreme good. All those motions, whether in animal bodies, or in other parts

---

[1] The moral judgment is here taken as the test for distinguishing uncaused causality from the merely physical laws that have been divinely established in nature. Conscience points to the *only* known power in the universe in pointing to the free agency of a person—a moral or immoral agent. Mere phenomena can only be established signs of other phenomena, and *a priori* any phenomenon might have been made the sign (physical cause or effect) of any other by the supreme moral power.

[2] So Cudworth (*Intellectual System*, b. I. chap. 3. sect. 12-14). A vein of speculation somewhat similar appears in Aristotle's *Physics*. The facts referred to, with many others analogous, have given rise to modern hypotheses of 'unconscious mental agency,' 'unconscious cerebral agency,' and 'automatic activity.' That our habits and instincts involve thought *of which the subject of the habits or instincts is unconscious*, is not, however, to be taken as evidence that thought issues from what is inferior to itself. It rather shows that our (unconsciously) rational instincts and habits are an expression of the Supreme Reason. An artist need not previously know *consciously* the *ideal* that determines the work he instrumentally produces.

of the system of nature, which are not effects of *particular wills*, seem to spring from the same general cause with the vegetation of plants—an æthereal spirit actuated by a Mind [1].

259. The first poets and theologers of Greece and the East considered the generation of things as ascribed rather to a Divine Cause, but the *physici* to natural causes, subordinate to and directed still by a Divine; except some corporealists and mechanics, who vainly pretended to make a world without a God. The hidden force that unites, adjusts, and causeth all things to hang together, and move in harmony—which Orpheus and Empedocles styled Love—this principle of union is no blind principle, but acts with intellect. This Divine Love and Intellect are not themselves obvious to our view, or otherwise discerned than in their effects. Intellect enlightens, Love connects, and the Sovereign Good attracts all things.

260. All things are made for the Supreme Good, all things tend to that end : and we may be said to *account* for a thing, when we shew that it is so best. In the Phædon, Socrates declares it to be his opinion that he who supposed all things to have been disposed and ordered by a Mind should not pretend to assign any other cause of them. He blames physiologers for attempting to account for phænomena, particularly for gravity and cohesion, by vortexes and æther; overlooking the τὸ ἀγαθὸν and τὸ δέον, the strongest bond and cement which holds together in all parts of the universe, and not discerning the Cause itself from those things which only attend it [2].

[1] In short, acts for which moral agents are responsible are the *only* effects in the universe which are *not* to be referred to the Supreme Mind; *persons* are the only secondary causes.

[2] In Berkeley's philosophy, as one cannot be too often reminded, the merely physical inquirer has to do only with *powerless phenomena*, and with the laws or rules which they are made to follow in their metamorphoses. Phenomena (*i. e.* the data of the senses—'ideas' of sense) are in all cases *effects*, not causes—in which Divine thought and Will are expressed to human minds : physical 'causation' is the divinely

261. As in the microcosm, the constant regular tenor of the motions of the viscera and contained juices doth not hinder particular voluntary motions to be impressed by the mind on the animal spirit; even so, in the mundane system, the steady observance of certain laws of nature, in the grosser masses and more conspicuous motions, doth not hinder but a Voluntary Agent may sometimes communicate particular impressions to the fine æthereal medium, which in the world answers the animal spirit in man. Which two (if they are two), although invisible and inconceivably small, yet seem the real latent springs whereby all the parts of this visible world are moved—albeit they are not to be regarded as a true cause, but only as an instrument of motion; and the instrument not as a help to the Creator, but only as a sign to the creature[1].

262. Plotinus supposeth that the soul of the universe is not the original cause or author of the species, but receives them from Intellect—the true principle of order and distinction, the source and giver of *forms*. Others consider the vegetative soul only as some lower faculty of a higher soul which animates the fiery æthereal spirit (sect. 178). As for the blots and defects which appear in the course of this world—which some have thought to proceed from a fatality or necessity in nature, and others from an evil principle—that same philosopher observes, that it may be the governing Reason produceth and ordaineth all those things; and, not intending that all parts should be equally good, maketh some worse than others by design; as all parts in an animal are not eyes; and in a city, comedy, or picture, all ranks, characters, and colours are not equal or alike; even so excesses, defects, and contrary qualities conspire to the beauty and harmony of the world.

caused, constant although arbitrary, connexion of sensible signs with the phenomena of sense which they signify.
[1] Cf. *Principles*, sect. 60–66.

263. It cannot be denied that, with respect to the universe of things, we in this mortal state are like men educated in Plato's cave, looking on shadows with our backs turned to the light. But though our light be dim, and our situation bad, yet if the best use be made of both, perhaps something may be seen[1].—Proclus, in his Commentary on the Theology of Plato, observes there are two sorts of philosophers. The one placed Body first in the order of beings, and made the faculty of thinking depend thereupon, supposing that the principles of all things are corporeal: that Body most really or principally exists, and all other things in a secondary sense, and by virtue of that. Others, making all corporeal things to be dependent upon Soul or Mind, think this to exist in the first place and primary sense, and the being of Bodies to be altogether derived from and presuppose that of the Mind[2].

264. Sense and Experience acquaint us with the course and analogy of appearances or *natural effects*. Thought, Reason, Intellect introduce us into the knowledge of their *causes*. Sensible appearances, though of a flowing, unstable, and uncertain nature, yet having first occupied the mind, they do by an early prevention render the aftertask of thought more difficult; and, as they amuse the eyes and ears, and are more suited to vulgar uses and the mechanic arts of life, they easily obtain a preference, in the opinion of most men, to those superior principles, which are the later growth of the human mind, arrived to maturity and perfection, but, not affecting the corporeal sense, are thought to be so far deficient in point of solidity and reality—*sensible* and *real*, to common

[1] The tone in this and other parts of *Siris* may be compared with that in the first five sections of the Introduction to the *Principles*, in which Berkeley attributes the difficulties of philosophy, not to mysterious facts in human experience, but to 'our having first raised a dust, and then complaining that we cannot see.'

[2] This well expresses the opposition between mere Materialism and Immaterialism. Proclus, the Neoplatonist, lived in the fifth century after Christ.

apprehensions, being the same thing. Although it be certain that the *principles of science* are neither objects of Sense nor Imagination; and that Intellect and Reason are alone the sure guides to truth [1].

265. [2] The successful curiosity of the present age, in arts, and experiments, and new systems, is apt to elate men, and make them overlook the Ancients. But, notwithstanding that the encouragement and purse of princes, and the united endeavours of great societies in these later ages, have extended experimental and mechanical knowledge very far, yet it must be owned that the Ancients too were not ignorant of many things, as well in Physics as Metaphysics, which perhaps are more generally, though not first, known in these modern times.

266. The *Pythagoreans* and *Platonists* had a notion of the true System of the World. They allowed of mechanical principles, but actuated by soul or mind: they distinguished the primary qualities in bodies from the secondary, making the former to be physical causes, and they understood physical causes in a right sense: they saw that a mind infinite in power, unextended, invisible, immortal, governed, connected, and contained all things: they saw there was no such thing

---

[1] This section is one of the best expressions of Berkeley's later philosophy, with its recognition of the Common Reason (νοῦς) as the highest faculty in the constitution of our knowledge—distinguishable from mere 'sense,' and also from the 'suggestions' to which sense experience or custom gives rise, while it is unconsciously involved in these suggestions. It may be contrasted with the attack on abstractions, in the Introduction to the *Principles*, and with the account of the elements involved in human knowledge in the *Principles*, sect. 1, 2. *Siris*, animated by the Platonic spirit, finds the essence of reality in 'principles'—universal relations of Reason—which are apprehended in perception and in suggestion only in a dim and a confused way. In the *Principles* (sect. 28-33, 36, 89), and in his other early works, Berkeley speaks as if scepticism consisted in doubting the reality of sensible things. Here he speaks lightly of that sort of reality. Can these views be reconciled?

[2] The two following sections are preparatory to those in which Ancient Idealism is used as a means for educating rational insight.

as real absolute space: that mind, soul, or spirit truly and really exists: that bodies exist only in a secondary and dependent sense: that the soul is the place of forms: that the sensible qualities are to be regarded as acts only in the cause, and as passions in us: they accurately considered the differences of intellect, rational soul, and sensitive soul, with their distinct acts of intellection, reasoning, and sensation; points wherein the Cartesians and their followers, who consider sensation as a mode of thinking, seem to have failed. They knew there was a subtle æther pervading the whole mass of corporeal beings, and which was itself actually moved and directed by a mind: and that physical causes were only instruments, or rather marks and signs [1].

* * * * * * * * *

270. [2] The doctrine of real, absolute, external Space induced some modern philosophers [3] to conclude it was a part or attribute of God, or that God himself was space; inasmuch as incommunicable attributes of the Deity appeared to agree thereto, such as infinity, immutability, indivisibility, incorporeity, being uncreated, impassive, without beginning or ending—not considering that all these negative properties may belong to nothing. For, nothing hath no limits, cannot be moved, or changed, or divided, is neither created nor destroyed.—A different way of thinking appears in the Hermaic as well as other writings of the ancients. With regard to absolute space, it is observed in the Asclepian Dialogue, that the word *space* or *place* hath by itself no meaning; and again, that it is impossible to understand what space alone

[1] This section deserves study both as showing what Berkeley had come to consider 'the true system of the world,' and also as a text for comparing, in the light of historical criticism, speculations about the universe among the ancient Platonists with those of the moderns, in the Cartesian period of philosophy in which Berkeley was educated.

[2] The dogmas of Space and Matter as independent entities, and of blind Fate or Chance, are contrasted in the following sections with the ancient and more spiritual conception of Anima Mundi and all-regulating Mind—especially as in the Platonists and Aristotle.

[3] See *Life of Berkeley*, p. 177.

or pure space is. And Plotinus acknowledgeth no place but soul or mind, expressly affirming that the soul is not in the world, but the world in the soul. And farther, the place of the soul, saith he, is not body, but soul is in mind, and body in the soul.

271. Concerning *absolute space*, that phantom of the mechanic and geometrical philosophers, it may suffice to observe that it is neither perceived by any sense, nor proved by any reason, and was accordingly treated by the greatest of the ancients as a thing merely visionary[1].

From the notion of absolute space springs that of *absolute motion;* and in these are ultimately founded the notions of *external existence, independence, necessity,* and *fate.*

Which *fate,* the idol of many moderns, was by old philosophers differently understood, and in such a sense as not to destroy the αὐτεξούσιον of God or man. Parmenides, who thought all things to be made by necessity or fate, understood justice and Providence to be the same with fate; which, how fixed and cogent soever with respect to man, may yet be voluntary with respect to God. Empedocles declared fate to be a cause using principles and elements. Heraclitus taught

---

[1] With Berkeley Space apart from and independent of phenomena presented in sense is an empty negation. Perceived and suggested sensible extension is the only space he recognises. Any other sort of Space, like any other sort of Matter, is for him a meaningless abstraction—'a thing merely visionary.' The Space against which Berkeley here argues is that of some ancient and modern mechanical philosophers—a huge. infinitely extended, self-subsistent Vacuum, supposed to be somehow an object of our knowledge, which so contained within it everything that could exist that spiritual or unextended beings were impossible. This illimitable phantom Berkeley rejects, because it is neither a *phenomenon* perceived or suggested in sense, nor what he calls a *notion.* Berkeley's Space is created—not infinitely divisible—a phenomenon revealed in course of the gradual development of sense perception through associations established between what we see and what we touch. He fails to note that, although Space cannot be perceived at all apart from presence of phenomena in sense, neither can sense phenomena be perceived as consisting of *partes extra partes,* and in that sense as external, without the presupposition of Space. Also he fails to appreciate the fathomless mystery of the boundless Space, unperceivable by us, yet forced upon us somehow in our perception of things extended.

Irrational Necessity and Provident Mind. 333

that fate was the general reason that runs through the whole nature of the universe; which nature he supposed to be an æthereal body, the seed of the generation of all things. Plato held fate to be the eternal reason or law of nature. Chrysippus supposed that fate was a spiritual power which disposed the world in order; that it was the reason and law of those things which are administered by Providence [1].

272. All the foregoing notions of fate, as represented by Plutarch, do plainly shew that those ancient philosophers did not mean by Fate, a blind, headlong, unintelligent principle, but *an orderly settled course of things, conducted by a wise and provident Mind.*—And as for the Egyptian doctrine, it is indeed asserted in the Pimander, that all things are produced by fate.—But Jamblichus, who drew his notions from Egypt, affirms that the whole of things is not bound up in fate; but that there is a principle of the soul higher than nature, whereby we may be raised to a union with the gods, and exempt ourselves from fate.—And in the Asclepian Dialogue it is expressly said that fate follows the decrees of God. And indeed, as all the motions in nature are evidently the product of reason (sect. 154), it should seem there is no room for necessity—in any other sense than that of a steady regular course [2].

273. *Blind fate* and *blind chance* are at bottom much the same thing, and one no more intelligible than the other. Such is the mutual relation, connexion, motion, and sympathy of the parts of this world, that they seem as it were animated

---

[1] The relation of Will to Reason is one of the difficult metaphysical problems.

[2] The works here referred to are (*a*) *Pœmander*, the most memorable of the Hermic works, probably Neoplatonic, and of the fourth century after Christ, though long ascribed to the Egyptian Hermes; (*b*) the *De Fato* of Jamblichus, the Neoplatonist (A.D. 278-333); and (*c*) the dialogue *De Natura Deorum* of Asclepius, a reputed disciple of Hermes.

The one 'necessity' that is *absolute*, i.e. in the very nature of things, according to the philosophy of *Siris*, is the necessity for Reason, as the power by which the material world is continually made actual to conscious spirits.

and held together by one soul: and such is their harmony, order, and regular course, as sheweth the soul to be governed and directed by a Mind.

It was an opinion of remote antiquity that the World was an *animal*. If we may trust the Hermaic writings, the Egyptians thought all things did partake of life. This opinion was also so general and current among the Greeks that Plutarch asserts all others held the world to be an animal, and governed by Providence, except Leucippus, Democritus, and Epicurus. And although an animal containing all bodies within itself could not be touched or sensibly affected from without, yet it is plain they attributed to it an inward sense and feeling, as well as appetites and aversions; and that from all the various tones, actions, and passions of the universe, they suppose one symphony, one animal act and life to result.

274. Jamblichus declares the world to be *one* animal, in which the parts, however distant each from other, are nevertheless related and connected by one common nature. And he teacheth, what is also a received notion of the Pythagoreans and Platonics, that there is no chasm in nature, but a Chain or Scale of beings rising by gentle uninterrupted gradations from the lowest to the highest, each nature being informed and perfected by the participation of a higher[1]. As air becomes igneous, so the purest fire becomes animal, and the animal soul becomes intellectual: which is to be understood not of the change of one nature into another, but of the connexion of different natures; each lower nature being, according to those philosophers, as it were a receptacle or subject for the next above it to reside and act in.

[1] The thought of a Chain (σειρά) in nature, connecting the phenomena of the universe with one another, and with immanent Mind, in a Cosmos or Order in which each phenomenon is rationally linked with every other—this governing thought in *Siris*, was common in the ancient world. This and the next section may be compared with Milton, *Par. Lost*, V. 469-490.

275. It is also the doctrine of Platonic philosophers, that *intellect* is the very life of living things, the first principle and exemplar of all, from whence by different degrees are derived the inferior classes of life: first the rational, then the sensitive, after that the vegetal; but so as in the rational animal there is still somewhat intellectual, again in the sensitive there is somewhat rational, and in the vegetal somewhat sensitive, and lastly, in mixed bodies, as metals and minerals, somewhat of vegetation. By which means the whole is thought to be more perfectly connected. Which doctrine implies that all the faculties, instincts, and motions of inferior beings, in their several respective subordinations, are derived from, and depend upon Mind and Intellect.

276. Both Stoics and Platonics held the world to be alive; though sometimes it be mentioned as a sentient animal, sometimes as a plant or vegetable. But in this, notwithstanding what hath been surmised by some learned men, there seems to be no Atheism [1]. For, so long as the world is supposed to be quickened by elementary fire or spirit, which is itself animated by soul, and directed by understanding, it follows that all parts thereof originally depend upon, and may be reduced unto the same indivisible stem or principle, to wit, a Supreme Mind — which is the concurrent doctrine of Pythagoreans, Platonics, and Stoics.

277. There is, according to those philosophers, a *life* infused throughout all things: the πῦρ νοερὸν, πῦρ τεχνικὸν, an intellectual and artificial fire—an inward principle, animal spirit, or natural life, producing and forming within as art doth without; regulating, moderating, and reconciling the various motions, qualities, and parts of this Mundane System. By virtue of this life the great masses are held together in

---

[1] Faith in the supremacy of mind and moral government is here supposed to be reconcilable with various forms of verbal expression; and in particular even with that which asserts the *immanence* of Supreme Mind, in the graduated evolution of vegetable into animal, of animal into rational life, and generally in the order of nature.

their orderly courses, as well as the minutest particles governed in their natural motions, according to the several laws of attraction, gravity, electricity, magnetism, and the rest. It is this gives instincts [1], teaches the spider her web, and the bee her honey. This it is that directs the roots of plants to draw forth juices from the earth, and the leaves and corticle vessels to separate and attract such particles of air, and elementary fire, as suit their respective natures.

278. Nature seems to be not otherwise distinguished from the *anima mundi* than as life is from soul, and, upon the principles of the oldest philosophers, may not improperly or incongruously be styled the life of the world. Some Platonics, indeed, regard life as the act of nature, in like manner as intellection is of the mind or intellect. As the First Intellect acts by understanding, so nature according to them acts or generates by living. But life is the act of the soul, and seems to be very nature itself, which is not the principle, but the result of another and higher principle, being a life resulting from soul, as cogitation from intellect [2].

279. If nature be the life of the world, animated by one soul, compacted into one frame, and directed or governed in all parts by one mind: this system cannot be accused of Atheism; though perhaps it may of mistake or impropriety. And yet, as one presiding mind gives unity to the infinite aggregate of things, by a mutual communion of actions and passions, and an adjustment of parts, causing all to concur in one view to one and the same end—the ultimate and supreme

---

[1] Compare sect. 257, and note on p. 314.
[2] 'Soul,' *i.e.* animating cause, as distinguished from its effects or manifestations. The effects constitute the visible and tangible world—that world being, by the supposition, animated organism. Soul ($\psi \upsilon \chi \dot{\eta}$) was distinguished from body ($\sigma \acute{a} \rho \xi$), on the one hand, and from reason ($\nu o \hat{u} s$), on the other—mediating between them. The ancient notion of the animation of the universe may be found, in one form or another, among physical philosophers of the sixteenth and seventeenth centuries. It is often difficult to distinguish from Hylozoism, or the hypothesis that the universe is eternal matter of which conscious life is an attribute, under certain conditions of physical organization,

good of the whole, it should seem reasonable to say, with Ocellus Lucanus the Pythagorean, that as life holds together the bodies of animals, the cause whereof is the soul; and as a city is held together by concord, the cause whereof is law, even so the world is held together by harmony, the cause whereof is God. And in this sense the world or universe may be considered either as one *animal* or one *city*[1].

284. * * Thus much the schools of Plato and Pythagoras seem agreed in, to wit, that the Soul of the World, whether having a distinct mind of its own, or directed by a superior mind, doth embrace all its parts, connect them by an invisible and indissoluble Chain, and preserve them ever well adjusted and in good order.

285. Naturalists, whose proper province it is to consider phænomena, experiments, mechanical organs and motions, principally regard the visible frame of things or corporeal world—supposing soul to be contained in body. And this hypothesis may be tolerated in physics, as it is not necessary in the arts of dialling or navigation to mention the true system or earth's motion. But those who, not content with sensible appearances, would penetrate into the real and true causes (the object of Theology, Metaphysics, or the *Philosophia Prima*[2]), will rectify this error, and speak of the world as contained by the soul, and not the soul by the world.

286. Aristotle hath observed there were indeed some who thought so grossly as to suppose the universe to be one only corporeal and extended nature: but in the first book of his Metaphysics he justly remarks they were guilty of a great mistake; forasmuch as they took into their account the elements of corporeal beings alone, whereas there are incorporeal

---

[1] The *De Legibus* of Ocellus Lucanus is here referred to—now, along with other fragments, rejected as spurious.
[2] With Aristotle these are one. See *Metaph*. lib. VI. c. 1, and lib. XI. c. 7. This section again contrasts 'sensible appearances,' the phenomenal data of *sense* and *suggestion*, with true causes, the objects of *reason* or *intellect*. (Cf. *Vindication*, sect. 9–13, and 42.)

beings also in the universe; and while they attempted to assign the causes of generation and corruption, and account for the nature of all things, they did at the same time destroy the very cause of motion.

287. It is a doctrine among other speculations contained in the Hermaic writings—that all things are One. And it is not improbable that Orpheus, Parmenides, and others among the Greeks, might have derived their notion of Τὸ ˚Ἑν, THE ONE, from Egypt. Though that subtle metaphysician Parmenides, in his doctrine of ἐν ἴστως, seems to have added something of his own. If we suppose that *one and the same Mind* is the Universal Principle of order and harmony throughout the world, containing and connecting all its parts, and giving unity to the system, there seems to be nothing atheistical or impious in this supposition.

288. Number is no object of sense: it is an act of the mind. The same thing in a different conception is one or many. Comprehending God and the creatures in one general notion, we may say that all things together make one Universe, or τὸ πᾶν. But if we should say that all things make one God, this would, indeed, be an erroneous notion of God, but would not amount to Atheism, so long as mind or intellect was admitted to be the τὸ ἡγεμονικὸν, the governing part[1]. It is, nevertheless, more respectful, and consequently the truer notion of God, to suppose Him neither made up of parts, nor to be himself a part of any whole whatsoever.

289. All those who conceived the universe to be an animal must, in consequence of that notion, suppose all things to be one. But to conceive God to be the sentient soul of an animal is altogether unworthy and absurd. There is no sense

---

[1] This would be a Theism difficult to reconcile with moral agency in men, and therefore with moral government, unless we exclude moral agents from the 'things.' But his disposition, especially in *Siris*, is to acknowledge that, even in ignorance of *what* God is, men may nevertheless struggle to become like God, and be victorious in the struggle.

nor sensory, nor any thing like a sense or sensory, in God. Sense implies an impression from some other being, and denotes a dependence in the soul which hath it. Sense is a passion: and passions imply imperfection. God knoweth all things, as pure mind or intellect; but nothing by sense, nor in nor through a sensory. Therefore to suppose a sensory of any kind—whether space or any other—in God, would be very wrong, and lead us into false conceptions of His nature. The presuming there was such a thing as real, absolute, uncreated space seems to have occasioned that modern mistake. But this presumption was without grounds [1].

290. *Body* is opposite to *spirit* or *mind*. We have a notion of spirit from thought and action. We have a notion of body from resistance. So far forth as there is real power, there is spirit. So far forth as there is resistance, there is inability or want of power: that is, there is a negation of spirit. We are embodied, that is, we are clogged by weight, and hindered by resistance. But in respect of a perfect spirit, there is nothing hard or impenetrable: there is no resistance to the Deity: nor hath he any body: nor is the supreme Being united to the world as the soul of an animal is to its body; which necessarily implieth defect, both as an instrument, and as a constant weight and impediment [2].

291. * * Nor is this doctrine less philosophical than pious. We see all nature alive or in motion. We see water turned

---

[1] Berkeley here rejects the supposition that sensible things exist *as phenomena of sense* in the Divine Mind. He says that they exist in God *intellectually*, whatever that implies. And the sublime mystery of infinite uncreated space again repels him.—Note what is said in this section of dependence on power *external to ourselves* being implied in the passivity of sense. Thus sense, by contrast with our own active consciousness, awakens in us the conviction of our individuality, rounded off by power other than our own.

[2] He assigns *resistance* (not extension) as the essential mark of external body. So too in his early philosophical works. Are tactual phenomena more the tests of sensible reality than visible phenomena; and are they in any respect the fundamental experience, into which that of the other senses has to be translated?

into air, and air rarefied and made elastic by the attraction of another medium, more pure indeed, more subtle, and more volatile, than air. But still, as this is a moveable, extended, and consequently a corporeal being, it cannot be itself the principle of motion, but leads us naturally and necessarily to an incorporeal Spirit or Agent. We are conscious that a Spirit can begin, alter, or determine motion; but nothing of this appears in body. Nay, the contrary is evident, both to experiment and reflexion [1].

292. Natural phænomena are only natural appearances. They are, therefore, such as we see and perceive them. Their real and objective [2] natures are, therefore, the same; passive without anything active, fluent and changing without anything permanent in them. However, as these make the first impressions, and the mind takes her first flight and spring, as it were, by resting her foot on these objects, they are not only first considered by all men, but most considered by most men. They and the phantoms that result from those appearances, the children of imagination grafted upon sense—such for example as pure space—are thought by many the very first in existence and stability, and to embrace and comprehend all other beings.

293. Now, although such phantoms as corporeal forces, absolute motions, and real spaces do pass in physics for causes and principles, yet are they in truth but hypotheses; nor can they be the objects of real science. They pass nevertheless in physics, conversant about things of sense, and confined to experiments and mechanics. But when we enter the province of the *philosophia prima*, we discover another order of beings —*mind and its acts—permanent being*—not dependent on

[1] Here he finds power in spirit through his own spiritual 'consciousness' but without the reference to conscience implied in sect. 257. He grounds his allegation of the impotence of body on our not having any corresponding perception of power in unconscious things.

[2] 'Objective'—here equivalent to phenomenal. Contrast its recent applications, either to something extended and independent of transitory phenomena, or to relations that are universal and necessary.

corporeal things, nor resulting, nor connected, nor contained; but containing, connecting, enlivening the whole frame; and imparting those motions, forms, qualities, and that order and symmetry, to all those transient phænomena, which we term the Course of Nature.

294. It is with our faculties as with our affections: what first seizes holds fast. It is a vulgar theme, that man is a compound of contrarieties, which breed a restless struggle in his nature, between flesh and spirit, the beast and the angel, earth and heaven, ever weighed down and ever bearing up. During which conflict the character fluctuates: when either side prevails, it is then fixed for vice or virtue. And life from different principles takes a different issue.—It is the same in regard to our faculties. Sense at first besets and overbears the mind. The sensible appearances are all in all: our reasonings are employed about them: our desires terminate in them: we look no farther for realities or causes; till intellect begins to dawn, and cast a ray on this shadowy scene. We then perceive the true principle of unity, identity, and existence. Those things that before seemed to constitute the whole of Being, upon taking an intellectual view of things, prove to be but fleeting phantoms.

295. From the outward form of gross masses which occupy the vulgar, a curious inquirer proceeds to examine the inward structure and minute parts, and, from observing the motions in nature, to discover the laws of those motions. By the way, he frames his hypothesis and suits his language to this natural philosophy. And these fit the occasion and answer the end of a maker of experiments or mechanic, who means only to apply the powers of nature, and reduce the phænomena to rules. But if, proceeding still in his analysis and inquiry, he ascends from the sensible into the intellectual world, and beholds things in a new light and a new order, he will then change his system, and perceive that what he took for substances and causes are but fleeting shadows: that

the mind contains all, and acts all, and is to all created beings the source of unity and identity, harmony and order, existence and stability [1].

296. It is neither acid, nor salt, nor sulphur, nor air, nor æther, nor visible corporeal fire—much less the phantom *fate* or *necessity*—that is the real agent, but, by a certain analysis, a regular connexion and climax, we ascend through all those mediums to a glimpse of the First Mover, invisible, incorporeal, unextended, intellectual source of life and being. There is, it must be owned, a mixture of obscurity and prejudice in human speech and reasonings. This is unavoidable, since the veils of prejudice and error are slowly and singly taken off one by one. But, if there are many links in the Chain which connects the two extremes of what is *grossly sensible* and *purely intelligible*, and it seem a tedious work, by the slow helps of memory, imagination, and reason [2]—oppressed and overwhelmed, as we are, by the senses, through erroneous principles, and long ambages of words and notions—to struggle upwards into the light of truth, yet, as this gradually dawns, farther discoveries still correct the style and clear up the notions.

297. The Mind, her acts and faculties, furnish a new and distinct class of objects, from the contemplation whereof arise certain other notions, principles, and verities, so remote from, and even so repugnant to, the first prejudices which surprise

---

[1] In this and the foregoing section thought or reason, with its constitutive power in the formation of knowledge, is recognised, in contrast with sense and its suggestions. We do not find this in Berkeley's earlier writings. In his *Commonplace Book* especially, 'mind' is little more than *sense*, and the common reason is not distinctly acknowledged as an element in the constitution of knowledge. 'Pure intellect I understand not' (*Commonplace Book*, p. 460). 'We must with the mob place certainty in the senses' (p. 454). 'If it were not for the senses mind could have no knowledge, no thought, at all' (p. 434). 'Mind is a congeries of perceptions. Take away perceptions and you take away the mind. Put the perceptions and you put the mind' (p. 438). 'Sensual pleasure is the *summum bonum*. This the great principle of morality' (p. 457).

[2] 'reason' is here used for reasoning, as in Locke and others.

Is God distinct from or immanent in Nature? 343

the sense of mankind that they may well be excluded from vulgar speech and books, as abstract from sensible matters[1], and more fit for the speculation of truth, the labour and aim of a few, than for the practice of the world, or the subjects of experimental or mechanical inquiry. * * *

298. There are traces of profound thought as well as primeval tradition in the Platonic, Pythagorean, Egyptian, and Chaldaic philosophy. Men in those early days were not overlaid with languages and literature. Their minds seem to have been more exercised, and less burdened, than in later ages; and, as so much nearer the beginning of the world, to have had the advantage of patriarchal lights handed down through a few hands. * * *

300. Plato and Aristotle considered God as abstracted or distinct from the natural world[2]. But the Egyptians considered God and Nature as making one whole, or all things together as making one Universe. In doing which they did not exclude the intelligent mind, but considered it as containing all things. Therefore, whatever was wrong in their way of thinking, it doth not, nevertheless, imply or lead to Atheism[3].

301. The human mind is so much clogged and borne downward by the strong and early impressions of sense, that it is wonderful how the ancients should have made even such a

[1] The 'abstract' is here contrasted with the 'sensible'—in a tone foreign to that of the *Principles*.

[2] This is confirmed by passages in Plato. As regards Aristotle the case is not so clear. He seems to distinguish Deity (*Actus Purus*) from nature, but not to regard God as a self-conscious person: nature with him is eternal—an endless succession of phenomenal changes, developed according to their several forms or essences. Berkeley reverts to Divine personality and unity in sect. 345-346.

[3] As in the *Principles* Berkeley expressly raised the question of what should be meant when we use the word *Matter*, so here and elsewhere in *Siris* (as previously in the *Vindication*) he raises the deeper question of what should be meant when we use the word *God*, and what Atheism essentially consists in. He says less here than in his writings on Visual Language about verifying faith in God by sense and its suggestions, and more about trying to find him in the constitution of reason, if not in the heart and conscience.

sense was science, is absurd[1]. And indeed, nothing is more evident than that the *apparent* sizes and shapes, for instance, of things are in a constant flux, ever differing as they are viewed at different distances, or with glances more or less accurate. As for those *absolute* magnitudes and figures, which certain Cartesians and other moderns suppose to be in things; that must seem a vain supposition, to whoever considers it is supported by no argument of reason, and no experiment of sense[2].

305. As understanding perceiveth not, that is, doth not hear, or see, or feel, so sense knoweth not: and although the mind may use both sense and fancy, as means whereby to arrive at knowledge, yet sense or soul, *so far forth as sensitive*, knoweth nothing. For, as it is rightly observed in the *Theœtetus* of Plato, *science* consists not in the passive perceptions, but in the reasoning upon them—τῷ περὶ ἐκείνων συλλογισμῷ[3].

306. In the ancient philosophy of Plato and Pythagoras, we find distinguished three sorts of objects:—In the first place, a *form* or *species* that is neither generated nor destroyed, unchangeable, invisible, and altogether imperceptible to sense, being only understood by the Intellect. A second

---

[1] The reference is to the *homo mensura* of Protagoras argued against in the *Theætetus* by Plato—with whom God, not man, least of all each individual man, is the criterion of truth.

[2] If there can be no 'knowledge' of what is 'flowing and unstable,' how do transitory sensations become knowledge in perception? Also, on the hypothesis of Empiricism, how can 'sequences' of phenomena become known as invariable? These questions hardly rise in Berkeley.

Here, as in his earlier writings, what he teaches is in harmony with *arbitrariness* in the creation of natural law. Throughout he resists the hypothesis that the law in nature is eternally necessary and independent of Divine Will, or that there is any thing thus necessary even in the space relations of things. To those who argue that in knowing nature at all we *must* conceive that the laws of its phenomena are uniform, and that the opposite conception is meaningless because irreconcilable with our having any physical experience—to such he might answer that, in this meaning of 'knowledge,' 'we *have* no knowledge or experience' of things sensible.

[3] Does this imply that phenomena of sense, in themselves, are unintelligible, and that we cannot, strictly speaking, be even conscious of them—unless by 'consciousness' is meant mere sensuous feeling?

sort there is, ever fluent and changing (sect. 292, 293), generating and perishing, appearing and vanishing: this is comprehended by Sense and Opinion. The third kind is *matter*, which, as Plato teacheth, being neither an object of understanding nor of sense, is hardly to be made out by a certain spurious way of reasoning—λογισμῷ τινι νόθῳ μόγις πιστόν[1]. The same doctrine is contained in the Pythagoric treatise *De Anima Mundi*, which, distinguishing Ideas, sensible things, and Matter, maketh the first to be apprehended by Intellect, the second by Sense, and the last, to wit, Matter, λογισμῷ νόθῳ. Whereof Themistius the Peripatetic assigns the reason. For, saith he, that act is to be esteemed spurious, whose object hath nothing positive, being only a mere privation, as silence or darkness. And such he accounteth Matter[2].

307. Aristotle maketh a threefold distinction of objects, according to the three speculative sciences. Physics he supposeth to be conversant about such things as have a principle of motion in themselves; Mathematics about things permanent but not abstracted; and Theology about Being abstracted and immoveable. Which distinction may be seen in the ninth book of his *Metaphysics*, where by abstracted, χωριστὸν, he understands separable from corporeal beings and sensible qualities.

308. That philosopher held that the mind of man was a *tabula rasa*, and that there were no innate ideas. Plato, on the contrary, held original ideas in the mind; that is, notions which never were or can be in the sense, such as being,

[1] As in the *Timæus*, where he distinguishes indeterminate *materia prima* from self-existent external Forms or Ideas, and also from the Cosmos of sensible things.

[2] The difference between positive and negative thinking—thinking that is concerned with what is realisable in imagination, and thinking that is not so realisable—with applications of the latter to solve problems of knowledge, have engaged some modern psychologists, especially since Kant. The phenomenon of 'negative thought' plays an important part in Sir W. Hamilton's philosophy, along with the cognate question of the mutual relations of belief and knowledge.

beauty, goodness, likeness, parity. Some, perhaps, may think the truth to be this:—that there are properly no *ideas*, or passive objects, in the mind but what were derived from sense : but that there are also besides these her own acts or operations; such as *notions*[1].

309. It is a maxim of the Platonic philosophy, that the soul of man was originally furnished with native inbred notions, and stands in need of sensible occasions, not absolutely for producing them, but only for awakening, rousing, or exciting into act what was already pre-existent, dormant, and latent in the soul ; as things are said to be laid up in the memory, though not actually perceived until they happen to be called forth and brought into view by other objects. This notion seemeth somewhat different from that of innate ideas, as understood by those moderns who have attempted to explode them[2]. To *understand* and to *be* are, according to Parmenides, the same thing. And Plato in his seventh Letter makes no difference between νοῦς and ἐπιστήμη, mind and knowledge. Whence it follows that mind, knowledge, and notions, either in habit or in act, always go together.

310. And albeit Aristotle considered the soul in its original state as a blank paper, yet he held it to be the proper place of *forms*—τὴν ψυχὴν εἶναι τόπον εἰδῶν—which doctrine, first maintained by others, he admits, under this restriction, that it is not to be understood of the whole soul, but only of the

---

[1] In this important sentence we approach the contrast yet correlation of Sen-e and Reason. Berkeley's 'ideas (phenomena) or passive objects' represent the former; his 'notions' are connected with the latter. What he says here is in curious contrast to what he says in his *Commonplace Book* (p. 457), where he expressly accepts the sensationalist answer— 'Nihil est in intellectu quod non prius fuit in sensu,' adding that if the schoolmen had stuck to this, 'it had never taught them the doctrine of abstract ideas.' Here, in *Siris*, he virtually accepts the famous addition of Leibnitz—'Nihil est in intellectu quod non prius fuit in sensu *nisi intellectus ipse*;' in which the activity of rational intelligence is recognised as a necessary element constitutive of knowledge. The *tabula rasa* of Aristotle is not inconsistent with the *potential* existence of pure reason. Cf. sect. 310.

[2] He probably refers to Locke's *Essay*, b. I.

Matter as conceived by Plato and Aristotle. 349

νοητικὴ; as is to be seen in his third book *De Anima*[1]. Whence, according to Themestius in his commentary on that treatise, it may be inferred that all beings are in the soul. For, saith he, the forms are the beings. By the form every thing is what it is. And he adds, it is the soul that imparteth forms to matter; τὴν ὕλην μορφῶσα ποικίλαις μορφαῖς. Therefore they are first in the soul. He farther adds that the mind is all things, taking the forms of all things it becomes all things by intellect and sense. Alexander Aphrodisæus saith as much, affirming the mind to be all things, κατά τε τὸ νοεῖν καὶ τὸ αἰσθάνεσθαι. And this in fact is Aristotle's own doctrine, in his third book *De Anima*, where he also asserts, with Plato, that actual knowledge and the thing known are all one. Τὸ δ' αὐτό ἐστιν ἡ κατ' ἐνέργειαν ἐπιστήμη τῷ πράγματι. Whence it follows, that the things are where the knowledge is, that is to say, in the mind. Or, as it is otherwise expressed, that the soul is all things. More might be said to explain Aristotle's notion, but it would lead too far[2].

311[3]. As to an *absolute actual* existence of Sensible or Corporeal Things (sect. 264, 292, 294), it doth not seem to

---

[1] 'Let us suppose the mind to be, as we say, white paper, void of all character, without any ideas—how comes it to be furnished?' (Locke's *Essay*, b. II. ch. i. § 2.) Locke in answering this question does not refer to the Aristotelian distinction of potential and actual ideas and knowledge. In the passage referred to, Aristotle identifies the αἰσθητικὸν with the αἰσθητὸν, and the ἐπιστημονικὸν with the ἐπιστητὸν, through their forms (εἴδη)—the potential intellect being with him, as with Plato, the place of forms—τύπος εἰδῶν.

[2] The passage in Aristotle that is referred to is one of several, in the *De Anima* and elsewhere, in which he seems to identify knowledge and existence, or at least to hold that until a thing is an object of knowledge it can have only a potential, not an actual, existence. A virtually creative activity of understanding is thus implied.

[3] In sect. 311–319, Berkeley, in contemplating the transitoriness of phenomena, and the implied 'notion' of 'mind' on which they all depend, returns (but in a more meditative and less argumentative spirit) to the favourite speculation of his youth—the meaning of the term *reality*, when asserted of *sensible things*, as well as of *visible* and *tangible space*. He summons Plato and Aristotle as witnesses, that their *actual* (not *potential*) existence is dependent upon a percipient; that unperceived Matter and Space are mere negations. ('Sensible things'

have been admitted either by Plato or Aristotle. In the *Theætetus* we are told that if any one saith a thing is, or is made, he must withal say, for what, or of what, or in respect of what, it is, or is made; for, that any thing should exist *in itself* or *absolutely* is absurd. Agreeably to which doctrine it is also farther affirmed by Plato, that it is impossible a thing should be sweet and sweet to nobody. It must, nevertheless, be owned with regard to Aristotle, that even in his *Metaphysics* there are some expressions which seem to favour the absolute existence of corporeal things. For instance, in the eleventh book, speaking of corporeal sensible things, what wonder, saith he, if they never appear to us the same, no more than to sick men, since we are always changing and never remain the same ourselves? And again, he saith, sensible things, *although they receive no change in themselves*, do nevertheless in sick persons produce different sensations and not the same. These passages would seem to imply a distinct and absolute existence of the objects of sense[1].

312. But it must be observed, that Aristotle distinguisheth a twofold existence—*potential* and *actual*. It will not therefore follow that, according to Aristotle, because a thing is, it must *actually* exist. This is evident from the eighth book of his *Metaphysics*, where he animadverts on the Megaric philosophers, as not admitting a possible existence distinct from the actual: from whence, saith he, it must follow, that there is nothing cold, or hot, or sweet, or any sensible thing at all, where there is no perception. He adds that, in consequence of that Megaric doctrine, we can have no sense but

---

are of course not to be confounded with the ἄπειρον of Plato, or the ὕλη of Aristotle.)
[1] See b. X. (XI.) ch. 6, where Aristotle argues against Protagoras, and in behalf of *permanence* in sensible things. He does not thereby contradict the doctrine of the *De Anima*, as to the creative activity of reason, and the share contributed by sense to the constitution of things. Only he implies that things are, potentially at least, more than the individual thoughts—more, *a fortiori*, than the individual sensations of a sentient thinker.

Existence as Potential and as Actual. 351

while we actually exert it: we are blind when we do not see, and therefore both blind and deaf several times a day[1].

313. The ἐντελέχειαι πρῶται of the Peripatetics, that is, the sciences, arts, and habits, were by them distinguished from the acts or ἐντελέχειαι δεύτεραι, and supposed to exist in the mind, though not exerted or put into act[2]. This seems to illustrate the manner in which Socrates, Plato, and their followers, conceive *innate notions* to be in the soul of man (sect. 309). It was the Platonic doctrine, that human souls or minds descended from above, and were sowed in generation; that they were stunned, stupefied, and intoxicated by this descent and immersion into animal nature; and that the soul, in this ὀνείρωξις or slumber, forgets her original notions, which are smothered and oppressed by many false tenets and prejudices of sense. Insomuch that Proclus compares the soul in her descent, invested with growing prejudices, to Glaucus diving to the bottom of the sea, and there contracting divers coats of seaweed, coral, and shells, which stick close to him, and conceal his true shape[3].

314. Hence, according to this philosophy, the mind of man

[1] This distinction of potential and actual, already referred to, is amongst the most fruitful in Aristotle, and one might reconsider Berkeley's theory of what is meant by the reality of the material world in the light of it. In this passage, potential (ἐν δυνάμει) is contrasted with actual existence (ἐν ἐνεργείᾳ, or ἐν ἐντελεχείᾳ); and the Megaric theory, limiting 'existence' to the latter, is identified with the sceptical subjectivity of Protagoras. Berkeley, on the other hand, may be supposed to imply that, as far as human percipients and agents are concerned, the things of sense always exist in ἐν δυνάμει, inasmuch as, when unperceived *by them*, they exist for them potentially in the Divine Reason and Will.—But what is to be understood by this sort of 'potential' existence? What is God? Is an 'object' in divine knowledge analogous to an 'object' in human knowledge? Is *something impercipient* a necessary datum, or is it voluntarily created by God? Berkeley hardly recognises these difficulties, but he rejects the supposition that the material world has a *sentient* existence in God, *i.e.* that it exists in the form of divine sensations.

[2] The *acquisition* of a habit implies previous potentiality, as well as the *exertion* of the habit. Hence the first and second energies of the Peripatetics.

[3] *Commentaria* of the Neoplatonist Proclus (A.D. 412-485).

is so restless to shake off that slumber, to disengage and emancipate herself from those prejudices and false opinions that so straitly beset and cling to her, to rub off those covers that disguise her original form, and to regain her primeval state and first notions: hence that perpetual struggle to recover the lost region of light, that ardent thirst and endeavour after truth and intellectual ideas, which she would neither seek to attain, nor rejoice in, nor know when attained, except she had some prenotion or anticipation of them, and they had lain innate and dormant, like habits and sciences in the mind, or things laid up, which are called out and roused by recollection or reminiscence. So that learning seemeth in effect reminiscence [1].

315. The Peripatetics themselves distinguish between reminiscence and mere memory. Themistius observes that the best memories commonly go with the worst parts; but that reminiscence is most perfect in the most ingenious minds. And, notwithstanding the *tabula rasa* of Aristotle, yet some of his followers have undertaken to make him speak Plato's sense. Thus Plutarch the Peripatetic teacheth, as agreeable to his master's doctrine, that learning is reminiscence, and that the νοῦς καθ' ἕξιν is in children. Simplicius also, in his commentary on the third book of Aristotle, περὶ ψυχῆς, speaketh of a certain interior reason in the soul, acting of itself, and originally full of its own proper notions, πλήρης ἀφ' ἑαυτοῦ τῶν οἰκείων γνωσέων [2].

[1] There is blind and passive suggestion, by association, of what has coexisted in past personal experience. It is to be distinguished from active 'reminiscence' of Ideas, *i.e.* development of necessary and universal thought.

[2] Themistius, the first-named of these Peripatetics, lived in the fourth century. To Simplicius, a Neoplatonist of the sixth century, we owe valuable expositions of Aristotle, especially the *De Anima*. He attempted to reconcile Aristotle with Plato. 'Plutarch the Peripatetic' seems to be Plutarch son of Nestorius, the Neoplatonist, who is said to have written a commentary, now lost, on the *De Anima*. With Aristotle, reminiscence (ἀνάμνησις) implies perhaps rational volition, but not all that Plato meant by pre-existing and latent ideals, evolved with a growing clearness through much reflective exercise in the individual.

316. And as the Platonic philosophy supposed intellectual notions to be originally inexistent, or innate in the soul, so likewise it supposed sensible qualities to exist (though not originally) in the soul and there only[1]. Socrates saith to Theætetus, You must not think the white colour that you see is in any thing without your eyes, or in your eyes, or in any place at all. And in the *Timæus*, Plato teacheth that the figure and motion of the particles of fire dividing the parts of our bodies produce that painful sensation we call heat. And Plotinus, in the sixth book of his second Ennead, observes that heat and other qualities are not qualities in the things themselves, but acts: that heat is not a quality, but act in the fire: that fire is not really what we perceive in the qualities, light, heat, and colour. From all which it is plain that whatever real things they suppose to exist independent of the soul, those were neither sensible things nor clothed with sensible qualities.

317. Neither Plato nor Aristotle by Matter, ὕλη, understood *corporeal substance*, whatever the moderns may understand by that word. To them certainly it signified no positive actual being. Aristotle describes it as made up of negatives, having neither quantity, nor quality, nor essence[2]. And not only the Platonists and Pythagoreans, but also the Peripatetics themselves declare it to be known, neither by sense, nor by any direct and just reasoning, but only by some spurious or adulterine method, as hath been observed before. Simon Portius, a famous Peripatetic of the sixteenth century,

---

[1] 'There' does not imply locality—*spacial* relation. The relations which are essential to the constitution of knowledge (whatever these may be found to be) are unconsciously involved in sense-perception.

[2] The ἄπειρον, or ἕτερον of Plato—according to Hegel, a *necessitated* 'otherness.' 'Matter,' as actually given in sense-phenomena, must not be confounded with the formless potential Matter of Aristotle. This is that dark, undefinable, presupposed *condition* of the actuality of sensible things, for which Berkeley substitutes God and constant creation, or divinely established order of sense-phenomena, which, as phenomena, are relative to a conscious mind, and, because orderly, are significant and interpretable.

denies it to be any substance at all, for, saith he, *Nequit per se subsistere, quia sequeretur, id quod non est in actu esse in actu*[1]. If Jamblichus may be credited, the Egyptians supposed Matter so far from including aught of substance or essence, that, according to them, God produced it by a separation from all substance, essence, or being, ἀπὸ οὐσιότητος ἀποχισθείσης ὑλότητος. That Matter is actually nothing, but potentially all things, is the doctrine of Aristotle, Theophrastus, and all the ancient Peripatetics.

318. According to those philosophers, Matter is only a *pura potentia*, a mere possibility. But Anaximander, successor to Thales, is represented as having thought the supreme Deity to be infinite Matter. Nevertheless, though Plutarch calleth it Matter, yet it was simply τὸ ἄπειρον, which means no more than infinite or indefinite.—And although the moderns teach that Space is real and infinitely extended, yet, if we consider that it is no *intellectual notion*, nor yet *perceived by any of our senses*, we shall perhaps be inclined to think with Plato in his *Timæus*, that this also is the result of λογισμὸς νόθος, or spurious reasoning, and a kind of waking dream. Plato observes that we dream, as it were, when we think of place, and believe it necessary that whatever exists should exist in some place. Which place or space, he also observes, is μετ' ἀναισθησίας ἁπτὸν, that is, to be felt as darkness is seen, or silence heard, being a mere privation[2].

---

[1] Simon Porta or Portius—a Neapolitan Professor of Philosophy at Pisa, and the most famous of the pupils of Pomponatius.

[2] Space, in abstraction from all experience in sense, is neither a 'notion' nor an 'idea' (according to Berkeley's use of these terms). We find we cannot when we try imagine space emptied of sense. On the other hand, sense cannot be conceived as *outward* apart from space, which is necessarily blended with the phenomena that we are conscious of when we perceive, giving them outwardness, making them capable of being conceived as outward, and connecting them with that boundlessness or spacial infinity which may well be considered one of the ultimate mysteries.

Berkeley finds in *phenomena of sense* and *notions* the two elements of knowledge. In his early philosophy he concerned himself chiefly with the former; in *Siris* rather with the latter. Abstract space,

319. If any one should think to infer the reality or actual being of Matter from the modern tenet—that gravity is always proportionable to the quantity of matter, let him but narrowly scan the modern demonstration of that tenet, and he will find it to be a vain circle, concluding in truth no more than this—that gravity is proportionable to weight, that is, to itself. Since Matter is conceived only as defect and mere possibility; and since God is absolute perfection and act; it follows there is the greatest distance and opposition imaginable between God and Matter. Insomuch that a material God would be altogether inconsistent.

320. The *force* that produces, the *intellect* that orders, the *goodness* that perfects all things is the Supreme Being. Evil, defect, negation, is not the object of God's creative power. From motion the Peripatetics trace out a first immoveable Mover. The Platonics make God author of all good, author of no evil, and unchangeable. According to Anaxagoras, there was a confused mass of all things in one chaos; but mind supervening, ἐπελθὼν, distinguished and divided them. Anaxagoras, it seems, ascribed the motive faculty to mind, νοῦς; which mind some subsequent philosophers have accurately discriminated from soul and life, ascribing to it the sole faculty of intellection.

321. But still God was supposed the first Agent, the source and original of all things; which he produceth, not occasionally or instrumentally, but with actual and real efficacy [1].

being neither a notion nor a phenomenon, must, he concluded, be an illusion. He did not contemplate space as a condition indispensable to the constitution of our experience of an external world.

Sect. 320-329, in accumulating authorities favourable to the dependence of all phenomena ultimately on Mind, approach the question of *what* God is. That He *is*, and that our true life is the struggle to realise Him in ourselves, is assumed.

[1] 'Not occasionally or instrumentally, *i.e.* not under the relation of phenomenal sign and phenomenal event signified, as in the scientific conception of causality, but with the productive power of an uncaused cause.

326. Now, whether the νοῦς be abstracted from the sensible world, and considered by itself, as distinct from, and presiding over, the created system; or whether the whole Universe, including mind together with the mundane body, is conceived to be God, and the creatures to be partial manifestations of the Divine essence—there is no Atheism in either case, whatever misconceptions there may be; so long as Mind or Intellect is understood to preside over, govern, and conduct, the whole frame of things[1]. And this was the general prevailing opinion among the philosophers.

327. Nor if any one, with Aristotle in his *Metaphysics*, should deny that God knows anything without himself—seeing that God comprehends all things—could this be justly pronounced an atheistical opinion. Nor even was the following notion of the same author to be accounted Atheism, to wit that there are some things beneath the knowledge of God, as too mean, base, and vile; however wrong this notion may be, and unworthy of the Divine perfection.

328. Might we not conceive that God may be said to be ALL in divers senses;—as he is the cause and origin of all beings; as the νοῦς is the νοητά, a doctrine both of Platonics and Peripatetics; as the νοῦς is the place of all forms; and as it is the same which comprehends and orders and sustains the whole mundane system? Aristotle declares that the Divine force or influence permeates the entire universe, and that what the pilot is in a ship, the driver in a chariot, the precentor in a choir, the law in a city, the general in an army, the same God is in the world. This he amply sets forth in his book *De Mundo;* a treatise which, having been anciently ascribed to him, ought not to be set aside from the difference of style; which (as Patricius rightly observes),

---

[1] He seems satisfied to accept either the conception of God as *external* to the dependent universe of things and persons, or that other conception in which Deity is regarded as *immanent* in the world of nature and spirit—provided only that we practically acknowledge physical and moral government in the universe, and our own personal relation to this.

being in a letter to a king, might well be supposed to differ from the other dry and crabbed parts of his writings[1].

329. And although there are some expressions to be met with in the philosophers, even of the Platonic and Aristotelic sects, which speak of God as mixing with, or pervading all nature and all the elements; yet this must be explained by *force* and not by *extension*, which was never attributed to the mind, either by Aristotle or Plato. This they always affirmed to be incorporeal: and, as Plotinus remarks, incorporeal things are distant each from other not by place, but (to use his expression) by *alterity*.

330. [2]These disquisitions will probably seem dry and useless to such readers as are accustomed to consider only sensible objects. The employment of the mind on things purely intellectual is to most men irksome; whereas the sensitive powers, by constant use, acquire strength. Hence, the objects of sense more forcibly affect us, and are too often counted the chief good. For these things men fight, cheat, and scramble. Therefore, in order to tame mankind, and introduce a sense of virtue, the best human means is to exercise their understanding, to give them a glimpse of another world, superior to the sensible, and, while they take pains to cherish and maintain the animal life, to teach them not to neglect the intellectual[3].

331. Prevailing studies are of no small consequence to a state, the religion, manners, and civil government of a country ever taking some bias from its philosophy, which

---

[1] The *De Mundo* is not now accepted as genuine.

[2] The eloquent protest on behalf of Plato and Spiritual Philosophy, as against Materialism, in the sections which follow, is the prelude to abstruse speculation as to the Personality and Trinity of God, which is omitted.

[3] This is Berkeley's way of recognising the divine reality presupposed in the material or phenomenal world. Is the world 'above sense' supposed by him to be possibly phenomenal though unrealisable, as colour to the born-blind, in *our* imagination?

affects not only the minds of its professors and students, but also the opinions of all the better sort, and the practice of the whole people, remotely and consequentially indeed, though not inconsiderably. Have not the polemic and scholastic philosophy been observed to produce controversies in law and religion? And have not Fatalism and Sadducism gained ground, during the general passion for the corpuscularian and mechanical philosophy, which hath prevailed for about a century? This, indeed, might usefully enough have employed some share of the leisure and curiosity of inquisitive persons. But when it entered the seminaries of learning as a necessary accomplishment, and most important part of education, by engrossing men's thoughts, and fixing their minds so much on corporeal objects, and the laws of motion, it hath, however undesignedly, indirectly, and by accident, yet not a little indisposed them for spiritual, moral, and intellectual matters. Certainly had the philosophy of Socrates and Pythagoras prevailed in this age, among those who think themselves too wise to receive the dictates of the Gospel, we should not have seen interest take so general and fast hold on the minds of men, nor public spirit reputed to be γενναίαν εὐήθειαν, a generous folly, among those who are reckoned to be the most knowing as well as the most getting part of mankind.

332. It might very well be thought serious trifling to tell my readers that the greatest men had ever a high esteem for Plato; whose writings are the touchstone of a hasty and shallow mind; whose philosophy has been the admiration of ages; which supplied patriots, magistrates, and lawgivers to the most flourishing states, as well as fathers to the Church, and doctors to the schools. Albeit in these days the depths of that old learning are rarely fathomed; and yet it were happy for these lands if our young nobility and gentry, instead of modern maxims, would imbibe the notions of the great men of antiquity. But, in these freethinking times,

God as the Universal Order. 359

many an empty head is shook at Aristotle and Plato, as well as at the Holy Scriptures. And the writings of those celebrated ancients are by most men treated on a foot with the dry and barbarous lucubrations of the schoolmen. It may be modestly presumed there are not many among us, even of those who are called the better sort, who have more sense, virtue, and love of their country than Cicero, who in a Letter to Atticus could not forbear exclaiming, *O Socrates et Socratici viri ! nunquam vobis gratiam referam.* Would to God many of our countrymen had the same obligations to those Socratic writers ! Certainly, where the people are well educated, the art of piloting a state is best learned from the writings of Plato. But among bad men, void of discipline and education, Plato, Pythagoras, and Aristotle themselves, were they living, could do but little good.

334. Socrates in the First Alcibiades teacheth that the contemplation of God is the proper means to know or understand our own soul. As the eye, saith he, looking steadfastly at the visive part or pupil of another eye, beholds itself, even so the soul beholds and understands herself, while she contemplates the Deity, which is wisdom and virtue, or like thereunto. In the Phædon, Socrates speaks of God as being τὸ ἀγαθὸν and τὸ δέον ; Plotinus represents God as order ; Aristotle as law [1].

335. It may seem, perhaps, to those who have been taught to discourse about substratums, more reasonable and pious to attribute to the Deity a more substantial being than the notional entities of wisdom, order, law, virtue, or goodness, which being only complex ideas, framed and put together by the understanding, are its own creatures, and have nothing substantial, real, or independent in them. But it must be considered that, in the Platonic system, order, virtue, law,

These doctrines harmonise rather with the view of God as the Ideal towards which moral agents are bound to struggle, in order to the realisation of their chief end, than with that in which God is thought of as a Person.

goodness, and wisdom are not creatures of the soul of man, but innate and originally existent therein, not as an accident in a substance, but as light to enlighten, and as a guide to govern. In Plato's style, the term *Idea* doth not merely signify an inert inactive object of the understanding, but is used as synonymous with αἴτιον and ἀρχή, cause and principle. According to that philosopher, goodness, beauty, virtue, and such like are not figments of the mind, nor mere mixed modes, nor yet abstract ideas in the modern sense, but the most real beings, intellectual and unchangeable: and therefore more real than the fleeting, transient objects of sense, which, wanting stability, cannot be subjects of science, much less of intellectual knowledge [1].

336. By Parmenides, Timæus, and Plato a distinction was made, as hath been observed already, between *genitum* and *ens*. The former sort is always generating or *in fieri*, but never exists ; because it never continues the same, being in a constant change, ever perishing and producing. By *entia* they understand things remote from sense, invisible and intellectual, which never changing are still the same, and may therefore be said truly to exist: οὐσία, which is generally translated substance, but more properly essence, was not thought to belong to things sensible and corporeal, which have no stability; but rather to intellectual Ideas, though

---

[1] Mark the contrast between 'ideas of sense,' and 'abstract ideas' as understood in Berkeley's early writings, on the one hand ; and, on the other, what he here and in the next sections appreciates in the Ideas of Plato. Without Ideas, according to Plato, the material universe could not exist actually ; by participation in them the relations of sensible things are constituted ; in discovery of them, as principles, philosophy finds its satisfaction. Inductive research is an incipient endeavour to resolve phenomenal things according to their implied reason. Its imperfect and tentative but useful generalisations, limited by the presented data of our experience, are far short of the all-embracing Thought from which the phenomenal world issues, and which the Idealist systems of philosophy have hitherto vainly tried to grasp and comprehend. Our physical inferences of the events of time and sense involve trustful 'leaps in the dark,' so that even this 'knowledge' of nature is rooted in faith.

discerned with more difficulty, and making less impression on a mind stupified and immersed in animal life, than gross objects that continually beset and solicit our senses.

337. The most refined human intellect, exerted to its utmost reach, can only seize some imperfect glimpses of the Divine Ideas—abstracted from all things corporeal, sensible, and imaginable. Therefore Pythagoras and Plato treated them in a mysterious manner, concealing rather than exposing them to vulgar eyes; so far were they from thinking that those abstract things, although the most real, were the fittest to influence common minds, or become principles of knowledge, not to say duty and virtue, to the generality of mankind.

338. Aristotle and his followers have made a monstrous representation of the Platonic ideas; and some of Plato's own school have said very odd things concerning them. But if that philosopher himself was not read only, but studied also with care, and made his own interpreter, I believe the prejudice that now lies against him would soon wear off, or be even converted into a high esteem for those exalted notions and fine hints that sparkle and shine throughout his writings; which seem to contain not only the most valuable learning of Athens and Greece, but also a treasure of the most remote traditions and early science of the East.

339. In the *Timæus* of Plato mention is made of ancient persons, authors of traditions, and the offspring of the gods. It is very remarkable that, in the account of the creation contained in the same piece, it is said that God was pleased with his work, and that the night is placed before the day. The more we think, the more difficult shall we find it to conceive, how mere man, grown up in the vulgar habits of life, and weighed down by sensuality, should ever be able to arrive at science, without some tradition or teaching, which might either sow the seeds of knowledge, or call forth and excite those latent seeds that were originally sown in the soul.

340. Human souls in this low situation, bordering on mere animal life, bear the weight and see through the dusk of a gross atmosphere, gathered from wrong judgments daily passed, false opinions daily learned, and early habits of an older date than either judgment or opinion. Through such a medium the sharpest eye cannot see clearly. And if by some extraordinary effort the mind should surmount this dusky region, and snatch a glimpse of pure light, she is soon drawn backwards, and depressed by the heaviness of the animal nature to which she is chained. And if again she chanceth, amidst the agitation of wild fancies and strong affections, to spring upwards, a second relapse speedily succeeds into this region of darkness and dreams.

341. Nevertheless, as the mind gathers strength by repeated acts, we should not despond, but continue to exert the prime and flower of our faculties, still recovering, and reaching on, and struggling, into the upper region, whereby our natural weakness and blindness may be in some degree remedied, and a taste attained of truth and intellectual life [1].

* * * * *

350. The displeasure of some readers may perhaps be incurred, by surprising them into certain reflexions and inquiries for which they have no curiosity. But perhaps some others may be pleased to find a dry subject varied by digressions, traced through remote inferences, and carried into ancient times, whose hoary maxims, scattered in this Essay, are not proposed as principles, but barely as hints to awaken and exercise the inquisitive reader, on points not beneath the attention of the ablest men. Those great men, Pythagoras, Plato, and Aristotle, the most consummate in

---

[1] The abstruse speculation which follows is omitted. Advanced students may refer to the *Works*, especially sections 342-349, which refer to the *personality* of the Universal Mind and Spirit. These may be compared with the 'notion' of mind, spirit, self, or *ego* (not an 'idea' or 'phenomenon'), with which Berkeley starts in the *Principles* (sect. 2).

politics, who founded states, or instructed princes, or wrote most accurately on public government, were at the same time most acute at all abstracted and sublime speculations; the clearest light being ever necessary to guide the most important actions. And, whatever the world thinks, he who hath not much meditated upon God, the human mind, and the *summum bonum*, may possibly make a thriving earthworm, but will most indubitably make a sorry patriot and a sorry statesman.

* * * * *

367. As for the perfect intuition of divine things, *that* Plato supposeth to be the lot of pure souls, beholding by a pure light, initiated, happy, free and unstained from those bodies, wherein we are now imprisoned like oysters. But, in this mortal state, we must be satisfied to make the best of those glimpses within our reach. It is Plato's remark, in his *Theætetus*, that while we sit still we are never the wiser, but going into the river, and moving up and down, is the way to discover its depths and shallows. If we exercise and bestir ourselves, we may even here discover something.

368. The eye by long use comes to see even in the darkest cavern: and there is no subject so obscure but we may discern some glimpse of truth by long poring on it. Truth is the cry of all, but the game of a few. Certainly, where it is the chief passion, it doth not give way to vulgar cares and views; nor is it contented with a little ardour in the early time of life; active, perhaps, to pursue, but not so fit to weigh and revise. He that would make a real progress in knowledge must dedicate his age as well as youth, the later growth as well as first fruits, at the altar of Truth [1].

---

[1] *Siris* concludes with sentences which suggest that neither our faith in God, nor our faith in the divinely established order, and therefore significance, of the phenomena successively present in sense, can be converted by man into perfect science, with the faith entirely eliminated; that we know enough to know that our experience in time, as interpreted in the highest attainable science, cannot be identical with Omniscience;

that our philosophy cannot reduce or solve all the questions to which physical and moral experience gives birth, but that, in its furthest advance, there must still be an ever extending horizon of faith. Moreover, the full speculative solution of the ultimate questions,—although by 'exercise,' if we 'bestir ourselves,' we may 'discover something,'— is happily not indispensable to our living wisely and religiously. 'Agony of thought' is not the only way for separating the gold from the dross in this transitory life, which may be a life of reasonable faith, even if it must be one of enlarging but ever unfinished knowledge.

INDEX.

Qualifying words in Italics are to be continued to each entry until the next similarly marked words occur.

A.

Abstraction, ordinary but unintelligible uses of word, 15-25, 97-100; various sorts of ideas said to be framed by, 15; the power of, said to distinguish man from brutes, 19; a cause of confusion in metaphysics, 135; the only intelligible sort of, 17, 25, 37, 123; Locke on, 19; Schoolmen on, 26; Stewart on, 29 n.

Accidents, 'unthinking matter the support of,' an unintelligible expression, 47, 87.

Activity, unconscious mental, 326 n.

Acts of the mind, are not ideas, 135; cannot be abstracted from mind, *ib.*

Æsthetic, Kant's, 207 n.

'Αγαθὸν τὸ, with Socrates the strongest bond of the universe, 327.

Agent, an idea is not an, 54, 284; notion of, 56; is always incorporeal, 319; moral, the only real, 321.

Agnosticism, 261 n., 275 n.

Alexander of Aphrodisias, 349.

Algebra, verbal signs like, 29.

Analogy, what, 268; the laws of nature founded on, 108, 323; does not lead to universal conclusions, 110; the doctrine that we know God's attributes only by, criticised, 268—defended by Bp. Browne and Abp. King, 270 n.; Butler's use of term, 108 n., 270 n., 273 n.

Anaxagoras, on νοῦς, 263, 355.

Anaximander, on matter, 354.

Angles, the supposed method of judging near distance by, 159, 182, 244.

Anima mundi, 336.

Animal, the world an, 334, 338.— Animals, the lower, are unconscious organisms with Cartesians, 19.

Annihilation of things of sense every moment, alleged to follow from Berkeley's principles, 67.

Antinomies, Kant's, 124 n.

A priori and *a posteriori*, reasoning, distinguished, 51 n.

Aquinas, Thomas, on the Divine attributes, 267.

Arbitrariness, 77 n.; of visual signs, 158-73, 243-49; of those of magnitude, 175-77,—and of situation, 196; rational not capricious, 167 n., 324; of artificial languages, 242.

Archetypes of ideas, cannot exist independent of mind, 43, 66, 95; must be in some other mind, 104.

Arguments, Berkeley's, against abstract matter, classified, 94 n.

Aristotle, his *materia prima*, 45; his four causes, 56 n.; on form or essence, 106 n.; on nature, 139 n.; on the association of ideas, 164 n.; on the universe, 337; on God, 343, 353; his threefold distinction of objects, 347; no innate ideas, 347-48; actual existence of sensible things, 350; their potential existence, *ib.*; on nature, 340; on matter, 349-55.

Asclepian Dialogue, 333.

Association, *the subjective tendency*, recognised by Berkeley, 164 n.; does not decide whether knowledge is to be resolved into, 135 n.; *objective*, or divinely established, also recognised by Berkeley, 77 n.

Atheism, founded on the doctrine of abstract matter, 61, 100, 116; disproof of, 127; meaning of, 356.

Atomic philosophy, 315.

Attraction, a mechanical principle, 106, 318; does not explain phænomena, 315,—not being an efficient cause, merely a rule or method followed in nature, 107, 317,—and itself to be accounted for, 320-23; Hippocrates and Newton on, 319.

Augustine, St., on force, 321.

B.

Bacon, xiv, 11 n., 55 n., 83 n., 323 n.

Bailey, Mr. S., on Vision, 303 n.

Bain, Dr., on the relation of colour and extension, 225 n.

Being, comprehends ideas and spirits, 98; of sensible things, to be perceived [*percipi*], 38; of God, various sorts of arguments for, 231.

Berkeley, why a good introduction to psychology and metaphysics, vii; outline of his life, viii-x; his precursors, xi-xxii; materialism, xxii; his new question, xxiii; outline of his system, xxiv-xxxv; his reply to Hume by anticipation, xxxviii; his nominalism, 3; his underlying principle, *ib.*; recognises a moral duality, 11 n.; aim of his speculations to reconcile philosophy and common sense, 12 n.; his 'ideas,' xix n., 14 n.; his 'notions,' 14 n.; outline of his early psychology, 34 n,—which is to be compared with Locke's, Hume's, and Kant's, *ib.*; Ueberweg charges him with begging the question, 38 n.; his theory of law in nature, 51 n., 81 n.; on causality, 54 n.; his Egoism, 57 n.; on the permanence and identity of sensible things, 68 n., 93 n.; on the ideas of God, 86 n.; on number, 118 n.; on the relation of free finite spirits to the divine, 131 n.; on death, 132 n.; germ of Kantism in, 134 n.; on our communication with other spirits, 136 n.; on necessary connexion in mathematics, 156 n., 157 n.; on suggestion, 160 n.; on unextended colour, 225 n.; does not contemplate the possibility of philosophical nescience, 275 n.; alteration of his views in *Siris*, 310; his 'phenomena' there equivalent to his earlier 'ideas,' xix n., 310 n.; grounds his philosophy on moral facts, 326 n.; on space, 332 n., 354 n.; ideas of sense existing in the Divine Mind, 339 n.

Biran, Maine de, on cause, 55 n.

Blind, *men born*, have no idea of distance, 166, 249, 301,—for they do not at first connect ideas of sight and touch, 183, 212; cases of restoration of sight to, 304.

Body, perceived in sense of resistance, 115, 339; connexion of soul and, 131; difficulty regarding the resurrection of the, 101.

Brown, Dr. Thomas, on causality, 55 n.; on colour and extension, 225 n.

Browne, Bp. Peter, analogical knowledge of the Divine Attributes, 270 n.

Brutes, cannot, according to Locke, attain to abstraction, are machines with Cartesians, 19.

Butler, Bp., on death, 133 n.; on conscience, 138 n.; on the imperfection of our knowledge, 142 n.; his use of term analogy, 108 n., 270 n., 273 n.; held probability to be the guide of life, 179 n.

C.

Caprice, not Berkeley's 'arbitrariness,' xxxix, 77 n.

Categories, Kant's, referred to, 37 n.

Causality, three views regarding, xl n.; Berkeley on, 54-57; Aristotle, Locke, Hume, Kant, &c. on, 54 n.; assumption of materialism

Index. 367

regarding, 72 *n.*; efficient the only proper, 314 *et passim* ; erroneous uses of the term, 74.— Spirits the only proper causes, 54 *n.*, 108, 315; ideas are not, 54, 75; natural philosophers do not reach a knowledge of, 108, 319; no idea, but a notion of, 56 *n.*; are not objects of sense, 284; but are objects of reason, 329.—Causes, *physical* or *corporeal*, may be granted popularly, 73; but have no real efficiency, 54, 74, 315-20; are merely established signs analogous to a language, 58, 83.— Causes, *occasional*, doctrine of, referred to, 85.
Chain, in nature, 334; in life, *ib.*; in mind, 342.
Cheselden's case, 304.
Chimeras, difference between real things of sense and, 59.
Christianity, does not teach the doctrine of abstract matter, 92; that doctrine has caused difficulties in, 100.
Clarke, Dr. S., his theory, xxxiii; on God and space, 116 *n.*; and Leibnitz, 256 *n.*
Coleridge, quoted, 257 *n.*
Colour, idea of, abstracted from extension, 16; and superficial extension, 225; abstract general idea of, 17; proper object of sight, 167, 210, 248; admitted not to exist without a mind, 43.
Common sense, attempt of Berkeley to reconcile philosophy and, 12 *n.*; Reid's argument from, xlii.
Comte, on causality, 54 *n.*
Conception, as a criterion of objective possibility, 51.
Concepts, 20 *n.*, 23 *n.*
Contingency and science, 77 *n.*
Contradiction involved in abstract matter, 48 *n.*, 52-4; and human finitude, 46 *n.*, 51 *n.*
Copies of sensible things cannot exist without mind, 42 *n.*
Cosmos, are human spirits part of the? 131 *n.*; Aristotle on, 139 *n.*; the objective, the correlate of our personal reason, 141 *n.*

Creation, objection that Berkeley's conception of matter involves continual creation, 67; Schoolmen on, 68; and miracles, 81 *n.*; and a pre-established harmony, 256.
Cudworth, on Democritus, 322; nature is *ratio mersa*, 325; on unconscious mental agency, 326 *n.*
Custom, explains faith in causal connexion; according to Hume, xliii, 55 *n.*; is the tie between visible and tangible ideas, 178—so Hume, 179 *n.*; Pascal and Wordsworth on, 250 *n.*

D.

Death, Berkeley and Butler on, 132 *n.*
Definition, and essence, 71 *n.*, 106 *n.*; *of a general term*, does not imply an abstract idea, 26 *n.*; nor any single idea, 27.
Democritus, Cudworth on, 322.
Demonstration, nature of, by Berkeley unexplained, 9 *n.*; the universality involved in, 24.
De Motu, referred to, 113; object of the treatise, 322 *n.*
Descartes, xi, xii; what he means by 'ideas,' xix *n.*, 168 *n.*, 170 *n.*; his mechanical explanation of nature, 316 *n.*
Dialectic, Kant's, 128 *n.*
Dialogues between Hylas and Philonous referred to,—Second, 87 *n.*, 92 *n.*; Third, 70 *n.*, 76 *n.*, 98 *n.*, 102 *n.*, 131 *n.*
Diderot, remark of, on vision, 305 *n.*
Dionysius the Areopagite, the writings on the Divine attributes ascribed to, 265 *n.*
Distance, is either in the line of vision (i. e. outness) or lateral, 156 *n.*, 166; *or outness*, admitted by all that it is not a direct object of vision, 156; also that remote distance is suggested by experience of signs which are arbitrary, 156; but near distance is said to be inferred necessarily, 157; this rejected, 158-9; the signs by which near distance is suggested, 160-65, —their arbitrariness, 156, 160-65, 245,—analogous to a language,

242; which is rational, 161 n., 325;
man born blind has no idea of outness, 166, 249, 303; *lateral*, is it
an original object of sight with
Berkeley? 225 n.
Distrust of the senses by philosophers, 96.
Divisibility of matter, 68; of extension, 120; Hume on, 126 n.
Dreams, 49; and reality, 51 n., 64.
Duality in existence—Manichæism,
143 n.
Duration of a finite spirit, what,
103.

E.

Effect, the world a singular, Hume,
143 n.
Effort, voluntary, and the percep-
tion of distance, 169.
Egoism, 57 n.
Egyptian philosophers considered
God and nature as making one
Universe, 343.
Empedocles, 327, 332.
Entity, an incomprehensible abstrac-
tion, 91.
Epicureans, 101, 260.
Esse, is *percipi*, in things of sense,
38; of spirits is *percipere*, 104 n.
Eternity, of matter, 100; of space,
and God, 116.
Evil, *physical*, no objection to God's
existence, 140; not without its
use, 328; *moral*, and the being of
God, 233, 272.
Evolution, in psychology, 135 n.
Existence, includes spirits and ideas,
97; abstract idea of, incomprehensible, 91; *of sensible things*,
supposed to be twofold, 97; but
it truly consists in being perceived, 38, *et passim*,—that is, by
some mind, 69; absolute, unintelligible, 52; potential, what,
70 n., 88 n.; ordinary view of, a
cause of scepticism, 96; *of spirit*,
dependent on consciousness, 103;
our own, comprehended by reflection, 36, 98; of other finite
intelligences, known by inference,
98, 136, 239; *of God*, known by
similar inference, 136, 255.

Expectation, acquired perception is,
xxviii, 58 n., 160.
Experience, teaches us the laws of
nature, that is, the significance of
sense ideas, 57, 290,—c. g. the
signs of distance, 65, and of
magnitude, 176; but the inferences
of geometry do not depend on,
157; nor does the knowledge of
causes, 329; is not infallible,
290.
Extension, exists only in a mind
perceiving, 44; so exists by way
of idea not of mode, 70, 174 n.;
infinite divisibility of finite, 120;
depth of, not an immediate object
of vision, 157,—is superficial?
156 n., 225 n.; no extension common to sight and touch, 208,—
and no necessary connexion between visible and tangible, 179;
abstract idea of unintelligible, 15,
206.
Externality, i. e. independence of
mind, denied of visible objects in
the *Essay*, 167, 200; and of all
sensible things in the *Principles*,
38, 166 n.; real meaning of, 97.

F.

Faculties, *human*, their finitude and
scepticism, 12; are not ideas, 135;
cannot be abstracted from mind,
ib.; gradation of, 344-45.
Faith, is at the root of science,
xlvi; cannot be converted into
science, 363 n.
Fate, various ancient views of,
332.
Ferrier, Prof., on Vision, 303 n.
Fichte, xxxii n., 99 n.
Figure: see Extension.
Finitude of human knowledge, an
alleged cause of scepticism, 12;
and apparently contradictory propositions, 48 n., 53 n.
Force is spirit, 55 n.; conservation
of, 72 n., 110 n., 139 n.; is not in
bodies, 317, 321.
Fore-knowledge, Divine, 261.
Form, of Aristotle, 56 n., 106 n.
Four Causes, Aristotle's, 56 n.

G.

General, how words become, 25.
Geometry, its object is extension, but not abstract extension, 120, 206, and tangible, not visible, extension, 221; the necessity in, 157.
Geulinx, denied the efficiency of sensible things, xiii, 74 n.
God, existence of, known by rational inference from sensible signs, with more certainty than that of any finite spirit, 137, 255; laws of nature depend on the Will of, 58, 108, 138,—and are His language, 65, 83, 250-58, 323-25; explain the permanence of sensible things, 67; the theory that matter is the occasion for Him to excite ideas in us, 84; His ideas the archetypes of ours, 89; supposed co-eternality of matter with, 100; and space, 116, 331; His infinity, what, 127 n.; the relation of free finite spirits to, 131 n.; objection from physical evil to the goodness of, 140; from moral evil, 234, 271; the difficulty as to what is to be understood by the word 'God,' 261; theory that we have only an analogical knowledge of, 268.
Grammar of Nature, 323.
Gravitation, not an efficient cause, merely a rule in nature, 107, 319; not a necessary rule, 107.

H.

Hamilton, Sir W., on the objects of perception, 41 n.; on representative perception and scepticism, 97 n.; on space, 124 n., 194 n.; on superficial extension, 226 n.; on our knowledge of matter, 287 n.; his objections to a representative sense-perception partly anticipated by Berkeley, 291 n.
Harmony, pre-established, Leibnitz, 256, 316.
Hegelians, on man's relation to God, 131 n.

Helmholtz, signs of distance, 165.
Heraclitus, on fate, 332.
Hermaic writings, on space, 331; all things are One, 338.
Hippocrates on attraction and repulsion, 319.
Hobbes, xvi, 260.
Hume, his philosophy in relation to Berkeley's, xxxv-xli; on abstract ideas, 15 n.; his impressions, 35 n., 60 n.; his psychology and Berkeley's to be compared, 37 n.; on substance, 48 n.; on causality, 55 n.; on Berkeley's argument against matter, 94 n., 100 n., 131 n.; on representative perception, 97 n.; his philosophical nescience, 100 n., 275 n.; on space and infinity, 126 n.; the world a singular effect, 143 n.; makes custom the physical cause of knowledge, 160 n., 179 n.

I.

Idealism, Berkeley's, 95 n.
Ideas, include phenomena of which we are conscious in sense, 35, 284; either (a) sense-impressions, or (b) passions and operations of the mind, or (c) recollections and imaginations, 35; nature of, explained, 14 n., 18 n, 33 n., 95; sometimes restricted to imaginations, 60; cannot exist in absolute independence of mind, *passim*; can be like nothing but other ideas, 41, 99; are sometimes used as equivalent to 'notions,' 18, 24; but properly to be contrasted with them, 14 n., 98, 130; and therefore not the only objects of knowledge, 98, 134; for spirits are not ideas, 36, 98, 130, 134; nor are relations, 98, 134; distinguished from 'modes,' 70; power to form, the test of truth, 32 n. Ideas *of sense*, their actual *esse* is *percipi*, *passim*,—potential, *esse*, in God, 40, 84; do not imply abstract substance, 48; imply spiritual substance, 100; are not

causes, 54, 106, 284; but are signs, 58, 82; are real things in contradistinction to imaginations, 57, 64, 96; in *Siris*, called phenomena, xix *n.*, 323. Ideas, *abstract*, where discussed by Berkeley, 14 *n.*; doctrine of, a cause of confusion in philosophy, 14-31, 122; tenet that sensible things exist absolutely depends on doctrine of, 39. Ideas, *general*, not denied, 21, 123. Ideas, *and language*, 27-34. Ideas, Plato on, 15 *n.*, 346, 360; Descartes on, 170 *n.*; Locke on, 15 *n.*, 18, 37 *n.*, 170 *n.*; Hume on, 15 *n.*, 37 *n.*, 60 *n.*; J. S. Mill on, 15 *n.*

Identity, of sensible things, 53 *n.*, 67, 94 *n.*, 102; of the object of different senses, 289.

Idomenians, Reid's, 223 *n.*

Ignorance, man's ultimate, 142 *n.*

Images on the retina inverted and perception of situation, 187.

Imaginations, one class of ideas, 35; contrasted with sense-perception, 57-64; is no proof that sensible things can exist unperceived, 52; Locke, Leibnitz, and Hume on, 59 *n.*; are representations of sensible things, 283.

Immaterialist, in what sense Berkeley an, 95 *n.*

Immortality of the human soul, the natural, what and how proved, 131; Butler on, 133 *n.*

Impressions, Hume's, 35 *n.*, 60 *n.*

Individuality, human, 131 *n.*

Induction, latent in acquired perception, xix *n.*, 160, 323.

Inference, contrasted with suggestion, 298 *n.*, 299 *n.*; is midway between sense and omniscience, 186 *n.*

Infinite, man's apprehension of the, 127 *n.*

Infinity of things, the supposed, a cause of contradiction, 12, 124; of space, 116; Hume, Kant, Hamilton and Mansel on, 124 *n.*; of God, 127 *n.*

Interpretability of nature, 323-25; Bacon on, 55 *n.*

Invisibility of distance assumed, 155.

J.

Jamblichus, 333, 334, 354.

Jones, case of William, born blind, 227 *n.*

Judgment, used as in Locke, for presumption of probability, 156 *n.*, 176 *n.*; judgments, ontological import of, 71 *n.*

K.

Kant, xliii-xliv, 36 *n.*; on cause, 55 *n.*, 70 *n.*, 84 *n.*; on twofold existence of objects of sense, 95 *n.*; on physical and mathematical science, 105 *n.*; on space, 124 *n.*, 206 *n.*, 207 *n.*; on knowledge of self, 130 *n.*, 131 *n.*; on the origin of knowledge, 134 *n.*, 135 *n.*; on the moral proof of the Divine existence, 138 *n.*; on the constitutive principle of knowledge, 160 *n.*; his ultimate nescience, 275 *n.*

King, Abp., on the knowledge of God merely analogical, 270 *n.*

Knowledge, *human*, objects of, 35; not given by sense, 345; does not require abstract ideas, 24; ideal, what, 102; real, what, 27 *n.*; origin of, 135 *n.*; imperfection of, 363; and custom, 250; intuitive and discursive, 267 *n.*; symbolical, Leibnitz, 29 *n.*; and opinion, Plato, 345.

L.

Language, consists of arbitrary signs, 298; nature and abuse of, 14, 31; does not require abstract general ideas, 19; the universality in, 25; ends of, 29; abuse of, how to be remedied, 31; *of vision*, 65, 83, 222, 249, 323; its arbitrariness, 220, 249; but it is reasonable, 161 *n.*, 323; how it differs from other languages, 251.

Law, God is, Aristotle, 356; in nature, the rules in accordance with which God presents phenomena of sense to us, 58.

Leibnitz, after Spinoza, xiv; symbolical knowledge of, 29 n.; on imagination and reality, 60 n.; our ignorance of nature, 142 n.; on vision, 213 n.; pre-established harmony of, xiv, 256 n., 316 n.

Locke, xv-xxi; on the primary and secondary qualities of matter, xvii, 42, 67 n.; on substance, xviii, xix, 48 n.; on cause, 55 n.; his ideas, xix n., 170 n.; his abstract ideas, xviii, 18, 22; his explanation of the perplexities of philosophy, 12 n.; holds that the power of abstraction distinguishes man from the brutes, 19; physical science probable, not demonstrable, with him, 44 n.; his use of the term judgment, 156 n.; on defects of memory, 186 n.; on sight and touch, 212; on innate ideas, 348 n.

Lotze, signs of distance, 165.

Love, as the binding principle of things, 327.

M.

Machines, Cartesians held brutes to be, 19.

Malebranche, xiii, 74 n., 138 n., 255 n., 316 n.

Manichæism, 143.

Mansel, Dean, 20 n., 124 n., 291 n.

Materia prima, Aristotle's, 45 n.

Materialism, xlvi, 71 n., 72 n.

Mathematics, and abstract ideas, 116; and space, 207 n.; Kant on, 105 n.

Matter, cannot exist unperceived, 38 *et passim*; ordinary but unintelligible definition of, 43; abstract, what, 43, 67; is not the support of accidents, 47; cannot be known, 48; is useless, 49, 73, 85; is either contradictory or unintelligible, 48 n., 53 n.; impotence of matter, 54-8; abstract matter a support to impiety and empty disputation, 61; not needed in Natural Philosophy, 71; origin of the belief in, 75; not the unknown occasion of our ideas, 84; nor the unknown support of unknown qualities, 90; nor is it an unknown somewhat, neither substance nor accident, 91; is the root of scepticism, 97; and of irreligion, 100; Scripture on, 101; Plato, Aristotle, and other ancients on, 349-56.

Memory, Locke on, 186 n.

Metaphysics, abstract ideas the supposed object of, 14.

Mill, J. S., on abstract ideas, 15 n.; on causality, 55 n.; on external world, 58 n.; his Manichæism, 140; on extension and colour, 225 n.

Mind: see Spirit.

Miracles, 81 n.; do not involve abstract matter, 93.

Mirandula, Picus of, on God, 266.

Molyneux, on inverted images, 189; his problem, 212.

Monism, its two extremes, xlvi.

Moral proof of God's existence, 248 n., 273 n., 274 n.

Motion, a so-called primary quality, 43; cannot be the cause of our sensations, 54; abstract idea of, unintelligible or contradictory, 15, 104; Newton on, 114; does it imply space? 226 n.

Mystery of the universe, 143 n.

N.

Nature, laws of, what, 58—and Divine Will, 109, 140; course of, 317; defects of, no disproof of God's existence, 140; its universal language, 220, 323; remarks on Berkeley's conception of, 48 n., 50 n., 53 n., 68 n., 74 n., 77 n., 81 n., 93 n., 108 n., 109 n.

Necessity, in physical causality, 108 n., 109 n.; in mathematics, 157; no necessity of connexion between visible and tangible signs, *ib.*; Divine necessity, Hippocrates, 319; ancients on, 332-34.

Nescience, 275 n.; Hume's, xxxv-xli, 100 n.

Newton, Sir Isaac, on motion, time, and space, 111; on gravitation, 319.

Nominalism, Berkeley's, 3.
Notion, 14 n., 18, 56, 57 n., 62 n., 98, 134, 348 n., 349 n., 354 n., 362 n.
Number, 45, 117; is no object of sense, 338.

O.

Occasional causes, xiii, 74 n., 316 n.
Omniscience, 186 n., 363 n.
Order in nature, does it presuppose independent material substance? 78-84, 94 n.
Organisation in nature and the direct efficacy of Spirit, 78.
Organism, the human, and mind, 72 n.
Οὐσία, 71 n., 106 n.
Outness: see Distance.

P.

Parmenides, 332, 338, 360.
Pascal, 248 n., 250 n.
Passivity, of ideas or phenomena, 54.
Perception, *immediate*, is, with Berkeley, consciousness of phenomena—mental or material, xix n.; *mediate, acquired, suggested*, what, 158, 171, 283-87; distinguished from imagination, 57-59; in the 'chain of faculties,' 344; representative, 41, 97 n., 291 n.; said to be of primary qualities only, 42 n.; the great difficulty of, 95 n., 97 n.
Phenomenon, in *Siris*, analogous to idea of sense in Berkeley's earlier works, xix n., 323.
Philosophy, modern history of, xi-xlvii; what, 11 n., 13 n.; sceptical tendency of, 12; Berkeley's aim to reconcile common sense and, 12 n.; contradictions in, 13; abstract ideas, the supposed object of, 14; *Natural*, does not imply abstract matter, 71; cannot reach efficient causes, 108, 315-27.
Pimander, on fate, 333.
Platner, on knowledge of space, 194 n.

Plato, Ideas of, xix n., 15 n, 361; cave of, 329; on the personality of God, 343; on knowledge and opinion, 345; on matter, 349; on innate notions, 347; on sensible qualities, 353; on space, 354.
Plotinus, 323, 324, 332, 353, 359.
Plutarch, 333, 334, 352.
Portius, Simon, 353.
Positivism and Berkeley, 100 n.; his philosophy a spiritual, 106 n.
Power, is moral and spiritual only, 55 n.; ideas are destitute of, 54, 284; no idea of, 56; but a notion of, 54, 62 n. Powers of mind are abstractions, 134.
Proclus, 329, 351.
Psychology, Berkeley's early, 36 n.; the ideas or phenomena with which it is concerned, 35-37; rational, Kant on, 130; abstraction, a cause of confusion in, 135.
Pythagoreans, 117 n., 330.

Q.

Qualities of sensible things, primary and secondary, 42-47, 67 n.; are all dependent on being perceived, 87. See Ideas.

R.

Reason, cause an inference of, 284; and necessary connexion, 287 n.; and sense, 329.
Reasoning, *a priori* and *posteriori*, what, 51 n.
Reid, xlii; on cause, 55 n.; on Common Sense, 74 n.; on perception, 97 n.; on suggestion, 160 n.; on geometry of visibles, 223 n.; the existence of God the only real fact that is necessary in reason, 236 n.; on matter, 287 n.
Relations, we have 'notions' not ideas of, 98, 134; presupposed in knowledge, 51 n., 113 n., 118 n., 135 n., 208 n.
Reminiscence, Platonic, 339.
Responsibility, the measure of really originative agency, 326.
Resurrection of human body and abstract matter, 94 n., 101.

S.

Sameness of sensible things, 70 n., 102 n.
Scepticism, xxxv–xli; its causes, 12, 97; how to be escaped, 127; modern, 64 n.; 248 n.
Schoolmen, and abstraction, 25; argued for a continual creation, 67, 70 n.
Science, the ideal of, 110; and probability, 77 n.; Plato on, 345; the special sciences and philosophy, 117 n.
Self: see Spirit.
Sensationism, 95 n.
Sensations, 37; called phenomena in *Siris*, 287 n.; can exist only in a mind perceiving them, 37; and objects are one, 37, 49; cannot be causes, 54; not due to the motion of corpuscules, *ib.*; space a succession of, 66 n.; are significant through God, 94 n.; contain nothing but what is perceived, 96; all sensible qualities are, 104; knowledge of an unrelated sensation assumed by Berkeley to be possible, 160 n., 285 n.
Sense, the primary qualities are relative to the organs of, 43; why the presentations of are called ideas, 62; abstract matter is not an object of, 48; nor spirit, 129; its trustworthiness, 168 n.; knows nothing, 324; and reason, contrasted, 286, 329; *ideas of* are real things, 59; distinguished from imaginations, 59, 64; need a substance, which is spirit, 99.
Sight, *objects of*, are not without the mind, 167, 181, 200; only colour, 167, 210—superficial extension, 225; *and touch*, are signs, the one of the other, 66; their ideas or phenomena are absolutely heterogeneous, 209.
Signs, the material world a system of, 55 n., 94 n.; physical causes are really, 82, 298; of other spirits, ideas or phenomena of sense are, 138.

Socrates, 324, 327.
Solidity, a reputed primary quality, 43; but exists only in the mind, 44; perceived by touch, 169.
Solipsism, 57 n.
Soul: see Spirit.
Space, what, 66 n., 115, 116 n.; no absolute, 115; are the relations of space necessary? 115 n., 118 n.; its eternity, 116, 331; is not an immediate object of sight, 170, 225; Clarke on, 116; Kant on; 124 n., 207 n.; Hamilton on, 124 n.; Mansel on, 124 n.; Hume on, 126 n.
Spencer, Mr. H., on the origin of knowledge, 135 n.
Spinoza, xiv; on God, 260, 274 n.
Spirit, what, 36, 56, 128–34; the only substance, 41, 54 n., 99, 128; the only efficient cause, 54 n., 108; thinks always, 41 n., 103; we have a notion, not an idea of, 56, 130, 134; existence of ideas dependent on, *passim*; is a thing, 63; why men suppose matter rather than spirit as the cause of what we are conscious of in sense, 75; the Supreme, how known, 58, 76, 235–42; *other finite spirits*, how known, 36, 57 n., 94 n., 136 n., 237.
Stewart, Dugald, on abstraction, 29; on cause, 55 n.; on suggestion, 160 n.
Suarez, 267.
Subject of sensible qualities, an unintelligible expression, 71; and object, Kant on, 130 n.
Substance, spirit the only, 41, 56, 100, 129; material, is unintelligible, 43, 48. See Spirit and Matter.
Suggestion, 65, 160, 283; contrasted with inference, 180, 299.

T.

Tangibile minimum, 179; no absolute, 184 n.
Themistius, 349, 352 n.
Thing, properly includes both spirits and ideas, 63, 97, but is also used to distinguish the real objects of

sense from the ideas of imagination, 59. See Existence, Being, Matter, Spirit.
Time, considered, 100, 111; Locke on, 103 n., 107; Hume on, 126 n.; according to Platner serves for space to the born blind, 94.
Toland's *Christianity not mysterious*, 270 n.
Touch, includes muscular and locomotive senses, 66 n., 169 n.; ideas of, do not exist without the mind, 66, 166 n.; its objects assumed to be more steady, 177; arbitrariness of the connexion between the ideas of sight and, 179—their heterogeneity, 209; extension of, is the object of geometry, 221-26.
Transubstantiation, and Berkeley's conception of matter, 94 n.
Truth, the test of, 32; the cry of all but the game of few, 363.

U.

Ueberweg, Prof., charges Berkeley with begging the question, 38 n.; on our knowledge of other spirits, 57 n.; on the permanence of sensible things, 70 n.; on law in nature, 81 n.; on miracles, 93 n.

Unity, the aim if not the result of philosophy, 11 n., 13 n.; and of science, 186 n.; of self-consciousness, Kant on, 130 n.
Universality, in language, what, 25; of mathematics, 94 n.

V.

Visibile minimum, 174; no absolute, 184 n.
Vision: see Sight.

W.

Will, 55; no idea of, 56; *Divine*, and the reality of sense-ideas, 58, 66, 78-80; and natural law, 108; *and intellect*, in nature, 161 n., 323-27, 326 n.
Wolff referred to, xlii.
Words, general, are the signs not of abstract but of several particular ideas, 19; do not always stand for ideas, 29. See Language.
Wordsworth, quoted, 250 n.
World, the material, a system of signs, 55 n.; is constantly dependent on rational will, 66-70, 325; system of the, 331 n.; an animal, 334.

THE END.

BERKELEY'S COMPLETE WORKS AND LIFE.
BY PROFESSOR FRASER.

1. THE WORKS OF GEORGE BERKELEY, D.D., formerly Bishop of Cloyne. Collected and edited, with Prefaces and Annotations, by ALEXANDER CAMPBELL FRASER, M.A., LL.D., Professor of Logic and Metaphysics in the University of Edinburgh. 3 vols. 8vo. *cloth*, 2*l*. 2*s*.

2. THE LIFE AND LETTERS OF GEORGE BERKELEY, D.D., formerly Bishop of Cloyne; and an Account of his Philosophy: with many writings of Bishop Berkeley hitherto unpublished. By ALEXANDER CAMPBELL FRASER, M.A., LL.D., Professor of Logic and Metaphysics in the University of Edinburgh. 8vo. *cloth*, 16*s*.

'It is highly creditable to the Delegates of the Clarendon Press to have proposed this edition of Berkeley's Works, and it is difficult to conceive their idea better carried out than it has been by Professor Fraser.'—*Quarterly Review*.

'All that zeal, industry, and untiring devotion can do for ascertaining the facts of Berkeley's life, and elucidating his doctrines, has been done by his accomplished and sympathetic editor. At length we have a complete edition of Berkeley's Works, which reflects honour alike on the Clarendon Press and the University of Edinburgh.'—*Edinburgh Review*.

'This splendid edition of Berkeley's Works is of very high value.'— *Contemporary Review*.

'"Complete" is the characterizing word that may be written on these superb four volumes. The diligence, the love, the faith of Professor Fraser, as an editor, are, to our belief, quite unsurpassed in philosophical literature. Had we but—to say nothing of the rest—a Hume, a Kant, and a Hegel, in such perfection of detail as a like untiringness of labour and research might extend them to us!'—*Dr. J. H Stirling, in the American Journal of Speculative Philosophy*.

'We are delighted with the splendid edition of Berkeley's writings with which Professor Fraser has enriched the world. His work may be designated as in every respect a masterpiece. At length justice has been done to Berkeley.'—*Professor van der Wijck, in the Dutch Tijdspiegel*.

'This edition is already the standard one of Berkeley, and will never be superseded.'—*Princeton Review.*

'Professor Fraser has given us a life of Berkeley which is in every respect admirable. He has done a real service to philosophy in this country.'—*British Journal of Mental Science.*

'The University of Butler and Hooker has done well to associate her name with that of Berkeley—one of the most eminent men who has ever sojourned within her precincts. The present publication is one of the best which has appeared under the auspices of the Clarendon Press, and is a worthy tribute to the fame of its subject. Professor Fraser's estimate of Berkeley as a thinker, and of his position in the world of science, is by far the most complete which has ever come under our notice. No commentator certainly has ever brought out with equal distinctness and power the deepest part of the philosophy of Berkeley— his theory of the Divine causation.'—*Times.*

'There is probably no one living to whom the task of re-introducing Berkeley to the world could have been so fitly entrusted as Professor Fraser; and the manner in which he has executed his work quite justifies the high expectations that had been formed of it.—*Athenæum.*

'We congratulate the philosophical world on the possession of this noble edition of Berkeley.'—*Spectator.*

'We have already spoken of the satisfactory manner in which Professor Fraser has treated the life of Berkeley; he has perhaps succeeded still better in editing the philosophical works. While anxious to do full justice to Berkeley, he has handled his views with an intelligent strength that is really more respectful than weak indulgence. His introductions to the several treatises indicate great learning and research; his explanatory notes are almost always concise and quite to the purpose. Berkeley has never before been laid before the world in a form at all comparable for convenience, completeness, and elegance, with that of the Clarendon Press Edition.'—*Guardian.*

SELECTIONS FROM BERKELEY, with an Introduction
and Notes. For the use of students in the Universities. Crown 8vo. *cloth*, 7s. 6d.

'Professor Fraser has rendered the younger students of philosophy a real service in condensing, in the form of a handbook, some of the ripe fruits of his studies on Berkeley. A study of Berkeley, as it is here defined, will be an invaluable preparation to the proper understanding of modern philosophy.'—*Examiner.*

www.ingramcontent.com/pod-product-compliance
Lightning Source LLC
Chambersburg PA
CBHW020122020526
44111CB00049B/861